STUDIES IN ECONOMICS AND POLITICAL SCIENCE

Edited by

THE DIRECTOR OF THE LONDON SCHOOL OF ECONOMICS
AND POLITICAL SCIENCE

No. 109 in the series of Monographs by writers connected with the London School of Economics and Political Science.

ECONOMIC DEVELOPMENT IN THE NINETEENTH CENTURY

By the same Author

THE INDUSTRIAL AND COMMERCIAL REVOLUTIONS IN GREAT BRITAIN DURING THE NINETEENTH CENTURY

ECONOMIC DEVELOPMENT IN THE NINETEENTH CENTURY

FRANCE, GERMANY, RUSSIA, AND THE UNITED STATES

By the late

L. C. A. KNOWLES

Reprints of Economic Classics

AUGUSTUS M. KELLEY PUBLISHERS

New York 1967

First Published 1932
Reprinted 1936, 1942, 1945,
1947, 1948, 1952, 1958 *and* 1964

Published in U.S.A. by Augustus M. Kelley, Publishers
New York
Library of Congress Catalogue Number
67-27703

PRINTED IN GREAT BRITAIN

CONTENTS

PAGE

PREFACE vii

PART I

GENERAL INTRODUCTION

Chapter 1. LEADING FEATURES OF THE ECONOMIC HISTORY OF THE GREAT POWERS IN THE NINETEENTH CENTURY . . 3

„ 2. MAIN PERIODS AND THEIR CHARACTERISTICS 14

PART II

THE AGRICULTURAL REVOLUTION

„ 1. PERSONAL FREEDOM AND THE AGRICULTURAL REVOLUTION . . . 35

„ 2. FRANCE AND THE AGRICULTURAL REVOLUTION 47

„ 3. GERMANY AND THE AGRICULTURAL REVOLUTION 60

„ 4. RUSSIA AND THE AGRICULTURAL REVOLUTION 75

„ 5. AGRICULTURAL DEVELOPMENT IN THE UNITED STATES 84

PART III

THE INDUSTRIAL REVOLUTION

„ 1. FRANCE AND THE INDUSTRIAL REVOLUTION 105

„ 2. GERMANY AND THE INDUSTRIAL REVOLUTION 153

PAGE

Chapter 3. Russia and the Industrial Revolution 175

„ 4. Industrial Development in the United States 188

PART IV

THE REVOLUTION WROUGHT BY MECHANICAL TRANSPORT

„ 1. Transport in France 209

„ 2. Transport in Germany 216

„ 3. Transport in Russia 225

„ 4. Transport in the United States . 229

PART V

NATIONAL COMMERCIAL POLICIES

„ 1. French Tariffs 239

„ 2. The German Zollverein 254

„ 3. Russian Fiscal Policy 275

„ 4. Tariff History in the United States 288

„ 5. National Expansion 305

PART VI

GROWTH OF STATE ACTION

„ 1. Aspects 339

„ 2. Causes 342

BIBLIOGRAPHY 351

INDEX 355

PREFACE

THE present book is to be regarded as the second volume of a survey of the economic development of the Great Powers which the late Professor Lilian Knowles planned before her death in 1926. The first volume was published in her lifetime under the title of *The Industrial and Commercial Revolutions in Great Britain during the Nineteenth Century.* The further Great Powers which she had chosen for the purpose of her survey were France, Germany, Russia, and the United States, and it is the economic development of these Powers that constitutes the contents of the present volume.

The scope and purpose of the book are perhaps best described in her own words, taken from the draft Preface which was found among her papers.

" My object in writing this book has been to sketch the economic development of a hitherto neglected and yet most important century. I have attempted to show the interaction of the Great Powers on each other and how far their general development was similar and how far it differed in each country. The nineteenth century is peculiar because it saw man for the first time able to control nature by mechanical appliances and science. Distance was abolished by the railway and the steamship and geographical barriers were circumvented. A certain amount has already been written about the industrial revolution in each country and the social results that followed, but far too little has been written about the world effect of machinery, and little or no stress has hitherto been laid on the political, commercial, financial, and social revolutions caused by the development of mechanical transport. This is one of the gaps that this book attempts to fill. The whole world became one area for economic purposes after 1870 and economic motives dominated the political situation from that time onwards. Everyone who wishes to understand modern national, commercial, or labour problems must get some idea of the evolution which has produced the modern situation, not merely the story of the economic development of Great Britain, but of the other countries as well.

There is such a fundamental difference between the nineteenth and the eighteenth centuries, that it is quite possible to consider the nineteenth century by itself. I have tried to break new ground and to show how important are the changes that have taken place, and how a world interdependence and exchange have been substituted for a national system of economics. The political history of the century can be but ill understood unless there is adequate appreciation of the economic factors which became more and more important as the century progressed."

It may be added that a good deal of space is given to the tariff history of the different countries dealt with and to the commercial and industrial depressions that have visited them in turn and from time to time. The experience of the nineteenth century should help to a solution of the fiscal and other allied problems that are besetting the nations in the twentieth.

The book has been prepared for publication, in part from the sections of completed manuscript left by Professor Lilian Knowles, and in part by correlating and expanding her lecture notes. In this work Dr. Allan McPhee has had a large share. His intimate knowledge of the sources from which Professor Knowles drew her material has been invaluable; the thoroughness with which he has checked facts and references has been of infinite service; and his wide general knowledge of the subject has enabled him to fill in certain lacunæ which became apparent. He has furthermore contributed the Bibliography and the Index.

In the work of amplifying and adapting the material left by Professor Knowles, valuable help was derived from the notes taken at her lectures by Mr. W. L. Kendall, M.Sc.(Econ.), which he generously allowed to be used for the purpose of the book.

C. M. KNOWLES.

PART I

GENERAL INTRODUCTION

CHAPTER I

LEADING FEATURES OF THE ECONOMIC HISTORY OF THE GREAT POWERS IN THE NINETEENTH CENTURY.

Four main features :—

I. The attainment of personal freedom due to French influence.
  (*a*) The abolition of serfdom (France, Germany, and Russia); slavery (United States and British Empire).
  (*b*) The reconstruction of the administration. Abolition of settlement restrictions and gild monopoly. Result free movement, free choice of occupation.
  (*c*) The reconstruction of agricultural methods and tenures.

II. The Industrial Revolution—the influence of Great Britain.
  (*a*) England and France the two industrial nations in 1815. Germany purely agricultural, divided, poor, exporting food and raw materials. Russia self-sufficing, serf agriculture. United States—exporter of tobacco and cotton.
  The nineteenth century witnesses the industrialization of the agricultural States. Germany after 1860, United States after 1880, Russia after 1890.
  (*b*) The industrial changes give rise to a new labour movement. Decay of gilds, rise of Trade Unions, Socialism. Activity of the state in industrial legislation.

III. The Transport Revolution. The Steamship and the Railway—influence of Great Britain.
  (*a*) The penetration of great land areas—result new Empires and new rivalries.
  (*b*) The new mobility of goods—bulky articles and foodstuffs.
  (*c*) The new mobility of persons—immigration problems.
  (*d*) The new finance.
  (*e*) The abolition of distance, world interdependence ; man's control over nature.

IV. The change in national policies and international commercial relations.
  (*a*) The continuation of mercantilism.
  (*b*) The liberal period. *Laissez-faire* in industry.
  (*c*) Return to protection and State regulation after 1870 in Europe.
  (*d*) National commercial rivalries find a new outlet in colonial expansion for raw materials and markets.
  The scramble for Africa and Asia.

DURING the nineteenth century two great economic forces were at work in the world—English invention, which for the first time gave man a control over nature, and the French conception of economic liberty which followed on the French Revolution.

The English had by the end of the eighteenth century attained a degree of personal freedom undreamed of by other nations, and England's continental colonies on the mainland of North America, which became the U.S.A. in 1783, had necessarily followed its tradition of individual freedom and initiative. Far other was the development of the continental countries still sunk in serfdom and feudalism in the eighteenth century. The peoples looked to the feudal lord or king for guidance and leadership, and what was done in Europe was done mainly by autocratic monarchs acting according to their own ideas or those of some prominent minister. In England, Burghley and Elizabeth worked after this fashion, so did Henry IV of France and Sully, Louis XIV and Colbert, but as late as the last quarter of the nineteenth century one finds that Kaiser William I and Bismarck and the Czar and Witte in Russia were the arbiters of the economic life of their countries. In England, after the execution of Charles I, changes came from below and were due to individual initiative. On the continent they still came from above and varied according to the ideas of monarchs.

With the French Revolution there came a great uprising from below, which represented an attempt to attain by revolution and suddenly that personal freedom which in England had been attained by an evolutionary process. Wherever the French armies went under their revolutionary leaders or under Napoleon, they freed serfs, abolished gilds, introduced new laws of property, organized mediaeval countries on new lines, and made it necessary for monarchs who wished to retain their thrones to attempt to do from above what France had done from below, that is to say, introduce personal freedom.

The interest of the evolution of Europe lies in the attempts of Central and Eastern European governments to remodel their economy under the stimulus given by the French invasions and French ideas. In so far as their evolution demanded machinery and railways, they borrowed their economic equipment from England. The two influences were, however, interdependent. It would have been impossible to fill factories, work blast furnaces, build and operate railways with a people who were tied to the soil or prevented from settling in new places. French influence provided the people, English invention their occupations. It was the French revolutionary ideas of personal freedom that gave the great impetus to the reforms of the period 1806–65 which abolished serfdom in Central and Eastern Europe. It was due to French initiative that the great liberal treaty system of Europe was completed between 1860 and 1870 which meant the abolition of so many commercial and colonial restrictions. It was England, however, that inaugurated the new employments for the people who were now able to migrate; it was England that provided the mechanism and much of the capital for transforming agricultural into industrial states; and above all, it was England that provided in mechanical transport the means for that almost incredible and romantic development of the interiors of continents and the new wandering of the peoples. Railways opened up inland countries; steamship companies advertised for and moved people in millions to the New World; the continent of Africa became the object of intense competition; and the whole world entered into a new economic phase. It is the play of the ideas and inventions of the two giants, England and France, on the feudal agricultural Empires of Central and Eastern Europe, that constitutes much of the fascination of the economic history of the nineteenth century.

It is, further, the reaction of the Old World on the New, transforming the United States, a great empty continent, into a huge food-producing and industrial entity, and the reaction of this New World with its grain and meat exports on the Old, which again helped to alter the whole character of the economic development of Europe after 1870. These stupendous world movements emanating from England and France, transforming Germany and Russia, spreading to the United States, permeating South America, impinging upon Africa and reconstructing India and Japan, reacting on China, colonizing Australia and making its influence felt in remote Pacific islands, constitute the world revolution we have to examine.

Our subject, therefore, embraces first of all the establishment of personal freedom, freedom to move, freedom to buy and sell, free choice of an occupation. After that comes the adoption of machinery, creating new classes, new towns, new wants in raw material, and new facilities of transport. Then follows the railway, making continental areas as accessible and as valuable as countries with large coastlines; and after that follows the steamship, aiding the great migration to those countrie and linking up the world in a system of common economic relationships. Inside this great system of world exchange of peoples and goods are the nations, and each nation has its own idea of what should be its proper policy with regard to its own people now that railways and steamships have made new things easily available and men have become capable of a new mobility. It has to develop a new policy for the purpose of expanding its own type of civilization and selling its own goods. Protection or free trade, colonies and markets, raw materials and food stuffs, coal and iron, the creation and control of mechanical transport by sea and land, the regulation of capital and labour—all these become increasingly the object of national concern. The feudal states were naturally the first to evolve state direction in these matters, but the individualist states did not lag far behind. The nineteenth century witnesses first of all a repudiation of state action and a general belief that the state can do no good thing, and ends with a violent reaction from *laissez-faire* to state control in most spheres of economic life.

The Great Powers fall into two distinct groups, the individualist and the feudal. The individualist countries are the United Kingdom [1] and the United States; and the feudal countries are France, Germany, and Russia with their tradition of royal control. Not merely did the upheaval in France against feudalism react powerfully on the other two, but it occurred just at the time when English mechanism provided new careers and the Americas new outlets. The feudal countries with their backward agricultural populations could not leave things to individual initiative, as did England and the United States. The direction and assistance from above was necessarily greater. Moreover, with the exception of Great Britain, and to a less degree Germany, the Great Powers even to-day are primarily agricultural communities, and agriculture and agricultural problems have been their main concern. The settling of the questions arising out of the abolition of serfdom, the alteration of the whole methods of agricultural production in the change involved from serf to free labour, the introduction of intensive agriculture—all these questions, remote from England, have been of primary importance on the continent of Europe, The task of England, with her

[1] Dealt with by Professor Knowles in *The Industrial and Commercial Revolutions in the Nineteenth Century.*

engineering and machine production and her labour questions, has been to work out the problems connected with the new industrial and urban developments. She invented the factory inspector and main drainage, the Factory Acts, trade unions, and co-operation. The task of Continental Europe has been, mainly, to solve the questions connected with a backward peasantry just out of serfdom and increased home production in agriculture, combined with protection from American imports. All this has meant in these countries a necessary continuance of direction from above. England, on the other hand, went over to free trade in 1846 and relied on imported foodstuffs. She was not preoccupied until after 1914 about her home production of food.

This late emancipation from feudalism and serfdom on the continent has had very important results in stimulating both co-operative societies and the amalgamation of businesses to form combinations. Accustomed to work together for common cultivation on a manor, co-operative societies in agriculture are almost natural to peasants in feudal countries such as Denmark, Germany, and Russia. Accustomed to being organized from above, businesses will fall easily into line for common action to regulate production or stimulate the export trade. The slow growth of co-operation and combination in England may be ascribed to its historical training in individual action. In the United States co-operation hardly makes any headway, while the typical combination there is the trust or single firm, not as in Germany a combination of firms all retaining their individuality but co-operating for common purposes.

Another grouping of the Powers is, however, possible. Instead of classing them as feudal or individualist states, they may be divided according to whether they are primarily agricultural or primarily industrial states. This brings into one category the two most industrialized Powers, England and Germany, in contrast with the two great agricultural Empires, the United States and Russia, while France holds a position midway between.

Each of these Powers has become conscious of its economic wants and each believes that it has a civilizing mission in the world. Hence the great expansion of Russia in Siberia; of the United States in Mexico, Alaska, the Philippines, and the region of the Panama Canal; of France with its great colonial Empire in Indo-China, Madagascar, in the Sudan and West Africa, to say nothing of its Mediterranean colonization in Algeria, Tunis, and Morocco; and England with its quarter of the globe. The Pacific became a new object of rivalry and spheres of influence in China were a manifestation of the new economic imperialism. Thus the various national policies were reinforced by a policy of expansion for national purposes.

Thus it is seen that personal freedom, involving agricultural reconstruction, engineering and machine production, mechanical transport, and national expansion for markets and raw materials, are the main economic features of the nineteenth century.

The attainment of personal freedom meant the final abolition of serfdom in France in 1789, in Germany and Austria-Hungary between 1806 and 1848, and in Russia between 1861 and 1865. The abolition of slavery in the British Empire in 1833, in the French dominions in 1848, and in the United States in 1862–3 followed as a matter of course. As, however, the feudal lord had been judge and administrator of his district, the abolition of his power over the serfs meant a complete recasting of the administration in rural districts. In the towns the gilds had restricted the choice of an individual's occupation and had circumscribed settlement within the urban areas. Personal freedom did not merely mean the abolition of serfdom; it meant the overhauling and liberalizing of gild restrictions. The gilds had, however, been largely responsible for town administration and their reform meant also the reconstruction of urban governments. Even free men, that is to say, men who were not serfs, had been prevented from moving from place to place by settlement laws. The food supply of each area was so precarious that all districts resented the intrusion of new comers and the gilds were always afraid of rural craftsmen who might work more cheaply and undercut prices; it is a phase of the perennial duel between town and country. It was characteristic of the trend towards personal freedom that, during the nineteenth century, these restrictions on movement were modified. The general result was free movement and free choice of an occupation, an intensified migration and the growth of towns.

This new personal freedom meant in Europe a complete reconstruction of agricultural life. Agriculture had been mainly based on the communal cultivation of strips in the open fields supplemented by great wastes for fuel and fodder when the crops were growing. With the abolition of serfdom there came the break-up of the communal system, the enclosure of the strips, the break-up of the wastes, and the introduction of separate and individual ownership and intensive cultivation with greatly increased yields. Agricultural tenures were altered no less than agricultural methods. In the United States the freeing of the slaves meant the break-up of the large estates of the South and equally a new system of agricultural tenures and methods. Everywhere the law had to be recast to fit the new conditions of ownership designed for persons who were free to buy and sell, free to move, free to acquire land, free to leave it by will, free to marry and free to emigrate, all of which things were new for the bulk of population in the nineteenth century, and it is in this direction that the influence of France has been paramount. Serfdom was inconsistent with liberty, equality, and fraternity. In his Codes, Napoleon provided a new legal basis on which the new systems of personal freedom could rest.

The industrial revolution hinged on the development of steam power, the use of coal, the smelting of iron, the rise of engineering, machines and machine tools, and the development of industrial chemistry. The two most highly industrialized nations in 1815 were England and France. Germany was purely agricultural, divided by innumerable internal tariff barriers and bad roads. She was a very poor country with little or no capital. Russia was a self-sufficing Empire, dependent upon serf labour for agriculture and for her industrial production upon serf workshops. The United States were, in 1815, a strip of Western territory bordering the Atlantic, cultivating cereals and exporting tobacco and cotton, and relying on imports for the bulk of their manufactured articles. The nineteenth century witnessed the inauguration of industrialism in these three great agricultural states. All three developed coal and iron, engineering and machine making; all three developed the textile manufactures; all three developed the inevitable concomitant of machine production, namely, mechanical transport, more particularly railways. The industrial revolution is a marked feature in New England after 1840, in Germany after 1860, and in Russia after 1890.

The industrial changes gave rise in each country to a new labour movement. The old gilds decayed, trade unions arose, and new theories for the reconstruction of society were enunciated to which were given the comprehensive title of Socialism. Alongside of these new theories there developed an industrial code of great elaborateness and intricacy, designed to prevent some of the worst evils of the change. Just as the agricultural changes had meant a new local administration and a new body of law, so the industrial changes meant a new administration by inspectors, a new code of industrial legislation, and a new educational system.

Mechanical transport, by means of the railway and the steamship, meant the penetration of great land areas, with the result that new Empires and new international rivalries were created. There was a new mobility of goods and bulky articles, and foodstuffs like wheat and meat were moved for the first time in large quantities.

There was also a new mobility of persons, and that not merely of Europeans but of Asiatics, creating new problems of race exclusion and colour rivalry and new questions as to the maintenance of the standard of life. Americans and Australians were faced with the necessity of preserving their standards of life as against Eastern European immigrants with their lower standards, and have had to devote much thought to the question of the exclusion of Japanese and Chinese.

The new transport developments led to fresh investments of capital all over the world and a new financial era. There were large investments of capital in the railways themselves; and there were large investments in new countries because the railways existed to move their produce. There was a contraction of distances and a world interdependence appeared. The towns and factories grouped on the coal and iron areas of Europe looked to the outer world for raw materials and foodstuffs and supplied the new world in return with economic tools in the shape of railways, machines, and manufactured articles generally.

The most striking thing in the new mechanism of manufacture and transport was the way in which man was made dominant over the natural obstacles which hitherto had held him bound. The terror of almost every country prior to 1850 was famine. The cost of transporting bulky articles like foodstuffs was so great that every area practically aimed at being self-sufficing. Import was never easy when necessity arose, owing to the fact that Europe generally experienced much the same kind of weather and a famine in one European country was usually the herald of a scarcity in all Europe. With mechanical transport the failure of the harvest in Europe may be made good by the harvest of Argentina, Canada, Australia, or India. There is the whole world to draw upon, and the nineteenth century enjoyed a security previously unknown. Nothing now seems impossible of accomplishment. Rivers that overflow can be dammed; water can be conserved for irrigation by great engineering works, as in Egypt and India; mountains can be pierced by tunnels as in the case of the St. Gothard and Simplon; waterways such as the Suez and Panama canals can be made to link up oceans and create new trade routes; rivers can be made navigable, and can be connected by inland waterways large enough to take sea-going vessels, as the Manchester Ship Canal, and the Dortmund–Ems and the Mittelland canals in Germany. In this way the geographical limitations of a poor or short coast-line can be mitigated. Railways can cross the Rocky Mountains and the Andes and penetrate into the Sahara. Modern communications can defy both the snows of Russia and the tsetse fly of Africa, so fatal to beasts of burden. Modern science is enabling man for the first time to win in the great duel between himself and the insect world. Science is equally enlisted against the mosquito to save man from malaria and against the cotton boll weevil to save the cotton crop.

Between 1830 and 1870 the nineteenth century was charged with the electricity of national aspirations which found expression in a united Italy and Germany, a freed Greece, Roumania, and Serbia. National economic policies attained to a new significance since they represented democracies trying to realize their new national destinies. The tariff, therefore, became a battle-ground between different schools of thought and was the test case of state control or individual freedom. The autocratic kings had without exception carried out a policy of mercantilism. A protective tariff was used to shut out or penalize foreign goods. The export of national goods was assisted by bounties on production or export and by retaining exclusive possession of colonies as markets. The import and export of goods was further regulated by Navigation Acts designed to stimulate national shipping. This policy, which was intended to increase national trade at the expense of the foreigner, was generally accompanied by state supervision of all sides of economic life. Trading companies were encouraged with grants of monopolies. The training of apprentices, the regulation of the quality of goods, the provision of a sufficient food supply and its proper distribution were all the subjects of state regulation.

The reaction against the autocratic monarchs brought this system into disrepute. England, the most highly protected country of all, was organized for world production and exchange and accordingly repealed her tariffs and her Navigation Laws between 1822 and 1854, threw open her colonial system to all comers, and allowed her colonies to trade where they liked. Free contract and *laissez-faire* in industry accompanied free trade in commerce. The railways, as they developed, made all tariff systems obsolete by promoting exchange on a scale hitherto unknown and by lowering freights so that no tariff was effective to keep goods out. Other countries to a greater or lesser degree followed the example of England. The abolition of old restrictions and a general freedom were the economic features of the liberal period which on the political side was characterized by the establishment of democratic constitutions and new nationalities. Autocracy and mercantilism had been connected, and now were rejected together. Liberalism meant interchange of peoples and commodities and was held to be the only proper policy for a cosmopolitan democratic era. *Laissez-faire* in industry accompanied *laissez-faire* in commerce.

After the defeat of France in 1870, the new democratic liberalism became moulded by an intensified nationalism, and a reaction took place. It seemed only right to protect the work of your own people against that of other nations, especially as the railways had engendered an intensified competition in the world. New national policies emerged involving a high protective tariff on the one hand and a new labour code on the other. Social insurance was developed in Germany alongside of a high tariff and was copied and developed in other countries, and the state completely abandoned the idea of *laissez-faire* in industry. The new working class, disappointed with the effects of democracy, which they had expected would produce a new Heaven and earth with great rapidity, began to fall back on economic rather than political measures. In many countries a fundamental reconstruction of society became the labour ideal. This seemed all the more pressing as combination became increasingly the feature of modern business organization with the enormous power of crushing opposition that it involved.

The new Imperialism noticeable after 1870 arose almost naturally out of this intensified nationalism. It envisaged continents instead of the islands or strips of coast-line which had been the characteristic geographical features of the old colonial system. The increasing industrialization of Europe led the older countries to look abroad for markets. New sources of raw material were needed, new food areas became imperative for the growing towns, and the new colonial era had for its objective the control of tropical areas as well as the development of the unoccupied spaces suitable for settlement by the white races. That meant in its turn a fresh control of emigration and immigration and served to strengthen the general tendency to abandon *laissez-faire*. Nations became Empires developing preferential tariff arrangements with their colonies as in the case of France, England, and the United States. All countries undertook to a greater or lesser degree the scientific exploitation of the raw material of their tropical regions. The scramble for and division of Africa in the 'eighties was essentially a scramble for tropical areas; the scramble for spheres of influence in Asia in the 'nineties was a scramble for markets. To reach those markets Russia built the great Siberian and the central Asian railways. The railway net of India was developed by the government largely as an insurance against famines; roads were built and metalled in the Malay peninsula to keep order; the Baghdad railway became the bone of international contention. The French offset the loss of India in the eighteenth century by developing Indo-China and in 1895 acquired Madagascar. The United States took possession of the Philippines and built the Panama Canal. A new ocean, the Pacific, was brought into politics. Democracy and nationalism, with their accompaniment of free trade and *laissez-faire*, gave way to Socialism on the one hand and Imperialism on the other. The expression of the latter was found in protectionist tariffs and preferential arrangements with colonies, and of the former in a great labour code which tends more and more to become international so that the cheap sweated labour of one country shall not undermine the higher standard of another country. A new democratic imperial mercantilism took the place of the national mercantilism of the autocratic monarchs.

CHAPTER 2

Main Periods and their Characteristics

1789–1848.

The leading economic characteristic of these years is the establishment of the new personal freedom in Western and Central Europe. The industrial revolution takes place in England and France.

1849–70.

This is the liberal era. It witnesses a breakdown of mercantilism, the conclusion of commercial treaties on liberal lines and the development of mechanical transport in England, France, and Germany. Russia frees her serfs and modernizes. France is still the dominating economic personality of Europe.

1871–1914.

These years are the period of German influence. There is a return to state regulation in almost every department of life. Russia and the United States develop as great agricultural exporting Empires. Germany becomes an industrial and commercial power of the first rank. The United States and Russia become industrialized and there is a renewed effort to dominate raw material producing areas and markets.

War has had an important influence during the century in stimulating economic changes.

FROM the point of view of economic development, the history of the great European Powers, after the French Revolution, falls into three periods, viz. 1789–1848, 1849–70, and 1871 onwards. The period 1789–1848 is chiefly concerned with problems arising out of the movement towards personal freedom inaugurated by the French Revolution and the French Wars. The Declaration of the Rights of Man had laid down in 1791 that "men are born and remain free and equal as to their rights". To make headway against the French invasion, Prussia was obliged to follow suit and free her serfs, and the rest of Germany where serfdom still remained followed her example. The questions whether gilds should be allowed to restrict the choice of an occupation and whether they should be allowed to restrict mobility by refusing to let new craftsmen settle within their jurisdiction were settled in France by abolishing all gild restrictions, and in Germany by a very considerable restriction of their powers. The freedom of the cultivator of the soil was gradually accomplished in the other states of Central Europe, including Austria-Hungary. Between

1806 and 1848 an abortive attempt was made at freeing some of the serfs in Russia. The question of limiting the extension of slavery as new territories were formed and admitted as states began to be discussed in the United States, and the slaves were freed in the English colonies in 1833. Save for the definite efforts to realize personal freedom, the excesses of the French Revolution and the poverty induced by the French wars had produced in Europe generally a period of economic stagnation. Nations clung to their commercial policies of high and exclusive tariffs and state regulation of all sides of economic life with all their accompanying corruption, confusion, and limitation of intercourse. Reform was postponed, partly because revenue was needed and the possible diminution of income due to any fiscal change could not be faced, and partly from sheer conservatism, since the liberalism of France in 1789 seemed to have produced for that country ten years of economic chaos and a long resultant depression.

All Europe was in the throes of an agricultural crisis in the early nineteenth century, and therefore agricultural protection seemed specially desirable to maintain the growth of foodstuffs at home at a time when railways had not developed and grain was transferred only near rivers and then only when famine prices made it worth while. There was no question of moving meat (except salted) or cattle. The meat went bad; the cattle died in the uncertain sailing ships. Moreover, tariffs alone seemed to the rulers to protect France, Germany, and the United States from the absolute ruin of their industrial life now that Great Britain had developed cheap textiles with her machinery and cheap iron with her blast furnaces and abundant fuel supplies. Much of the mercantilism of the period was sheer self-defence against England. Inside these tariff walls France began to develop, at first slowly, then more rapidly after 1830, a machine industry of her own. Of machinery in the other European countries except England and France there was no trace.

Towards the end of the period it became obvious that the awakening from the lassitude left by the French wars, which was to result in the European upheavals of 1848, was to be accompanied by a movement for greater freedom of economic intercourse between nations. Prussia had been occupied since 1818 in abolishing the internal tariff barriers in Germany through the instrumentality of the Customs

Union, which first took definite form in 1834, and although this was merely in the nature of a treaty made for twelve years with no certainty of renewal at the end of each period, Germany had begun to count as something approaching an economic entity and a modern state. Free trade doctrines were increasingly discussed on the continent while England made drastic alterations in her tariff between 1842 and 1849, sweeping away the protective duties on corn and considerably lowering those on manufactures and at the same time removing restrictions on shipping. The English changes remained, however, without imitators for a time, because the circumstances in England were held to be exceptional.

The years from 1849 to 1870 are characterized by the spread of the belief in the efficacy of free international intercourse and there is an almost universal reaction from the old principles of state regulation and restrictions. Napoleon III came to power in 1849 with the clear purpose of restoring order in France after the troubles of 1848. He believed the mission of France to be that of an arbiter in Europe in the economic as well as the political sphere. He initiated and carried a scheme of reduced tariffs in France from 1853 and concluded a series of commercial treaties in Europe which led to reduction of duties all round. It is true that Europe had been prepared for this by the free trade crusade inaugurated by the economists. Adam Smith had shown that exchange would not take place unless each party required the thing he received more than the thing he gave in exchange, both sides thus seeming to gain by the transaction. It would be foolish, so free traders argued, to place obstacles in the way of an obvious benefit to both sides. Exchange was even invested with a religious halo. An all-wise Providence had endowed different countries with different climates and aptitudes, obviously intending that the wines of France should be exchanged for the coal of England. Who then could be presumptuous enough to set up tariff barriers against the will of the Almighty? It is true that in 1841 List had published his *National System of Political Economy* which advocated protection for backward countries, but in the 'fifties few educated persons outside Germany read German, and if they had they would have said that List was wrong.

The current trend of thought in favour of freer international dealings was not created by economic writers and teachers alone; a certain impatience of and disgust with the older system also existed. There had been a great deal of corruption among traders and certain government officials; and smuggling was an extensively practised and a by no means dishonourable profession. The sheer difficulty of getting any satisfactory result from the unreformed Civil Service led people to feel that the less government they had the better. Under the mercantile system of the seventeenth and eighteenth centuries the idea was that colonies should contribute to the power of the mother country by supplying her with bullion, raw material, and tropical products, and should also provide her with markets for manufactured goods. These raw materials should not be disposed of to any other country except the mother country nor should any other country except the mother country supply the colonies. There was no surplus population or capital in those days, therefore to allow people to emigrate was a definite loss unless they created wealth for the mother country somewhere else. The mother country had the burden of their defence if its people emigrated. Its liabilities were increased by the migration, and colonies must therefore contribute to the mother country's welfare or the very mainsprings of defence would be destroyed. The general idea was that colonies were valuable as monopolies and were estates that should be worked for the benefit of the mother country as well as for their own. Hence in all the colonizing nations—Spain, Portugal, Holland, England, and France—there was formulated an elaborate code of laws intended to make of colonies remunerative assets. The thirteen of England's American colonies[1] revolted in the eighteenth century, while France lost the bulk of her overseas possessions during that period, as also did the Dutch, as a result of defeat in war. Yet during the first half of the nineteenth century both England and France were the richest countries in Europe: the loss of their colonies had not ruined them—far from it. Trade went on between England and the United States in a larger volume than it had ever done between England and the continental colonies in America. Where then lay the benefits of the restrictions of the old colonial system? Free traders were prepared to argue that colonies had no

[1] Their population in 1800 only numbered 5,308,483, of which 1,002,037 were negroes. *Abstract of Thirteenth Census*, p. 78.

value and that colonial trade should be thrown open to all comers. In addition, the reaction against the older system of bounties, prohibitions, drawbacks, and export and import duties was helped by the fact that it had become almost impossible to work or understand it from its very complication. Trade was growing; new articles were entering into commerce; and no trader could master the hundreds of statutes or ordinances under which he was supposed to carry on his business.

Another factor which combined to make for freedom of trade was the railway. After 1850, countries were being linked up by steam transport and it became possible to exchange heavy goods with a facility, rapidity, and cheapness that had never before been attainable. The railways were overriding all tariffs and reducing them to futility since, with the reduction in freights owing to mechanical traction, goods could no longer be kept out by existing tariffs. The lowering of the cost of moving goods was in itself equivalent to an all round reduction of tariff. All tariffs would have to be overhauled in view of the new economic feature: why therefore maintain obsolete arrangements?

Again, the movement towards freedom was stimulated by the fact that Continental Europe and the United States were anxious to equip themselves with economic tools. They wished to purchase from England the textile machinery, the rails, the locomotives, and the steam engines which should enable them to share in the new progress. Tariffs enhanced the price of these articles: why should they pay more for these essential things than they need? Europe accordingly was prepared to receive the Napoleonic overtures favourably. Just as France had inaugurated freedom of movement, so in this period she led the movement for greater freedom of trade. She concluded a treaty with England in 1860 and made drastic reductions in her favour, offering to do the same for other countries that would lower their tariffs on French goods. Those that would not do so remained on the higher tariff basis. As no nation could afford to see England specially favoured in the French market, the reductions were made. Again, a treaty having been concluded between Belgium and France with reductions by Belgium in order to get the benefit of the reduced French duties, other nations could not afford to see France enjoy a substantial preference in Belgium. They were obliged to approach Belgium to get similar concessions, and to get something they had to offer something. They also had to lower duties for France to get the same privileges in France as Belgium enjoyed. In this way Europe was soon covered with a network of treaties in which all the contracting Powers made reductions to get reductions. Inspired by the liberal sentiments prevailing, they all bound themselves under "the most favoured nation" clause to extend any further reductions they might make to all the other treaty Powers.

In the United States also this period was one of lower duties up to the time of the outbreak of the Civil War. The Southern States, which were concerned with the export of cotton to Europe, wished to obtain their manufactures on the cheapest possible terms without tariff hindrances and threw all their weight against the protection desired by the North for their small but growing industries.

During this period, Germany, France, Italy, Austria-Hungary, Holland, Belgium, and England not merely joined in concluding treaties which substantially lowered the prevailing rates of duty, but also proceeded to other free trade measures. Colonial trade was thrown open by France and Holland, following the example set by England in the period 1824–49. Henceforth any country could trade with the colonies of another country, and colonies could send their goods where they liked and buy from whom they pleased. The numerous restrictions on shipping, such as the additional duties on goods brought in foreign ships, the prohibition of ships from bringing certain classes of goods from anywhere except the place of origin, the additional harbour and pilot dues payable by foreign ships, the regulations which prohibited the conveyance by foreign ships of certain kinds of goods from any place whether it were the country of origin or no, the prohibition of foreign ships from engaging in the coasting trade—all these were abandoned or very considerably modified so as to confer upon foreign ships national treatment in matters of navigation. In almost all cases, aliens trading within a country were allowed to trade on the same basis as natives in all the territories of the Great Powers, with the exception of Russia. Bounties were given up, and internal tariff barriers such as those which remained between Russia and Poland, Austria and Hungary, between the Swiss Cantons, between the remaining German States, between the Italian States, between Sweden and Norway, between the Canadian Provinces, and between Moldavia and Wallachia were removed. In these twenty-two years, 1848–70, as might be expected, there was an almost unparalleled expansion of trade and commerce.

Meanwhile the movement in the direction of greater personal freedom already inaugurated was much accelerated. Austria freed her serfs after 1848; France the slaves in her colonies the same year. About 40 million peasants in varying degrees of subjection were freed in Russia after 1861 as a result of the liberal era which followed the disasters of the Crimean War of 1854–6. Russia felt that those disasters showed that she must modernize. The first requisite was a free population—hence the entire abolition of serfdom before which the German emancipation, important as it was, falls into insignificance. This was followed by the freeing of four million slaves as a result of the Civil War in the United States.

The expansion of trade between countries was accompanied by the spread of the industrial revolution in other countries than France and England. The United States began to tap their coal resources and equip themselves with rails and machines from England, while the European emigration after the troubles of '48 supplied a population to work the American mines and factories. Germany, too, between 1850 and 1870, was increasingly equipping herself with economic tools, many of which were purchased in Great Britain. Her coal and iron mines began to be developed along modern lines, and the opposition of the iron and textile industries became a factor to be reckoned with when framing the low tariffs between 1862 and 1873. Nevertheless, up to 1870 France continued to be the dominating economic personality in Europe. It was the most populous state in Western Europe at the beginning of the century, even after the losses of the Napoleonic Wars. Its population in 1789 had been 26 millions; in 1816 it was 29·5 millions; by 1870 it was 38,440,000.[1] Great Britain had 11,970,116 inhabitants in 1811,[2] and the United Kingdom 31,256,535 by 1870. Germany had a population of 24,833,000 in 1816. By 1870 Germany had

[1] E. Levasseur, *Population Francaise*, i, p. 308.

[2] The Irish Census was not taken till 1821, but it is estimated that the population of Ireland was about 5 millions in 1801. It was 6,801,827 in 1821. G. O'Brien, *Economic History of Ireland from the Union to the Famine*, p. 71.

38,891,000[1] and the United States 38,558,371.[2] Accordingly, France, the most populous country in 1815, was in 1870 still as populous as Germany or the United States and more populous than the United Kingdom. In sheer numbers France loomed large as well as wealthy in comparison with her contemporaries. It is not surprising, therefore, that France, which had given the impulse to personal freedom, was able to usher in greater freedom of trade through the Napoleonic treaty system of 1860–70. England might be treated as an exception by other nations. France was always an inspiration, and although free trade had been an accomplished fact in England in the 'forties, and though the European movement was based originally on English economic writers, yet it needed the French advertisement and Napoleon III to make it European. It is difficult for us to realize the glamour which this France, rejuvenated after the wars of 1815, was able to exercise on its contemporaries in the first three-quarters of the nineteenth century.

The shock of French defeat in 1870 with its terrible completeness created an epoch which brought with it not merely a change in commercial policy but a new economic model—the German. With the coming of Germany there was a repudiation of *laissez-faire* and a return to protective tariffs in every country but England. There was a revival under the stimulus of the German victorious organization of a belief in the efficacy of state action; the humiliation of France led the European nations to doubt the wisdom of so much individual liberty. There was increase of armaments with an intensification of national feeling and international rivalry. The working of coal and iron, the manufacture of machinery and chemicals, the erection of blast furnaces, and the establishment of engineering works led the European population, now accumulating rapidly on the coal and iron fields of Europe, to look for markets abroad and to defend their markets at home. Hence continental states considered that higher tariffs were needed to pay for armaments and to preserve the home market. The desire to sell abroad led to a renewed struggle for new colonies. France began its great expansion in Africa and Asia not so much for the purpose of markets

[1] *Statistisches Jahrbuch*, 1914, p. 2.

[2] *Abstract of Thirteenth Census*, p. 22. Russia did not take an official census till 1897, but is estimated to have had 45 millions of population in 1815. See *Statesman's Year-Book*, 1914, p. 1229.

as for the purpose of acquiring a set-off to the loss of Alsace and Lorraine. It raised its colonial territory from 166,075 square miles in 1870 to 2,219,575 square miles by 1906, while the colonial population under French rule increased from 2,375,252 to 33,804,370, not including Algeria and Tunis.[1] Germany, not to be out-distanced by its rival, appeared for the first time as an effective colonial power. Belgium and Italy entered the field as colonial aspirants, and the scramble for and the partition of Africa was the result, while the 'nineties witnessed the extension of spheres of influence in Asia.

The new protection was, however, something essentially different from the old. In the first place, thanks to the reformed civil administrations found by this time in most European countries, a tariff when made was scientific and was systematically enforced, while modern searchlights, telegraphs, swift cruisers, and now wireless communication make evasion difficult, and smuggling no longer an easy or lucrative profession. The bulk of land traffic now passes by train and is fairly easily examined on the frontiers. Modern steamers can only enter ports which have proper accommodation and there goods can be systematically dealt with. An eighteenth century tariff was partly evaded by bribery and smuggling: a modern tariff is in the main effective. Moreover a tariff is now far more scientifically drafted than formerly. Anyone who looks through the elaborate classification of, say, the German tariff of 1906, with its endless subdivisions and minute specifications, and compares it with one of the old English Books of Rates, will see the fundamental difference between the old general and the modern specialized tariff. But, in addition, the new protection had new weapons of which railways were the chief. Railway rates are so integral a part of modern intercourse that a modification or increase in their freights has all the effect of a new tariff. With state-owned railways on the continent, the freight rates were used to promote the export or hinder the import of goods. By means of rate reductions and preferences in respect of those goods which the state desired to encourage and by high rates on those articles the import of which it wished to discourage, and by manipulating port facilities and port dues, a second effective line of protection could be sent up, and this was done. The State not merely threw its weight into the scales

[1] Hon. R. Lister, *Report on French Colonies* [*Cd.* 3883], 1908, p. 67.

by regulating trade through its railways; it also in certain States, such as England, France, and Germany, took up the work of diffusing among traders information as to openings, markets, and contracts, either privately or through the organization of the Consular service. In the growing keenness of competition between States there was a development of shipping subsidies, and restrictions were placed by Russia, Italy, Austria-Hungary, France, and the United States of America on foreign shipping. A movement grew up to re-establish closer relations between the mother country and her colonies, not by excluding foreigners as in the olden days, but by a system of preferential arrangements which give the mother country a predominance in the colonial markets. France, the United States, and the United Kingdom all became the centre of a network of preferential arrangements with their various colonial possessions.

Although the return to protection and the emergence of Germany as the new model were two of the great transformations after 1870, another dominant feature characterizes the period, namely, the development of Russia and the United States as corn exporting countries. With the accelerated railway building which took place in the United States after the recovery from the effects of the Civil War, and with the migration of those who had taken part in that war and of those affected by the depression of 1873, there was a rapid colonization of the Middle West in the United States. The virgin soil was broken up for wheat and maize which the railways carried at cheap rates to the seaboard and the steamers took rapidly and cheaply to Europe. Distance was no longer a barrier: it was no longer the case that it only paid to move grain when it was at famine prices. The price of wheat freights from New York to Liverpool dropped from 10*s*. 6*d*. a quarter in 1874 to 4*s*. in 1884, and from San Francisco it dropped from 67*s*. a ton in 1874 to 40*s*. in 1885 and 22*s*. 6*d*. in January, 1893.[1]

This produced a veritable agricultural revolution in Western Europe. In France and Central Europe there was a peasantry not long out of serfdom or its equivalent slowly and laboriously learning better methods, and with the great drop in prices they were threatened with ruin.

[1] See *Report on Agricultural Depression*, 1894 [*Cd.* 7400], p. 662. For particulars of a 50 per cent drop in inward freights between 1884 and 1903 see *Second Fiscal Blue Book, 1904* [*Cd.* 2337], chart, p. 253. The decline in outward freights during that period was 30 per cent.

No country could afford to see the decay of its numerous peasant population. Both Germany and France were also convinced for military reasons of the unwisdom of depending on foreign food supplies. Hence the protective era, already approaching for revenue reasons, was helped on by the idea of assisting agriculture through corn and meat duties. Only in the United Kingdom was the force of the American competition allowed to have full sway. Military considerations did not count in the United Kingdom and there were few small farmers to protect. The type of agriculture was that carried on by the capitalist large farmer and landlord. They were not as helpless as the continental peasant and the effects of free trade were allowed to proceed unchecked. In Ireland, where there was a large cultivating peasantry, the results were disastrous, and even Great Britain was forced to abandon *laissez-faire* so far as Ireland was concerned and start the series of Acts beginning with fair rents fixed by the State instead of free contract and leading up to the elimination of the landlord by the gradual advance of money, estimated to reach two hundred million pounds, to the Irish tenant to buy his landlord out. In other words, the abandonment of *laissez-faire* by England was so complete that it has ended in one of the biggest schemes of land nationalization of modern times.

In every country the agricultural depression which ensued between 1875 and 1895 produced a quickened interest in the production of better crops and in making farming pay. Scientific methods and co-operation in agriculture became a leading feature of both German and French rural life and France became practically self-sufficing as regards wheat, while the rapid increase in the yields and of the arable area in Germany[1] is in striking contrast with the British experience of nearly 3½ million acres turned from arable into pasture between 1870 and 1914.[2]

Russia, which had been the main European granary in the first half of the nineteenth century, continued to export even larger quantities of grain in the 'eighties and 'nineties. It, too, was affected by the drop in prices because it had to sell its wheat and rye cheaper in competition with American grain; and as it had to pay the interest on

[1] T. H. Middleton, *Recent Development of German Agriculture*, 1916 [*Cd.* 8305], pp. 7, 64.

[2] *Report of Reconstruction Committee on Agriculture*, 1918 [*Cd.* 9079], p. 10.

its debt to Western Europe for railway building by its corn exports, it had to sell increasing quantities to make up the amount due. In this Russia was helped by its railways and by the special reductions in corn freights which enabled it to export an ever larger amount, especially to England. This drop in the price of its principal article of commerce had very serious effects on the standard of life of the Russian peasant, who was just emerging from serfdom and trying to accustom himself to a money economy.

Neither Russia nor the United States remained outside the general tendency towards protective tariffs, though in neither case was it accompanied by the feature so marked in Central and Western Europe, namely, a resuscitated belief in the general beneficence of State action in all the industrial sphere and not merely in regulating trade by higher customs duties. In Western and Central Europe the State railways, shipping subsidies, legislation for the poorer classes, commercial and technical education, agricultural and scientific research financed by the Government, are instances of the extension of the spheres of state action, while Russia and the United States confined themselves to the ideal of making themselves as far as possible self-sufficing. Hence both these great agricultural countries transformed themselves into industrial powers. In the United States an almost prohibitive tariff, put on during the Civil War and reinforced at intervals in the 'eighties and 'nineties, helped that country to attract capital and utilize its immense natural resources. In the 'eighties the chief feature was the development of its great steel industry and cotton factories. In the 'nineties, too, under Witte, Russia began, with the aid of foreign capital, to develop further its cotton mills both in Poland and round Moscow, its iron and coal in the Donetz basin and its petroleum at Baku and Grozny. Behind a high tariff wall foreign capital for a time earned good dividends and started new industrial areas. Neither of these countries affected Western and Central Europe in the nineteenth century by their manufactured exports: they merely filled their own home markets. It was the export of grain and meat products and the reduction in price that reacted so disastrously on a European peasantry without much capital or staying power.

The period is not merely remarkable for the industrialization of Russia and the United States but for the rapid transformation of Germany from an agricultural to an urban industrial state also. The victories over France restored its self-respect and its belief in its own capacities. The Gilchrist Thomas process brought out in 1878 enabled Germany to utilize its iron which, containing a considerable proportion of phosphorus, had hitherto been almost useless for steel. The railways and canals brought the iron of the newly acquired province of Lorraine to the coal-fields of Westphalia with the rapid development of the German iron industry as a result.[1]

The textile industry developed rapidly, reinforced as it was by the spindles and cotton printing of the ceded province of Alsace—a great cotton making region. Factories and iron smelting and railways demand coal: so there was a growing demand for that mineral and for miners to extract it and a rapid development of the German coal areas. The crude steel ingots produced in the furnaces became the basis of a machine-making[2] industry, locomotive building, ship-building and the like. Westphalia, the districts bordering the Rhine, Saxony, and parts of Silesia and Bavaria became huge workshops instead of merely rural areas. In France the momentum was less, and France, though equipped for the "great industry", remained predominantly a land of domestic workers.

This industrialization, which cannot proceed without workers, led to the formation of new industrial groups and gave rise to class struggles in which French ideas prevailed for the first half of the nineteenth century—till 1848 in fact, to be in turn succeeded by the ideas of social democracy culled from Marx. The German model was again predominant in the latter part of the nineteenth century. Prince Bismarck had, however, decided to deal with the question by means of social reforms from above and he developed the system of social contributory insurance already at work in parts of Germany, which has been imitated by all the other Great Powers of Europe in some degree or other. The English inventions of the factory

[1] As a rule iron goes to coal because it takes about 3 tons of coal (according to quality) to smelt one of iron, but the return trucks which would otherwise be empty often take back coke and a secondary iron industry springs up on the basis of this return traffic either at the iron fields or in its proximity.

[2] Sombart, quoting from the Occupation Census of 1907, gives 385,225 persons in the industry of machine-making in 1895 and 907,048 by 1907, and adds that Germany has "completely emancipated herself from foreign countries in this respect". *Deutsche Volkswirtschaft*, 1913, p. 155.

and mine inspectors, main drainage, and preventive medicine, have also been widely adopted, the one to check the worst abuses of the new mills and mines, the other to make the herding of masses in towns a healthy possibility. The last quarter of the century was remarkable for the amount of legislation intended to benefit the new industrial class and to check the worst evils of the change. From regulating the work of women and children the activities of the State have been extended to include the regulation of the work of men. From merely dealing with its citizens at work, State intervention has advanced to the point where it takes account, with variations according to the country, of their early years—their education and the sanitary condition of their homes. From giving children merely the elements of a literary education, it has come more and more to look into their feeding, physical welfare, and technical training. In this period it was also natural that German economic writers should exercise an important influence on economic thought. List, who had written in 1841 opposing the ideas of Adam Smith, now became the protectionist prophet. He set out to show that cosmopolitan free trade did not necessarily benefit the smaller unit of the nation over a long period of time. His *National System of Political Economy* was widely translated, being rendered into Russian, for instance, by no less a person than Count Witte himself, and the views therein urged were put into practice in Russia.

It is to be noticed how closely the economic and political events of the periods react on one another. The chief political movement of the period from 1815 to 1848 was a re-establishment of absolutism by the Congress of Vienna and the constant revolts against it. The period of the absolute Kings coincides with the idea of state direction from above in economic matters. Hence the retention of the protective paternal policy known as mercantilism until the 'forties. With the general outbreak of revolution in 1848 there was ushered in a period of new nations and new constitutions. This successful revolt against absolutism produced a sentiment in favour of freedom all round, not freedom to vote merely, but freedom of trade and industrial production, hence the period of national revival and constitutional liberties finds its parallel in the free trade movement of the 'fifties and 'sixties. After 1870 the chief political characteristics are the growth of imperialism, the revival of kingship, and the belief in authority.[1] These phenomena were partly due to disappointment that democracy and nationalities should have accomplished so little, partly to the fact that statesmen had learnt how to outmanœuvre their parliaments and secure control, and partly to the growth of huge armies and organized police forces which made revolutionary outbreaks unlikely to succeed. The result in the economic sphere is an increasing state direction from above of industry and commerce and an enormous impetus to colonization and trade expansion in other countries. The general dissatisfaction in some quarters with the growing helplessness of the mass as confronted with governments found its expression in proposals to eliminate government entirely, as in syndicalism, or to utilize it in only a very moderate measure, as in gild socialism.

In this period so closely are political and economic considerations interwoven that nearly all the political action of the Great Powers is conditioned by economic motives. Germany's desire to dominate the markets in the Balkans and reach out from there to the Levant and Asia Minor was one of the main causes of the European War of 1914.[2] Germany's desire to obtain more colonies, especially those belonging to France, and to obtain a better sea outlet through Antwerp than its North Sea ports afforded to a great industrial power, led to the invasion of Belgium and France. Germany's action was, however, not unconnected with the desire to obtain the great fields of minette iron ores lying just beyond its boundaries in the Briey and Longwy districts.

There stands out from this general preliminary survey the striking manner in which great wars create new epochs in economic history. The freedom of movement in Germany which followed the French wars was almost a direct consequence of the French invasion and the Prussian defeat. Reorganization was found to be absolutely essential if Prussia was to beat Napoleon. Serfdom, gilds, and tariffs were all reconstructed and the rest of Germany could not afford to remain behind. Again, the Crimean war of 1854–6 led to the freeing of the Russian masses. Russia

[1] See Hobhouse, *Democracy and Reaction*, chap. ii, and H. A. L. Fisher, *The Republican Tradition in Europe*, chap. xiii.

[2] G. W. Prothero, *German Opinion and German Policy before the War*, 1916, pp. 28–33.

had been defeated through defective organization. If Russia was to be a modern state, able to hold its own with Western nations, it must have a free population whose energies could be diverted into new channels. After the lapse of years Russia discovered, as the English had discovered in Ireland, that giving a man a farm did not make him a farmer. The Russian peasant was grindingly poor, unable to pay his taxes, and famines devastated the country periodically. The defeats of the Russo-Japanese war were followed by agrarian risings which threatened to inaugurate a second French Revolution. The Government was forced to take action, the peasants could not longer be neglected, modern agricultural methods had to be introduced in Russia. Hence a great period of agricultural reforms, all the more remarkable as they affect one of the great grain areas of the world and a country which in size is two-thirds of Europe. The Crimean War did not leave England unaltered. It hastened on the Civil Service reforms which had been so often discussed. The great administrative breakdown of the war gave point to those who urged the appointment of civil servants by examination and not by patronage. In another way it lessened the opposition to the sanitary reforms for which the Health Movement stood and which had encountered so many difficulties. Florence Nightingale gave a practical demonstration of the efficacy of preventive and sanitary measures. The illness and mortality from preventable causes in that war brought the whole question of preventive medicine, isolation hospitals, and so forth to the front, and people who had regarded illness as a discipline from the Lord began to think that perhaps the Lord meant people to help themselves in this matter.

War not merely brought to a head questions of personal freedom. It has had an important influence in hastening the coming of steam power and machinery.

Napoleon restarted the industrial revolution in France to make the continent independent of England's manufactures and incidentally to ruin his most formidable enemy and raise up France in its place as the provider of iron and textiles.[1]

[1] There had been cotton machines and modern iron works in France before 1789, but the collapse of economic life after 1789 ruined the beginnings of the French Industrial Revolution. There was no capital or security forthcoming for industrial enterprises; labour was largely

Germany received its industrial impetus later from the war of 1870. No contrast is more striking than that between the divided, backward, poverty-stricken, agricultural mosaic which bore the geographical designation, Germany, in 1815, and the unified nationalized country welded together by a victorious war in 1870–1. The acquisition of Alsace and Lorraine with their skilled workers, revenues, iron deposits, and cotton spindles was one reason for the rapid development of German industry after 1870.

The increase of self-confidence felt by the whole German nation at having shattered a power whose credit had stood so high and whose population was equal and wealth greater than its own was remarkable. Germany had been humiliated to the dust in 1806 by France ; Sedan restored the self respect which Jena had forfeited and the whole of German national life received a new impetus to national effort. A new morale was created. If Germany could triumph easily over France in war, why should it not win in the economic sphere ? So why not let the national effort, so efficacious in war, be applied to trade and industry ? Hence the attention to technical education, to the development of state railways, and the provision of cheap water transport by canal building. A victorious country finds it easy to attract capital either from its own people or from foreigners. The banking system was organized in Germany with the special view of directly assisting industrial and commercial development. Germany, by the end of the nineteenth century, was still a great agricultural country, but was also the second great industrial country of Europe. Russia, too, experienced a considerable impetus to industrial development through war. The Russo-Turkish war of 1878 occasioned a marked growth of national feeling, which found expression in the wish of Russia to provide for its own wants by its own efforts. The succeeding decades witnessed a period of rapid railway building, high tariffs to keep out foreign goods, and a development of the iron and textile industries at home.[1]

Not merely did the freeing of serfs and industrialization receive a great impetus from war, but much of the colonial expansion during the nineteenth century is directly traceable

absorbed by the wars ; and if French machine industry was to start again it would have to be started from above.

[1] G. von Schulze Gaevernitz, *Volkswirtschaftliche Studien aus Russland*, pp. 250–3, 272.

to the feelings of rivalry aroused by the Franco-Prussian war. France was becoming a great African power. Germany could not see itself out-distanced by its rival. At the same time Germany wished to imitate the trade expansion of England and secure markets and raw material for its new industrial development. One element in the English success was thought to be England's possession of colonies: hence, partly, the German desire to acquire colonies. The Russo-Turkish War, which prevented Russia getting to a warm water port in Europe—Constantinople, led that country to push out towards warm water in the Pacific, with the result of the building of the Siberian railway and the accelerated colonization of Siberia. The Turkish war also gave a tremendous impetus to the Russian colonization of its Central Asiatic provinces.

Wars have left their traces not only on colonization but on tariffs. Wars must be paid for and the financial effects of wars last long after the actual fighting. The high tariffs of the period 1815–48 are partly to be attributed to the need for revenue after the French wars, for huge na tional debts had been piled up on which interest had to be paid. Hence the retention of high tariffs, even in England, when a large part of the world had been prepared by the argument of eighteenth century philosophers for greater freedom of intercourse.

The Franco-Prussian war again, though not the only factor, was an important element in the return to high tariffs during the last quarter of the nineteenth century. All nations relearnt the art of war in 1870. Europe became after that date a great armed camp, and that was expensive. Revenue reasons were one of the causes of the protectionist reaction from the liberal period of 1848–1870. Again, the effect of wars on tariffs was clearly seen in North America. The great result of the war between the North and South was to lead to the welding together of the United States. Previously it had consisted of two divergent areas, the North and the South, divided in tariff policy, on the question of land tenures and in political ideals, and differing fundamentally on the question of slave or free labour. After the war there was only one policy and one system, and high tariffs expressed the ideal of a national America seeking to be self-sufficing. Protection received a halo, since it seemed to stand for the national development of the resources of a great country.

Accordingly the economic effect of wars has been considerably to accelerate certain tendencies already at work and to lead to the reconstruction of national policies and national and social life. The effort which had been put forth for the military struggle was continued and applied to the things of peace on a scale hitherto regarded as impossible.

PART II

THE AGRICULTURAL REVOLUTION

CHAPTER I

Personal Freedom and the Agricultural Revolution

The implications of serfdom. The personal status of the serf and the obligations attached to land holding. The methods of cultivation: (*a*) estate management of farms let to tenants; (*b*) manorial cultivation by the feudal lord with astriction of the cultivators to the soil and labour dues.

The problems of the serf countries (France, Germany, and Russia) differ fundamentally from those of the non-serf countries (the United Kingdom and the United States).

In the serf countries men became personally free and a change in agricultural methods, taxation, and administration was necessary; a new legal system had to be evolved to give effect to the new personal freedom. The urgency of taking ex-serfs over to intensive cultivation made government intervention in agriculture inevitable.

In the non-serf countries the policy of the United Kingdom was to introduce new methods and thereby increase yields, but meanwhile the increased imports from the United States were a disturbing factor in all Europe. In the United States it has been a question of bringing unoccupied land under cultivation and attracting settlers by gifts of free land.

ONE of the leading characteristics of nineteenth century economic development has been a reconstruction of the whole of agricultural life and methods of cultivation in Europe and the United States. This was all the more important as agriculture was, and still is, the great predominant interest on the continent and in America. While the problems confronting Great Britain were those connected with the rise of a new industrial class collected in factories and massed in towns, the problems of the continent for the first three quarters of the century centred round the freeing of a people attached to the soil. After that date the chief agricultural question was one of defence against the imports from the United States and the development of intensive farming.

In Central and Eastern Europe, at the end of the eighteenth century, the bulk of the agricultural population consisted of serfs tied to the soil. In France, though there were but few serfs remaining at the time of the French Revolution, the peasant was subject to onerous taxation and feudal payments of such a nature that he was as much bound to the soil as if he had been legally a serf. In neither case was there the possibility of free movement or free development of the agricultural population. It was the task of the French to hasten by their revolt in 1789 the abolition of the feudal régime based on privilege and the substitution of a modern economic system based on personal equality. Serfs in Europe and slaves in America were both made free during the nineteenth century.

In the Middle Ages, the typical agricultural classes were the overlords and the unfree tenants or serfs, although there were also free men who held land from an overlord or feudal superior. Serfs were liable to two sets of obligations, one in virtue of their status as serfs and one as a result of holding land. To his feudal superior, seigneur, or overlord, the serf owed certain dues and services and was under certain obligations, simply because he was that overlord's man. The obligation attached to his person. A serf without land was still liable to attend the lord's court, had to ask permission to marry, and had still to make a payment if raised to the status of free man, while all his property reverted in theory to his overlord at death. Even if he purchased land and became a landowner himself, these obligations of his serf status attached to him as long as he was not emancipated.

To his landlord, who was generally, though not always, the same person as the feudal superior, the serf owed services in return for the land by which he lived. The theory was that the lord endowed the serf with a holding, protected him and kept him safe, and in return the serf kept the lord by his work.

Under the system of cultivation which prevailed all over Europe in the Middle Ages and which was still in force in continental Europe in the eighteenth century, the land on an estate was divided into three portions, arable, meadow, and waste. The arable land was divided into strips and each man cultivated a number of these strips, but no two strips lay together—they were all intermingled with those of other persons. Thus all tenants had a share of the good and bad land alike. The arable fields were divided so that part should be left fallow each year to rest and recover, and this was another reason for the division into scattered strips. Were the land not distributed, there would be years when all a man's land would be in the fallow area and he would have nothing for that year. The ploughing, sowing, and reaping were done in common and each man had to plant the same cereal crop as his neighbour. It was a fixed system of cultivation allowing of no variation. The curious point about it was its universal adoption all over Europe from France to Russia and the fact that this method of agricultural production has lasted right up to our own time in Eastern Europe. The reason for its prevalence is to be found in the fact that it was difficult to devise any other method by which the cattle could be fed. Cattle were essential for ploughing and on the existence of the plough-oxen depended the corn harvest Oxen can now-a-days be fed on hay, roots, or grain in winter. Up to the eighteenth century artificial pastures did not exist in any of the great continental countries. The hay grew in the meadows near streams and there was very little of it. Roots were not grown, and the result was a great shortage of winter food. Grain was too scarce for human beings for it to be allotted to cattle. In the spring and summer, when the hay and corn were coming on, the animals had to be pastured on the wastes, and thus wastes were an indispensable adjunct to this type of cultivation. As the wastes did not give enough food in the winter, the cattle were turned over all the arable fields after harvest and picked up a scanty living with the whole resources of the estate at their disposal. Even then it was hopeless to keep a large proportion of animals over the winter. They were thus killed in autumn when fat and salted for household consumption.

The lord of the manor was in theory the owner of all the land. A certain portion was kept in hand by him and called the domain. The rest was allotted to the serfs, who cultivated the domain as well as their own land in return for their holdings. In some cases, as in France, the lord's strips were intermingled with the tenants; in others, notably in England, the lord had succeeded in either rearranging or consolidating his strips so that they formed a compact area to which he could add by new intakes from the waste, which equally belonged to him subject to certain well-defined rights of the tenants to cut wood and pasture their cattle and plough oxen. The value of the lord's estate and his own existence depended upon having serfs to work for him. Thus the unfree tenants were bound to the soil as were also their children. In return, however, the lord was supposed to defend the serf and keep him safe from outside aggression and to feed him in famine years. If the lord had to be constantly in arms to prevent his land being invaded or his serfs taken away, someone else had to provide his food. In the same way in Russia, when the Czars wanted the nobles for purposes of administration, someone had to maintain the nobles while they fulfilled their obligations to the Czar. If the peasants were at liberty to leave in their lord's absence he might starve. To avoid this the peasants were attached to the soil in Russia in the early eighteenth century. Where the overlord was specialized for military purposes, as in France, or for administration, as in Prussia or Russia, his serfs paid such taxes as were levied. If the noble was incapable, owing to his other preoccupations, of keeping himself, it was considered that he would be unable to pay taxes. His tenants must, therefore, furnish the payments. The bulk of the taxation levied in continental Europe prior to 1789 was paid by the peasantry. The towns and middle classes also contributed ; but the noble class were privileged and escaped.[1] In his capacity as local administrator and keeper of order, the lord was the serf's judge in civil and usually in criminal matters.

As the centuries passed, this type of agricultural partnership between the lord of the manor and his unfree tenants which we may term *manorial cultivation* became modified in certain countries into what may be called *estate management.* Instead of cultivating a large portion of the manor himself with serfs, it had paid the landed proprietors in France and England to let their domains to tenants who paid a rent for the portion they received according to the value of the land. The lord who had let the domain no longer required the services of unfree cultivators on his land and the tendency was for the services to be commuted into payments in money or in kind. On an estate there would therefore be tenants paying a rent and other cultivators paying, not according to the value of the land, but according to the value of the lapsed services. In England these latter persons were called copyholders and they enjoyed virtual security of tenure as long as they made their payments, especially after the sixteenth century. Is some cases the lord did not merely let land but sold it outright, the man who bought being a freeholder.

[1] This is not true of the non-serf countries—England, Scotland, Ireland, and the colonies.

The obligations attaching to the serf personally tended, with the passing of centuries, to disappear or become merely nominal. In France, however, this was not the case. The personal obligations due to the overlord were so onerous that they were one of the causes of the revolution of 1789.

When the lord once received money payments or payments in kind in lieu of the services he did not require, he would be indifferent as to whether a particular serf stayed or left as long as he could get fresh tenants. The lord did not want the man, he wanted the money. Hence, where the lord ceased to do his own cultivation, compulsory astriction to the soil disappeared and considerable personal freedom existed, and men bought or leased land freely.

The fixed payments in lieu of services gradually became nominal as the value of money fell, until there was little to distinguish the copyholder and the freeholder. The object of the owner who let his land was to get a definite yield of money or goods and the skill consisted in the management of the estate and not in its method of cultivation by the proprietor.

Where the lord did not lease or sell his land, but retained and worked the domain himself, that is to say, where he continued the system of *manorial cultivation*, his prosperity depended on the number of cultivators he could control. In this case the serf would be bound to the soil and his children also would be forced to take up holdings to increase the manorial labour force.

Where the system of manorial cultivation prevailed, the serf worked so many days in each week for his lord, furnishing part of the ox-teams or merely giving hand service as the case might be. In return he received a holding which, in the case of the man providing oxen, was supposed to be sufficient to keep him and his family. The man giving hand services would not have so large a portion of land. The holdings consisted of portions of arable land and meadow for hay, and carried with them the right to cut fuel or timber or turf or litter from the wastes. The serf had also the right of turning a certain number of beasts or poultry over the wastes and of turning the cattle over the arable and meadow land of his own and his neighbours' strips in winter. As long as the usual services were performed with any extra services that might be customary at harvest or hay time, which varied from place to place, the serf could not be ejected. He could not leave, but he usually did not wish to do so. Meanwhile he had complete security of tenure, not merely legally, but because labour was scarce and it was to the lord's interest to keep him if possible. Up to the beginning of the nineteenth century, labour was difficult to obtain in every great European country.

When the peasant was free he could leave; but if he left he surrendered his land because it was only held on condition of certain services being performed and certain dues in kind being paid. Moreover, even if he were a free man he could not easily migrate, because the gilds would be an effective barrier to his taking up remunerated industrial employment. He simply would not be allowed to "settle" in any place where he could gain his living by industrial work as long as the gilds were the principal municipal authorities in the town. And where gilds were weak or non-existent, as in country districts, the poor relief administration would prevent a new comer from settling unless he could prove that he was not likely to fall into poverty.

Therefore to the peasant the mere title of "freeman" meant nothing. What he really wanted was to own his land without the obligation to give services and dues. Hence in the nineteenth century the question was not merely to free the serf but rather so to adjust the relations between the lord and the ex-serf that the latter could have his land as a piece of individual property without the ruin of the former land-owner resulting.

In France the system of estate management was almost universal by the eighteenth century, and there was consequently little serfdom, but the personal obligations to the feudal superior were still enforced and were becoming more oppressive. In Western Germany there is found at that date a mixture of the two systems. Manorial cultivation and estate management existed side by side, and, owing to the prevalence of the latter, serfdom was of a mild nature. Further East the system became harsher. In Prussia, in the greater part of Austria-Hungary, and over the whole of Russia, we get the system of manorial cultivation with the people bound to the soil.[1]

[1] As this book is only concerned with the Great Powers, the serfdom which existed in the eighteenth century in Denmark, Norway, Sweden, Roumania, Switzerland, and elsewhere, is not touched on. For further information as to serfdom in the smaller States see article "Bauernbefreiung", in Conrad's *Handwörterbuch*, and references.

In England the system of manorial cultivation had given place to estate management and serfdom had disappeared by the beginning of the sixteenth century. At that date the typical cultivators were small freeholders or yeomen, copyholders to whom the title of yeomen was sometimes extended, and small tenants on lease. Out of these, large farmers were slowly being evolved by the eighteenth century. Scotland had never developed serfdom, and personal freedom was established by the end of the sixteenth century in Ireland, when the authority of the clan chiefs was overthrown.[1] When, therefore, England expanded overseas, there was no question of the colonists taking the institution of serfdom with them.

While, accordingly, the bulk of the agricultural population of continental Europe was unfree in varying degrees in the eighteenth century,[2] the people of England, Scotland, and Ireland had enjoyed personal liberty in the economic sense for about three centuries. There is, therefore, a fundamental distinction between the agricultural problems of the serf and the non-serf countries in the nineteenth century, and this affects not merely their agricultural life, but the whole of their economic development.

Being short of labour for tropical agriculture, the colonists in the West Indies and the Southern belt of the United States, although free themselves, employed negro slaves in the seventeenth century. With the general prevalence of serfdom, personal liberty was so uncommon that slavery did not shock public sentiment till the end of the eighteenth century. The problem for the United States in the nineteenth century was to effect the freeing of these slaves, and it was only done at the cost of a civil war.

The emancipation of the slaves was carried out in the British Empire in 1833 and in the French colonies in 1848. Although compensation was paid to the owners, it was inadequate. The West Indian planters were partially ruined by the loss of control over their labour supply; and the methods of the emancipation led to friction with the Cape Dutch which sowed the seed of a bitter racial struggle.

Thus all the five great powers—France, Germany, Russia,

[1] Bonn, *Die englische Kolonisation in Irland*, i, pp. 237, 260–2.

[2] Schmoller considers that from 60–90 per cent of the European land system was in bondage up to the beginning of the nineteenth century *Grundriss*, i, p. 282.

the United States, and the British Empire—have been occupied during the past century with questions of emancipation and personal freedom and solving the problems resulting therefrom.

As far as continental Europe was concerned, this meant a complete change in the legal and economic relationship between individuals. The legal systems which had been devised for a feudal state had to be reconstructed to fit the new institutions of private property and personal liberty. To make human mobility possible, the laws of settlement which prevented migration from place to place had to be altered. If the lord of the manor were no longer the principal judicial element of the area and the manor court no longer the compulsory court for the mass of the agricultural population, what was to take its place? A new local government system had to be created in France, Germany, and Russia for both rural and urban areas. A man might be legally free to leave the land when he ceased to be a serf, but it was an entirely different thing for him to be allowed to settle down somewhere else. The place to which he might wish to go was sure to have restrictions on the right of settlement. The gilds especially had been hostile to the migration of countrymen to towns for fear they might constitute a cheap labour force. As the gilds were the chief administrative organs of the towns, they were able to prevent new-comers taking up a trade which was confined to those apprenticed to it. During the nineteenth century not merely were the laws of settlement modified to permit free migration in rural areas, but the town authorities were reconstructed and the gilds were no longer allowed to restrict men in their choice of an occupation. It was now open to the ex-serf to forsake agriculture for industry if he wished or he could leave his own country for another. He was free to choose his occupation or his domicile as he had never been free before. New town authorities were set up in place of the gilds and municipal reform was one of the results of the great emancipation of the nineteenth century. Taxation had to be entirely recast in France to secure personal freedom in that country and the privileged exemption of the upper classes was abolished where it existed in other countries.[1]

[1] In the United Kingdom taxation was also remodelled, but for other reasons. When the country went over to free trade, direct taxation in the form of the income tax was revived in 1842 to make up the loss of

The general result of the break-up of the system of manorial cultivation which occurred in the nineteenth century was that the peasant, when once emancipated, was free to rise in the world or free to go under, free to stay or free to go where he pleased. He was able to buy, sell, or mortgage his property, he could cultivate it as he chose, while he only paid a fair share of the taxation that was borne by all. He did not require protection from his lord, as the new governments with their military forces and police kept order, but he could no longer look to his lord to tide him over bad times. He had to rely on himself with such help as the state would afford. He thus attained to independence, self-dependence, and the status of equal citizenship. Not merely was he free personally, but he had free choice of occupation once the gild power was limited and the settlement laws modified. The change meant enormously increased possibilities for the individual personally, and this personal freedom constitutes the fundamental difference between the eighteenth and nineteenth centuries so far as Central and Western Europe were concerned. In Russia, though the serfs were freed in the 'sixties, the full implications of this freedom—freedom of movement, free choice of occupation, individual ownership and user of land—were only being realized after the revolution of 1905.

To substitute free and wage-paid labour for unfree labour giving day work as labour dues meant new methods of farming, and the result was a revolution in agricultural methods in every continental country. This had become pressing, as the population was already outgrowing the visible food supply. Under the system of manorial cultivation no artificial manures were used: there were few cattle as it was difficult to keep them over the winter and therefore animal manure was scarce. Rotation of crops was not understood and the yields of grain were scanty. As long, however, as there was plenty of land, portions of the waste could be broken up and brought into cultivation as the population slowly increased.

revenue from the customs, while the death duties were extended in 1853 to landed property. The tendency has been to rely more and more on direct taxation and to penalize the richer classes by heavier taxation on larger incomes and higher estate duties on large fortunes left at death, while incomes below a certain level are exempted altogether. In other words, the trend in England in the nineteenth century has been the exact opposite of the privileged exemption so characteristic of the eighteenth century.

Up to the end of the seventeenth century there were only little oases of cultivation in the midst of marshes, heaths, commons, forest, brushwood, and sandy plains. In the eighteenth century and particularly towards the end of it, population began to increase rapidly. The general result was that the available land was in process of being rapidly used up and people had somehow to get more out of the existing land they held.

The introduction of better methods of farming was a constant preoccupation after 1750 in both France, which was over-populated for its food resources, and in Great Britain with its growing industrial population. In the latter country, improving landlords popularized turnips which provided winter food for cattle. It was therefore possible to keep the animals alive during the winter instead of killing them off in autumn. Fresh meat and milk thus became obtainable during the winter months. The winter fodder was reinforced by clover, and artificial grass lands increased the pastures. Turnips cleaned the ground for the next cereal crop, while clover stored up nitrates in their roots which formed a valuable food for grain when sown after clover. Thus clover and turnips served the double purpose of augmenting the winter food supply for cattle and increasing the grain yields. As they improved the soil, both clover and turnips could be planted in the fallow year and thus they increased the cultivated area as no land need lie vacant to recover. Thus they became the basis of larger grain yields and new scientific cattle breeding.

French land-owners, in attempting to emulate English farming methods, fell foul of their peasantry and precipitated the Revolution of 1789. Great Britain, however, carried out the change to intensive methods in the eighteenth century. In the nineteenth century France and Germany were both obliged to take their people over to intensive methods to avoid scarcities. As cattle could be kept during the winter on hay and roots, the great wastes were no longer necessary as grazing grounds. Nor were they required for fuel once coal became available in quantities. Therefore the nineteenth century witnessed in both France and Germany what the eighteenth had already witnessed in Great Britain, namely, the reclamation of wastes and commons, drainage and irrigation, the dividing up of the commons between individuals and the abolition of the rights of common pasture. The strips were being gradually abolished by the process of enclosure—a rearrangement of the land so that each man should be at liberty to farm a compact area in his own way without reference to other people's method of cultivation.

Even in farming methods the tendency was to introduce liberty. The ex-serf had, however, to be taught to follow a proper rotation of crops, and he had to learn the value of manures, the way to increase yields from a small area and how to fill in the fallow periods with roots or clover. All this meant a radical change from extensive to intensive cultivation which could only be carried out in the case of an ignorant peasantry just out of serfdom by guidance from above by the central or local authority. The transition occupied the governments of France and Germany during the whole of the nineteenth century, and at the end of the century the transition was still incomplete.[1]

The Russian Government did not free its serfs until the 'sixties and therefore came later to the question of taking its people over to intensive methods. For forty years after the emancipation there were constant famines and scarcities in Russia in spite of a great extension of the area cultivated in both the Steppes and Siberia. The population, with its backward methods of cultivation, had outgrown the land by which it lived, as the French had outgrown their resources before 1789. The Russian peasants, clamouring for more land, joined the constitutional reform party in 1905 and precipitated a revolution. The Russian government, realizing that the peasants must be taught how to get more out of the land they already held, was engaged in carrying out a far-reaching scheme of enclosure with reclamation of wastes and the introduction of clover, roots, and artificial manures, when the war broke out in 1914, and their energies became absorbed in military matters. A peasantry will not willingly adopt intensive cultivation as long as there is vacant land available. In both France before 1789 and Russia before 1905, the peasants clamoured for a distribution of the land held by King, nobles, and church. In France there was a vast land redistribution after the Revolution, and there the cultivators settled down eventually to get more out of the existing land when no more land was available for distribution. In Russia the peasants were in process of acquiring the land of the Crown

[1] Austria-Hungary, Norway, Sweden, Denmark, and Roumania have been similarly occupied.

and the nobles before 1914, the financial facilities being provided by the Government. In Ireland also a great land transfer was being effected, the tenants buying out the landlords by means of loans advanced by the Government of the United Kingdom.

In the middle of the difficult transition from serfdom to freedom and from extensive to intensive cultivation came the cheap meat and wheat imports from the United States, causing wide-spread agricultural depression. It quickened the pace of the change to intensive cultivation in Germany ; it promoted agricultural co-operation in both France and Germany ; it increased the agricultural difficulties in Russia ; it made the Irish question acute and created a radical transformation of English agriculture. No European country remained unaffected. It stimulated a return to protective tariffs on the continent of Europe and state assistance to agriculture in Germany, France, and the United Kingdom.

The problems of the people of the United States were two-fold. After freeing the slaves, the agriculture of the South had to be reconstructed on new lines, and the result was a great increase in the production of raw cotton. Elsewhere it was the question of opening out a continent, attracting emigrants, arranging for the alienation to settlers of vast unoccupied areas of land, providing the railways by which alone the penetration of the continent could be effected and finding a market for the surplus agricultural products in Europe. The result was that the United States became the greatest producer of surplus food products in the world and the disturbing factor in European agriculture. In the twentieth century it, too, has used up its vacant land and is faced with the problem of introducing intensive methods.

CHAPTER 2

France and the Agricultural Revolution

Before 1789. The cultivated land mostly in the hands of the peasants as owners or tenants. Little actual serfdom, but French peasant in effect bound to land by feudal dues and taxation.

The movement by the seigneurs to create large farms and break up commons and wastes was one of the causes which led to the French Revolution.

After 1789. All serfdom and feudal dues abolished. Lands of King, nobles, and church sold; commons divided; taxation reformed; free user of land. Redistribution of land resulted in new landed aristocracy. The problem of better farming. Gradual improvement in methods. The problems of subdivision of holdings and mortgage indebtedness.

As has already been stated, economic development in the nineteenth century was the outcome of French ideas of personal liberty combined with English inventions, which placed within the grasp of the man who had attained the new personal freedom new possibilities as to choice of occupation and change of abode. It is in connection with the freedom of the agricultural worker that the French influence is most clearly seen.

In France, in 1789, there was little serfdom except in the Eastern region on the borders of Germany.[1] The peasants had acquired more and more land as the centuries progressed, so that in the period immediately preceding the Revolution they owned a large part of the land of France. The great French landowners cultivated very little of their own land owing to its being intermingled to such a large extent with the peasants' strips.[2] The result was that apart from the immense wastes, forests, and commons, they let their arable land either for a rent or on the métayer system

[1] The number is estimated to have been 1,500,000 in 1789. (Lavisse, *Histoire de France*, p. 255.) It had existed in certain parts up to 1779. Louis XVI abolished it on the royal domains in that year and interdicted it in the rest of France. (M. Kovalevsky, *La France économique et sociale à la veille de la Révolution*, p. 259.) Peasants were, however, still bound to the soil in places in Auvergne, Nivernais, Burgundy, Franche-Comté, and in certain parts of Champagne (Chaumont, Troyes, and Vitry), as well as in the Marche and Bourbonnais, in 1789. (Kovalevsky, p. 258.)

[2] J. Luchitsky, *État des classes agricoles en France*, pp. 56–60.

by which they received a share of the produce. The bulk of the cultivated land of France was thus in the hands of the peasants before 1789 either as tenants or owners, and the lords had no occasion to insist on services, which therefore tended to lapse, as in England in the fifteenth and sixteenth centuries, and small money payments or payments in kind were substituted. The prevailing system was that of estate management, but the lords had sold a great deal of their land outright to the peasants, who were thus increasing their share of the land of the country while that of the nobles was diminishing. The ownership of the peasants was, however, limited by the fact that they had to make certain feudal payments to their seigneur or overlord, which were relics of their old serf status. Tenants had, moreover, to make these payments in addition to their rent.

Of these feudal dues one item consisted of *banalités*, viz. the obligation of the peasant to take his corn to the lord's mill to be ground, or his grapes to the lord's wine-press to be made into wine, a payment in kind being taken for the services rendered. In the case of grain the actual amount due was one-sixteenth, but in practice the miller often took more. Whenever land was sold, a proportion of the sale price varying from one-fourth to one-sixteenth had to be given to the seigneur (*lods et ventes*). Another due, known as *cens* or *champart*, was an annual payment in kind varying in amount from place to place, but usually consisting of one sheaf in ten or twelve. This had to be carted by the grower to the seigneur's barn. In addition, there was a payment when a man inherited his land, usually amounting to a year's rent. Furthermore, the seigneur had the right of administering justice and taking fees for so doing. Only in criminal matters had his jurisdiction been diminished by 1789. He was also entitled to levy tolls on all goods in transit as well as on goods exposed for sale in the market. Probably the most unpopular of all the feudal dues were the hunting rights, which caused the spoiling of much produce and interfered with the course of agriculture.

These payments were in addition to the taxes paid to the King and the tithe paid to the Church. Where the man was an owner, he had not merely to pay taxes and tithe but these seigniorial dues as well. All land just before the Revolution, except recent reclamations of waste, was burdened in France with three sets of payments, royal, seigniorial, and ecclesiastical. The tenant paid rent in addition. Taine estimated that out of a peasant's income of 100 francs, direct taxes took 53·15, the tithe 14·28, and the seigniorial dues another 14·28, making 81·71 francs in all, leaving the peasant only 18·29. It is, however, generally acknowledged that this estimate is excessive, and modern writers are inclined to accept M. Marion's tentative estimate as nearer the truth, viz. 13–14 per cent for the tithe, the seigniorial dues 11–12 per cent, and the direct taxes 36 per cent, that is to say, about 60 francs out of every 100.[1]

The privileged classes, the nobles, the Church, and the officials escaped certain taxes, such as the heavy *taille*, altogether and managed to evade the greater part of the rest. In the case of the poll tax, for instance, the nobles were assessed according to their personal declaration, and were "estimated to pay only one-eighth of their fair contribution, while the peasantry contributed eight times their equitable quota",[2] and the towns, having commuted, were either free or assessed very lightly. Not merely did the burden of taxation fall on the poorest class, but it was very unequally levied on those that did pay; thus, while some escaped lightly, others had a double burden.

For the most part the payments to the seigneur and the Church were made in kind, and up to 1787 thirty days' compulsory work on the roads was due from the peasant each year.[3] As long as a man had to pay a certain amount of corn and wine and oil or work on a definite piece of road, he had to stay in one spot to produce those things or perform those obligations. Moreover, on so narrow a margin as that afforded by the 40 per cent left him after his direct taxes and dues were paid and out of which he still had to pay the indirect taxes such as the salt tax, there would not be much chance of real personal freedom. The French peasant, though not legally bound to the soil, was in actual fact as much fixed by taxation and feudal obligations to one spot as the German serf east of the Elbe.

In the thirty years before the Revolution, a movement grew up in France to create large farms. It was copied from England where intensive large scale farming not merely

[1] *Impôts directs*, p. 120. "Classes rurales en Bordelais" in *Revue des études historiques*, 1902, pp. 133, 216, 235.

[2] H. Higgs, "Finance," in *Cambridge Modern History*, viii, p. 69.

[3] M. Marion, *Impôts directs*, p. 113. Although legally abolished in 1774 and a tax substituted, many districts did not dispense with the corvées, which were again abolished in 1787.

paid well but gave an increased food supply to a growing population. The average French landowner was a poor man, he felt the pinch of rising prices and wished to increase his income. France was over-populated for its available food supply, famines were of almost yearly occurrence, and the desire to increase agricultural yields was stimulated by the physiocrats, who taught that agriculture was the sole productive force. Rousseau, with his idea of returning to nature, still further roused the enthusiasm for improved agriculture in France. The French peasant who did the bulk of the food producing was, however, a backward farmer, hence the desire of the landowners to cultivate the land themselves *à l'anglaise* and form large farms. This, however, meant ousting the small tenants for the sake of the big farmer. Matters got worse when the lords began to raise rents and break up commons, thus depriving the peasants, both owners and tenants, of winter pasture and wood for fuel and building. As wastes were essential to their type of cultivation, it meant that their very existence was threatened. At the same time, the seigneurs, needing money for agricultural improvement, increased dues and revived claims to feudal payments which had fallen into disuse or were years in arrear. The general agricultural discontent thus engendered was one of the most potent causes of the Revolution.[1] Hence, while the middle classes wanted a constitution and reformed taxation, the French peasant wanted more land and that land free from financial and feudal burdens.

The Assembly, after declaring on 4th August, 1789, that all persons should be free and that certain "usurped" seigniorial dues should be abolished without compensation, appointed a committee to fix the terms of compensation for the rest.[2] In 1793 the government was forced by the

[1] L. C. A. Knowles, "New Light on the Economic Causes of the French Revolution," *Economic Journal*, April, 1919, pp. 1–24.

[2] Buchez et Roux, *Histoire Parlementaire*, ii, pp. 259 ff. The decree runs as follows:

I. The National Assembly hereby completely abolishes the feudal system. It decrees that in the case of rights and dues both feudal and copyhold all those originating in real or personal serfdom or personal servitude as well as the rights and dues representing these shall be abolished without any indemnification. All other dues are declared redeemable, the terms and mode of redemption to be fixed by the National Assembly. Those of the said dues which are not extinguished by this decree shall continue to be collected until indemnification shall take place.

revolutionary outbreaks among the peasants to sweep away all the feudal dues without compensation. As the tithe was also abolished the French peasant-owner became a real freeholder instead of a limited owner.

The tenant did not gain much by the abolition of the tithe and the seigniorial dues, as his rent increased to balance it, but he got new chances of getting more land in the land sales after the Revolution. Arrangements were further made for dividing the commons among the individuals of the commune and abolishing the rights of common pasturage over the arable fields in winter, so as to have only one proprietor instead of several with rights of user over other people's land.[1] The Revolution thus introduced freedom in the use of land.

The main thing, however, was that taxation was equitably adjusted and the peasantry paid only their fair share. No longer overweighted by taxation, they were able to buy, sell, lease, and mortage land freely. Payments in kind ceased except where land was let on the métayer system. There was therefore no obligation which fixed a man to the soil if he wished to move.

Thus in France, instead of actual serfdom, the survivals of it had resulted in a system of taxation, seigniorial, ecclesiastical, and royal, which had the virtual effect of

II. The exclusive right to maintain pigeon-houses and dove-cotes is abolished.

III. The exclusive right to hunt and to maintain unenclosed warrens is likewise abolished and every landowner has the right to kill or have destroyed on his own land all kinds of game.

IV. All seigniorial courts are hereby suppressed without indemnification.

V. Tithes of every description as well as the dues which have been substituted for them under whatever denomination they are known or collected . . . are abolished.

VII. The sale of judicial and municipal offices shall be suppressed forthwith. Justice shall be dispensed gratis.

X. Pecuniary privileges personal or real in the payment of taxes are abolished for ever. Taxes shall be collected from all the citizens and from all property in the same manner and in the same form.

XI. All citizens without distinction of birth are eligible to any office or dignity whether ecclesiastical, civil, or military.

These were the principles which the French revolutionary armies were going to spread and which would be fatal to feudalism and privilege all over Europe, involving a new agricultural system (I–III), a new judicial system (IV and VII), a new system of taxation (V and X), and new opportunities for a career and occupation (XI).

[1] G. Bourgin, " Les Communaux et la Révolution Française," in *Nouvelle revue historique du droit français et étranger*, Nov.–Dec., 1908. For documents see Bourgin, " Le partage des biens communaux," in *Collection des documents inédits.*

serfdom, that is to say, the deprivation of the power of movement or initiative. The result of the reforms and the land distribution was that the French peasant was freer and better off and fought valiantly for the Revolution. He submitted to conscription and formed the backbone of the finest army in Europe because he was fighting for the land that was now really his own, and wherever he went he carried not merely the tricolour but this gospel of personal equality resulting in the freedom of the individual and the land. What had galled the French peasant was the onerous nature of the dues which attached to him personally and for which he received no tangible equivalent. He was therefore above all things the apostle of personal freedom or equality.

As population increases, the peasant has either to get more out of the same soil or more land has to be given to a starving people, since with antiquated methods of cultivation there is not enough for all to live. In France, the cry of the peasants, consequent upon the increasing population before 1789 and the backward methods of cultivation, was for more land. When the lands of the church, the nobles, and the King had been sold there was no more to be had and circumstances forced them to make the best of what they possessed.

In other words they were forced to make the change from extensive to intensive agriculture. How necessary this was may be judged from the fact that Dupont de Nemours, an agricultural expert, estimated that in France 18 million *arpents* were cultivated on the system of alternate crop and fallow and 12 on the three field rotation of two crops and a fallow.[1] Thus 13 million *arpents* out of 30, or nearly half the arable land of France, would lie uncultivated every year. In addition to the fallow land there was in France an enormous extent of heath, forest, and marsh. Arthur Young said that between a sixth and a seventh of the whole kingdom was occupied by wood, a necessity in a country where wood was the only fuel, but it seriously contracted the cultivated land. Arthur Young also estimated that 40 million acres of land were sheer wastes.[2] His view is also confirmed by another agricultural expert, the Marquis de Turbilly, who speaks of half the country being waste.

[1] His report is quoted in Pigeonneau, *L'Administration de l'Agriculture*, 1785–7, p. 268. An *arpent* may be taken for rough purposes of reckoning as equivalent to an acre. It varied in size in different parts of the country.

[2] *Travels in France* (ed. 1794), vol. i, pp. 373, 472; ii, p. 96.

It was estimated by the Committee of Agriculture in 1786 that there were only 1,800,000 cows, 1,200,000 calves, and 1,700,000 horses in all France.[1] "The proportion of farm animals is insufficient and does not furnish the necessary manure for cultivation," was the verdict. The soil was so subdivided that a man who cultivated 30 *arpents* was said to be obliged to take them in a hundred different plots at a considerable distance from one another.[2]

The Revolution prevented the consolidation of holdings and of strips into large farms by the nobles and therefore preserved the peasant in France. The distribution of the commons enabled some peasants to increase or consolidate their holdings, while the land sales after the Revolution gave a chance to those peasants who had money to acquire land very cheaply in depreciated paper money, which was accepted by the State at its face value as the Government would not acknowledge the existence of depreciation. Hence the larger peasants increased their holdings and many others got more land who had previously had very small portions, mere scraps in fact.

The proportion of land obtained by the different classes varied enormously in the different parts of France.[3] It is, however, a disputed point as to whether the French Revolutionary land sales increased the numbers of the French peasant proprietors to any large extent. It must be remembered that even before 1789 the possession of land, either as tenant or owner, was very widespread in France. Even the beggars were said to own land in the district round Bordeaux.[4] The French Revolution did not, therefore, in any sense create the French peasant proprietor, but it did free him from burdens, and gave him a chance to enlarge his holding. Any increase in numbers may have been due to the operation of the new law of inheritance passed in the year II but made retrospective to 1789. By this a man might only leave a tenth of his property away from his family or a sixth in the case of collaterals. The rest had to be divided equally among his heirs. It might not be left to one and entailed as in England. There would thus be a constant redistribution of land which

[1] Pigeonneau, *L'Administration de l'Agriculture*, p. 19.

[2] *Journal Économique*, Feb., 1763, p. 61.

[3] J. V. Luchitsky, *Quelques Remarques sur la Vente des biens nationaux*, chaps. ii–v, and Appendices 1 and 2.

[4] M. Marion, "Classes rurales dans la généralité de Bordeaux," in *Revue des études historiques*, 1902, p. 99.

would make for equality and its widespread possession,[1] and must have led to an increase of proprietors. This law of equal inheritance was modified by Napoleon in 1801 in his civil code, and the amount the testator was free to leave as he chose varied between a half and a quarter according to the number of his children. Entails were permitted to one degree.[2]

Whether the number of proprietors was increased or not, the revolutionary land sales had unexpected results, inasmuch as they created a new landed aristocracy in the place of the nobles. The possession of land passed to a considerable extent into the hands of the middle classes who had capital enough to buy large quantities. Thus the revolutionary land sales actually promoted the formation of large farms.

There were three great national attempts at land transfer during the period 1789–1914. There was the confiscation and sale of the lands of the Crown, the Church, and the *émigrés* in France. There was the sale of the lands of the Czar, the imperial family, and the nobles to the peasants through the banks, which had occasioned a great change of land-ownership in Russia, especially between 1905 and 1914. From 1885 onwards and more particularly after 1903, the Irish landlord was being bought out by the tenant cultivator. Of all these changes the French was the most dramatic and the most rapid. Starting with wholesale expropriation, the land was quickly distributed among a population only too eager to acquire land. It is interesting to trace the stages by which this work was accomplished. In 1789 the confiscated land was divided into small portions, the purchaser was to pay 12 per cent of the purchase money and the rest in instalments spread over twelve years. This gave the opportunity to the small man to purchase gradually. The revolutionary government had destroyed one system of taxation and could not make another work, and as a result they needed money badly and they wanted it at once. After November, 1790, land was sold in large quantities; 20 per cent of the purchase price had to be paid at once and the rest in periods ranging

[1] G. Bourgin, "L'agriculture et la révolution française" in *Revue d'histoire des doctrines économiques et sociales*, 1911. Sagnac considers that the number of proprietors increased considerably. "La division du sol pendant la Révolution et ses conséquences" in *Revue d'histoire moderne et contemporaine*, v, 1903–4, p. 464.

[2] H. A. L. Fisher, "The Codes" in *Cambridge Modern History*, ix, p. 160.

from $2\frac{1}{2}$ to $4\frac{1}{2}$ years. This put a premium on purchase by the wealthier classes. By 1793 the lands of the *émigrés* had been confiscated and the policy was to sell this land at very low price and as speedily as possible in order to win the purchasers over to the side of the Revolution and prevent the emigrated nobles from recovering their property and power. The nobles' land was thus rapidly distributed and the Bourbons could not return in 1814 until they had agreed not to upset the revolutionary land settlement. The general result was to create a new territorial aristocracy alongside of a peasant democracy which had increased its share of the land, but the merchants and bourgeois of the towns acquired as much and often more than the peasants.[1] They were able to keep the property intact far more frequently than the peasant, as there was generally other capital which would form the subject of division at death and the landed property might go intact in one share. The result is that by the end of the nineteenth century France was a country with a considerable proportion of large properties and large farms. As life became more secure, the bigger men began to put business methods and capital into land management, as did the English merchants who bought land after the Reformation and the Civil War. The great difficulty till 1815 was labour, so many men were absorbed by the constant wars, and Napoleon himself, though keen on promoting industrial development, did not really understand agriculture.[2] He wanted wool for cloth for his soldiers and the flocks of sheep increased, and he

[1] P. Sagnac, "La propriété foncière et les paysans" in *L'œuvre sociale de la Révolution française*, pp. 254 ff.

[2] J. A. C. Chaptal, *Mes souvenirs sur Napoleon*, p. 295.

"The Emperor placed agriculture in the first rank among the useful arts. He had, however, no knowledge of its working. He had indeed on this subject an ignorance which passed all bounds. . . . Napoleon feared the people, he feared insurrections and it is this fear which led him constantly to adopt false measures. His principle was that corn ought to be sold at a very low price because riots nearly always arose from dearness or scarcity of bread. As a result he did not permit the export of grain except when the agriculturist threatened to no longer cultivate it. . . . No, he willed that corn should be cheap and he dried up public prosperity at its source. In the two periods of famine which took place during his reign one has seen him take all the measures capable of aggravating the scarcity.

"This system of ruin for the country joined to the requisitions and conscription ought to have made the Emperor abhorred by the peasant. But one would be mistaken. His warmest partisans were among them, because he was their insurance against the return of the tithe, feudal dues, the restitution of the goods of the *émigrés* and the oppression of the overlords."

wanted beet to make sugar because that would make Europe independent of the sea-borne sugar supply threatened by the English sea-power, and where that was developed it meant improved rotation of crops. Still, agricultural methods were improving slowly, even at the end of the eighteenth century. The reconstruction of the roads and canals carried out by Napoleon for military purposes increased the possibilities of sale and where the armies were quartered for a long period, as they were round Boulogne for the invasion of England, they had to be fed from the district and agriculture became more intensive with increased possibilities of sale.

"If one compares agriculture with what it was in 1789, one is astonished at the improvements that have been secured. . . . Harvests of all kinds cover the soil, numerous and strong animals labour and manure the land, food is wholesome and abundant, houses are clean and comfortable, there is simple but decent clothing; such is the share of the inhabitants of the fields. Misery has been banished and ease has been born of the power of the free disposal of all products." [1]

This view of the good standard of living of the French peasant is born out by an English traveller, Birkbeck, who made a voyage there just after the peace. When one reads, however, the annual survey of agriculture in the *Mémoires* of the *Société Centrale de l'Agriculture* one realizes how much still remained to be accomplished, and one gathers that the real improvement in methods—the abolition of the fallow period, improved rotation of crops, better breeds of cattle, the break up of wastes and marshes—took place much more rapidly after 1830 than before. It was after that date that the industrial revolution really became effective in France. That meant that a great deal of country industry would be destroyed, and labour, the great difficulty before, would be increasingly available for intensive cultivation.[2] Apart from the fact that the growth of the town population consequent on the industrial revolution would require more food and would thus stimulate production, there would be an increasing demand for raw material produced by the French peasant, such as silk and wool.

[1] J. A. C. Chaptal, *De l'Industrie française*, i, p. 152.

[2] E. Levasseur, ii, p. 537 n., shows how the persons engaged in the mining industry had to choose between agriculture and becoming *ouvriers fixes* in the mines. They chose agriculture.

Then, too, capital was being rapidly accumulated after 1830. By that time industry had recovered from the economic destruction of the revolution. Much of this was being invested in agriculture by business men who bought estates and were willing to improve production. The industrial revolution in France, as in England, reacted upon agriculture. Another great impetus was given to French agriculture by the coming of the railways, which equalized agricultural prices in the different districts of France and provided not merely a better market but the chance of getting artificial manures in large quantities. The free trade treaties of the period 1860–70 opened out large markets abroad for French wines and stimulated the production of the vineyards.

The progress made in the first half of the century can be seen from the following figures:—[1]

	1789. Million hectares.	1848. Million hectares.
Fallow	10	5
Wheat	4	6
Artificial pasture . .	1	3
Roots	$\frac{1}{10}$	2

(A hectare is approximately 2½ acres.)

Increased Yields.

	1789. Million hectolitres.	1815. Million hectolitres.	1848 Million hectolitres.
Wheat . .	34	44	70
Potatoes .	2	20	100
Wine . .	17	35½	40

(A hectolitre = 22 gallons.)

These figures show that the fallow land had been reduced by half in the 59 years in question and while the wheat area had increased by fifty per cent the yields had doubled.

After 1884 it was possible to start Agricultural Co-operative Societies in France, as the law against syndicates was repealed, and whether it was due to their efforts or to the protective tariff of 1883, the progress is no less striking, as

[1] These figures are from an article by Lavergne in the *Revue des deux Mondes*, 1858, p. 436. He has compiled them from Lavoisier, 1789, Chaptal, 1815, and the *Statistique Générale de la France*, 1848. As to the progress in the eighteenth century, see Levasseur, "Du progrès de l'agriculture française dans la seconde moitié du XVIIIe siècle" in *Revue d'Économie politique*, 1898.

appears from the following statistics [1] relating to annual averages over successive decades, which should be read bearing in mind that 1831–50 was the period when the industrial revolution was reacting on agriculture; that 1851–80 was the railway era; and that from 1881 onwards not only railway development, but also high tariffs and co-operative societies are factors which have to be taken into account.

	Wheat.		Wine.		Potatoes.	
	Hecto-litres (millions).	Yield per Hectare.	Hecto-litres (millions).	Yield per Hectare.	Quarters (millions).	Yield in Hecto-litres per Hectare.
1815–1820	45·6	9·89	—	—	—	—
1821–1830	58·29	11·9	—	—	36·1	76·15
1831–1840	68·63	12·77	—	—	59·06	95·99
1841–1850	79·61	13·6	—	—	71·34	96·10
1851–1860	90·07	14·01	29·68	13·81	63·09	87·80
1861–1870	98·9	14·27	51·73 [2]	22·53	86·8	102·62
1871–1880	98·09	14·21	49·21	20·8	91·01	99·05
1881–1890	109·06	15·13	29·44 [3]	14·80	106·65	84·79
1891–1900	110·5	16·17	39·98	23·54	122·99	80·25
1901–1910	115·3	17·56	51·76	31·86	127·64	84·56
1911–1913	114·9	17·5	49·5	31·6	135·6	87·87

The introduction of improved methods has been a constant preoccupation of the Government,[4] which has given a great deal of assistance to agriculture in the form of tariff protection, cheap water transport in the shape of free canals and assistance to agricultural credit and co-operative societies, while it has encouraged agricultural scientific experiment and education. The transition to root crops has been stimulated by the bounties given to beet-sugar production. The constant subdivision of the land among the children on the death of the owner has often led to the creation of such small properties that they cannot adequately be cultivated and this has to a certain extent stood in the way of improved methods. This process, known as *Morcellement*, has been the subject of much anxiety in France. For one thing, it makes it difficult to introduce machinery. On the other hand, the widespread desire

[1] From *Annuaire Statistique*, 1914, p. 43.
[2] The Free Trade Treaty era.
[3] The period of the phylloxera.
[4] See *Société Centrale de l'Agriculture, Mémoires*, in many volumes.

to possess land has led to the French peasants buying more land whenever they can get it so that to counteract the splitting up of farms there is this strong tendency to enlarge properties by constant purchase. Another difficulty has been the constant mortgage indebtedness of the small farmer, and here, as elsewhere, the government has had to devise methods for "peasant rescue".

CHAPTER 3

Germany and the Agricultural Revolution

In Germany there has been a marked difference between the history and tenures of the land lying East and West of the Elbe.
In Germany West of the Elbe the serfs were in a more favourable position than in the East, where serfdom had only developed since the sixteenth century.
In Western Germany there was a good deal of estate management with serfs paying dues in money or in kind and not in work. Many were free to move on payment of a fine. In the East manorial cultivation prevailed.
The French hastened the abolition of serfdom in the West. In the East emancipation was carried out by the Prussian King following the French example.
During the nineteenth century the West is predominantly the region of small farms and the East that of the large landowners or Junkers.
After personal emancipation the second stage is to make the peasant free of labour dues. His " day works " were commuted either for a money payment or for a surrender of part of his land to the overlord.
A free land-owning peasantry was thus created by the process known as " regulation ".
The third stage is the introduction of better methods or intensive cultivation.
To do this the land had to be rearranged and enclosed, and commons broken up.
Regulation, enclosure, and the introduction of intensive methods have occupied the governments of the German states all through the nineteenth century. It was not completed in 1914.
Great agricultural progress has been made in all directions. The subsidizing of beet-sugar introduced rotation of crops, and co-operative credit (Raiffeisenbanks) assisted the peasantry, just out of serfdom. The Imperial government provided cheap transport facilities and protected agriculture with a high tariff.
The scarcity of agricultural labour has been a great problem in Germany since 1880–90.

IN Germany there is a fundamental difference between the country East and West of the Elbe. In 1914, East of the Elbe were to be found the large estates cultivated by the landowners or Junkers themselves. It was the granary of the German Empire and the bulk of the population were engaged in agriculture, most of them as day-labourers for the cultivating landowner, and even in 1914 the relations between the two classes were semi-feudal. It is from this region that the strength of the agrarian party was drawn. Everything that is typically Prussia falls East of the Elbe. West of the Elbe are to be found the bulk of the small peasant properties and their main occupation is pasture farming and cattle rearing. Here also is to be found the great industrial region of Westphalia and the Rhineland, acquired by Prussia in 1815, which has been ever since an excrescence on the original Prussia—never typically Prussian. It is, for instance, Catholic in religion as opposed to Lutheran Prussia.

To understand this fundamental cleavage in the German Empire up to the European War of 1914, one has to remember that Germany was a creation of the colonizing movement of the Middle Ages. The regions West of the Elbe, which were the earliest to be settled, presented the usual type of feudal lord with his cultivating serfs. The East was taken from the Slav and the conquering noble necessarily started out with free companions and only gradually in the sixteenth century did serfdom emerge.

In Western Germany, by the beginning of the eighteenth century, serfdom where it still existed was only a mild survival of the Middle Ages and manorial cultivation was merging into estate management. The eighteenth century saw it disappear still more rapidly and a system of payments was substituted for labour dues. On the other hand, East of the Elbe it had become a very harsh system.

A serf in the Western and Southern districts was under two sets of obligations, one to his overlord in virtue of his status as a serf and one to his landlord who provided him with a holding. Sometimes both lordships were united in the same person, often they were not. Persons in a village would sometimes own obedience to several lords; there was no principle of "one area, one lord", as there was in the East. In virtue of the personal status the unfree man's property by feudal law reverted at death to his overlord. Gradually this had become modified in the West and South-West to the surrender by the heir of the best beast or best chattel. The serf had to ask permission to marry and make a payment if such permission were granted; he could not become a free man without his lord's permission and even then a payment had to be made. The lord had the right of taking all the serf's children into his service if he wished and could sell or exchange his rights over the serf. In addition, the unfree person owed certain services to his landlord for his holding. He could not leave the land without permission of the landlord and the feudal superior could force the serf to take up a holding whether he wished it or no. He was then bound to cultivate his lord's land as well as his own.

In Western Germany money payments had gradually been substituted in many places for these rights and between the sixteenth and eighteenth centuries many peasants had become virtually free. The great bulk of the ecclesiastical rulers had their territories West of the Elbe. They were not cultivating landowners themselves and could not hand on their estates to their descendants. They therefore preferred money payments and payments in kind to services. Sometimes the peasants had even been freed without compensation,[1] as in Münster and Baden in 1783. To this disappearing serfdom came the French invasion to make a clean sweep of the system.

When the French made the country as far as the Rhine part of France, they freed the peasantry. Napoleon created three new states beyond the Rhine, the Kingdom of Westphalia under his brother Jerome, the Grand Duchy of Berg, and the Grand Duchy of Frankfort. Here too serfdom and feudalism were abolished.[2]

Then Napoleon enlarged the territories of three German potentates—Baden, Würtemberg, and Bavaria, to which the Tyrol was added—and here again the French influence was naturally paramount. It was impossible for these Kings, owing as much as they did to the French Emperor, not to carry out some of the liberal principles for which France stood. When the Confederation of the Rhine was formed the effect was the same. Bavaria abolished serfdom in 1808 and Baden in stages from 1783 onwards. In Würtemberg the abolition was promised in 1798 and carried out in 1817. In Hesse, where the Elector had restored serfdom on his restoration in 1813, it was abolished in 1831, and the last place where it lingered in the West was Hohenzollern-Sigmaringen, where it lasted till 1833.

Emancipation does not mean that the peasants' labour dues and services were abolished, only that his status as an unfree man ceased to exist. The services went later. Nor does it mean that the ex-serfs ceased to be judged by their overlords. What it did mean was that they were free of the obligations belonging to their status, though not necessarily free of the obligations belonging to their

[1] T. Knapp, *Gesammelte Beiträge*, p. 370.

[2] H. A. L. Fisher, *Studies in Napoleonic Statesmanship and Germany*, pp. 230, 232.

land. They became free to move, but if they did so, their land was lost to them.

Very different, however, was the course of events East of the Elbe. Men were free in Brandenburg, Pomerania, Mecklenburg, Holstein, and East Prussia when those in the West were serfs. East of the Elbe they were able to leave the land, they were not limited as to their marriage or choice of occupation nor were their children forced to serve in the lord's house. They could leave their property by will and buy and sell land. From the sixteenth century onwards they lost these rights. Not till the nineteenth century did the bulk of them regain the favourable position they enjoyed in the fourteenth and fifteenth centuries.

The day's work or labour dues were at first very slight in the East as the landlord was a fighting man and spent his days either in the service of his prince or elector or as a raider on his own account. He did not possess nor did he need much land; other people kept him. He saw to it that they did.

With the development of standing armies in the sixteenth century, soldiering and raiding were not the professions they had been and the knightly adventurer had to become an agriculturist for his living. He therefore sought to extend his land in order to get an adequate livelihood and he needed peasants to cultivate it. As labour was scarce it had, as in Russia later, to be attached to the soil. The lord had considerable power if he chose to exercise it. He combined in himself, East of the Elbe, the two lordships which were often separate in the West. He was both feudal superior and landowner, while he alone dominated his village. In the West one lord might be appealed to against the other, and with several lords in one village there was competition for adherents. In the East there was no such relief.

The tendency to get hold of peasant properties and make large landed estates out of them is marked in the sixteenth century, but was greatly stimulated by the Thirty Years' War (1618–48). In that dreadful period whole villages were swept away; in other places the inhabitants were reduced to one-tenth of the original number; and the lords rapidly formed large landed estates. The surviving peasants, in their miserable condition, were only too glad to get protection and food on any terms. In addition, the landowners and the King, who was the largest landowner, energetically promoted colonization from other parts, and the new-comers were planted out as serfs. Peasant properties were said to disappear "like snow before sunshine". The lords rapidly altered the old land tenures to suit their convenience. Land was only granted for life. The lord was free to add the peasant's land to the domain on the death of the tenant or he could give it to whom he liked, not necessarily to the cultivator's son. There was the usual stipulation about the lord's consent before marriage. The forced service of children who could not leave and the restriction on movement were conditions which were also imposed.

Of all the characteristics which were introduced, the unmeasured and unpaid services on the lord's land that were now demanded were the most onerous. We find peasants working four and five days a week for the lord and providing the teams themselves. In times of pressure they had to work the whole week and many instances of six days a week at other times are common. Thus while payments more or less light were being substituted for services in the West, services in the East became more oppressive. The Kings of Prussia did a good deal towards improving the condition of the serfs on the royal estates between 1719 and 1777. First in East and West Prussia, then in Pomerania and Brandenburg, the conditions of the royal serfs became much better, so that by the end of the century whole villages had been freed and their payments turned into money. Under the stimulus of the French example West of the Elbe the King of Prussia went still further, and in 1799 the royal peasants were all made free in his dominions and their services turned into money payments or they gave up part of their land instead. Many private persons followed suit. What was accomplished by the decree of October 9, 1807, was to sweep away any remnants of feudalism on the royal estates and bring the peasants on the estates of private lords into line with the privileged peasants on the royal domains.[1]

Frederick the Great (1740–1786) had also done something to prevent the growth of the large estates at the expense of the peasants, but in the lands surrounding Prussia, such

[1] T. Knapp, "Zur Geschichte der Bauernbefreiung in Ost und West Preussen, 1719–1808," in *Gesammelte Beiträge*, pp. 333 ff. "Ueber Leibeigenschaft," in *Deutschland seit dem Ausgang des Mittelalters*, ibid., p. 346 ff.

as Holstein, Mecklenburg, and Swedish Pomerania, the tendency to form large estates went on all through the century. It is interesting to see how the same tendency to create large farms was at work during the 18th century in such different countries as England, France, and Eastern Germany, while the late enserfing with its onerous nature is a characteristic both of that region and Russia, whose population was not really fixed to the soil till the time of Peter the Great, though the tendency was becoming apparent in the seventeenth century.[1]

The Emancipatory Edict of 1807 for Prussia[2] declared that there was no longer such a thing as the status of serfdom, nor could any man in future become a serf by birth, marriage, or contract; that anyone might acquire any land whatever his rank; that a peasant might become a townsman or a townsman a peasant; and that the peasant no longer required the lord's permission to learn a trade.

The services then had to be turned into money to make this freedom really effective, a process called in German "Regulation". In 1808 the peasants on the royal domains had their services fixed at a cash value and these were capitalized at 5 per cent, that is to say, if a peasant's dues were reckoned as worth £20 a year he could by paying £400 become owner of the land he had hitherto held on condition of giving labour dues. In 1811 this was applied to the land on the nobles' domains, but instead of the money payment the peasants could give up land to the lord varying between a half and a third of what they held, according to their tenure. They would then be the owners of the rest. Where the nobles and peasants could not agree about the compensation the state would intervene, and a Commission was appointed for every province to arrange the capital sum or the amount of land to be surrendered. It is interesting to notice that this still further tended to increase the size of the large estates. The outcry among the landowners who lost possession and control of their labour was so great that the plan had to be modified. They were left with more land and no one to work it. Hence in 1810 it was decreed that the commutation of services should only relate to the larger peasants'

[1] Sir D. M. Wallace, *Russia*, pp. 468–70.

[2] The freeing of the serfs in other parts took place as follows: Nassau, 1812; Waldeck, 1814; Baden, 1818; Hesse-Darmstadt, 1820; Saxe-Coburg-Gotha, 1821; Mecklenburg-Schwerin and Mecklenburg-Strelitz, 1820.

holdings, those supplying the plough teams. The holdings where the peasants gave hand services were not "regulated" till 1853.[1] As Prussia acquired fresh territories these arrangements were extended to them. Services were not commuted for the whole of Germany till the first half of the 19th century was over.

The revolutions in 1848, which brought about the freeing of the serfs in the dominions of the Habsburgs, also quickened the process of making the Prussian peasant a landowner free of labour dues. In 1850 the legislation on the subject was codified, the smaller properties were freed from services, and a law was passed providing for the erection of a bank in every province which should advance the capital sum still due to the lord. The peasant was to mortgage his land to the bank at 4 per cent and pay off the capital sum by instalments in 41½ or 56½ years. The same plan was adopted by other provinces at a later period. Thus when the war broke out in 1914 some German peasants were still in process of redeeming their labour dues. The adjustment of compensation was a task of peculiar difficulty which in some States took years to carry out.

The next great step was to induce the freed cultivator to improve his methods. He only understood a system which at best was a triennial one of two cereal crops and a fallow and often a biennial one of crop and fallow alternately, and he had to be induced to try a rotation of crops by growing clover, turnips, beet, or other roots alternately with a cereal crop. To do this the right of the villagers to turn their cattle over the common fields after harvest had to be abandoned because the cattle would be fatal to a root crop not pulled till late autumn or winter.

As has been pointed out, however, there was not food enough for the cattle over the winter unless they could feed on all the arable fields as well as on the wastes. Therefore artificial pastures and larger supplies of winter food must be provided. These had to come out of the wastes which had to be brought into cultivation. The wastes, however, had been necessary for cutting fuel as well as for the animals. As coal became available in the nineteenth

[1] The regulation began in Baden from 1820, in Saxony from 1824, Bavaria 1825, Hesse-Darmstadt 1827, Hanover 1830, Oldenburg 1831, Brunswick and Electoral Hesse 1832, Waldeck 1837, Coburg and Gotha 1835, Wurtemburg 1836, Lippe 1838. The rest of Germany followed suit in the 'forties. The process continued through the 'fifties.

century, owing to better methods of getting it out of the pit and transporting it, the wastes were no longer essential for fuel. Thus an enormous amount of uncultivated land could be brought into use for purposes of intensive cultivation and a larger food supply.

One of the great obstacles to intensive farming lay in the nature of the scattered strips. It was essential, if good farming was to be introduced, that these strips should be consolidated so that a man should have his holding in one place. On a large estate the strips might lie miles apart, and in Russia, for instance, some of them were two or three days' journey distant from the homestead. Not merely was much time wasted in going from strip to strip for purposes of sowing, reaping, or spreading manures, but there was a great waste of actual land. Each strip had to be separated from every other by a ridge of land or turf balk, and this was uncultivated. There were constant disputes, too, about encroaching on other people's land to increase your own share or to turn the plough,[1] while the whole of the arable fields were intersected with pathways causing a further waste of land. The system of common ploughing and reaping gave no opportunity to the man who wished to effect changes or initiate improvements. To give a good farmer a chance to show what he could do, the system of common cultivation must give way to a system of individual farming carried out on an enclosed area.

The whole scheme of strips, fallows, and wastes had meant a backward system of agriculture and scanty crops, and as there was a difficulty about the importation or transportation of grain in every continental country owing to the bad state of the roads, it often meant scarcity and famine.[2] To increase the food supply and introduce better methods, not merely was enclosure a necessity, but more cattle were also wanted. They were required for manure as well as for meat. This was a further stimulus to enclosure. The

[1] Cf. the sentence in the Commination Service in the English Prayer-book, which gives some idea of the difficulties which arose. "Cursed is he that removeth his neighbour's landmark." This comes third in the list of offences of which ten are enumerated.

[2] So serious was the famine in 1709 in France that the population, which had probably been about 19 millions in 1709, dropped to between 16 and 17 millions by 1714. Bonnemere speaks of 30 famines in France between 1700 and 1789. *Histoire des paysans*, pp. 631–2. There are two occasional prayers in the English Prayer-book against famines as well as a petition in the Litany, also two prayers against excessive rain in order that "we may receive the fruits of the earth in due season".

village herds which pastured on the commons were constantly afflicted with various infectious diseases such as foot and mouth disease or scab, and, as isolation was impossible, cattle plagues spread rapidly. It was not until a man could keep his cattle to himself and feed them over the winter that it was worth while to improve the breeds.[1] Accordingly, the abolition of the fallow period, the substitution of rotation of crops, the enclosure of the strips so as to form a compact farm, the break up and division of the commons, the increase of artificial pastures and root crops to feed cattle in the winter—all these were tasks confronting the rulers of the various German States.

After enclosure was carried out, the chief method adopted to bring about better rotation of crops and increased cattle breeding was the encouragement of the growing of beetroot. A man who grew sugar beet was obliged to follow out the regular sequence of rotation; he was forced to manure the land to get his beet to thrive; he had a valuable root for sugar, while the refuse provided him with a winter cattle food.[2] The root was, however, chiefly valuable for the intensive cultivation it entailed. Thus all the continental governments that wished their peasantry to farm better went in for subsidizing beet sugar. By the Sugar Convention in 1903 France, Germany, Austria-Hungary, Holland, Belgium, and Denmark agreed to give up the bounty system, their agriculture having successfully developed root crops, but backward agricultural countries like Spain and Russia were still adhering to it in 1914.

The redistribution of the land was provided for in Prussia in 1821 and enlarged by further ordinances in 1850 and 1872. By 1866, in the eight older provinces of Prussia, 15,262,100 hectares belonging to 1,600,510 owners had been redivided. When the new provinces—Hanover, Brunswick, and Nassau—were acquired in 1866, the process was extended to them. In 1872 a measure of compulsion was applied. If the person or persons who owned half the land wished for division, it had to be carried out by the Commission appointed for the purpose. Thus one large landowner might cause a redivision whether his peasants wished it or no. In Saxony,

[1] Milk must have been almost unprocurable in winter until the nineteenth century as there was no winter fodder for cows and cows do not give milk unless they are fed. Perhaps this partly accounts for the heavy child mortality and the slow increase of population.

[2] T. H. Middleton, *Recent Development of German Agriculture*, 1916 [*Cd.* 8305], pp. 38–40. Beet also provided a winter occupation.

where redivision might be carried out in 1834 if two-thirds of the inhabitants desired it, by 1861 the proportion was reduced to half. The process of redistributing the land and abolishing common rights was still going on in 1914.

West of the Elbe the tendency was different. Redivision came much later, and proceeded less drastically.[1] The West is mountainous and it is very difficult to arrange land in hilly regions so that such a division shall be fair. Each bit of land varies in mountain districts according to whether or not the sun strikes it; the soil has often been carted there laboriously in baskets as in the vineyard region of the Rhine—to re-allot it is almost impossible. Moreover the peasants of the West clung to their common rights and rights of pasturage on which their cattle-rearing depended. It was a different economy from the great corn growing areas of the East. Hence enclosure did not proceed very far or very rapidly in Western Germany.

It is one thing for a peasant to be able to leave his land, it is another thing to be allowed to "settle" somewhere else. The *Code Napoleon* had decreed that no one should be prevented from settling, and where the French influence ran, in the French provinces and the Confederation of the Rhine, obstacles to settlement were swept away. It was not until 1867, however, that free settlement was possible in all the German territory.[2] It was not till 1849, after the revolution, that the private manorial courts of justice were abolished in Prussia, and 1877 for the Empire. Not till 1861 in Prussia was taxation readjusted so that the landowner should bear his fair share of taxation, though of course West of the Elbe this had occurred from Napoleonic days.

The preliminary to the introduction of proper rotation of crops had thus been successfully surmounted in Germany and France. The land has been re-sorted in Eastern Germany and to a lesser extent in Germany West of the Elbe. In France enclosure also took place during the nineteenth century. In Russia it was the main agricultural problem after 1905 and was proceeding rapidly before 1914.

A people just emerging from serfdom must have guidance and leadership in instituting new courses of agriculture;

[1] The dates are: Nassau 1852, Wurtemberg 1862 and 1886, Baden 1856, Hesse-Darmstadt 1857 and 1871, Bavaria 1861 (if four-fifths of the landowners desired it) and 1886, the Rhine Provinces 1885. It is only since 1883 that provision has been made for redivision in Austria

[2] Meitzen, "Freizügigkeit" in *Schönberg's Handbuch*, ii, p. 157.

they also require capital. A small man is often ruined by two bad years; he falls into the hands of the money-lender and he has no capital or initiative for improvements. Hence two further problems arise, the problem of instruction and the problem of credit. The larger farmer is more alert, he can try experiments, he is not so hide-bound in his conservatism as the small peasant farmer, a good government experimental station will give him hints which he will gradually carry out. There will be various societies for the promotion of agriculture which will do their best to diffuse knowledge by publications and agricultural shows. But the small peasant is remote from these influences. Moreover, if a large farmer grows a thing profitably it does not mean that the small man can or will do so. Even if he sees a large farmer do well on certain classes of produce, he often has not the capital for the necessary outlay.

At the beginning of the nineteenth century, the lead in improved agriculture seems to have rested with large landowners and large farmers in Germany, France, and England. Then as science developed the State took the matter up and carried out experiments and started agricultural schools and colleges.

Special measures, however, became necessary to assist the small farmer. He became involved in a mesh of mortgage indebtedness. He subdivided his holding in Western Germany, where the Napoleonic Codes prevailed, till it became uneconomic, and then in the 'eighties he began to feel the effects of the American meat exports. He had gone in for keeping pigs and cows, whereas the big cultivating landowner was chiefly a corn or potato grower. The German Junkers combined to demand a protective tariff, which they obtained in 1878. The small peasant was equally protected by the tariff but was saved by co-operation. The Raiffeisen banks started in 1849. They were a system of mutual guarantee by peasants amalgamated in small groups and this guarantee enabled members who needed credit to obtain it at cheap rates from the banks, instead of at exorbitant rates from moneylenders. Other forms of co-operation also developed. The peasants learnt to co-operate to buy manures and good seed, to hire machinery, and to set up power stations to supply electricity to the farms. They combined to found beet-sugar factories and dairies. They co-operated not merely for production but for sale, as agricultural produce fetches a larger price in quantities, properly packed and graded. They also combined into all sorts of insurance societies, especially for cattle.[1] This combination for various purposes has a great educational effect and the small peasant is reached by these means when the scientific experimental stations and government schemes of agricultural education leave him untouched. This agricultural co-operation is often subsidized and always encouraged by the central government in both France and Germany as well as in other countries. It is the most effective method of " peasant rescue " yet devised.

The combined action of large farmers and peasant-owners led to their having considerable political influence in Germany, and they were able to bring pressure on the Government in the matter of corn laws and tariffs and the construction of canals and other public works for the benefit of agriculture. The same pressure could be, and was, brought to bear by the agricultural co-operative societies in France, and to a lesser degree in Germany. Hence organized agriculture was a real political power in those countries.

Improved agriculture and better yields seem to be the leading characteristic of the agriculture of France, Germany, and England during the nineteenth century.

In Germany, after the large landowners had survived the difficulties of the emancipation period, progress was remarkable. They did not, as in England, let their land to farmers, but they retained it in their own hands and became cultivating landowners, farming for their livelihood and operating on a large scale. For a time they were hampered by lack of capital to carry out intensive agriculture. The abolition of the Corn Laws in England gave them a new market out of which they made money, prices rose between 1850 and 1870, and agricultural methods improved. Threatened with disaster by the importation of cheap grain and meat from America after 1870, they obtained a protective tariff in 1878, increasing as the price of grain dropped in the 'eighties. The German Government, during the last quarter of the nineteenth century, regarded the agricultural interest much as the English regard the navy, namely, as their principal means of defence. It was held that the land furnished better soldiers than the towns, and was the backbone of the army. The food supply, so it was

[1] Cahill, *An Enquiry into Agricultural Credit and Agricultural Co-operation in Germany*, 1913 [*Cd.* 6626], pp. 292–302.

thought, would be safer in time of war if increased production took place at home. Whether it be due to Government encouragement, or to the tariff, or to the excellence of their agricultural research and education, or to their organization in co-operative societies, or to their system of co-operative credit, or to a combination of all these, the results are striking. The progress has been accomplished in spite of the fact that "only one-fifth of the soil of Prussia . . . can be classed as good; two-fifths consists of indifferent loams; and two-fifths is very poor. The climate of Germany . . . is certainly not so well suited for the growing of large crops of grain, potatoes, roots and hay as our own." [1] The test of the abolition of the fallow and the growing of root crops is very illuminating. For 1878 Sir W. H. Dawson [2] gives the amount of fallow for all Germany as 2,308,474 hectares or 8·89 per cent of the arable and garden area. By 1900 it was reduced to 1,230,626 or 4·69 per cent. There were, in 1911–12, 505,000 hectares under beet.[3] The German forests cover one-fourth (25·7 per cent) of the whole area of the country, viz. 13,875,644 hectares. They have been made a great financial success and the German forestry methods are the model for the world.

Verily Germany is a triumph of art over nature! The result may be seen from the following figures:—

	Average total production.[4]		*Average per acre.*	
	Rye, Wheat, Oats, Barley. Million tons.	*Potatoes. Million tons.*	*Cereals. Centals = 100 lb.*	*Potatoes. Centals = 100 lb.*
1879–83	13·2	21·1	10·24	3·05
1909–13	26·9	45·0	17·86	5·46

The total yield of cereals has, therefore, doubled, and of potatoes it has more than doubled. This is not due to the reclamation of fresh land, but to the process of getting more out of the same land, as the yield per acre has risen enormously. Nor has this been carried out at the expense of the livestock.

	1883. Thousands.	*1913.*[5] *Thousands.*
Horses	3,522	4,516
Cattle	15,787	20,154
Sheep and Goats . .	21,839	9,172
Pigs	9,206	21,885

[1] T. H. Middleton, *Recent Development of German Agriculture*, 1916 [*Cd.* 8305], p. 7.

[2] *Evolution of Modern Germany*, p. 232.

[3] Middleton, op. cit., p. 72.

[4] Middleton, op. cit., p. 8.

[5] Middleton, p. 9.

It is interesting to observe that 93 per cent of the land of Germany was owned in 1916 by the men who cultivated it, and that small holdings under 50 acres comprised nearly half the total area. The great agrarian looms large in politics, but he only owns a little over half the land. Small holdings covered 38,644,382 acres, i.e. 48·5 per cent, while large ones covered 40,942,803 acres, or 51·5 per cent. In that total, moderate-sized holdings between 50 and 125 acres covered 17,053,248 acres.[1] An interesting feature is that small holdings tend to increase in number, which seems to invalidate the socialist argument that big businesses and big estates will swallow up small ones.[2]

While France in 1789 and Russia in 1905 carried through revolutions largely to improve agricultural conditions, this element has been absent in Germany. Both in France and Russia a starving peasantry wanted more land to live. In Germany the paternal Government helped them to make the best of the land they already held, and as the yields increased during the century in proportion to the population, the causes of agrarian revolution were eliminated.[3]

Possibly, however, this is due to the " land flight " which has been another striking feature of German agriculture during the century. The German has not perhaps made a revolution, because he could and did get away. He had an alternative in the factories or in the United States. Many of the peasants were unable to hold on after the disappearance of the old communal methods of farming. They could not adapt themselves to the new ways. An agricultural depression set in all over Europe after 1815, which intensified the crisis for the incapable. The result was that many of them became agricultural labourers, engaged on a yearly contract, under which they were given a holding and a certain amount of food by their employer and a small money payment. This was the typical method of

[1] Middleton, p. 12.

[2] W. J. Ashley, *Progress of the German Working Classes*, p. 65.

[3] A comparison of German and English agriculture is interesting, especially as it was from England that Germany originally learnt intensive farming at the beginning of the nineteenth century.

On each 100 acres of cultivated land—

The British farmer—	The German farmer—
Feeds 45 to 50 persons.	Feeds 70 to 75 persons.
Grows 15 tons of corn.	Grows 33 tons of corn.
Grows 11 tons of potatoes.	Grows 55 tons of potatoes.
Produces 4 tons of meat.	Produces 4½ tons of meat.

Middleton, p. 6.

hiring East of the Elbe before 1914. West of the Elbe, day labour was more common; the small peasants did not require all their time on their holdings, and were willing to work for the larger farmers. Nevertheless, the labourers refused to stay on the land, and there was a labour famine only mitigated in the East by the annual importation of between 300,000 and 400,000 migrant Russian or Galician workers who came in for the harvest. It was said that the system of education unsettled the agricultural labourers, that they were attracted to the towns where they had passed their military service. Wages had risen, it is true, but not as rapidly as in industry, and they were under severe penalties for breach of contract, which did not apply to artisans. They were also not allowed to form trade unions, and only in 1911 were the insurance laws compulsorily extended to agricultural workers. The general tendency has been for the peasant in the West of Germany to emigrate to America, and for the Eastern labourer to migrate West and take his place, or go into the mines and factories. The reason for the Western emigration has been said to be the excessive subdivision of holdings consequent on the application of the French law of inheritance. On the other hand, many of the peasants from the East, especially Pomerania and Schleswig, have also emigrated to the United States. It must, however, be remembered that 42·6 per cent of the German population were still living in the country in 1905. A comparison with 1875, however, shows the predominantly rural nature of the Empire at the earlier date [1] :—

	Total population.	*Urban (over 2,000 people).*	*Urban to Rural.*
1875	42,727,360	16,657,172	39 per cent.
1905	60,641,278	34,818,797	57·4 ,, ,,

It is from these figures that one realizes the overwhelming importance of agriculture in 1875, when 26 out of 42 million people were still living under rural conditions, and although a much larger proportion was gathered in towns in 1905, even then over 25 million were still living in communities of less than 2,000 people, which meant that the bulk of those 25 million would be concerned or connected with agriculture in some form or other.

[1] *Fiscal Blue Book*, 1909, [*Cd.* 4954], p. 17.

CHAPTER 4

Russia and the Agricultural Revolution

After 1856.

Period of Reform. Emancipation of the Serfs.

The emancipation carried out on the initiative of the Czar by the nobles' committees, 1861–5.

The object to make every peasant a landowner.

The authority of the landowner replaced by the *Mir*, which became responsible for the payment of the taxes.

Peasants to pay compensation for their services to the landowner. The Government to advance the landowner four-fifths and the peasants to pay the other one-fifth. The peasants to pay the Government in gradual instalments.

Result :—

About 40 million people freed—all males received land.

The *Mir* became all powerful and prevented freedom of movement to ensure payment of taxes.

Intensive agricultural methods prevented by periodical redistribution of land, general ignorance, lack of capital, and strip system.

Sale of grain immediately after harvest to get money for taxes. Export of the good grain, impoverishment of the food supply.

Gradual buying out of the proprietors, rise of inequalities among peasants.

After 1906.

Legislation to break up the *Mir*.

Land obtainable in individual ownership.

The sorting of the strips.

Cancelling of the redemption payments.

Attempt to encourage better agriculture—technical centres.

Government facilitates sale of nobles' land to peasants through Land Banks.

RUSSIA has been subjected alternately to the influence of France and Germany, and her intellectuals have usually responded to it by ardently advocating views of French liberty or German administrative methods, as the case might be. There has been a strong undercurrent of feeling, however, that the Slav had after all a better civilization than the West, and there was a desire to keep Russia from the contaminating influence of these foreign ideas. All these forces made themselves felt in turn in agricultural questions. Under the stimulus of French ideas, Alexander I, who was nothing if not liberal, was in favour of freeing the serfs. He was followed by a reactionary Czar, who reverted to a purely Slav attitude and outlook. It was against this autocratic monarch that England and France commenced the Crimean War in 1854. Incidentally they meant to free Turkey, but they also conceived that they were fighting the cause of freedom. They won. Nicholas died, it was thought as a result of the defeat he had experienced, and he was succeeded by a liberal Czar, Alexander II, who intended to free the serfs and modernize Russia. The advantage of an autocrat is that if he intends to have a thing done it has got to be done without argument. The Lithuanian nobles appealed to him to be allowed to revise the working arrangements with their serfs (the inventories). The Czar chose to assume that they were asking permission to free them, which they were not. He graciously granted permission to them to do this. He sent all over the Empire extolling the public spirit of the Lithuanian nobles and recommending the others to follow their example. He also enclosed a copy of the fundamental principles on which such an emancipation should take place. Such a communication was not a hint but an order. In 1858 the nobles formed committees in every province to carry this out. The great idea was to avoid the evils that were typical of the West, especially the landless labourer. The possibility of creating a mass of homeless wanderers who should form a "proletariat" was the nightmare of those who were going to carry out the emancipation. The committees sent in their reports and a Government Commission sat to codify them, the governing principle being that the serf was not merely to be free, he was to be a landowner with a stake in the soil. This, it was thought, would prevent the revolutions of the West, such as those of 1848, which Russia had escaped. It was also hoped that the peasant would stay on the land if he owned it, that the growth of great modern towns would be avoided and "Holy Russia" would preserve her essential characteristics unaffected by the devastating effects of industrialism as seen in other countries.

Between 1861 and 1865 the serfs were freed. The personal obligations that were thus abolished were much the same as those prevailing in Prussia,[1] but whereas in Prussia, after emancipation, the peasant had been free to leave the land if he liked and take up a trade, in Russia he could not

[1] One great difference lay in the fact that domestic serfs were serfs in the lords' household for life. In Prussia it lasted till a man was 35.

leave without the passport of his *mir* or commune. The *mir* was set up as the governing unit in place of the lord. It was made responsible as a whole for the taxes, and the ownership of the land of the community was, as a rule, vested in this body.[1] Thus a man did not own land that he could mortgage or sell, but he had a claim to land somewhere in virtue of being born a member of the commune. The land was not his to treat as he liked, but he cultivated it in common in the same way as his neighbours, and his share was an equal one with theirs. A large family would have a larger aggregate number of holdings than a small one, but reckoned per head the idea was equalitarian. So heavy were the taxes that land was a burden rather than a privilege. The possession of land meant taxes and the *mir* was responsible as a whole for their payment. If one member failed the others had to make the deficit good. Thus the *mir* did not give a man his passport to leave his village unless it were quite sure that his share of the taxes would be forthcoming, and without a passport a man could not move in Russia. Hence personal freedom was as much restricted by taxation considerations in Russia as it had been in France before 1789. Even if the Russian were allowed to leave he had to send back money to the commune for his quota of the land taxes. It was not until 1905 that the *mir* ceased to be financially responsible *en bloc*. When those who stayed behind no longer had to make good the deficits of those who had left, there was no reason to refuse passports, and it was expressly forbidden to refuse them by a ukase of 1906. Hence freedom of movement was not gained in Russia till the twentieth century.

Russia, too, had to arrange compensation to the landlords, and did it in somewhat different fashion from Prussia. The land to be held by each male person was a fixed quantity, the *nadiel*, which varied, however, in different districts. If the land the serf was holding did not reach the size fixed as the minimum for his district, the lord had to make up the difference. If the man held more than the prescribed maximum, he gave up the extra amount of land to the lord. On the whole, the peasant's share of the land was increased. He also made a money payment in redemption of services,

[1] K. A. Wieth-Knudsen states that 81·4 per cent of the land was given into communal ownership, 18·6 per cent into individual possession. The *mir* was responsible for taxes even in the latter case. *Bauernfrage und Agrarreform in Russland*, p. 35.

four-fifths of which was advanced by the State to be repaid by the ex-serf in instalments over a long period of years. These redemption payments were paid at the same time as the taxes. The burden of these payments in addition to the taxes created an impossible state of things for the tenant, and, unlike the similar German payments, the arrears outstanding were cancelled in 1905. Thus the State partly found the money to pay compensation to the overlords in Russia. The task of resettling the lives of 40 million emancipated persons [1] over an area which was two-thirds of the size of Europe was a stupendous one, and apparently neither side was satisfied with the results, but it remained as a settlement until the Revolution of 1905 forced the reconsideration of agricultural tenures on the Government, with a further transference of land from the lords to the peasants.

Agricultural improvement did not take place to anything like the same extent in Russia as in the two other countries that have been considered. The Russian peasant still continued to farm in strips for the next forty years. The reason for this lay in the fact that the Russian peasant was extremely conservative and he also possessed the tradition of common work and co-operation. Indeed, he frequently combined into a sort of co-operative society or *artel* [2] to carry out any piece of work. He was, moreover, very ignorant, and as the Government had carefully eliminated both the priest and the former landowner from the *mir* he had not much intellectual guidance. The communal system of cultivation needed little skill or initiative; a man did everything in exactly the same way as his neighbours, because there was no other way possible. He contributed to the plough teams which broke up ground at the same time as everyone else's teams; he was obliged to sow the same crop, rye or oats in the spring, wheat in winter; he reaped at the same time as his neighbours. The cattle of the village were turned over the reaped fields at a certain time fixed every autumn. In the same way he mowed his bit of meadow at the appointed time. Under this system a potentially good farmer gained little advantage as compared with a bad one. It left nothing to his judgment. Of course, even with equal shares there would be inequalities. A delicate man with an ailing wife and many young children is

[1] Sir D. M. Wallace, *Russia*, p. 503.

[2] F. H. E. Palmer, *Russian Life in Town and Country*, p. 241.

necessarily in a different position from a strong man with an active wife and several grown-up sons able to help him; but, on the whole, the chances of a man rising or falling were less under this fixity of methods of cultivation.

It was precisely the fact that improved agriculture was impossible as long as these practices obtained that led Germany and France to sort out strips and enclose them into compact farms. But the matter was complicated over large parts of Russia by the fact that the land did not belong to the individual but to the *mir* or commune and that each male child that was born had a right to land. Thus the land of the *mir* had to be redivided periodically to provide for the new citizens. Each man's portion got smaller and smaller, and he ceased to be able to live on the holding allotted to him. Nor was he willing to improve his land, as he might lose it at the next redistribution. The decline in the size of the average *nadiel* is seen from the following figures[1]:—

	1860.	*1880.*	*1890.*	
Nadiel	4 desiatines	3·3	2·6	Central industrial region.
	8·4 „	5·2	3·2	North-Eastern regions.

The result was that, as the Russian did not know how to farm intensively, he wanted more land to farm extensively. As in France before the Revolution, there was a steady purchase of land from the nobles, whose share declined, while that of the peasants rose. Between 1877 and 1905 no less than 24,597,383 *desiatines* were transferred from the former to the latter class.[2] Inequalities became, therefore, more pronounced among the tenants. Those who could afford to purchase more land tended to form a separate class, as they had done in France before 1789. A rich peasant, known in Russia as a *kulak* or "fist", from his supposedly grasping nature, would hold his strips in the commune, but what he purchased from the lord would be his own private property. It was on the dislike of the smaller peasant for the richer that Bolshevism played and got its hold on the lower class of agricultural population. The tradition of Russia is markedly equalitarian, and the new peasant class had violated this tradition.

With the diminution of the *nadiel* in size as population increased, Russia became more and more a prey to famines. It was said that there was a small famine every spring, and a

[1] K. A. Wieth-Knudsen, *Bauernfrage und Agrarreform in Russland*, p. 40. A *desiatine* is 2·7 acres.

[2] Wieth-Knudsen, p. 41.

big one every seven years. Meanwhile, Russia began to export corn in increasing quantities. There was, therefore, the anomaly of a starving country with large food exports.

Corn Export.

	Million poods.
1881–1885	269·1
1886–1890	367·9
1891–1895	377·5 [1]

The proportions of the harvest of wheat, oats, rye, and barley exported were :—

Average.	
1862 to 1866	4·6 per cent exported.
1871 „ 1875	9·1 „ „
1875 „ 1879	14·3 „ „
1883 „ 1888	13·6 „ „
1888 „ 1893	14·1 „ „
1893 „ 1897	15·7 „ „

The growing quantity of grain exported did not benefit the peasant. This was due to the fact that the redemption payment and the taxes had both to be paid after the harvest. In order to meet his obligations, the moujik had to sell his corn at once to get money, and he sold it either to a Jewish or German middleman. As the price of grain on the world's markets steadily fell between 1875 and 1894, owing to the quantity of the American supplies, the peasant had to sell more corn to get the same amount of money, to pay his taxes, and had less for seed and food, especially as he sold the best grain and kept the worst. As the cattle were killed off in a scarcity and manures, therefore, got more scanty, the yields grew less. It was a vicious circle. The peasant, who was the lightest taxed man in Europe if mere figures only are regarded, was probably the heaviest taxed man if it were a question of his ability to pay. In addition he had to meet his redemption payments, which steadily fell into arrears. It is scarcely to be wondered at that a stream of emigration set in towards America or that they wandered out in thousands to gather in the German harvests. Germany was as much affected in some respects by the Russian corn exports as she was by the American wheat. The Russian exported rye in considerable quantity, which is a crop Germany also produces and consumes.

In 1905 matters came to a head. Taxation had been

[1] Wittschewsky, *Russlands Handels-, Zoll- und Industriepolitik von Peter dem Grossen bis auf die Gegenwart*, p. 253. A *pood* is 36 lb.

increased to carry out the industrial revolution from the 'nineties onwards, and the costs of the Japanese war seemed to promise a further rise. The railway trucks which should have taken the grain to market were in Siberia, and the Russian peasant could not realize his harvest. The result was that all over the Empire the peasants rose to demand more land.

Before 1905 only feeble attempts had been made to solve the problem of intensive cultivation. It is true that, driven by sheer starvation, methods had somewhat improved in the Northern zone,[1] but nothing effective had really been done for all the Russias. The blame had been laid on the *mir*, which was said to strangle all progress by its insistence on maintaining the communal system of agriculture and the redistribution of land, but it was regarded by the Slavophils as so purely Russian in character that it was an almost sacred institution. After 1905, however, the agrarian problem was really faced, and the result was an attempt to provide more land, and to set up at the same time individual instead of communal ownership of land with the consequent break up of the *mir*. There was to be free sale and free movement, and not merely was the redistribution of land to cease where it still existed, but the strips were to be re-sorted. This meant a break up of the whole collectivist régime of land-holding, the buying out, over a vast Empire, of the nobles, and the establishment of a kingdom of peasant proprietors.

By a series of ukases between 1906 and 1911, afterwards confirmed by the Duma, Commissions were set up in the various provinces, consisting of officials, members of the Zemstvos or County Councils, and the peasants. These had to decide on the needs of the peasants for more land and the possibility of satisfying it by selling them the land of the nobles, the state lands, and the lands of the imperial appanages. The lands were to be sold to Land Banks, the business of which was to resell to peasants whose lots were under the average size of the region. Advances were also made to peasants to enable them to buy direct from the landowner. The Commissions were supposed to help to establish better agricultural methods at the same time. The nobles found such difficulty in getting labour, and had had so much friction with the peasants, that offers to sell

[1] Sir D. M. Wallace, *Russia*, pp. 533–6.

flowed into the banks in quantities. The banks were allowed to sell either to communes or to individuals, but their whole endeavour was to be directed to selling to individuals so that the land should be held as private property. The banks thus sold on easier terms to individuals than to communes, and they endeavoured before selling to rearrange the properties as compact farms. In addition the Russian in the *mir* could demand that he should be given his strips in individual ownership and the Government was willing to re-sort the land of any commune into compact areas should two-thirds of the people desire it. Wieth-Knudsen says that in most communes one man's share, consisting of 20, 30, 40 and even 100 strips, might be 15–20 kilometres apart.[1] A man was thus separated from his land by whole days' journeys. The difficulty was that if the land was redistributed, some people had to live in the outlying parts, away from the stream or water supply. The task of the Government was not merely to re-sort the land, but to dig wells for the people and make roads. The land in the black mould zone is so porous that the water often lies at a considerable depth, and the sheer capital expenditure, not merely of sinking the well but of ropes and windlass, would be beyond the capacity of the peasant. The Government was, however, just beginning to undertake the work before the War broke out. The peasants did not prove to be so attached to the system of communal agriculture and redivision as the Slavophils had thought. The demands to have the land redivided flowed in rapidly; the lack of trained surveyors was the only drag on the wheel. The peasants were so used to measuring land for their redivisions and were so accustomed to the idea of redivision, that enclosing was proceeding at a phenomenal rate before 1914. There is, moreover, so little variation in the quality of the land of a district that the difficulties which arose in the mountainous districts of Western Germany were entirely absent in Russia. The object of the Commissioners was to get people to leave the village and settle on their own enclosed farms, but they also tried to create new villages, thus carrying out a sort of inner colonization.

Thus before the European War broke out Russia was engaged on the most stupendous agricultural revolution of modern times, and was accomplishing it quite rapidly. The

[1] Op. cit., pp. 81–2. See also the sketch-maps.

result should have been greatly increased yields, the creation of a new granary for Europe, and a higher level of life for the peasant. Had the land been all sold to the peasants, they would have had to cultivate intensively, having exhausted the available supply of land for extensive cultivation. As, however, the big owner who farmed better than the peasant would have been eliminated, the State would have had to inculcate the knowledge of improved methods. This was being tried through the Zemstvos and through the new land commissions, while co-operative societies were forming rapidly, as the Russian has a genius for co-operation.

The communal system, however, made it difficult for a man to fail entirely, as he did every thing inthe same way as the others and at the same time. When matters are left to individual initiative, certain people with better capacity prosper, others fail ; the latter cannot adjust themselves to the more strenuous type of farming, hence they lose their land and become a landless class. The nineteenth century witnessed the growth of this class, almost a new class, in France and Germany, and the twentieth saw it beginning in Russia. Indeed, a new word was invented in Russia to designate this growing social distinction among persons who were formerly equals ; it was *differentiation* (differentsia).

CHAPTER 5

Agricultural Development in the United States

North *versus* South.
- Extensive methods of cultivation in the South where "cotton is King".
- In the North the homestead the typical holding.
- The South free trade; the North protectionist.

The Expansion West and the question whether new States to be "slave" or "free".

The maintenance of slavery necessary to preserve the political preponderance of the South.

Reasons for defeat of the South in the Civil War:—
- South depended on export of cotton and import of food and manufactures:—
  - Both prevented by the North.
  - South numerically inferior.

Effects of Civil War.
- Transformation of the South.
- Abolition of slavery leads to break-up of old plantation system.
- Growth of small farms in South.
- Approximation of economic conditions of South to North.
- Great increase in cotton production.
- Problem of the negro as a cultivator.

Reaction of United States on Europe.
- Enormous export of corn due to—
  - Cheap freights.
  - Railways and elevators.
  - Agricultural machinery.
  - Virgin soil and cheap land.

Development of the Middle West.
- Railways.
- Migration from East to West. Immigration to fill the gap.
- The Homestead Acts.
- The refrigerator car and the meat trade.
- Spring wheat.

THE agricultural problems of a new and non-serf country like the United States have varied considerably from those of Europe. Just as in Germany there was a radical difference between East and West, so in the English colonies of America there was a fundamental distinction between North and South. The Southern States were founded either by men with capital or by chartered companies to grow staple products not produced in England. The idea of English colonization both in the West Indies and in the Southern region was to promote a self-sufficing Empire. Tobacco was obtained through the arch-enemy Spain. Virginian tobacco would take its place, although both James I and Charles I disapproved of the practice of smoking. Sugar from the West Indies would deliver this country from dependence on the other great rival, Holland. From the very first the South was developed on the lines of capitalistic agriculture growing for an oversea market and importing its manufactured goods. Large plantations were set up, and as the labour difficulty was acute, negro slaves were imported. A certain number of whites were also brought over as indentured servants and these formed the overseer class. It is mainly from these latter that the " poor whites " of the South are descended. If they acquired land they could not afford to purchase slaves—the basis of the great plantations—and so they took up land on the hilly and less fertile districts and carried on small farming of a rather miserable type. The South cultivated its land extensively. An area would have a fire kindled to burn the timber and brushwood, the ashes would manure the ground, tobacco would be planted, a crop would be taken and then the land would revert to its former wild state not to be touched again for something like twenty years. There was plenty of land and this was the most economical form of cultivation, demanding no particular skill from the negro. The South, however, needed more food than it produced and imported its pork and corn from the North, while it obtained its manufactures from England. By the end of the eighteenth century the South began to develop cotton rapidly.

The invention of the cotton gin in 1793 disposed of the difficulty of the seeds left in the cotton. The cotton factories were developing in Great Britain and were ready to absorb larger and larger supplies. Hence the South expanded vigorously along the lines of cotton, cultivating it in the same extensive manner as tobacco, which it soon out-weighed in importance. Cotton became the great Southern staple and the saying ran in America, " Cotton is King."

The North, on the other hand, had developed quite a different type of agriculture. The climate was not suitable for tropical or semi-tropical products ; the settlers had not the capital to buy many slaves ; and coloured labour did not thrive in the colder climate of the North. Hence the typical holding was the " homestead ", a piece of land of a size that could be cultivated by a man and his family.

The Northern settlers aimed at providing for their own wants and therefore grew foodstuffs. They lived in villages or townships and the concentration of population in groups in the North is in striking contrast with the scattered nature of the population on the plantations in the South. Towns therefore developed in the North. In the South the great estate was a kingdom to itself. The North was too poor to buy manufactures as did the South and therefore was obliged to be as far as possible self-sufficing. They earned money, however, in the eighteenth century by carrying on a flourishing shipping and ship-building trade, varied by occasional smuggling. They also bought slaves in Africa with the rum distilled in the West Indies, and sold them to the South. The West Indies and the Southern States were the best markets for the surplus food products of the North, especially for pork and corn. The South was to a large extent dependent on the North for food.

There were thus in the United States two civilizations, the South and the North, and they differed not merely in their type of agricultural labour and land tenure but in their attitude towards the tariff. The South was for free trade, in other words, low duties; while the North was protectionist. The North wished to develop industrially and felt that unless their infant industries were sheltered from English competition they had little chance of becoming industrial. The South, on the other hand, did not see why it should pay more for its manufactures in order to start the North on a new career of prosperity during which the North might become more important than the South.

With the expansion of the United States beyond the Alleghanies, the burning question was whether this fundamental cleavage was to be perpetuated in the new territories. Were they to be "slave" or "free"? There was no question at first of freeing the existing slaves. It was not a question of personal freedom but of the clash of two types of civilization. The South could not carry on without slaves—its whole economy rested on them. If the new States were to be free States they would belong to the civilization of the North, and as they obtained votes in the Senate they would in time swamp the Southern vote. The aristocratic Southern gentleman would be dominated by the Yankee bagman and have to take his orders from the despised Northerner. Southerners felt that this was not to be tolerated. The South must expand *pari passu* with the North and take their slaves and their great plantations with them. The cotton cultivation was being pushed further and further West: how could they continue to produce it without slaves? Free labour, it was felt, meant extinction for the South.

By 1819, of the twenty-two States in the Union, eleven were slave and eleven were free. Meanwhile a "free soil" party had grown up and a battle was fought over the question as to whether Missouri was to be slave or free. Was the system to be extended to the Louisiana purchase and the lands beyond the Mississippi?

A compromise was arrived at in 1820 and further modified from time to time, but by 1860 the South saw itself outvoted by the "free" states. Lincoln's election marked the victory of the North, and seven Southern States, headed by South Carolina, left the Union.[1] Both South and North were fighting for their respective types of civilization.[2] The North intended to force the South back into the Union and the Civil War broke out at Fort Sumter in 1861.

That the North succeeded is not surprising. The South had a population of 12 millions, of whom 4 millions were slaves. The Northerners were twice as numerous. The South depended on its export of cotton to purchase manufactures and food. The North had the shipping and maintained a blockade which made it impossible for the South to sell. And as they could not sell they could not purchase either food of war materials. Nor had they manufactures which could produce the necessary munitions and stores.[3]

They lost their only two large trade centres, New Orleans and Charleston, in the first year of the war. The revenue

[1] The States that seceded were South Carolina, Georgia, Florida, Alabama, Mississippi, Louisiana, and Texas. North Carolina, Virginia, Tennessee, and Arkansas joined after the war broke out.

[2] Surprise is frequently expressed that England should have been so sympathetic to the South—to a slave régime—during the Civil War. It has been attributed to the fact that she wanted raw cotton and that Lancashire suffered from a cotton famine and unemployment during those years. As a matter of fact England stood, especially at that period, for the right of nationalities to determine their own destiny. She had helped Italy, which had almost achieved unity by 1860, and had fought to prevent Turkey being crushed by Russia in 1854. The North seemed, with its enormous preponderance, to be crushing another nationality that wanted to be free and was trying to force it into the Northern mould as Russia was Poland in 1863.

[3] J. C. Schwab, "The South during the War (1861–5)," in *Cambridge Modern History*, vii, p. 621.

depended on the custom duties, and, as nothing came in, money failed; nor was it easy to raise a revenue from the planters as their financial strength lay in cotton which could not now be realized. Moreover, as the bulk of the food supply of the South came from the North, the South was starved out. The South had no training in business; their commissariat was mismanaged; their labour was slave and not efficient, although it remained loyal to its masters. The mystery was that the war lasted four years, 1861–5. It left the South in a state of complete financial collapse. The North suffered far less. Their surplus foodstuffs were readily absorbed by the army. Their industries now working for war received an enormous stimulus, especially railways and iron making. Many new industries were started, and as they had white labour it was more intelligent as well as more numerous than the Southern coloured labour force. Taxation was heavy, but it could be borne, and the Western expansion went on all the time, as the armies afforded such a good market for foodstuffs. The utilization of agricultural machinery economized labour to such an extent that it has been said that the issue of the Civil War was decided by the reaper. "Overwhelming material superiority, it turned out, was with the North; but she had also another and greater advantage: she was to fight for the Union and for the abiding peace, concord, and strength of a great nation." [1]

One result of the war was that in 1863 the slaves were declared to be free in all States. Personal freedom was thus attained in the United States at the same time as Russia was emancipating her serfs. The two great agricultural Empires were also alike in that they both began in the next decade to develop a corn export which produced confusion in European agriculture.

In Russia the emancipation meant the break up of the nobles' estates; in the United States the end of the Civil War saw a complete change of tenure and the break up of the great plantations and the reconstruction of the South. Most planters were heavily in debt by the end of the war and were forced to sell their estates so far as they could find purchasers. Many others found that they could not continue with free labour and so leased their lands if they could find tenants. To the sons of the planters the life

[1] Woodrow Wilson, "State Rights (1850–60)," in *Cambridge Modern History*, vii, p. 442.

offered no career and they migrated, chiefly to the cities. Much of the land lapsed temporarily into wilderness, but the chief effect was the rise of the small farm. The people who bought were mainly the poor whites; sometimes they were negroes. Frequently the former owner let his land to negroes on condition of receiving a share of the produce. As these small farmers could not feed or supply themselves, stores had to grow up, and towns were formed in the South as in the North. The typical estate of the South, as of the North, became the average sized farm,[1] and instead of one-half the Union differing in its habits from the other a similarity of economic conditions emerged. The United States justified its name for the first time by being economically unified.

The effect of this transformation was a great development of cotton growing, an event of world importance, since cotton became more and more in demand as the industrial revolution developed in Europe. When the plantations were broken up into small estates, cotton could no longer be grown extensively. More had to be got out of the same area if the small man was to live. Hence he had to put in manures as he could not go on continually changing his land. Marl and phosphates were discovered in the South and with the use of these fertilizers the yield of the crop quadrupled.[2] Transport also assisted the expansion of the cotton belt, while a new use was found for the waste cotton seed extracted from the wool in making cotton seed oil, which considerably increased the value of the crop and the impetus to grow it.

The small man, however, needs credit. He must live for a year at least before he can grow and sell his cotton crop. Hence he runs an account with the local storekeeper. The storekeeper will not give the farmer food and implements without security, therefore the cotton grower, white or black, has to mortgage his crop in advance. Moreover,

[1] *Average Size of Farms.*

	Acres. 1850.	1900.
North Atlantic . .	112·6	96·5
S. Atlantic . .	376·4	108·4
S. Central . . .	291	155·4

U.S.A. Census 1900, *Agriculture*, v, p. xxi.

[2] M. B. Hammond, "The Cotton Industry," in *American Economic Association Publications*, New Series, No. 1, pp. 135–7. Other crops were also grown, as rice, tobacco.

the storekeeper is often the agent of some big firm of cotton merchants, who will not supply goods except cotton be produced, and so the farmer has to go on growing cotton whether he likes it or no. "The high prices which he has been obliged to pay for his merchandise, and the low price which he receives for his cotton leaves the balance of the account each year standing in favour of the merchant. The contract which the farmer has entered into with the merchant binds him to continue his business with the latter until the old debt is paid, and as the end of each year finds him unable, in his own words, 'to pay out,' he begins again the weary struggle for existence, with new burdens laid upon him, but still deluded by the vain hope that 'more cotton' will enable him to escape from his load of indebtedness".[1] With this heavy indebtedness it does not seem that personal freedom was much more of a reality in the South than it was in Russia prior to 1905.

Meanwhile the negro as an agriculturalist, in spite of brilliant exceptions, was notoriously unsatisfactory. He was a careless cultivator and it was said of him that he can "grow cotton but he cannot grow corn",[2] the idea being that the former stood neglect better. With the spread of the cotton boll weevil,[3] however, and the constant watchfulness that the methods of prevention entail, even this crop was endangered, as the South has not labour enough to cultivate cotton on a large scale without the negro.

The enormous preponderance and importance of the American cotton supplies and its growth since the Civil War may be seen from the following table:—

World's Sources of supply.[4]

	U.S.A.	*Brazil.*	*W. Indies.*	*India.*	*Egypt.*
			Million pounds.		
1851–55	1254·7	27·1	6·3	134·8	60
1861–65	531·7	36·2	14·6	491·3	191·4
1871–75	1682·3	108·8	42·3	538·5	238
1881–85	2717·2	54·1	11·6	540·3	292·5
1891–95	3773·6	50·5	13·6	453·4	455·7
1901–05	5115·6	42·9	22·4	409·9	596·5
1906–08	5850	43·6	43·2	494·2	653·3

The value of raw cotton in 1909 was estimated to be worth

[1] Hammond, pp. 151–2.

[2] C. Kelsey, "Evolution of Negro Labour," in *Annals of the American Academy*, 1903, pp. 55–76. Also P. A. Bruce, *The Rise of the New South*, pp. 25–6.

[3] J. A. Todd, *World's Cotton Crops*, pp. 105–6.

[4] *Fiscal Blue Book*, 1909 [Cd. 4954], p. 154.

$703,619,000, and the seed $121,077,000, the total value of the United States crop being only second to maize.

While the United States have not had to face the problems of Europe such as the freeing of the serfs and the readjustment of strips, they have had to solve the problem of making the negro cultivator efficient, and his wasteful methods become more difficult of toleration as the unoccupied land grows yearly less and less. The solution of this question with its reaction on cotton does not merely affect the United States but all the cotton-making countries [1] and their operatives who depend on the raw material for their livelihood. It is a striking instance of world interdependence.

While the South was undergoing reconstruction a great expansion was going on in the Middle West, and the United States began to react on Europe with its grain and meat exports. One effect of the Civil War was to give a powerful stimulus to railway building East and West to make up for the loss of markets to the South. The great trans-continental lines were subsidized by huge land grants, the Union Pacific obtaining 12 million acres of land and the Central Pacific, opened in 1869, 11 million.[2] The filling up of the region between the Mississippi and the Rocky Mountains is the most striking event of the decade 1870–1880 and was only made possible by the railway. The railways further stimulated the opening of the Middle West by advertizing for emigrants, partly to make their own land grants valuable, partly because they could not get freight unless people settled on the land and produced the grain, etc. They granted free passes to home seekers and ran emigration bureaux. The railways, therefore, made the West accessible and facilitated colonization to develop the traffic.

The rapid increase in grain production and export may be seen from the following tables. It should be noticed

[1] The following figures of the consumption of raw cotton in average periods of five years are suggestive :—

	Great Britain.	*Europe.*	*U.S.A.*
		Million pounds.	
1851–55	750·1	451·4	281·4
1881–85	1444·1	1314·9	856·7
1901–05	1662·1	2535·2	1989·9
1906–08 (3 years)	1887·1	2877·8	2319·4

Fiscal Blue Book, 1909 [*Cd.* 4954], p. 154.

[2] Professor H. C. Emery, "Economic Development of the United States," in *Cambridge Modern History*, vii, p. 705.

that the maize was not merely exported as maize but in the shape of the beef and pork fed on the maize.

WHEAT.[1]—*Winchester bushels*

Annual Average.	*Production.*	*Exports.*
1880–84	463,973,317	140,469,416
1885–89	435,417,000	113,527,522
1890–94	476,678,028	167,330,604
1895–99	529,477,802	181,113,550
1900–04	626,194,816	164,248,229
1905–08	681,732,365	130,641,405

INDIAN CORN.—*Bushels*

1880–84	1,575,194,108	55,755,909
1900–04	2,182,585,716	86,917,993
1905–08	2,724,095,158	74,747,740

It would seem from the following figures as if the United States produced something like a quarter of the wheat of the world at the end of the nineteenth century.

	1897.	*1898.*
	Bushels.	
World	2,269,352,000	2,907,000,000
U.S.A.	530,149,168	710,000,000 [2]

The value of the meat products exported rose [3]

In 1865	$ 35,072,000	worth of meat	was	exported.
,, 1880	$113,769,000		,,	,,
,, 1900	$175,226,000		,,	,,

The total value of the exports of agricultural products, which would include lumber and cotton, increased as follows [4]:

1870	361	million	dollars.
1875	430	,,	,,
1880	686	,,	,,
1885	530	,,	,,
1890	630	,,	,,
1895	553	,,	,,
1900	836	,,	,,

The primary cause of this stupendous development is, as has been said above, the conquest of the new lands by the railway; but the railway is useless without people who provide something to carry, and people needed something to attract them on to the land. Those attractions were found in the fact that new markets were opened in Europe where

[1] *Fiscal Blue Book*, 1909 [*Cd.* 4954], p. 179.

[2] *U.S.A. Industrial Commission*, vi, p. 95.

[3] Emory R. Johnson and others, *History of Domestic and Foreign Commerce of U.S.*, ii, p. 67.

[4] *Domestic and Foreign Commerce of U.S.*, ii, p. 69, quoting *U.S. Bureau of Statistics Monthly Summary*, April, 1903, p. 3249.

the settlers could sell their surplus, that the land laws of the United States enabled them to obtain land for nothing, and that new inventions came in which opened up new vistas of profit in wheat and cattle growing. Thus while a stream of immigrants began to set in from Europe, the native-born moved West.

To open up markets in Europe, two things were necessary. First, the stuff raised in America must be sold in Europe at a price that would compete with the grain grown in proximity to its market. Wheat produced in California, for instance, must be sold in Liverpool at or about the same price as wheat grown in Essex or East Prussia. Secondly, not merely must wheat be sold at or about European prices, but other countries must be willing to allow it to come in. American farmers grew more than America could take; if they could not export the surplus the colonization of the Middle West was useless. The question was how to place the surplus in Europe.

The chief factor in the matter of American food exports was the phenomenal fall in freights after 1870. So low did the cost of carriage fall that distance ceased to be a barrier to the marketing of American products. This fall in freights was due to three causes; the use of a new material—steel, competition among the railways for traffic, and competition between the steamer and the sailing ship. The steel rail lasted about three times as long as the iron rail, therefore the maintenance and renewal of the railway lines cost less. In 1880 less than three-tenths of the railroad mileage was equipped with steel rails. It rose to eight-tenths by 1890.[1] The steel rail would also bear a heavier truck, so the cars themselves were gradually made of steel, beginning with wheels and axles, and they were made larger in the stronger material. Locomotives also increased in size and power,[2] and the average train load carried increased from 177·42 tons in 1890 to 270·86 in 1900 and 362·57 in 1909.[3] It was the large freight car that specially favoured the development of the meat traffic, as live cattle take up much space. The decrease in the cost of handling

[1] *Industrial Commission*, xix, p. 291.

[2] The average weight of the locomotive increased from 90,000 lb. at the end of the Civil War to 250,000 lb. in 1900. In 1885 the locomotive hauled as a maximum load 3,600 tons on a level, and in 1890, 4,000 tons. In 1894 the locomotive hauled on an average over the year 32,000 tons, in 1899, 46,000 tons. *Industrial Commission*, xix, pp. 292–3

[3] *United States Stat. Abst.*, 1910, p. 268.

goods owing to the larger loads and the cheapening of maintenance were two reasons which brought American corn cheaply to the sea-board.

The second cause of cheap freights is to be found in the great speculative era of railway building which set in between 1870 and 1880. The mileage, which had been 35,000 at the end of the war, was 52,000 miles in 1870 and 93,267 in 1880. It reached 128,320 by 1885 and was 167,191 by 1890.[1]

Scarcely one third of the railways built were justified by the existing business and they began to compete wildly against one another for freight. The result was that rates for carrying grain dropped something like 60 per cent between 1867 and 1896,[2] with a corresponding drop in wheat and maize prices. It varied of course on the different lines, the fall being 24% on some and as much as 74% on others.

In addition to the competition of the railways there was a special reason for a big drop in freights to the coast, because the railways had not merely to compete with one another but with water as well. Wheat from Chicago to Liverpool could either go by water via the lakes, the Erie Canal and New York, or by the lakes to Montreal, or by rail all the way to New York. It could equally go from Kansas or St. Louis down the Mississippi and out by Galveston or New Orleans or by rail down the same route. Furthermore, the towns on the coast competed amongst themselves to obtain the great grain shipments. Thus New York and New Orleans were equally in competition with Baltimore and Chicago, hence towns bought or guaranteed railway bonds and tried to see that the railways served their particular port in the matter of grain exports.

The third reason for the drop in prices is to be found in the competition of the steamer and sailing ship. Between 1870 and 1886 there existed a surplus of tonnage. The new iron steamers made many more voyages than the old sailing ships, and the capacity of the shipping of the world outgrew the cargoes to be carried. Thus there was a fierce struggle among sailing and steam ships to convey the heavy shipments of grain. The result was that whereas the average

[1] *Fiscal Blue Book*, 1909 [*Cd.* 4954], p. 131.

[2] See Chart, in the *U.S.A. Industrial Commission*, vol. vi, p. 90 (1900). On the Rock Island and Pacific it cost in 1865, 1·985 cents to move 1 ton of grain per mile to Chicago. It cost ·958 in 1897. The drop continued till 1900, after which a rise took place.

rate for carrying wheat from California to Liverpool per ton in 1869 was £4 5*s*., it sunk to £1 17*s*. 3*d*. in an iron ship and £1 3*s*. 9*d*. in a sailing ship in the years 1896–7.[1]

Cheap corn in Europe was mainly due, therefore, to competition; competition between the railways, between railways and water-ways, between the sea-board cities and between the ships for cargo. Grain was often transported below the actual cost of service,[2] and the price dropped much below the average which had prevailed in Europe previously.

This competition with Europe was still further stimulated by the fact that elevator companies set up all along the railway routes. They collected, stored, and graded the grain, which not merely diminished the cost of handling it, as it could be despatched in huge loads, but it also helped the farmer to dispense with barns and expensive buildings. Moreover, the elevator companies, by grading the grain, enabled the merchants to know exactly what they were buying and greatly facilitated the working of the marketing through the produce exchanges.

The United Kingdom had abolished protective tariffs between 1846 and 1860, and all foodstuffs of the kind the United Kingdom produced were admitted free. Great Britain, therefore, offered an unexampled market for grain and meat in her great industrial towns. The low price of the wheat and meat exported from America enabled those products to conquer the continental market as well, until the continent began to dyke up against the flood by tariffs in the 'eighties which were increased as the American exports grew in volume. The United Kingdom, however, remained free trade and provided a great stimulus to the American settlement of the prairies.

While cheap railway and steamer rates enabled the American farmer to find a market for the surplus the United States did not require, the system of the disposal of the unoccupied land was another inducement to settlers to move out and open up the centre of the continent.

During the Civil War the policy of the United States with regard to its unoccupied land underwent a change. The vacant lands forming the hinterlands of the thirteen colonies had been ceded by the States to the Federal Government and formed the Public Domain by 1802. The

[1] *U.S.A. Industrial Commission*, p. 99, vi.
[2] Ibid., p. 113

policy of disposing of these lands varied. It was sometimes sold in large blocks to speculators to pay off the National Debt, sometimes it was disposed of at cheap rates in small quantities to would-be cultivators. From 1844 onwards there was an Anti-Rent movement which aimed at "free homes for free men", and Bills were brought in to grant land at nominal rates to settlers on a small scale. The South was opposed to this as it would upset its traditional methods of agriculture, namely, the large plantation; hence it was not until the Civil War broke out that the policy of free land grants on a small scale could be successful. The Civil War decided the question whether it should be a system of large farms and sparse population or subsistence farming and vigorous colonization.

The Homestead Act of 1862 declared that any citizen over 21 could have 160 acres of public land without payment if he cultivated it himself for five years. Soldiers who had served during the Civil War were allowed to count their years of service as part of the five years and many availed themselves of this privilege. In 1873 this was followed by another Act giving a man 160 acres if he would plant one-sixteenth of it with trees and protect them for eight years. In 1877 the Desert Land Act granted 640 acres of lands not suitable for arable and on this concession the ranches were built up.

Under these Acts it has been possible for a man to get land for nothing and this prospect has had a tremendous effect in stimulating emigration, especially from Germany. With the excessive subdivision of land taking place in Western Germany, a man was powerfully attracted by the prospect of the free gift of what would be in Europe a good average sized farm.

The third inducement to the settlement of the Middle and Far West was provided by the new inventions of agricultural machinery, the refrigerator car, and the new process of milling spring wheat.

It would have been of little use for a man to go into the prairies unless there had been a development of agricultural machinery. Where all can get land there is not likely to be much surplus labour. The new settler could not have got in his harvest by hand at a cost that would have enabled him to sell in Europe, even had the labour been there, which it was not. Between 1850 and 1860, however, came the invention of agricultural machinery; the reaper and binder were successfully developed and later the steam thresher and steam plough. In 1850 the value of farm implements was $151 million dollars. By 1890 it was $494 millions, by 1910 $1,265.[1] The farmer was bound to have machinery, and he had to mortgage his land to obtain it, and in 1890 there had accumulated a tremendous amount of mortgage indebtedness.[2]

The ease, however, with which large quantities of grain were sown, reaped, and threshed by machinery was another reason for the cheapness of American grain and consequently for its ability to compete in Europe.

The soil, moreover, was virgin land; it needed no manures and all the settler had to do was to take crop after crop until the land was exhausted and then move on and "prove up" another homestead. It is this continual robbing of the land that is one of the great problems of American agriculture. On the other hand, with few farm buildings necessary because of the elevators, with no manures, little labour and cheap freights, it is not surprising that the effects of the American grain surplus should have fallen like a blight on European agriculture. English wheat fell in price from 56*s*. 8*d*. in 1871 to 22*s*. 10*d*. a quarter in 1894.[3]

The development of the meat trade in the United States was largely due to the invention of the refrigerating process, coupled with the means of adapting that process to transporting the meat in the refrigerator car. The packing industry consists of the curing of pork in various ways, the canning of meat products, and the slaughtering, chilling, and transporting the frozen or chilled meat, chiefly beef. The centre of the meat packing industry was first of all Cincinnati and then Chicago outstripped the former town in importance, therefore such meat as was intended to be "packed" for distribution within the country had to be brought to these centres in the Middle West and distributed from there. It was here that the refrigerator car came in. Meat could be received or despatched in a perfectly good and sweet condition in the middle of summer as well as

[1] Census 1910, *Agriculture*, v, p. 84.

[2] Census 1910, *Agriculture*, v, p. 158. Of 3,142,746 farms in 1890, 875,052 or 28·2 per cent. were mortgaged. In 1910 there were 1,312,034 farms mortgaged or 33·6 of the total number of farms. Mortgage is thus on the increase.

[3] House of Commons Return showing for every year from 1800–1910 price of British wheat per quarter, No. 339 of 1912, p. 4.

winter both for home and export. The curing of hogs, which had only been possible in winter, was equally possible in summer when the chilling of the carcases enabled them to be kept from deteriorating in the heat. Thus an all round market was provided in both winter and summer.

By 1875 the refrigerator cars were developed sufficiently to revolutionize the packing industry, and the export of fresh beef began in 1876, when 19,838,000 pounds were despatched. By 1880 it had reached 100,622,000 pounds, by 1890, 182,500,000, and by 1892 it had become 233 million pounds. In Chicago, whereas about 20,000 hogs were killed in 1850–1, by 1890–1 the figure had reached 6,071,000. All this naturally reacted on the cattle-raising interests both of the Middle and Far West and South-West. The very concentration of the beef and pork industries in a few centres led to the development of bye-processes. Out of the waste products of horns, hoofs, bones, and blood are made glue, oil, tallow, fertilizers; while the hair, hides, and wool are the basis of other manufactures. "To-day a large packing plant depends largely for its profit on the intelligent utilization of those so-called waste materials which in the early days of the packing industry were thrown away."[1] So much profit was made from bye-products that the meat itself could be sold cheaper and it was placed in Europe at prices which affected vitally the price of second and third class meat.[2]

The demand of the meat packing establishments stimulated the cattle interests of the Central West and reacted on the developing of cattle ranches in the Far West. The cattle traffic was favoured, like wheat, with low railway rates, and as the trucks grew larger, owing to the use of steel in their construction, the price of meat products fell and European agriculture again felt the effect. The cattle raised in the Far West were often sent into the Central West to be fattened on the maize grown there, and thus the grain and cattle raising interests stimulated each other.

Another invention which affected the method of milling wheat was introduced in the early 'seventies into Minneapolis, which still further increased the stimulus to

[1] Armour, "The Packing Industry," in *One Hundred Years of American Commerce*, ed. Depew, vol. ii, p. 383.

[2] Ibid., p. 122.

grain raising in the more northern parts of the Middle West. By this process the growing of spring wheat was made highly remunerative. The danger in the northern sections of sowing the wheat in the winter is that the thaws may force the wheat out of the ground and it may be killed by the frost. The ground in the northern parts of the Middle West is not, as in the east, covered with a thick "eider-down coverlet" of snow which protects the grain. Apart from the frosts, biting winter winds are often fatal to the growth of the winter-sown wheat where there is no snow to protect it. Wheat sown in spring generally escapes the danger of the "winter kill", but it must be a special kind of wheat which matures quickly. This wheat used to be inferior to winter wheat when ground, as it was impossible to remove all the particles of bran, and the flour being a poor colour it fetched a low price. Therefore wheat-growing in the North West was a speculative affair, as winter wheat was apt to be killed and spring wheat sold badly. By the new process the flour produced from hard spring wheat was as fine as any and commanded an even higher price than winter wheat. This was a great incentive to settlement in such states as the Dakotas, Nebraska, and Minnesota.

The railways, the Homestead Acts, agricultural machinery, the refrigerator car, and the new milling inventions would all have been ineffective but for the hordes of settlers who poured into the new districts. Emigration, as will be seen from the table hereunder, set in rapidly towards the United States from England, Ireland, Germany, and Scandinavia after 1848.[1] The majority of the English were skilled

[1] Average Annual Immigration into the U.S.A. from various countries during the years 1825–1914 :—

	All Countries.	*United Kingdom.*	*Germany.*	*Italy.*	*Austria.*	*Scandinavia.*	*Russia.*	*Greece, Roumania, Turkey.*
				000 omitted.				
1825–34	32	14	4	—	—	—	—	—
1835–44	71	41	19	—	—	—	—	—
1845–54	294	168	95	—	—	2	—	—
1855–64	150	79	49	1	—	2	—	—
1865–74	334	134	113	3	3	22	2	—
1875–84	389	103	109	13	17	45	10	—
1885–94	453	119	98	47	48	56	38	—
1895–04	463	56	28	114	102	38	77	18
1905–14	1,012	96	34	220	235	41	199	57

Report on Shipping, 1918 [*Cd.* 9092], p. 14.

workmen, engineers and miners, and they did not go on the land except for cattle ranching. The Irish stayed in the towns and amongst other things worked the lifts and the trams and ran the saloons and the town governments of their adopted country. A great many Germans were agriculturalists and about a quarter of them went on to the land as did also about forty per cent of the Scandinavians.[1] The great agricultural development was, however, carried through by the American himself. One of the most extraordinary features of American life to an English observer is the migratory character of the population and the way in which it can change not merely its habitat but its occupation and turn from one industry to another and from industry to agriculture. It is almost impossible for an English farmer whose family has been for 150 years or more on the same farm under the same family of landlords to conceive the ease with which an American will give up his farm several times during his life-time and "move West".

In 1873 there came a great depression in the United States. Works were closed down; merchants and artisans put their savings together and moved out. Whole colonies left Brooklyn and New York every week. The high wages paid to artisans enabled them to accumulate savings and they poured into Wisconsin, Minnesota, the Dakotas, and Nebraska to take up farms. In no case, however, did the foreign out-number the native element, and so the foreign element was easily absorbed and the national characteristics were preserved. The tendency of the foreign immigrants has been to settle in the cities. The new-comer generally has to seek employment at once and starts afresh in a hand trade or shopkeeping, or carries on mechanical and mining operations. The colonization of America has therefore been the work of the second generation at least and has been a native effort of expansion.

Some idea of the extent of the work may be gathered from the following figures:—

The number of farms in	1850	was	1,449,073
	1860	,,	2,044,077
	1870	,,	2,659,985
	1880	,,	4,008,907
	1910	,,	5,361,502
	1920	,,	6,449,998

[1] Professor H. C. Emery, "Economic Development of the United States," in *Cambridge Modern History*, vii, p. 702.

The land area brought into cultivation in farms out of 1,903,289,600 acres was :—

	Acres.
In 1850	293,560,914
„ 1880	536,081,835
„ 1890	623,218,619
„ 1910	878,798,235

The percentage of the total land in farms was 15·8 in 1850 and 46·2 in 1910.

It is interesting to notice that while the United States intended to create a race of landowners, tenancy has been gradually increasing and the number of persons who rent their land has gone up from 25·6 per cent of all farming in 1880 to 37 per cent in 1910. During the thirty years from 1880 to 1910, the number of tenant farmers increased 1,330,075 or 129·8 per cent, while farms operated by their owners increased 1,022,520 or 34.3 per cent.[1]

In the decade 1900–10, there was a slackening in land occupation, an average of 4 million acres a year being taken up instead of 15 millions as in the thirty previous years. The unoccupied land was getting used up and the problem now before the United States was that of making farms out of wet and dry lands, the one by drainage, the other by irrigation,[2] before the homesteads could extend much further.

On the other hand, the great problem is to make people get more out of the land they have already got. The white settler of the Middle West has to be taught that he cannot rob the soil beyond a certain point and that there comes a time when instead of always taking out he must begin to put in; in other words, the introduction of intensive cultivation is nearly as pressing in the United States as in Russia. The boll weevil down South presents still another problem.

The State has taken the lead and with its agricultural experimental stations and schools has been trying to introduce some method of alteration less wasteful for the future, and to devise means for combating the boll weevil. Hitherto their efforts have been chiefly confined to training people to teach intensive cultivation. Of 46·2 per cent of

[1] U.S.A. Census, 1910. *Agriculture,* v, p. 102.

[2] In 1902 a law was passed providing that irrigated lands should be sold and the proceeds devoted to further irrigation—thus one piece recovered pays for the next.

land farmed, 25·1 per cent, or 478,451,750 acres, was said to be "improved" and 21·0 per cent, or 400,346,575 acres, unimproved.[1]

While the average European visualizes the United States as a great industrial country with huge towns, it is interesting to notice that only 33·1 per cent of its population lived in urban areas in 1900, i.e. 50,485,268 out of the huge population of 75,477,467 lived in the country at the beginning of the twentieth century. The United States and Russia were at that date the most rural of the Great Powers, the latter having 87 per cent and the former 66·9 of her people grouped in areas of less than 2,000 people.[2]

Meanwhile, in the early years of the twentieth century, the population was growing and the U.S.A. was ceasing to be a great wheat and raw material exporter. Fewer people in proportion to the total population were in the country districts and more in the towns. Agricultural machinery is seen to be more and more taking the place of human beings, the gasoline engine being a particularly important factor.

In America people talk of the crops as people in England talk of foreign trade. During the whole of the nineteenth century, of agricultural exports, cotton stood first, and wheat second. These formed the backbone of American internal commerce and comprised, during the period 1860–90, 77 per cent of the value of the exports.

In the twentieth century food and cotton exports are seen to be declining, the proportionate figures being:—

Period.	*Wheat.*	*Cotton.*
1896–1901	210	176
1912–1914	144	42

Meat exports declined from 951 million pounds in 1906–9 to 489 in 1912–14. Actually the importation of foodstuffs balanced the exports just before the Great War, and the United States became a food importing nation.

[1] U.S.A. Census, 1910, *Agriculture*, v, pp. 30, 34.

[2] The total number of persons over 10 who were quoted as occupied in the American Occupation Census of 1910 (published 1914) was 38,167,336. Of these 12,659,203 were said to be occupied in agriculture (p. 53).

PART III

THE INDUSTRIAL REVOLUTION

CHAPTER I

France and the Industrial Revolution

French predominance in the world of economic ideas.
- The advertisement of liberty.
- The advertisement of socialistic ideas—the National Workshops, 1848.
- The carrying through of the free trade movement in Europe, by Napoleon III, from 1860.
- The new development of the working class movement—syndicalism.

Periods :—
- 1789–1799. The French Revolution and economic collapse.
- 1799–1815. Napoleonic reconstruction.
- 1815–1848. Intensified protection and industrial change.
- 1848–1870. Free Trade era.
- 1870–1914. Era of social legislation.

Pre-Revolutionary manufactures and organization through the gilds.

The Eden Treaty, 1786.

Multiplicity of tariffs, legal and administrative units.

The Convention (1792) and the Directory (1795).
- Financial collapse and economic ruin.
- The assignats.
- The financial and industrial chaos leads, aften ten years' misery, to the rise of Napoleon.

The Reconstruction of France by Napoleon I.
- Napoleon III's dictum : " Our existing Society is nothing more than France regenerated by the Revolution of 1789 and organized by the Emperor Napoleon I."
  - Centralized administrative system created.
  - The Civil Code.
  - Financial system reorganized—Bank of France founded.
  - French industry developed along the lines of machinery.
  - To protect and encourage this industry the protective system was developed, especially against England—The Continental System.
  - The prohibition of combinations. The Conseils de Prud'hommes.

After Napoleon.
- General progress of French industry.
- Growth of use of machinery—steam power.
- Influence of St. Simon, Fourier, Louis Blanc.
- The national workshops—their failure.

After the Revolution of 1848.
- Rapid industrial development.
- Railways.
- Liberal and free trade movement.
- The Labour Movement and increase in wages.

The Third Republic.
- A slowing down.
- Lack of coal as handicap in iron industry.
- Domestic work survives in textiles.
- Social legislation.

New Labour Movement.
- The Syndicate Law of 1884.
- Syndicalist movement.
- In 'nineties, political methods less prominent than economic (general strike).

FRANCE had aimed in 1789 at creating a new state of society based, not on socialism, but on individual liberty. Each man was allowed to own property and he was to be free to deal with his own property as he liked, to choose his own occupation and carry on his trade or business free from control or hindrance. Although the result of this freedom was to produce a collapse followed by regulations that were the very negation of the liberty aimed at, the idea was always present in the minds of Frenchmen that a new state of society could be rapidly attained if only people chose to have it, either by some form of mutual consent or by another revolution. "We do not make a reform in France," said Napoleon III, "we make a revolution." The Frenchman is so logical that with him there is no half-way compromise; it is all or nothing. The effect of the events of 1789 on other parts of Europe was momentous. French revolutionary ideas operated to bring about freedom of industry and freedom of trade. In Germany the break-up of the gilds was the result of the spread by French conquests of the ideas of the French Revolution. Again, Napoleon introduced free trade in the part of Germany that he annexed, and so paved the way to the Zollverein, while his Continental System was the precursor of the later protection.

With the spread of the industrial revolution and the dislocation it inevitably involved, it seemed perfectly feasible to some Frenchmen to try and establish a new state of society. St. Simon laid down plans for a Utopian state. Fourier, Proudhon, and Louis Blanc evolved others. In 1848 the French working men in Paris proceeded to try and carry into effect the idea of Louis Blanc, and the French Revolution of 1848 re-echoed all over Europe. Everywhere except in England, Sweden, and Russia revolutions broke out, and in Austria the serfs were freed as a consequence. The revolutions which broke out in Europe were, it is true, not due to economic causes, except in Austria, where the desire of the serfs to be free was only one of the motives of the rising. The revolutions were due to the wish to attain either a more liberal government, as in Prussia, or to achieve national expression, as in Italy or Hungary. So great was the influence of France on political thought and action that a revolution in France caused largely by economic motives[1] was sufficient to start political revolts over a large part of the continent. These political revolts led, after a period of reaction, to more liberal constitutions, and this reflected itself in the economic sphere in a great period of "free trade" treaties, i.e. treaties which lowered the protectionist tariffs all over Europe. Thus France, by giving the momentum to political liberalism in 1848, stimulated economic liberalism as she had done after the French Revolution.

Again, in 1860, when Napoleon III put himself at the head of the free trade movement in Europe, he continued the work the revolution of 1848 had begun. Using the treaty concluded with England in 1860 as a basis for negotiations, he inaugurated the change to greater liberty of trade for all Europe.

Although defeated in 1870 in war, France was once again to be influential in the realm of ideas. Its syndicalist movement, though weak in numbers, struck a new note in the 'nineties and provided a new inspiration to the Labour movement. Even if anarchic and impracticable, it seemed to provide an alternative to men disappointed with the slow progress of Marxian socialism. The underlying idea of syndicalism was direct action by the workers, arising from an impatience with all government. The proposal was that society should be overturned—this is typically French! —but this time not by political action but by a general strike. Society would then consist of organized groups of trades or professional associations, each a law to themselves, without the existence of any governmental machine.

The result of the discussions was to lead to the formation of groups professing similar ideas in other countries. The Industrial Workers of the World in the United States owe their origin to the syndicalist movement. The Gild Socialists of England have also been inspired by the French doctrines. The general trend in England to associate the workers more closely in the management of the business

[1] The disgust of the French with Louis Philippe's timorous foreign policy was another reason as well as his tendency to outmanœuvre his Parliament and to create an absolute monarchy under constitutional forms.

may possibly owe something to the discussion of syndicalist doctrines.

Therefore, on four separate occasions in the period under consideration, France has been influential in affecting the economic current of ideas or actions, after 1789, after 1848, after 1860, and from the 'nineties onwards.

All through the century two separate and opposed traditions are at work in France. There was a long tradition of control from above, and that persisted, being confirmed by Napoleon. On the other hand, there was a pride and belief in the efficacy of individual liberty as embodied in the principles of the French Revolution.

From the reign of Henry IV (1589–1610), and even earlier, the King had been a sort of economic providence in industry. This was intensified under Colbert who, when he was in power from 1661–83, nationalized the control of industry. The Crown during the eighteenth century had itself created or subsidized many new industries owing to the absence of liquid capital in France; and whenever times were bad the workmen looked to the King for relief. This was distributed through his *intendants*—royal officials whose business it was not merely to administer their *généralité* but to report on the state of industry in their province, carry out the orders of the government in industrial matters, collect the taxes, relieve the poor, regulate the corn trade, and as far as possible secure the prosperity of their district. How great was the economic power and discretion of the *intendants* may be seen by the brilliant work of Turgot in his *généralité* of Limousin. There were also royal inspectors of manufactures who saw to the quality of the goods produced. Direction from above, paternalism and elaborate government control were perfectly familiar everyday things to Frenchmen. A reaction against the excessive fostering and regulation of industry took place in the last half of the eighteenth century. The physiocrats preached that agriculture was the only true source of wealth and that freedom, not regulation, was the only way in which prosperity could really be secured. It was a Frenchman who invented the phrase, "*Laissez-faire, laissez-passer.*" Under Louis XVI a great deal had been done towards securing this freedom. The gilds were abolished in 1774, though they did not disappear; taxation was being reformed; the grain traffic was left free—to be restricted later—and a country industry was allowed to grow up after

1762. The French Revolution was an attempt not merely to get a constitution and revise taxation but to realize this freedom more rapidly and thoroughly.

Ten years of economic misery, following 1789, resulted in the rise to power of an autocrat who centralized the government machine but restored order and a certain degree of prosperity. Revolutions are very expensive things, and even Napoleon could not bring France back to the pitch of economic well-being it had enjoyed in the 'eighties. He interfered very little, however, with individual liberty in industry or agriculture; but with his roads, his codes, and his police, he provided a framework in which the French ideas of freedom might work themselves out. He did not initiate, but he made effective, the high protective tariff that the Directory had drawn up; and he intensified it by his Continental System which, by excluding the goods of his only rival, England, gave a chance to French industry slowly to struggle to its feet again. He revolutionized communications and restarted machine industry in France. Since that date the Frenchman believed, on the one hand, in a protective tariff and central control, and, on the other, in complete personal liberty. The first is the Napoleonic tradition; the second the revolutionary tradition.

During the nineteenth century a high tariff was maintained in France, except for the interlude between 1860 and 1883. It was almost natural, since the state had made and managed the roads and the canals from the time of the great Emperor, that the railways should grow up with state assistance and on a uniform state plan and not as a patchwork system as in England, and that many of them should be owned and worked by the state. On the other hand, one cannot but notice the very great reluctance of the French government to abandon *laissez-faire* individualism in industrial matters. It is rather remarkable how late the French were in permitting workmen's combinations to exist at all; not till 1884 did workmen really have full liberty to combine. They were also late in adopting effective factory legislation, insurance, a weekly day of rest and other methods devised to protect the working classes from the evils of modern industrialism. It is really not till after 1870, when the revolt of the Commune showed for a second time in twenty-two years how deep was the desire of a certain section of workmen and intellectuals for a new state of society, that the French government really began to adopt "interventionisme" instead of *laissez-faire* and to develop a modern labour code.

The periods of French industrial development during the nineteenth century may accordingly be divided as follows: (1) The French Revolution and the economic collapse, 1789–99. (2) The Napoleonic reconstruction, 1799–1815. (3) The intensification of protection and the development of the industrial revolution, 1815–48. (4) 1848–70. The Free Trade Era. (5) 1870–1914. The era of social legislation.

1789–99

To trace the beginnings of the industrial revolution it is necessary to go back to the period before the French Revolution. In the eighteenth century France, like England, was a country with a great cloth industry. It was distributed all over the country and not concentrated, as it is now, in the North. The chief manufacturing centres were either those places in which wool was grown in the vicinity or where it could be imported easily from Spain. Flanders, which had always been a great cloth-making region even in the Middle Ages, still preserved its skill; and one of the great centres of cloth-making was Lille and the surrounding towns. Picardy was another great textile region with the manufacture based on Amiens and Abbéville. A third was in Normandy, with Rouen and Elboeuf as its centres. A fourth was in Champagne, where there were large flocks of sheep; and the principal towns were Rheims, Sedan, Mezières, and Rethel. A fifth region centred round Carcassonne and was based on the sheep kept in Languedoc and on the import of Spanish wool. This region supplied the Levant with cloth.

After woollen cloth, linen and hempen goods came next in importance. Flanders was a great linen region, but Normandy was the linen area *par excellence*. Silk was the third great industry, and was located in the Rhone Valley with Lyons as its chief centre. The mulberry trees grew there and raw silk could be imported from the Levant to supplement the home supplies. Iron was made in little forges dispersed over the country and the ore was smelted by charcoal.

In addition, a small cotton industry was growing up which

was worked by machines in factories. Englishmen were responsible for the introduction of the new mechanism into France. One of the principal agents was Holker, a man from the neighbourhood of Manchester, who, having been a supporter of the Pretender in 1745, was forced to fly, and he took refuge in France. He received considerable financial encouragement from the government and set up a manufacture of cotton velvet. As there was a difficulty in getting spinners he brought over two English women named Hayes and Law to teach spinning in the country districts, and the government assisted him by setting up spinning schools. At a later date he introduced Hargreaves' spinning jennies. Another Englishman, Milne, installed Arkwright's water-frame. The general result was that before 1789 there were three or four large factories at Neuville, L'Epine, Louviers, and Orleans.[1] The various Englishmen who introduced these new methods and machines received substantial pensions and subventions from the government. The minister Tolozan complained bitterly that there were not capitalists in France large enough to introduce machines on their own account, which shows how fundamentally France differed at this date from England,[2] where the Duke of Bridgwater spent £220,000 in building his canals and Arkwright obtained £12,000 to complete his water-frame by entering into partnership with two other men.

In the same way there was the beginning of a modern iron industry at Creusot. Various enterprising Frenchmen had gone to England to study the new methods and one of them had succeeded in interesting the great iron master, John Wilkinson, who sent his brother, William Wilkinson, to France. The latter organized the beginnings of a modern iron industry, using coke at Creusot in 1781 instead of charcoal. This is the origin of the famous Creusot works.[3] Thus the beginnings of modern large scale machine industry existed in France before the Revolution and in all cases founded on English technique.

Industrial organization in France before the Revolution was mainly centred in the gilds. They had been reconstructed by Colbert and had to work under a system of

[1] On the whole subject, C. Schmidt, "Les débuts de l'industrie cotonnière en France 1760–1806" in *Revue d'histoire économique*, 1913.

[2] Schmidt, op. cit., p. 32.

[3] C. Ballot, "La révolution technique et les débuts de la grande exploitation dans la metallurgie française," in *Rev. d'histoire des doctrines économiques*, 1912.

national control which was instituted at the same time. An elaborate system of rules to ensure quality was set up by the government, and to these all work had to conform, and royal inspectors were instituted to see that the rules were observed. The regulations were so elaborate that they were said by an official in 1787 to fill eight quarto volumes. An attempt was made to dissolve the gilds in 1774, but they survived, and industry was largely in their hands in 1789 as far as town industry was concerned. The gilds saw to the training of workmen and instituted as far as possible a trade monopoly for their own benefit by limiting numbers and excluding country workers. They also opposed new methods. When a man was out of his apprenticeship it was the custom for him to travel, and in order that he might be properly entertained and employed the journeymen formed associations known as *compagnonnages*. These were, in the nineteenth century, when trade unions were prohibited, the only working men's associations.

Alongside of the gilds with the masters, journeymen, and apprentices working in small workshops, there existed certain large establishments. Colbert, in reorganizing industrial life, had made arrangements for the setting up of new manufactures or privileged establishments outside gild control. These were created by letters patent and were known as *manufactures royales*. The minister thus provided for the development of large scale industry or new inventions while the gilds still retained the control of domestic industry. The "great industry" was, however, directly under the control of the state, from which it derived its licence to exist. Spinning was extensively carried on in the country districts by women and children, but the other processes were grouped in towns under gild supervision. It was part of the general movement towards freedom noticeable after 1750 that there should be an attack on the gild monopoly, and the result was the creation of a country industry outside the gilds somewhat similar to the movement which took place in England at the beginning of the sixteenth century.

By two edicts, 1762 and 1765, any person might engage in industrial production without belonging to a gild, so long as he observed the general regulations for the conduct of industry laid down by the Government.

The general result was a widespread extension of industry

in the rural districts nearly all over France.[1] The pieces of cloth woven in such a poor district as Brittany rose from 118,000 in 1767 to 249,000 in 1775,[2] and these were worth between 14 and 15 million livres. Indeed, one of the inspectors chronicles that " there are few villages in France in which woollen or linen cloth or stockings are not being made ".[3]

Arthur Young noticed this prevalence of domestic industry and considered that it was harmful to agriculture, as the people were so occupied with their industrial bye-employments that they did not apply themselves to increasing the agricultural yields. The Government favoured the extension of this country industry and in 1779 relieved it of all restrictions. The country workers were not even obliged as heretofore to conform to the general regulations laid down by the Government. This was only acknowledging an existing state of affairs, since industry had become so widespread that inspection was impracticable. Some of these peasant workers, as in England, sold straight to the consumer; the majority appear to have worked to order for a merchant whose agents collected the goods. Sometimes the peasants supplied the raw material and delivered over the finished article made on their own looms; sometimes the agent or the merchant supplied the raw material and more rarely the looms. We find all degrees of dependence and independence.

Into this prosperous hive of industry with its growing export the treaty of 1786 with England came as a sort of thunderclap. The Eden treaty was of such an extraordinarily liberal nature for its time that most of the import duties, heretofore on a prohibitive level in both countries, were reduced to between 10 and 12 per cent *ad valorem*.[4]

This treaty came into operation in May, 1787, and was almost immediately followed in France by a great industrial crisis. English goods which had always had a certain vogue among the rich in France now flooded the market. The imports, which had been 24 million livres in 1784, rose to 58½ million in 1787, of which 33 million were manufactured goods. By 1788 the imports of English goods had risen

[1] E. V. Tarlé, *L'industrie dans les campagnes en France à la fin de l'ancien régime*, 1910.

[2] H. Sée, " Les Classes rurales," in *Bretagne du XVIe siècle à la Révolution*, p. 449.

[3] Tarlé, *L'industrie dans les campagnes à la fin de l'ancien régime*, p. 13

[4] E. Levasseur, *Histoire du Commerce de la France*, i, p. 540.

to 63 million livres. The French exports to England, on the other hand, declined somewhat, being 37½ million in 1787, 34 in 1788, and 36 in 1789.[1]

This large import of foreign goods coincided with a shortage of raw material in France, so that while some merchants ceased to give out orders because they could not give out raw material, others ceased to place orders because they could not sell the goods made, the English goods having ousted French products. The result was an appalling industrial crisis,[2] the effect of which was compared to the revocation of the Edict of Nantes.

From all the big manufacturing centres, Rouen, Elboeuf, Sedan, Carcassonne, the tale is the same—a diminution in the number of looms, workmen emigrating, merchants ruined. The *intendants* sent in requisition after requisition for money for poor relief, and in spite of the desperate condition of the finances no less than 1,500,000 francs were sent by the Government at the end of 1788 and the beginning of 1789 to relieve the distress. The inspectors of manufactures considered that by the end of 1788 there were 200,000 workmen unemployed in the towns, and this crisis had then lasted a year and a half. Many had, however, emigrated.[3]

While the Eden Treaty was blamed for the depression, there were many other contributory causes. There was a failure, for instance, of the silk-worm, and a scarcity of raw silk in the year 1787–8. The French clip was not sufficient for the growing cloth industry and Spanish merino wool was a necessity to mix with the native wool to produce good quality cloth. There was increasing difficulty, apparently, in obtaining this, as the English also required Spanish merino wool and were more expert in obtaining it. They kept agents at Bilbao to purchase it and were able to ship direct to England.

Moreover, in certain lines of trade the English were ousting the French, especially in the Mediterranean. They supplied a better cloth at a cheaper price and thereby ruined the cloth trade of Carcassonne, which depended on the Spanish and Mediterranean market. This would have happened treaty or no treaty, but it was not obvious to the people at the time. When anything went wrong the Government was blamed. Hence the crisis was considered

[1] E. Levasseur, p. 542.
[2] C. Schmidt, "La crise industrielle de 1788," in *Revue Historique*, vol. xcvii, 1908, pp. 78 ff.
[3] Schmidt, op. cit., p. 91.

to be the fault of the Government which, with its liberal ideas, had abandoned the traditional policy of prohibition.

Overtaxed and already smarting under the increasing weight of the seigniorial dues, incensed by the enclosure of commons, eager for more land and seeing no prospect of getting it, and now deprived of the industrial bye-employment, is it to be wondered at that the French peasant was willing to support the middle classes in a revolution? The town artisan who had felt the crisis acutely was ready to join the peasant. Matters were precipitated by the fact that 1788 was a year of great food scarcity and ended in one of the coldest winters of the century, when even the port of Marseilles was frozen. The result was the outbreak of 1789.

In spite of the temporary set-back caused by the Eden treaty with England it must not be forgotten that France was a great industrial country in 1789 and that the export of her manufactures was not merely large but was increasing rapidly. Her colonial trade was greater in 1789 than that of England in 1771–2, when the latter still possessed all her North American colonies. While the import and export trade between Great Britain and her colonies in that year was £9,535,390,[1] that of France amounted to over £10½ millions, reckoning the livre as the equivalent of a franc and 25 francs as equal to an English pound.

The following figures show how important was the French trade and how rapidly it had grown from 1715, also the magnitude of her distributing trade in colonial products. It is interesting to notice that the exports and imports did not reach this point again till 1830.

	Livres. 000's omitted. 1715.	1787.
Total Imports	94,623	590,173
Total Exports	118,352	517,600

	1716. Million livres.	*1789.*
Products of French industry exported .	45	133
Re-export of American colonial products	15	152
Re-export of Indian products . .	2·6	4·1
Re-export of foreign merchandize . .	6	46

	Import.	*Export.*	*Import.*	*Export.*
Trade with French colonies	16·7	9·1	192	78·9[2]

[1] Sir C. Whitworth, *State of the Trade of Great Britain in its Imports and Exports, 1697–1774*, 1776, p. 76.

[2] E. Levasseur, *Histoire du Commerce de la France*, i, pp. 517–18.

Of the exports of textiles 39 millions went to Europe, 10·3 to Africa, and 27·2 to America. France was the foremost industrial country in the eighteenth century and only gradually was England beginning to catch up, favoured by her capital accumulations, her banking system which made her capital readily available, her coal, her inventors, and her good transport facilities. In this last respect, however, France was improving rapidly before 1789.

Before the revolution of 1789 France had no national economic unity. She had a geographical name and observed a common obedience to the King and his *intendants*. From the thirteenth century the Kings had been adding the great fiefs to the domains of the crown. Fresh territory had also been taken in war, and each district thus acquired had its own traditions, history, and customs, which were retained when they were added to the area ruled by the French monarch. Each province and each district even had its own code of law. There were no less than 360 regional codes in force in France before 1789.[1] There were four great systems of law which obtained to a greater or lesser degree in various parts of France—the Roman Law, the Customary Law, the Feudal Law, and the Canon Law, and all these were modified by royal edicts which again were differently applied by the thirteen *parlements* which registered these edicts. It is almost impossible to give an account of the economic condition of France in 1789 which should be true for the whole country, the conditions of agriculture, trade and taxation varied so enormously in different parts. The King ruling with his Council was the one link between the whole. Under him were his *intendants*, administering districts called *généralités*, and under them again delegates having charge of an *élection*. The *élections* did not exist, however, in the *Pays d'état*, though the *intendants* ruled there also. France was therefore divided again into the *Pays d'élection* and *Pays d'état* and, as we have seen above in the case of the roads, the royal power was stronger in the former than the latter. Corresponding to the multiplicity of these divisions, tolls, tariffs, legal, and administrative systems were the differences in weights and measures, and their divergency was one of the great hindrances to internal trade.

It was part of the reforming movement of the French

[1] P. Sagnac, *La législation civile de la Révolution*, p. 1.

Revolution to sweep all these barriers away. As a result France was re-arranged into eighty-six "départements", which ignored the old historical boundaries. A common decimal system of coinage, weights, and measures replaced the old confusion. The internal customs were abolished. The laws were gradually unified and embodied in the Napoleonic codes. Napoleon made France really a unity by re-making the roads which linked up the whole kingdom with Paris. The Revolution stood for unity as well as freedom.

It was quite in keeping with the idea of individual liberty that the gilds should be abolished. In March, 1791, a measure was passed declaring that on and after April 1st every individual should be free to exercise any craft or profession whatsoever provided only that he should equip himself with a licence from the public authorities. These were inexpensive and easy to obtain. Thus the gild monopoly was broken though there seems to have been little or no demand for the abolition of the gilds from any quarter. To maintain complete liberty the Assembly on June 14, 1791,[1] prohibited all combinations of workmen or masters and declared all combinations, strikes, and agreements between workmen to refuse to work or of employers to refuse to give work to be contrary to the Declaration of the Rights of Man and to be punishable.

The Assembly also abolished all privileged companies for commerce, such as the East India and Levant Companies.

The Assembly had found the cultivator in some places a serf, and the peasants oppressed with feudal dues and taxation. It made both free. Industry was said to be hampered by inspectors, gilds, and a multiplicity of indirect taxes and privileges to special persons. These too were abolished. Trade, in so far as it had been hampered by internal tolls and internal customs barriers, was freed from those restrictions. When the Assembly retired all citizens were equal before the law, the roads were open to all, all taxes were equal in principle though not yet in fact and apportioned to the capacity of the taxpayer. France was united under one administration instead of a multiplicity of administrations. She had not as yet much peace to enjoy these things, but she had been made a nation

[1] J. B. Duvergier, *Lois*, iii, p. 22.

in the economic sense, i.e. she had a real economic unity. It is not surprising that Frenchmen should refer to the Revolution as "the glorious Revolution", forgetting the ten terrible years which followed until Napoleon organized a system of national law, national roads, and national internal peace which made the unified national system effective and allowed liberty to flourish when order was maintained.

The chief characteristic of economic life under the Convention (1792–5) and the Directory (1795–9) was the financial collapse caused by the shock to property and the ruin of industry owing to the floods of depreciated paper money or *assignats*. There was a drastic return in some cases to that state regulation which the Revolution had repudiated. For instance, maximum prices had to be fixed, but the real trouble lay in the absence of any security for trade or property. The utter weariness of the people with the financial and administrative disorder led them to acquiesce in the dictatorship of Napoleon. He gave them order and they gave him a free hand to reconstruct the economic system at will. During this period of collapse the agricultural population was much better off than the people of the towns. The peasant could supply himself with food and if he had a surplus to sell he obtained high prices for it. He was free from feudal dues and the tithe, and he distinctly gained from the Revolution. He could pay his rent in depreciated paper and buy land in the same currency very cheaply. Indeed, a story is told of a man whose rent was 600 livres, which was paid with half a sack of flour, a sack being worth 1,200 in *assignats*. On the other hand, the man engaged in industry lost. His customers were either killed or impoverished or had emigrated. The gilds which had tided him over bad times were broken up; raw material, especially wool from Spain, was almost unobtainable; and cotton and silk were difficult to get after 1793, when the English declared war and kept the seas. The workers joined the armies; no more men were being trained; apprentices could not be obtained as there were no prospects ahead if they did train; and the whole tradition of industrial training was discontinued.

The old taxation had been swept away and the new revenue was raised by direct taxation. There was a land tax, a poll tax, and a tax on personal property, while the taxes on industry and professions were to take the form of payment for licences to trade or practice. In addition the customs duties were retained and a low tariff was set up in 1791. Indirect taxation was supposed to be abolished, but Napoleon found it necessary to revive it, and 40 per cent of the total revenue was derived from this source in 1811. The articles chiefly affected were salt and liquors, while tobacco was made a government monopoly. These financial changes were in themselves good, but they had abolished taxes before they had devised a method of collecting the new ones and there was not a sufficient revenue to carry on the government. There was the enormous debt of the old monarchy to be met and an additional one for compensation for the offices that had been abolished. As assets the government had the confiscated land, valued at two milliards, and they issued paper bearing interest based on this land which might be tendered for payment of land purchased. As the financial difficulties grew, fresh issues were constantly made, and these new issues did not bear interest. Between 1790, when they were first started, and November, 1795, no less than 29,430,481,623 livres of assignats had been issued and they dwindled to 1/250 or 1/300 of their original value. Coin disappeared; prices rose enormously and varied in the most bewildering fashion as no one knew in what currency to calculate, and the value to-day would not be the value to-morrow. The people who held stocks of merchandise refused to sell for fear of the depreciation of the assignats in their hands. The populace broke out in riots and raided the markets. Laws were passed against monopolies in 1793 and maximum prices were fixed in 1793 and 1794. The enforcement of these prices was impossible when the assignats fluctuated so wildly in value and the maximum was suppressed in 1794. To refuse to receive the assignats at less than their face value was made punishable by a fine of 3,000 livres and imprisonment for six months. Then the penalty was increased to 6,000 livres and twenty years in irons; and finally for a second offence the punishment was death. Manufacturers were ruined by having to accept at its face value worthless paper money in payment for their goods.

The following are some samples of the rise of prices given by M. Levasseur, quoting from the *Gazette française*[1]:—

[1] E. Levasseur, *Hostorie des Classes ouvrières de 1789 à 1870*, i, 223.

	1790.	1795.
Boisseau of flour (2¾ gals.)	2 liv.	225 liv
" barley	2 " 16 sols.	50 "
" oats	2 " 18 "	50 "
" beans	4 "	120 "
" peas or lentils	4 "	130 "
A *demi queue* of Orleans wine	80 "	2,400 "
A *voie* of wood	20 "	500 "
A pair of shoes	5 "	200 "
" stockings	3 "	100 "
Ell of cloth of Elboeuf	18 "	300 "

The rapid variation in prices may be seen from the following :—

The louis (20 livres) was worth :

130	livres in assignats	in January, 1795.
227	" "	by March, "
750	" "	" June, "
1,200	" "	" Sept., "
2,500	" "	" Oct., "

There was a complete collapse of internal trade, while external trade by sea was interrupted by the English men-of-war. Brigands roamed over France and pillaged farms ; the roads were infested with thieves and gradually became impassable as they were not kept in repair ; and the canals had become useless.[1] The cloth industry of Sedan and other centres was ruined. The workmen had emigrated or joined the armies ; some of the employers had been guillotined ; and as the rest had to accept assignats at their face value they ceased to produce. Public relief works became a necessity and all the larger communes were forced to distribute bread and food to the people. To meet these expenses the Government threw all the resources of the country into hotchpotch. The salaries of the clergy ceased to be paid, forced loans, forced gifts, requisitions in kind or in money, the seizure of the church plate and the melting of the church bells were all temporary expedients resorted to for tiding over the difficulty ; while the large sum of 500 million livres was drawn from the countries occupied by the armies of the Republic. It must not be forgotten that all this while the Republic was conducting a successful war which had not merely kept foreign invaders out but had extended the frontiers of France to the Alps and the Rhine.

So great was the misery and the paralysis of industry that the Directory succeeded the Convention. They

[1] Levasseur, op. cit., i, pp. 260–1.

attempted to abolish the assignats and reconstruct economic life. They were forced, however, to issue *mandats*, also based on land and which also depreciated. The *mandat* of 100 livres was said to be worth 20 sous in 1797.[1]

In 1797 the Directory prohibited the circulation of both mandats and assignats and tried to return to coin. This meant ruin for people who had any paper money as it was now worthless. It was nothing more or less than national bankruptcy and repudiation, and the unfortunate holders of paper money had to suffer. It was this collapse after ten years of constant struggle that made France welcome Napoleon. The destruction was not universal. The country districts did not suffer to anything like the same extent, though they, too, had felt the effect of the requisitions and lacked a market for their raw material. The younger workmen probably suffered less than the small masters, as they could join the armies. The manufacture of armaments gave a certain stimulus to the iron industry and to sulphur and saltpetre works, but France was so exhausted that it could not revive without assistance. Fortunately for France it found the man in the First Consul and he gave the momentum which created the new France.

In some things the Directory had anticipated Napoleon. France had returned to a high protective tariff in 1793 and the Directory went still further and ordered that a large number of commodities, whatever their origin, should be *reputed* to be British produce and should be seized wherever they were found. In this we have the forerunner of the famous Continental System. It also tried to encourage industrial development by subventions, partly to revive industry, partly to deal a blow at the English.[2] The Directory was, however, too discredited by the financial ruin to be able to accomplish anything effectual.[3] There was an utter lack of confidence and the great requisite was security for person and property. This explains the power of Napoleon, who gave both. He was an artillery man and knew what artillery could do against a mob. His army would obey him and would use the guns as directed. For him, therefore, the *canaille* had no terrors and he had

[1] Levasseur, op. cit., i, pp. 236, 238–47.

[2] See reasons given for assisting a cotton and muslin factory at Versailles, Levasseur, op. cit., i, p. 274.

[3] The current price of government annuities of 5 per cent was 7 francs in 1799. In 1800 they were 44 francs. G. Pariset, "The Consulate, 1799–1804," in *Cambridge Modern History*, ix, p. 2.

already stamped out incipient revolutions in Pavia and Cairo before he successfully overawed Paris and tackled the Directory and dispersed them in November, 1799, to secure his own rise to power. He had, therefore, the instruments as well as the capacity and the will to restore order, and could rely on popular support if he did so. The situation with which he had to deal has been summarized by a great authority on Napoleon as follows :—

"The needs of France were such that only the highest powers of technical administration were adequate to meet them. Ten years of anarchy had broken up the roads, disorganized the hospitals, interrupted education, and thrown all the charitable institutions of the country out of gear. Forty-five of the departments were reported as being in a state of chronic civil war. Robber bands two, three, eight hundred strong, scoured the country, pillaged the stage-coaches, broke into the prisons, flogged or slew the tax collectors. . . . No one obeyed the law. . . . The mobile columns who were entrusted with the duty of policing the disturbed regions had to forage for themselves and lived on rapine. Commercial credit had disappeared, for the currency had been depreciated, the State had declared partial bankruptcy, and English cruisers had long since interrupted foreign trade. Such had been the violence of the Revolution that almost all the talent and virtue of the country had been driven out of public life. . . . The bureaucracy was immense, but stained with the habit of pillage and corruption . . . and many mayors were unable to sign their name." [1]

To the task of restoring order in this terrible state of affairs Napoleon brought a passion for improvement, a genius for acquiring technical information, a wealth of administrative inventiveness, "a rare power of driving and draining the energies of men," [2] and the capacity of working eighteen or twenty hours at a stretch.[3]

1799–1815

The task of Napoleon Bonaparte as First Consul and then as Emperor was to reconstruct a modern state out of the

[1] H. A. L. Fisher, *Bonapartism*, pp. 25–6. See also H. A. L. Fisher, "Brumaire," in *Cambridge Modern History*, viii, pp. 665–6.

[2] H. A. L. Fisher, *Bonapartism*, p. 26.

[3] "Working up to 20 hours a day one never perceived either his spirit fatigued, nor his body crushed, nor any trace of fatigue," J. A. C. Chaptal, *Mes souvenirs sur Napoleon*, p. 56.

principles laid down by the French Revolution. He had to make liberty work and provide it with guarantees. He had first of all to restore confidence and order, then re-establish the finances, provide cheap credit, and revive industry by direct government encouragement. To achieve this last he gave subventions and orders to manufacturers, he encouraged the production of machine-made goods and rewarded inventors, he pushed the sale of French goods in other countries, he tried to provide raw material, and he shut out the products of France's great rival, England, and gave French manufacturers the whole European continent as their market.

Napoleon clearly understood that his hold on France was that of a restorer of order. Chaptal said of him that he feared the slightest unrest among the workers more than a lost battle. His interest in industry arose partly from the fact that he wished to provide employment as an antidote to revolution, and partly from his hatred of England. He also wished to set up France as the great industrial power in place of England. He would thereby ruin his greatest opponent by striking at her trade, which enabled her to find the money to oppose him and to subsidize the continent against him. France would have developed machine industry sooner or later in any case, but there had now come to the head of the government a man whose great interest was to further the development of trade and manufactures. "You must never lose sight of the fact that if English commerce triumphs at sea it is because they are stronger there. It is then right and proper (*convenable*) that, since France is the stronger by land, she should make her commerce triumph there, without which all is lost," [1] was what he wrote to the Viceroy Eugène.

The French conquests were, therefore, made to subserve the purposes of French industry. There was an economic motive in Napoleon's military campaigns and in his struggle with the English, and that economic motive was the revival of French industry. Before the French Revolution, France had been the great industrial nation and England second. Napoleon wished to restore France to its ancient pride of place. France must therefore adopt machinery, and Napoleon must find markets for the manufacturers. French goods were to go over Europe as freely as French soldiers, and he

[1] Correspondence, Napoleon I, 2160, 23rd August, 1810.

expected his officials to follow up his victories and fill the shops of the conquered countries with French products. He expected his kinglets to be commercial travellers as well as good patrons for French goods. He filled that rôle himself in France. "It is perhaps not sufficiently widely known that Napoleon possessed a general staff trained in economics as well as a military one, and that he sent commissioners along with his officers and diplomats to all parts to learn their economic condition and to further French trade."[1] One of the most important men on this staff was Isnard, who did a great deal to promote French trade in Italy (1806–7). In France, Napoleon was ably seconded in his designs by the famous scientist, Chaptal,

[1] P. Darmstädter, "Studien zur Napoleonischen Wirtschaftspolitik: 2—Über die auswärtige Handelspolitik Napoleon I," in *Vierteljahrschrift für Social- und Wirtschaftsgeschichte*, vol. iii, 1905, p. 126. It is remarkable that so little has been written on Napoleon's economic policy. In addition to the chapters in Levasseur, i, pp. 319–535, the two best studies known to me are the article of Darmstädter quoted above and another by the same writer, "Studien zur Napoleonischen Wirtschaftspolitik: 1—Die Krisis von 1810–11," in *Vierteljahrscrift für Social- und Wirtschaftsgeschichte*, vol. ii, pp. 559–615. Brandt, *Beiträge zur Geschichte der französischer Handelspolitik von Colbert bis zur Gegenwart*, devotes part of the book to the consideration of Napoleon's policy. Rocke, *Die Kontinentalsperre und die Einwirkung auf die französische Industrie* (1894), also deals with the question of the effect of the Napoleonic measures on French industry.

The economic side of the Continental System is dealt with in E. F. Heckscher, *The Continental System*, Kiesselbach, *Die Kontinentalsperre*, and Lumbroso, *Napoleone e l'Inghilterra*, as well as in the *Cambridge Modern History*, vol. ix, *c.* 13. Miss Cunningham has dealt with Napoleon's interest in financial questions in *British Credit during the last Napoleonic War*. A detailed study of Napoleon's work in finance is much needed. Melvin, *The French and British License System*, University of Pennsylvania, 1913, treats of another aspect of the Continental System.

The influence of Napoleon on German industry is traced in C. Schmidt, *Le Grand Duché de Berg*; P. Darmstädter, *Das Grossherzogtum Frankfurt*; Zeyss, *Die Entstehung der Handelskammern und die Industrie am Niederrhein: Ein Beitrag zur Wirtschaftspolitik Napoleon I*; A. König, *Die sächsische Baumwollindustrie*.

For Switzerland, Cérenville, *Le système continental et la Suisse 1803–1813*, and Chapuisat, *Le commerce et l'industrie à Genève pendant la domination française*.

While this list is probably not by any means exhaustive, these are the principal works known to me and it is a very small list considering the importance of the subject. Most of the books are concerned not with Napoleon's really great constructive work for French industry but with the Continental System. There is great need for a detailed study of Napoleon's economic policy at home and abroad. It would probably affect our whole conception of Napoleon's military aims. It would be interesting to see, for instance, how far the expedition to Spain was due to mere lust of conquest or whether the desire to get merino wool for cloth for the soldiers and a further market for French goods had some weight in determining Napoleon's Spanish policy.

Minister of the Interior from 1800. It is true that a great collapse followed in 1811, but the administration which Napoleon set up continued to work after his fall and survived the revolutions of 1830, 1848, and 1870. His framework held the economic life of France together as a "going concern" all through the nineteenth century. Napoleon had set French industry on its feet and started it on a new career. Handicapped as France was by dear coal it was, nevertheless, the second great industrial power during the first three-quarters of the nineteenth century. From the time of Napoleon it is merely a question of tracing in the statistics the increase of coal used, the growing number of steam engines and spindles, the rise in the volume of raw cotton imported and of iron produced, in order to trace the progress of the industrial revolution in France.

Napoleon did not, however, merely modernize France. Where he went he introduced a new financial and a new administrative system, which did much to modernize the economic system of Germany and Italy. Apart from the abolition of serfdom and gilds, the abolition of the internal customs barriers over large parts of Italy and Germany formed a great object lesson for the German Customs Union and Italian unity. Under the stimulus given by Napoleon, Germany and Italy were bound sooner or later to realize economic unity.

To restore order Napoleon had to gather the administration into his own hands. The difficulty that earlier revolutionary governments had experienced was to get their commands carried out by the local authorities. Napoleon re-centralized the administration which had been decentralized at the Revolution; it is often said that he overcentralized it: but he had to get a grip on the whole machine, which was not working, and he had to concentrate it in such a manner that he could control it and make it work. He governed with the assistance of a Council of State; at the head of the departments he placed his prefects—the old *intendants* under another name—choosing many of them from among the trained officials of the *ancien régime*. They were to be to him the economic instruments that the *intendants* had been to the King. He thus had directly under his hand the personnel to carry out an effective economic policy. He found great disorder and demoralization; he created a bureaucracy more competent, active, and enlightened than any which Europe had seen,[1] although they deteriorated later under the Empire and the great temptations incidental to being in undisputed power over conquered peoples. "By his strict system of national accounts no less than by his personal example he did much to correct the singularly loose code of pecuniary morality which prevailed even among the most distinguished public servants of the French state." [2] He acted through Councils of Commerce, which he set up in 1801 in all the principal towns. These consisted of merchants and manufacturers with the prefect as President.[3] Their function was consultative. They had to advise on all matters relating to trade. Alongside of these were set up Chambers of Manufacturers in April, 1803. They had to advise the government as to the state of manufactures and means of improving them. They contained representatives of domestic and factory industry. Above these there was a General Council of Manufacturers and a General Council of Commerce.

Probably one of the greatest services Napoleon rendered to the reconstruction of France was the promulgation of the Codes. An intelligible system of law is the first requisite of order, and the Codes were the guarantee of that equality which the Revolution had proclaimed.[4] Napoleon abolished the judges elected by the people and substituted lawyers appointed by himself. He thus tightened his hold on the administration of justice, which again would make for order without which economic progress cannot take place.

He reorganized the financial administration, and the taxes commenced to flow regularly into the Treasury. He made the conquered countries pay heavily both in money and men. The money was expended in France, while the men helped to win Napoleon's victories and so spared the French population. No less than 10,000 Swiss were lost in the Russian campaign of 1812. The French population had increased from the 26 millions at the time of the Revolution to 30 millions in 1811. Between 1806 and 1810 Napoleon had drawn over a milliard of francs

[1] H. A. L. Fisher, *Studies in Napoleonic Statesmanship: Germany*, p. 375.

[2] Ibid., p. 375. For a more detailed account of the administrative system see P. Ashley, *Local and Central Government*, pp. 244 ff.

[3] R. Zeyss, *Die Entstehung der Handelskammern und die Industrie am Niederrhein*, p. 10.

[4] For details, H. A. L. Fisher, "The Codes," in *Cambridge Modern History*, ix, chap. vi.

as a war contribution from the conquered countries.[1] This money no doubt helped to base the circulating medium on coin and prevented any return to depreciated paper. It is interesting to see how closely Napoleon studied banking,[2] and how anxious he was about a "reserve of several millions as the basis and foundation of credit", as "the imagination of the people is still impressed by remembering the time when the paper fell in value at a most rapid rate". He intended to have a sound currency. He also studied banking because he wished to gauge where the strength of the English lay and to sap it if possible, and he also desired to create a sound banking system in France. His ambition was that French manufacturers should be able to borrow at 4 per cent: "only then can manufacturers thrive."[3] The one great asset in which England had surpassed France during the eighteenth century was her ready command of capital, and to this her excellent banking system contributed. There was a remarkable absence of any banking institutions in France. Only four banks of any importance existed at the beginning of the nineteenth century, and they were quite recent: the Caisse des Comptes Courants, founded in 1796; the Caisse d'Escompte du Commerce, 1797; the Comptoir Commercial, 1800, and the Société Général du Commerce de Rouen. In 1801 Napoleon founded the Bank of France, which absorbed the first two of these banks. The difficulty was to raise the capital of 30 million francs for the Bank. Napoleon took shares and, to help it to get funds to start, the government deposits, forming part of the sinking fund, were placed with the Bank. It was employed to pay the interest on the government loans, and it was given the sole right of issuing notes in 1803. Napoleon appointed the chief officials after 1806. The Bank not merely did a good deal of the government business but it discounted bills of exchange and other commercial paper. It supplied a long felt want in the provision of some important establishment which would give credit facilities.[4] Whether it was due to the introduction

[1] P. Darmstädter, *Die Krisis von 1810–11*, p. 563, n. 1.

[2] A. Cunningham, *British Credit in the last Napoleonic War*, chap. v, "Napoleon's views."

[3] P. Darmstädter, *Die Krisis von 1810–11*, p. 562.

[4] There is a remarkable contrast here with the Bank of England, which was founded by private merchants, who received the right to found a bank in return for a loan of £1,200,000 to the government. It was the English

of a stable government or the result of the establishment of the new banking system, the rate of interest fell from 9 or 11 per cent to 6 or 7 per cent.

Napoleon did everything in his power to encourage French industry. He founded the Society for the Encouragement of National Industry. He gave large orders on behalf of himself and his court. He promoted technical instruction. He rewarded inventors. He gave loans to manufacturers. Between March 27, 1807, and October 8, 1809, Napoleon lent no less than 1,175,925 francs to manufacturers, of which only 250,271 francs was repaid.[1]

One of the most important inventions of the time was the Jacquard loom, by which mixed stuffs could easily be made by machinery. Napoleon made the town of Lyons buy Jacquard's machines, and give him a pension of 3,000 francs. He was also given free board and lodging at the Hospice of Antiquaille.[2] The prefects had to send workmen to a model factory at Passy to learn to work the flying shuttle. A Scotsman, named Douglas, was set up in a government workshop to make machines and teach French manufacturers and workmen how to use them. The state gave him a large grant, and the bigger manufacturers were formed into a commission to watch the results. He made machines for opening out wool, for carding and weaving, and in two years he had sold 340 of them. The machines themselves were far from perfect, but this did not daunt the government. It sent circulars round to the prefects of the provinces pointing out the advantages of machinery, enclosing Douglas' circulars, and stating that the government was willing to make advances to assist would-be purchasers. He was very active in promoting an increase in the herds of merino sheep to provide the wool needed for cloth.

The general result was that the cotton industry began to revive and to employ machines. France began to make its own muslins and piques. Ghent became a flourishing

bank that financed the government from the very start, not the government the bank, as in France. On the whole question of the founding of the Bank of France, see Léoni Lévi's chapter, "Currency and Banking in France," in the *History of British Commerce*; also Liesse, "Evolution of Credit and Banks in France," 1909, translated in *American Monetary Commission*.

[1] C. Ballot, "Prêts aux Manufactures," in *Révue des Études Napoléoniennes*, vol. ii, 1912, p. 77.

[2] Charléty, "La Vie Economique de Lyons sous Napoleon," in *Vierteljahrschrift für Wirtschaftsgeschichte*, vol. iv, 1906, p. 374.

cotton centre, where the enterprising Bauwens[1] had no less than 1,000 workmen in his factory working English cotton machines. Alsace also became a great cotton centre, especially when the raw cotton from the Levant was diverted overland *via* Vienna and Strasburg when the English held the seas. The whole of Belgium and the incorporated provinces of Germany on the left bank of the Rhine shared in the revival. The Emperor was particularly anxious to establish cotton, as he considered it would be a blow to the English. To one manufacturer, Oberkampf, who was printing cotton by cylinders, he said: "You and I, we both make war on the English, but your war is the better."

There was a general revival of industry. The biggest manufacturers in France began again to make woollen stuffs in large quantities. Its Cashmere shawls made the fortune of Rheims. The iron industry was flourishing with the demand for munitions, though this specially affected Belgium, now included in France. The Lyons silk industry, in which Napoleon took a special interest, was prosperous. The number of looms there had risen from 3,500 in 1800 to 10,720, and the workers from 5,800 to 15,506. About 80,000 persons were said to be employed in the silk industry altogether.[2]

Napoleon wearied his ministers with almost daily correspondence in his desire to ascertain the exact condition of French industry. "It paid better," Chaptal says, "to lie boldly than to delay in order to tell the truth." Hence the figures presented to the Emperor are not always as reliable as they might appear. Yet we do have figures as we get them for no other country at the time. Napoleon insisted on information and the prefects had to make reports. In one of these estimates the value of the textiles produced is said to have risen from 22 to 500 millions of francs.[3] Hat making, watch making, and furniture making all revived. The machinery that was installed was worked by water, not steam; only in one place, Creusot, was iron smelted by coke; the rest was smelted with charcoal. France

[1] Levasseur, op. cit., i, p. 421. Chaptal estimated that in 1806 the production of cotton thread was worth 66 millions of francs. Levasseur, op. cit., i, p. 435, note.

[2] Levasseur, op. cit., i, p. 441.

[3] Levasseur, op. cit., i, p. 444, n. 1.

was technically backward in the matter of machinery when compared with Great Britain. But it is when we come to industrial chemistry that we witness the triumph of France. Leblanc had been the pioneer of the French chemists and had created a factory for the production of artificial soda in 1787. He was followed up by other French chemists, who produced nitric, muriatic, and sulphuric acids, the three principal agents in industrial chemistry, while bleaching with chlorine was another triumph for the chemists, as it was no longer necessary to expose cotton and linen cloth for months in the open to whiten them. In the matter of dyes, Prussian blue was invented to supplement indigo. The art of tanning was also revolutionized.[1]

With all this increasing production of French industry, markets were necessary and overseas markets were increasingly difficult to reach as long as the English dominated the seas. M. Levasseur warns us that French industry, although reviving, had not regained the level of prosperity that it enjoyed before the Revolution.[2] We have only to look at the figures to see how French trade had dropped [3] since 1789, and although there was a steady rise in the volume of trade, there was still much leeway to be made up. Napoleon, therefore, set out to get markets abroad throughout Europe by means of a series of treaties whereby allied countries favoured French goods and also by means of the Continental System, whereby English goods were excluded.[4]

French industry seemed for a time to flourish enormously under the prohibition of English goods. Germany, Italy, Holland, Spain, Russia seemed to compensate for the loss

[1] Levasseur, op. cit., i, p. 429.

[2] Ibid., i, 405.

[3] Ibid., i, p. 493, note. French trade had totalled 1,108 million francs when the Revolution occurred.

	Imports.	*Exports.*	*Total.*
In 1787	590,200,000 fr.	517,600,000 fr.	1,108,000,000 fr.
„ 1799	253,000,000 „	300,000,000 „	553,000,000 „
„ 1800	323,000,000 „	272,000,000 „	595,000,000 „
„ 1801	415,000,000 „	305,000,000 „	720,000,000 „
„ 1802	465,000,000 „	325,000,000 „	790,000,000 „
„ 1803	430,000,000 „	347,000,000 „	777,000,000 „
„ 1804	441,000,000 „	380,000,000 „	821,000,000 „
„ 1805	492,000,000 „	375,000,000 „	867,000,000 „
„ 1806	477,000,000 „	456,000,000 „	933,000,000 „

[4] Dealt with in part v, chap. i, *post*.

of the colonial and American trade.[1] Although raw cotton was expensive to obtain, the chief source of supply was the Levant, and much of it was able to come by land and evade the English, the route being *via* Vienna and Strasburg, and at a later date by the Illyrian provinces and Italy. The cotton industry was prosperous as was also the Lyons silk industry. Trade was diverted to new land routes, and Strasburg became a busy centre of distribution for Europe. The French and continental ports were, however, ruined. The great land power had turned its armies into customs officers, and the great sea power had turned its navy into smugglers, and the war of the two great nations became a war for markets. The English were organized for world trade and needed markets for their growing machine products. They knew that whatever they could sell in Europe would keep out French goods. They had no wish to see France become the workshop of the world. Moreover, it was not easy for the English to sell elsewhere. The United States had passed a Non-Intercourse Act in 1809 and trade with them was suspended. The cotton goods sold in tropical countries were paid for in colonial products, such as tea, coffee, and sugar, and Great Britain had to make her profit on these by resale in Europe.[2] The Continental

[1] The fall in trade may be seen from the following figures of French exports and imports :—

	Imports.	*Exports.*	*Total*
1805	492,000,000 fr.	375,000,000 fr.	867,000,000 fr.
1806	477,000,000 ,,	456,000,000 ,,	933,000,000 ,,
1807	393,000,000 ,,	376,000,000 ,,	769,000,000 ,,
1808	320,000,000 ,,	331,000,000 ,,	651,000,000 ,,
1809	288,000,000 ,,	332,000,000 ,,	620,000,000 ,,
1810	339,000,000 ,,	366,000,000 ,,	705,000,000 ,,
1811	299,000,000 ,,	328,000,000 ,,	627,000,000 ,,
1812	308,000,000 ,,	419,000,000 ,,	727,000,000 ,,
1813	251,000,000 ,,	354,000,000 ,,	605,000,000 ,,
1814	239,000,000 ,,	346,000,000 ,,	585,000,000 ,,

[2] The diversion of English foreign trade may be seen from the following figures which show the loss of trade with Northern Europe and the United States. It also shows the rise in the value of the trade carried on from the smuggling depôts like Gibraltar and Malta and the value of Portugal :—

	1805.	*1811.*
North of Europe and France . .	£16,647,474	£3,483,091
Spain	£186,660	£1,495,865
Portugal	£2,027,650	£6,164,858
Gibraltar, Malta, Sicily, the Levant	£1,574,156	£7,393,390
Ireland, Man, Guernsey, and Jersey	£6,400,363	£7,210,699
Asia	£3,111,748	£3,063,971
Africa	£1,156,955	£409,075
U.S.A.	£11,446,939	£1,874,917
Other parts of America and W. Indies	£8,557,186	£12,843,754

Chalmers, *Historical View of the Domestic Economy of Great Britain*. 1812, p. 468.

System cut at her manufactures and her entrepôt trade[1] and created great unemployment.

Napoleon also wanted markets. He had to keep France contented, prosperous, and employed. The English had cut off the very valuable colonial trade; they had ruined the whole overseas trade; the ports and the sea-coast towns were in a terrible state in spite of his efforts to continue building ships; hence he had to seek compensation in reviving the inland markets.

Apart from the necessity to provide an outlet for French industry, Napoleon also believed that he could best eliminate the English opposition by excluding English goods from the continent. He carefully studied finance, as we have seen. He had lived through the terrible period of the assignats himself; he had seen the inextricable misery and confusion that could be created by a collapse of the currency and he sought to produce a similar confusion in England by shutting English goods out of Europe. He seems to have reasoned as follows: If the English cannot sell goods they must export gold; their currency in the absence of bullion would not be based on anything stable and would fluctuate wildly as did the assignats in France; and English industry would collapse as did the French under the Convention. With the collapse of her industry she would no longer be able to finance the continent or continue the war and industrial France would rise on the ruins of English industry.[2]

The progress of French industry under Napoleon's forcing policy had been too rapid. The banks had financed the growing cotton industry, which found ever-growing difficulty in getting raw material, cotton, which was 3 francs a pound in 1806, and was 7.50 francs by 1810.[3] The cotton manufacturers could not meet their debts to the banks. The latter were also in difficulties, as they had speculated in colonial products, and had been hit by the Trianon Tariff enacted by Napoleon in 1810. This had raised the price of colonial goods and had checked consumption,

[1] In the Great War we tried to keep Germany from getting goods but we had plenty of markets elsewhere. There was no unemployment here as in 1811, because the army absorbed such numbers. In 1808 a petition from Bolton was signed by 30,000 persons who were in want of bread. Leone Levi, *History of British Commerce*, p. 127.

[2] A. Cunningham, *British Credit in the last Napoleonic War*, pp. 3–7.

[3] On this whole question, Darmstädter, "Die Krisis von 1810–11," in *Vierteljährschrift für Social- und Wirtschaftsgeschichte*, vol. ii, pp. 559–615.

and the stocks, on which the banks had advanced money, could not be realized.[1] The financial situation was complicated by the fact that there was a failure of the silk and corn harvests. When Spain revolted a very important market for French goods had been lost. The Russians, once such good customers, were unable to purchase, as they paid for French goods by selling their timber, flax, wax, and furs to London, and the money was transmitted from London to France. There was a slackening in demand for manufactures in Central Europe also, where the people were groaning under the burden of the heavy taxation and the rigour of conscription. The high prices and difficulty of obtaining colonial goods under the Trianon Tariff, while it incensed them, made them bad customers for French goods. The collapse of the banks in France was the last straw for French manufacturers who were working so largely on credit. Napoleon did all he could to tide over the crisis. He lent money to manufacturers on condition that they should not dismiss their workmen; he started great schemes of road building and canals to give employment; he gave large orders for goods; but it was all in vain. His policy abroad ruined the French markets; his system of plunder made it impossible for them to be good customers, even if English goods were shut out. French industry had developed on credit to fill this continental market; the banks had over-speculated; there was a cessation of trade and wide-spread bankruptcy and unemployment. Even Bauwens, the famous cotton manufacturer, failed with the rest. The result was that Napoleon lost the confidence of France, and his fall was inevitable. The military situation might have been retrieved, but the economic situation made it impossible. When a government plays the part of economic providence, it always has to bear the blame of a failure.

The French revolted against the government. The English workmen who were discontented or starving vented their indignation on the employers by breaking up machinery or burning ricks. They were unaccustomed to the constant interference of a highly centralized government and did not turn upon it in revenge when trouble came, as did the French.[2]

[1] The wholesale price of sugar, which had been 118 Dutch guilder in 1801, was 720 in 1811. Zeyss, op. cit., p. 155.

[2] A. Cunningham, *British Credit in the last Napoleonic War*, p. 77.

Napoleon had no social policy for the workers. He was unsympathetic with the workmen and prejudiced in favour of the masters. He was thoroughly bourgeois. Therefore nothing was done in his time towards the settlement of working class questions. The prohibition of combinations was included in the Codes. On the other hand, the real capital versus labour question had not yet arisen. Only a small proportion of the manufacturing output of France was as yet produced in factories. To settle industrial disputes, Napoleon set up Councils of Experts or *Prud'hommes* in 1806. They were conciliation boards, on which both workmen and employers were represented. In his time there were twenty-six in France. The procedure was cheap, and they are still one of the most successful institutions in France. In 1847 the seventy-nine Councils then existing dealt with 19,271 cases, of which only 259 could not be arranged by conciliation.[1]

The mark which Napoleon left on the economic and administrative life of France has never been effaced. So thoroughly had he reorganized the economic life, that from this time forward France continued to advance in wealth, in machine industry, and in agriculture. It was impossible for the Bourbons to revive the gilds of the *ancien régime*, or to upset the land distribution. There have been revolts, such as that of the Commune in 1870 against the system of centralization, but the advance continued. The Continental System left a strong tradition that industry could flourish inside a high tariff barrier, and that the French producer ought to have protection as a sort of natural right. Napoleon had created a class of manufacturers, who expected that the state would continue to exclude foreign goods for their benefit, and they made their influence felt in the tariff policy of France all through the nineteenth century. As Napoleon III declared: "Our existing community is simply France regenerated by the Revolution of 1789 and organized by the Emperor Napoleon I." This was particularly true of France before 1870.

1815–48

The fall of Napoleon made no difference to the trend of economic development in France. Machine industry

[1] Levasseur, op. cit., i, p. 390, n. 2.

continued to develop along the lines he laid down, and his successors, the Bourbons, continued his policy of subsidizing and developing roads and canals.

Napoleon had not attempted to solve the question of capital and labour, nor did his successors attempt to deal with the matter. The French Revolution had chiefly benefited the middle classes or bourgeoisie, and their interests were the main consideration in France up to 1870. But it had left behind a tradition that a revolution was the way to bring about economic improvement and had made a revolution a possible weapon not merely for the French working class but for the working classes all over Europe at a time when such ideas were likely to bear fruit. As a result of the industrial changes and better communications people were herded into towns or could easily reach each other, so that general discussion and comparison of views between neighbours or fellow workmen was facilitated. They needed a new gospel to replace the idea of ordering themselves lowly and reverently to their betters in the shape of a feudal lord, and the French Revolution of 1789 supplied new ideals. "Liberty," to the people of those days, did not really mean freedom to do as one liked, but it meant to them democratic government, that is to say, liberty to take part in the government of the country. "Equality" did not mean the equal sharing of property. The Declaration of the Rights of Man was emphatic "that property is an inviolate and sacred right and no one shall be deprived thereof except where public necessity legally determined shall clearly demand it and then only on condition that the owner shall have been previously and equitably indemnified." While it did not mean a new social order based on common property, it did mean the abolition of privilege and monopolies, of serfdom and feudalism.

In the nineteenth century, however, the French were to go further in this matter and to formulate plans of Utopian Socialism, largely based on the abolition of private property. The French Revolution of 1789 had shown that a successful revolt against aristocracy was possible; the French Revolution of 1848 afforded a further object lesson of successful revolt, this time in the direction of communism.

The international importance of French economic development lay in the fact that anything that happened in France was bound to react on continental Europe.

Every country except England and Russia was radically affected by the French Revolution of 1848. Although the movement started first in Italy, it became international when it got to France. The retention of a high protective tariff in France after 1815 strengthened the whole movement for protection in other countries, while the adoption of a low tariff by Napoleon III meant the lowering of duties all over the continent. While the continent equipped itself with the new tools furnished by Great Britain, it looked to France for economic leadership.

In 1815 French industry was in danger of being overwhelmed by English competition, so France adopted high protection. Inside this high tariff barrier machine industry progressed. By 1830 the iron industry was in certain parts using coke for smelting, and had adopted the English methods of puddling. They were making steel, which facilitated the production of scythes, files, needles, table-cutlery, and knives. The chemical industry went ahead. In the textiles there was much progress owing to the fact that sheep had increased in numbers and France was no longer dependent for her material on Spain. Mechanical wool spinning had been adopted, which helped the weavers, and fine woollen stuffs were the result. Cotton had made great strides with the facilities for obtaining raw material. Rouen developed because of the ease of getting raw material. After the peace France had developed a large variety of cotton textures and had a growing export of light cotton piece goods such as muslins, gauzes, and tulles. Cotton printing was also carried on by means of cylinders as in England. Alsace, which had been a calico printing centre, developed cotton spinning and had one-third of all the spindles in France by 1847. The spinning of silk had been perfected, and the development of cotton helped the silk industry by assisting the manufacture of mixed stuffs. Glass, crystal and pottery all shared the progress of the time. In 1815 there were only 15 establishments using steam engines. By 1830 there were 625, and machinery was becoming increasingly dependent on steam instead of water. This meant, as in England, a vital change. As long as water was used industry would be carried on where there was water power in hilly country districts. When steam was used the industries either settled on the coal areas or moved into towns which would be supplied with coal regularly for household purposes. Therefore the 625 factories using steam meant concentration in towns and the development of urban areas.

By 1830 the French had probably got back the same level of prosperity that they had enjoyed before the Revolution. For a generation politics and war had diverted the workmen and prevented the training of the young artisan. Capital had to accumulate and security to be really established before money would be invested in industrial enterprises to a large extent. The new society was reconstituted on a more liberal basis, but there had been much leeway to make up, as the old society, though narrow, was prosperous.

After 1825 the export of many varieties of machines was permitted by England, and France was able to equip itself more rapidly with machines than heretofore.[1] But, with the introduction of machine tools, the French made rapid progress between 1830 and 1841 in producing their own machines. "Their machinery was very inferior to ours ten years ago but now it is inferior to a small extent only," was the verdict of an expert at the Select Committee of 1841, concerned with the export of machinery, though France even then was importing largely.[2] Much had been done between 1815 and 1830 by Englishmen who had emigrated to France and had set up there. Douglas, so valuable to Napoleon, was still busy under the Bourbons, and when one encounters among French manufacturers such names as John Collier, Manby, Wilson, Waddington, and Edwards, the manager of the factory of the brothers Chaillot, one sees how strong was still the influence of English technique on France.[3]

In 1830 there were two important industrial nations, Great Britain and France, the latter technically inferior but making great progress. It is wonderful what had been

[1] The following figures, taken from a return showing the value of machinery exported between 5th January, 1823, and 5th January, 1827. *Accounts and Papers, 1826–7*, xviii, p. 163, show that France was Great Britain's largest customer for machinery, also the growth of the exports in 1826 and 1827 with the removal of restrictions :—

	Europe.	*France.*	*Of which steam engines were*
1823	£52,359	£40,203	£31,977
1824	£46,056	£24,455	£18,129
1825	£42,739	£18,878	£12,581
1826	£80,836	£42,782	£23,393
1827	£136,623	£69,765	£52,136

[2] The figures for 1840 are: Machinery £72,600, of which steam engines were £56,247. *Parliamentary Papers*, 1841, vii, p. 263.

[3] Levasseur, i, p. 612 and 629, nn. 2 and 3.

accomplished by 1830 in spite of two invasions, the occupation of France till 1818 by foreign armies and a famine in 1818. Although there was an increase of factory industry, the predominant type of work was that of the small domestic workshop. This was to change rapidly after 1830 with the import of English machinery, and the coming of the railways which facilitated the concentration of industry and retail trading and the use of raw material in masses. As in England, the railways in France gave a vigorous impulse to the iron industries and to the formation of large businesses and joint stock company trading. The railway companies were the biggest single undertakings in France outside the Bank of France.

The rapid spread of the industrial revolution in this period (1830–48) in France may be gauged from the evidence given by expert English observers before the Select Committee on Export of Tools and Machinery in 1841. They were told by one witness that " there is no machine the French cannot make if they have a good model ". The general opinion seemed to be that the cost of machinery would average 35 per cent more than in England. " The French iron is not good iron, but if they get English iron and English copper and brass they can make as good machinery as far as quality goes as we can." They could not, however, apparently make anything like as good machine tools. They were making locomotives themselves in 1841 from English models but the attempt to make a marine engine at Creusot was attended with disaster. It was tried on the Rhone and blew up the boat and some of the engineers with it. The success of the French in making flax-spinning machinery was very striking. In 1838 it was introduced by Maberley, an Englishman. By 1841 five French concerns were making flax-spinning machinery and were turning out machines equal to the English.[1] This proves that the linen industry was in process

[1] The story told by the witness Marsden is as follows : " He went over to Mr. Maberley with 100 English artisans and £6,000 worth of tools and material. The French flax-machinery makers who followed in his footsteps were said " to have purchased excellent tools of all descriptions from Manchester and Leeds and purchased one specimen of the best models of machines from the different machine makers in Leeds and other parts of the country and have established works for the purpose of making machines ; they have taken over the cleverest Englishmen they could get, not looking to the salary in the first instance but paying very enormous salaries to induce the cleverest men to go and having got the tools together

of transformation. This verdict of English observers is confirmed when we turn to the statistics.[1]

The Census of 1851 recorded 1,331,260 persons in the "great industry", of which 124,133 were masters with 675,670 men and 531,457 women workers. In domestic industry there were 1,548,334 masters and 1,434,224 journeymen or apprentices and 1,730,468 women.

This transformation of industrial life could not fail to produce a great deal of theoretical discussion in France. Two men had already set out schemes for a new social order and they were eagerly discussed. Those who prospered under the new factory system saw no need for a change; but the loss of the spinning for women, the consequent readjustment of wages, and the loss of independence by the workmen—all these prepared a favourable soil for those who were advocating a change.

St. Simon, whose works were published between 1817 and 1825, seemed to advocate a new society in which all the existing capital should be put into the hands of the most capable, directed by a priesthood. These were to distribute it and allot the tasks. All men were to work, reward was to be proportioned to merit, and inheritance was to be abolished. The whole was permeated with the idea of organizing society according to ethical and Christian principles. St. Simon did not work out any practical details. He gave his message, and he seems to have expected that people would promptly and willingly dissolve the present society, when shown the better way, and reconstruct it according to his principles. He failed to realize that most people were quite satisfied with society as it was.

Fourier, whose work was published in 1820, was more

with those clever men and the models of the machines smuggled out of this country they have been able to make machines . . . quite equal to any that I have seen made in England." Report, *Parliamentary Papers*, 1841, vii, p. 91.

[1]

	1827.	*1847.*
Coal extracted (thousand tons) . .	1,691	5,142
,, imported	—	2,943
Pig Iron (thousand quintals) . .	2,200	5,916
Cotton imported (thousands of kilos) .	29,683	45,522
Wool imported	—	15,628
Steam Engines	616 about (10,000 h.p.)	4,853 (61,630 h.p.)
Import of raw material (million francs)	276	547
Export of manufactures (million francs)	348	699
Exports and Imports (million francs)	1,211 (1830)	2,340

Levasseur, op. cit., ii, p. 163; also pp. 846 and 857.

practical. He did not believe in a state or government. The population was to be divided into groups of 1,600 to 2,000 persons. In this *phalanstère*, as it was called, every one was to take part in productive industry, but each person was to be allowed to select his task. A bare subsistence wage was to be paid to all workers and the surplus produce was to be distributed, by which Labour received five-twelfths, Capital four-twelfths, and Talent three-twelfths. Some of these Fourier settlements were actually tried in France and in the United States, but they all collapsed.

To a country that had carried out the Revolution of 1789 there seemed nothing fantastic in the possibility of completely changing the structure of society from top to bottom. One must remember the impossibility of working men's opinion making itself felt in any ordinary constitutional manner in France at that date. There was a very narrow franchise which excluded the working-class. No trade unions were allowed by law. The *compagnonnages* had declined since 1830. They had been mainly composed of journeymen travelling to perfect themselves, and existed to provide lodging, fellowship, and employment. With the coming of machinery it was no longer so necessary for journeymen to travel, and the railways made travelling perceptibly easier, and these associations weakened in consequence. *Sociétés de résistance* had been formed in the 'thirties, but they were revolutionary and illegal. There was no way for the French working classes to assert themselves effectively except by a revolutionary upheaval.

It has been pointed out that a characteristic of the French labour movement is its want of continuity.[1] It undergoes a staggering blow amounting to complete destruction for the time being. When it again emerges it is a fresh creation, with a new and complete theory. This happened at the time of the French Revolution, and the French labour movement disappeared with the advent of Napoleon. It began to grow again after 1830 and came to a head in 1848. It then suffered a complete eclipse, when it was driven back on the ideas of Marxian socialism on the one hand and co-operative consumption on the other. The Commune in 1870 was another attempt to equalize property and again

[1] G. D. H. Cole, *World of Labour*, p. 58.

there was a break lasting for twenty years. The labour movement revived again, with syndicalism as its intellectual aim, in the 'nineties.

The French labour movement has not built itself up piecemeal as has the English trade union movement, following the tradition of the English turnpike roads and the English canals, but, like the French railways or French industry under Napoleon, it has been fashioned after a complete pattern in somebody's mind and not slowly developed as circumstances altered. It therefore has an intellectual basis from the very beginning and is moulded on someone's ideas, preferably with that someone for a leader. Thus in France one has to start with a book or a man in examining the history of French working class movements. The works of St. Simon and Fourier prepared the ground by attacking the whole scheme of society based on private property.

Louis Blanc focussed the unrest of the years 1830–48, made it articulate and gave it something definite to aim at in his book, *L'Organisation du Travail,* published in 1839. He said that everyone had a right to live by his labour, that there was a "right to work". He proposed to transform the existing state of society gradually by setting up co-operative workshops which should gradually take over the control of all industry. As these workshops would require capital, the government must raise a huge loan to start them. All workmen of good character must be admitted. The government would assign to each their work, but later this would be done by popular vote. The proceeds of these workshops were to be divided into three portions, one for the workers, one for the sick and infirm, and one for renewals of plant. The trades were to federate and gradually extinguish private competition.[1]

Now here was a people already discontented, already prepared to strike at the very basis of society only not knowing how to accomplish it, a people who not sixty years before had electrified Europe by sweeping away feudalism, and here was something tangible to aim at, namely, a state of society organized on the basis of co-operative production

[1] The book is reprinted by the Clarendon Press, 1913, edited by J. A. R. Marriott, and it is from his excellent historical introduction that the following account of the Revolution has been summarized.

financed by the state and taking over the control of all industry.

There was a movement on foot to demand constitutional reforms and a more democratic government. A reform banquet proved the signal for a successful outbreak of revolution in which the workmen joined. The year 1846–7 had been a famine year in France as in Ireland, and the acute distress no doubt helped to bring the workmen into line. Two parties brought about the revolution. One wished for a republic, that is to say, political reforms in a liberal sense; and the other was socialistic and desired to abolish the regime of private property.

So great was the pressure brought to bear on the provisional government by the workmen that it had to promise to establish national workshops. Louis Blanc, the author of the *Right to Work*, was one of the provisional government. He was set up at the Luxembourg as President of a Workmen's Commission of 700 to work out his schemes of co-operative production.

The government had promised national workshops, and the Parisian populace, among whom there was a large amount of unemployment, declined to wait for Louis Blanc's schemes to mature. The republican party in the government were anxious to outbid Louis Blanc and the socialists and to attract adherents to themselves, and so they set up an opposition scheme under Émile Thomas, the circumstances being those in which no scheme of national workshops could possibly succeed, that is to say, in revolutionary times, when there was no work for workpeople to do as there was no effective demand. There were thus two opposing movements, one of the Working Men's Committee at the Luxembourg, and the National Workshops organized by Émile Thomas. Men understood, however, that these workshops were the outcome of the ideas of Louis Blanc. They were regarded as his workshops though he indignantly repudiated them. The government national workshops were intended to provide immediate employment for all applying, but there was only navvies' work to be done, and the men were occupied in digging up the Champ de Mars. Those who worked got 2 frs., those who could not get work were paid 1·50 per diem.

The actual work accomplished was trifling and the numbers of the unemployed joining the workshops rose. Thomas organized these men like an army, in companies and brigades, but he could not provide work, and still the numbers rose. In March there were 14,000, in April 66,000, in May 120,000. The so-called workshops were very expensive and quite useless, though had there been more time no doubt some works of utility might have been evolved. As it was they were a menace to public order. It was found that private employers could not keep their men, who flocked to join the unemployed and were joined by others from the provinces.

When the elections were held the moderate party was returned with an enormous majority, and this enabled the republican government to pass Louis Blanc over completely when setting up the Executive Commission. He was furious and tried to upset the government. On his failure he had to fly to England. His schemes collapsed with him, but he left behind him a tradition of co-operation that the workmen of France spent the next twenty years trying to realize, and he was the parent of the modern syndicalist movement in France.

The national workshops were another story. The new government quickly saw that they would have to be dispersed. Arrangements were made for the men to be drafted on to railway-building and into the army and also for them to enter the service of private employers. The workmen in the national workshops declined to accept this and rose. A horrible four days' street fighting followed; the army used artillery, and the numbers killed were put at 16,000 by the British ambassador. The socialist millennium had ended in a disastrous failure. When a president had to be elected, so greatly did the ordinary citizens dread any renewal of the disorder that they voted in overwhelming numbers for Prince Napoleon, who declared that his name stood for "order, nationality, and glory". He got 5,434,226 votes; Cavaignac, who suppressed the national workshops, got 1,448,107; and Lamartine 17,910. The importance of this lies in the unrivalled position it gave Napoleon for carrying out any economic policy he chose. Nevertheless, the belief in a possible social transformation of society became a tradition in France, and Napoleon was regarded by the middle classes as the saviour of the social order. From this time onward, however, the government began to abandon the idea of *laissez-faire* and showed more solicitude for the worker. But even then only about a quarter of the French population was urban.

1848–70

The revolution of 1848 and the menace of the national workshops had led to the rise of another Napoleon in December, 1848, to restore order. Under his regime, first as President and then, from 1852 onwards, as Emperor, we get a brilliant and rapid period of industrial development, which coincided with the building and development of the railways on a uniform system after 1853. There was a considerable development of banking and joint stock companies and France entered on the second phase of the industrial revolution which accompanied the facilities for the increased transport of goods. France became the pioneer after 1860 of the free trade movement in Europe and the centre of the European treaty system. This period ended with the capture of the Emperor at Sedan and the taking of Paris by the Germans. The great economic strength of France was seen by the comparative ease with which she paid the indemnity.

By 1850 France had began to recover from the dislocation caused by the revolution of 1848. There ensued during the next twenty years the most brilliant period of French economic development. In spite of the cholera epidemic, the scarcity of 1854, and the Crimean War, never had French industry and commerce made more rapid strides. The railway mileage developed and the railways were merged into six great systems. They created a new demand for iron for their construction, they provided a wider market for agriculture, and they stimulated industry by better distribution which increased sales. Banking and credit institutions developed; companies of all kinds increased. The *Crédit Foncier* helped the building of the towns and the great constructional works generally, while the *Crédit Mobilier* was founded to assist industry. Science was increasingly applied to industrial problems and the *expositions* showed the progress the French were making. Indeed, both the London Exhibition of 1851 and the Exposition of 1855 in Paris proved that the French were able to hold their own against English products.[1]

So great was the progress that Napoleon III was not afraid to throw France open to British competition by the Cobden

[1] So marked was the superiority of the French in the decorative arts in the Exhibition of 1851 that the Museum of Arts and Crafts at South Kensington was founded to stimulate English design.

Treaty of 1860. He followed it up by making treaties on a low tariff basis not merely with the other great industrial country, Belgium, but with all the other important continental countries. This breaking down of tariff barriers within Europe still further increased the volume of French trade. Wages rose rapidly in France as in England ; there was a great extension of the co-operative movement ; the prohibition of trade unions was somewhat relaxed ; but no attempt was made during this period to grapple with the labour question as a whole.

The expansion of trade was due first of all to the railways. This is easily seen from the following figures[1] :—

Foreign Trade.

	Year.	*Million francs.*	*Average.*	*Million francs Increase on preceding period.*
Under the Protective Tariff . . .	1850	2,553	—	—
	1847–50	—	2,288	213
Railways and Protective Tariff . . .	1859	5,412	—	—
	1851–59	—	4,265	2,859
Liberal Tariff and Railway Extension .	1869	8,003	—	—
	1860–69	—	7,128	2,591

Thus the increase in the period of high tariff and railways was as great as that of the low tariff and railways. It was the development of the railway net that gave the first great impetus to trade expansion.

If one turns to examine the effect of this twenty-one years on French industry and commerce one finds that machinery had begun to assume an ever larger place in French industry. Coal mining, which is the crucial test, had expanded and had nearly trebled in amount. The amount of iron produced had more than doubled and import was falling off. The import of raw cotton had more than doubled while that of wool had sextupled. The import of raw materials was nearly four times as much as it had been twenty years before. The amount of horse-power used had more than quadrupled ; while steam engines were nearly five times as numerous. The import and export trade had increased 206 per cent between the beginning and end of the Empire.

[1] Levasseur, op. cit., ii, p. 858.

	1847.	1867.
Coal extracted (thousand tons) .	5·142	12·738
,, imported (,, ,,) .	2·943	7·422
,, miners	34,800	84,900 [1]
Pig Iron (thousand quintals) . .	5·916	12·600
,, imported	1·042	916
Cotton imported (thousand kilos) .	45·522	95·903
Wool imported (,, ,,) .	15·628	93·205
Import raw material (million francs) .	547	1·972
Export of manufactures (million francs)	699	1·530
Steam engines (thousands) . .	4·8	23·4
Horse-power (,,) . .	62	289
Wine export (million francs) . .	97 (1852)	261 (1869)

The table of general exports and imports show the rapidity of the progress in exchange with other countries during this period.

	Million francs.				Growth of special commerce.
	General Commerce.[2]	Special.			% increase of one period over the preceding.
		Imports.	Exports.	Total.	
1827–36	1366	480	521	1001	—
1837–46	2112	776	713	1489	+ 48%
1847–56	3175	1077	1224	2301	+ 54%
1857–66	6280	2200	2430	4630	+ 101%

The increase between the beginning and end of the second Empire (18 years) may be put in a still stronger light as follows :—

1851	General commerce, million francs	2,614	+ 206%.
1869		8,002	

In the 'sixties, with the increasing spread of the factory system and the rapid growth of communications due to the railways, we get developments in the labour movement.

After the Revolution of 1848, universal suffrage was retained; the working classes had, therefore, a much greater leverage in politics than they had ever had before. In the first ten years of his reign Napoleon sternly repressed all workmen's associations and most of them perished or disguised themselves as Friendly Societies. In the 'sixties more latitude was allowed and a great development of co-operation ensued, carrying on the tradition of Louis Blanc. The members were unbusiness-like and absorbed in political discussion,[3] and the movement was practically

[1] Levasseur, op. cit., ii, p. 537; for the table see ii, p. 846.
[2] Levasseur, op. cit., ii, p. 856.
[3] Levasseur, op. cit., ii, p. 638.

ruined by the bankruptcy of the *Crédit du Travail* in 1868, in which the co-operators had invested their money. Co-operation as a means of transforming society seemed to be a failure. The working classes then began to throw themselves energetically into the "International", i.e. the revolutionary socialism of Karl Marx, the leading idea of which is that the working classes should transform society by seizing political power and then legislating in their own interest; should abolish the capitalist and take possession of the means of production.

Meanwhile the government had begun to assume a more liberal attitude with regard to trade unions. Many of the Paris workmen who had been sent over to the Exhibition in London came back enthusiasts for trade unionism and demanded to be allowed to organize. In 1864 they were allowed to strike but they were not allowed to "assemble". As it was difficult to see how a strike could be organized without some "assembling" the concession was illusory. All associations of over 20 persons were, in any case, illegal. In 1868 the Minister of Commerce announced that without modifying the law on coalitions the government would tolerate working men's organizations. They therefore had no legal right to exist, only a permission accorded by the government, and such toleration could be easily withdrawn.

Then came the Franco-Prussian War, the attempt to carry out socialistic ideas in the Paris Commune, the ruthless executions to restore order, and the eclipse of the working class movement for another ten or twelve years.

During the years 1850–70 wages rose rapidly. Levasseur calculates the rise at about 41 per cent in the provinces and 32 per cent in Paris. In the cotton industry in Alsace the rise was 50 per cent. He considers that it would not be an exaggeration to say that the average wage in France rose in the first three-quarters of the nineteenth century between 60 and 70 per cent, and that this rise took place chiefly after 1850.[1]

1870–1914

From 1870 to 1914 France was hampered by the slow growth of its population and the loss of Alsace and Lorraine, which meant the transference of 1½ million people

[1] Levasseur, op. cit., ii, p. 872.

together with a great cotton industry in Alsace and a great field of iron ore in Lorraine. France was left with a big war debt and a lowered prestige. At the end of the 'seventies France was still further depressed by the phylloxera which ravaged the vineyards and was said to have caused a bigger financial loss than the indemnity paid to Germany. The vineyards were gradually replanted with American stocks which were supposed to be immune and considerable impetus was given to state intervention in agriculture, not merely by the financial assistance afforded in the replanting but by the necessity of preventive measures such as spraying with copper. After 1870 French industrial development was slower than that of the other great powers measured by export and import statistics.[1] Those forty-four years were characterized by a certain amount of labour legislation, by the rise of trade unions and co-operative societies after 1884, by the development of syndicalist ideas, and by the rise in wages and the standard of comfort of the artisan. In France, as in the United Kingdom, Germany, and even the United States, there was an increased tendency to state regulation in all directions.

All through the century France has been hampered by the difficulty of obtaining sufficient coal at cheap rates for industrial purposes. Coking coal for iron had to be imported from either Durham or Westphalia. Its textile industries were concentrated on the coal measures in the North of France. It seems possible that the phenomenal development of electricity as a motive power which took place during the war in connection with munition making, may lead to France becoming in the future an even greater industrial nation, since it will no longer be hampered by dear motive power. In the Pyrenees, in the Alps, and in the central plateau, France has abundant waterfalls, and it is quite possible that industry may migrate to new areas and depend on electrical power.

On the whole, French industrial progress after 1870 was slow until 1892, after which progress became faster. The chief seat of the iron industry was in the north. Here, as elsewhere, the lack of good coking coal was a severe handicap, and iron was exported in enormous quantities over the border

[1] What one cannot measure by these statistics is the amount of profit there is behind them. It might possibly be that Germany doing a large trade in figures might yet be doing an unprofitable trade and that France might be making a larger profit on a smaller figure.

into Germany. Algeria, with its iron measures, sent most of its ore by sea to Middlesborough, and passed by coalless Marseilles. In engineering, the French showed much skill, though more in light engineering than in heavy engineering, in the manufacture of machines and motor-cars. Coal mining expanded steadily throughout the period, but its growth could not be compared with that of England or of Germany.

During the period the leading characteristic of the textile industries was the importance of domestic work on a small scale. The reasons for this backward state of affairs were that the goods produced were often of an artistic type, that the occupations were frequently bye-employments, and that coal was costly and put a premium on hand methods and small scale workshops. The woollen industry in the north was organized on large scale lines since it was close to coal supplies, but elsewhere in France hand-loom weaving still survived. The cotton industry was much more mechanized and carried on in factories. But industrialization was slow, and as late as 1896 the average staff per industrial unit was 5·5, which proved that the typical industrial unit was still the workshop, and not the factory.

Before the War, French industry held its own in the supply of the local market with ordinary goods and in the supply of foreign markets with luxury goods where good taste was important. On the other hand, French industry did not produce cheap goods on mass production lines: these were introduced from Germany, despite the tariff, and possibly prevented the development of mass production in France. In any case, mass production is alien to the French genius. This state of affairs relieved France from a pressing social problem which afflicted Germany, England, and United States periodically. With a steady market, a stable population, and a scattered industry France did not require to deal with the questions of unemployment, of industrial training, of capital equipment and of new markets, questions which arose in countries that expanded rapidly and revolutionized their technique from time to time. This may help to explain the backwardness of France in social legislation in the period before the War.

In the matter of social legislation France lagged behind other industrialized countries, despite the fact that Socialism was preached longer in France than in any other country. As a matter of fact, there was less practical Socialism in

France before the War than in Germany or Great Britain. In addition to the economic backwardness of the country, the very preaching of Socialism, by scaring bourgeois France, may have retarded its development. By 1914 the industrial code regulating conditions of employment, workmen's compensation, and similar matters had not progressed very far. As to nationalization, one railway system had been taken over by the State, an unfortunate example from every point of view. In nationalization, of course, the tide had set against the State with the rise of syndicalism, and in favour of workers' control through the trade unions. This was another factor helping to explain the lag of social legislation in France before the War.

The labour movement suffered eclipse after the extinction of the Paris Commune, and for many years Socialists had to tread warily. But by 1880 things were reviving. Guesde had displaced Barberet as leader for the time being, and the French labour movement was ready for an advance, but an advance with a brand new programme.

In 1884 the Syndicate Law was passed, giving both trade unions and co-operative societies the right to exist. This tardy recognition of trade unions in France explains why they never built up the solid movement by slow growth as happened in England, where the trade unions had been recognized 60 years before. It also explains their tendency to violent and unconstitutional methods, unlike the trade unions of England, which had learned to work through the existing Parliamentary machinery.

Between 1884 and 1914 the dominating influence in French trade unionism came to be that of syndicalism, which inevitably detracted from a strong political labour movement and undoubtedly weakened the position of the Socialist parties in the legislature. Social Democracy was too slow for the French temperament in obtaining control of politics. Socialists were apt to compromise: they might even accept office as did Millerand, "the traitor." Even should the political machine fall into the hands of the Socialists, it would only be exchanging the existing tyranny for the tyranny of a bureaucracy. Accordingly, the idea arose of organizing all trades so as to make possible a general strike which should paralyse the government machine. Economic action, or direct action, was to replace political action.

All strikes were to be encouraged, because they bred

ill-feeling between employers and employed, and made for solidarity among the workers. The movement existed to wage ceaseless war against the existing industrial regime. There were no "benefits" amongst French syndicalist associations, and no financial stability was aimed at. A strike was not a misfortune, as it was in Germany and England, but a method to be used as frequently as possible, because every strike was a preparation for the general strike which would ultimately bring about the social revolution. Meanwhile, other methods of *sabotage* were in frequent use, such as bad work, slow work, putting machines out of gear, and so forth. Anti-militarism was always one of the syndicalist cries, since the general strike might fail before a disciplined army prepared to shoot. Finally, when the existing system was destroyed, it was intended that the mechanism of industrial and social life should continue, but organized in local groups of industries. Here the theory was based on French conditions with small and localized industries and with each locality largely self-sufficing.

The importance of French syndicalism lay in the impetus it gave to the philosophy of the labour movement rather than in its numerical strength. An estimate of 1910 put the paying membership of the syndicalist unions at 357,814.[1] Another estimate in 1912 assessed their numbers at 400,000 out of 11,000,000 wage-earners, and it was thought that even out of the 400,000 some 250,000 were opposed to violent action and to revolutionary doctrines.[2] The influence of syndicalism was scarcely less important abroad, particularly in England and the United States. In England syndicalism helped in the revival of trade unionism about 1908–10 and ultimately produced a similar philosophy adapted to English needs and circumstances. This was Gild Socialism, which advocated industrial unionism, direct action, workers' control of industry, and a joint control over prices and goods by producers and consumers. In the United States, syndicalism issued forth in the Industrial Workers of the World, an organization which attempted to organize the under-dogs of industry and advocated the seizure of power by direct action. In Germany and Russia, on the other hand, the influence of syndicalism was small, since there Marxism held the field.

[1] L. Levine, *The Labour Movement in France*, p. 181.
[2] J. R. Macdonald, *Syndicalism*, p. 33.

Syndicalism achieved little or nothing in France beyond stiffening the backs of the bourgeoisie against much needed reforms. France was really unsuitable soil for such a philosophy. The majority of French workers before the War were still engaged in domestic industry and were dependent on family and not on individual earnings.[1] The typical trade unions were small, local bodies, marked by incessant quarrels, and subscriptions very much in arrears. Then came the War, and for the time being theories and programmes were swept on to the scrap-heap.

[1] *Report on Industrial Conditions in Europe to the American Department of Commerce and Labour*, by H. Studniczka, 1910, Series No. 38, p. 55.

CHAPTER 2

GERMANY AND THE INDUSTRIAL REVOLUTION

To 1871. Leadership of Prussia in the formation of a new and united Germany.

Natural features of Germany.

Long frontier; consequent burden of defence.
The centre State.
Rivers flowing north.
Poor outlets to sea.
Continental climate and poor soil.
Minerals.

Economic position in early years of nineteenth century.

Mediaevalism.
Natural economy.
The handicap of the Thirty Years War.
Different tariffs, coinage, weights and measures, laws, in the various States.

The Leadership of Prussia.

Piecemeal formation of the Kingdom of Prussia.

German industry in eighteenth century crushed by competition of French, English, and Dutch goods.
Prussia's economic task in eighteenth century was to improve communications; make Prussia the centre State; develop Prussian industry and agriculture.

After Jena (1806) Prussia carried out six great reforms: Educational reform—Union of Prussian territories, 1818, and internal markets freed from barriers—Freeing of serfs; commutation of labour dues for money and division of land—Removal of restrictions imposed by gilds on settlement and choice of trade—Reform of municipal government—Legal reform. The other German States slowly follow

Industrial freedom brought about by reform of the gilds.

Exclusiveness of the gilds abolished in Prussia in 1810, in other German States between 1825 and 1860. Freedom for the whole Empire, 1872. Reconstruction of the gild system by Bismarck, 1881.

Administrative reform—Reform of the municipalities, 1808.

After 1871.

Growth of coal, iron, and steel industries. Engineering, chemical industries and textiles follow.

Industrial organization in Kartells.

Protection of the Industrial Worker.

Social Insurance.
The Trade Union Movement.

ONE of the most striking features of the nineteenth century is the rise of three new and vigorous nations. The United States of America, where the country was blank

—a blank page on which something had to be written—has evolved into one of the most individualistic states of the New World where everything is new, enterprising, big. Then there is the rise of Russia, the greatest socialist state of modern times, its mediaevalism and the passivity of its people contrasting violently with the newness and the individualism of the United States and the pushfulness of the Americans as a race. Then there is the third, Germany. At the beginning of the nineteenth century Germany was merely a geographical expression. At the end of that century Germany had been welded into Imperial unity, for which the way was prepared by a Customs Union. The leader in this movement was Prussia.

After the war of 1870, in Germany as in other countries, there came a great industrial advance—in iron, in electricity, in chemicals, in textiles—and an expanding population, making it necessary to import food. But unlike those other countries, Germany had no unoccupied area in which to expand, so that it had to find an outlet either by means of peaceful penetration, by emigration, or by developing manufactures to employ its people, which means the cultivation of markets. The position of Germany became that of a prolific nation outgrowing the physical condition of its surroundings. Up to 1870 Germany was reorganizing its internal condition under the leadership of Prussia, a poor country, with machinery only just developing, enormously behind England and France. "Before 1870, the economic revolution had already begun, and Germany would have become more and more industrial every year by the very necessity of things, but the development would have been gradual and there would have been no abrupt break with the past. The war, the indemnity, and the new Empire together gave the material enterprise an abnormal impetus, an impetus so strong that it has never since suffered check."[1] So whereas the chief problem up to that date was the establishment of a united Empire system of free trade internally, the chief problem after that time was industrial development, and the one prime necessity an outlet.

The problems of Germany have been essentially different from those of France. France is a rich country with a thrifty population, a large sea-border facing three great

[1] W. H. Dawson, *The Evolution of Modern Germany*, p. 7.

highways of commerce, the Channel, the Atlantic, and the Mediterranean. It has a northern and a southern climate, and an almost stationary population. It is the next greatest colonial power after England. Agriculture has developed inside its tariff walls and it is practically self-sufficing as regards food, while, as to exports, its taste creates a demand for them which is unique.

Germany is a country which developed as a nation in comparatively recent times. Before, it was a mass of scattered States all differing from one another, divided by one of the most powerful solvents, religious differences, and united only in jealousy of Prussia. And even when unity was achieved its economic security was threatened all the time by Socialists, by religious difficulties, by the Polish question, and by the possible break-up of North and South, since there were before the War really three Germanies: the Rhineland, Bavaria, and Prussia. It had a growing population, so that in spite of its increased production of food within its own borders additional food had to be imported. Germany must either export people or find new markets. Germany has an unfavourable soil. The pasture lands are not good as in England and France; there is no Black Earth Zone as in Russia; and there is a great deal of sterile waste and moor and sand, forest and mountain. The sterile land in Prussia is said to be two-fifths sand and moor. Berlin has arisen in the middle of a sandy desert. The country has a very poor coastline but wide rivers, which, however, flow partly into the Baltic, with its ice and difficult navigation. Also the continental climate means cold for long periods in winter, so that in East Prussia it is difficult to do any agricultural work from November to May, and in the extreme North-east the period of vegetation lasts only four or five months. The effects of a poor soil and a not very favourable climate were that the German, like the Englishman, was compelled to work and work steadily. At the same time conditions are not so depressing as in Russia, where one gazes out on the great expanses of snow in winter, or flat brown plains in summer. Its natural advantages in the possession of coal and iron in considerable quantities in Silesia, the Ruhr district, Westphalia, and the Saar, provided an outlet for the early industrial energies of Germany; but until the introduction of railways it hardly paid to work them because of the cost of bringing the coal and iron together.

It is wonderful that out of such a poor country, with its necessarily heavy military burdens, and possessing so few natural advantages, such a powerful state should have arisen, the industrial development of which is one of the most striking phenomena of our day. It is still more wonderful when we contrast the mediaeval condition of Germany and its poverty at the beginning and throughout the first half of the nineteenth century with that of any of the other great Powers of the time.[1] But what it lacked in coastline it made up in artificial waterways. To a poor soil it consistently applied chemical manures. By sheer scientific education it wrested chemical industries from England and was the first to develop and build up the electrical industry. It developed a shipping second only to Great Britain and a growing export trade. It organized its finance on quite new lines. It developed its railways. There is no more interesting study than to try and find out to what this development is due.

Two characteristics of the Germans during the nineteenth century have to be noted. First, the very high birth rate. During the period 1871–1910 it attained a maximum of 42·6 per 1,000. Where there is a large family, the members of that family must work. The parents cannot hope to save enough to leave them all competencies. Hence the German has put his money on education and on fitting his children for the battle of life. On the other hand, the Frenchman saves and scrapes in order to leave his children a competency. Hence the necessity for the German to press on to a career and the comparative stagnation of the Frenchman. Hence also, the surplus with which to build up industries.

In the second place, by reason of their geographical situation, the Germans had to be a nation in arms. This was specially true of Prussia from the days of the Great Elector. The people had to submit to military discipline all through the nineteenth century—and earlier in Prussia, and this has developed a capacity for discipline which has given them, according to Sombart,[2] the best schoolmasters, the best army, and the best organized State in the world. It has also given them a capacity for combined action by means of trusts and co-operative movements. Among the

[1] In 1853 the German fleet was sold by auction.
[2] *Die deutsche Volkswirtschaft im neunzehnten Jahrhundert*, 1903, p. 125.

Germans the individualism of the American or the French is impossible. Sombart also considers that their having been citizens of petty States rather than of a united nation so long made the German modest and adaptable, and that their being without national pride until quite recent times made them such good business men. Then he considers that their tradition of autocratic rule kept the best brains from going into politics and attracted them instead into business. " It was the complaint, even in ultra-bureaucratic Prussia, that the best business men were found, not in the state service, but at the head of industrial, commercial, and financial undertakings." [1]

There are two other points to be noticed. The first is that the poverty caused by the Thirty Years War left the initiative in all things to the state, which alone had the necessary money or energy. The second point is that German development was a conscious development. It began from above, was carried out by an autocrat in each State, and was systematic and designed to a definite end. Partly because German development was so late, it could see whither it was going. Compare English education, which has been sheer compromise, with the systematic reconstruction of its educational system by Prussia from the Universities downwards, with compulsory attendance as long ago as 1808. The circumstances of Germany did not allow for drift or absence of mind.

While Western and Northern Europe came rapidly forward between 1550–1700, Germany retrogressed, chiefly owing to the Thirty Years War. In 1650, in many parts of Germany, the population had been halved; the production of cattle and wool was entirely ruined; capital was destroyed; and most of her little States and communities were bankrupt. Many thousands of houses in town and country were burnt down. The price of land had sunk to one-fourth its normal value. The brewing, wine, paper, mining, printing, wool, and linen industries were either ruined outright or had dwindled almost to nothing. The rate of interest was ten to thirty per cent. Germany had sunk back into a state of natural economy and politically it broke up into a multitude of completely self-contained small States. There were only some ten or fifteen reasonably large territories, and these were scattered

[1] W. H. Dawson, *The Evolution of Modern Germany*, p. 9.

and participators in the universal decay. On all sides Germany was outstripped by other nations. Holland ruled the Lower Rhine. France dominated the Upper Rhine and corrupted the German courts with pensions and subsidies. Sweden controlled the mouths of the Weser and the Oder and made the Baltic a Swedish lake. Denmark threatened to annex Hamburg. Poland was threatening East Prussia. The German Hanse League was broken up. The splitting up of the country into so many separate territories prevented any common effort. Prussia in the North and Austria in the South alone were developing a national policy.

In 1815 Germany had again been devastated by war and by the Continental System, which necessitated drastic measures of reconstruction. In 1800 the people on the land were serfs in an infinitely worse condition than were the French in 1789. The gilds survived in the towns, a circumstance which reflected a backward state of industrial organization in comparison with other European nations. There were the usual elaborate restrictions as to the number of apprentices and the purchase of raw materials, with the idea of providing a living and with the usual consequence that there grew up outside a number of people who could not get a living at all. Most necessaries were made at home; in other words, the German household in 1800 was nearly self-sufficing. The houses in the country would be made of wood, with thatched roofs, and would be built with the help of neighbours. Clothes were all made at home with the flax and hemp which were sown very generally. Itinerant tailors would make them up. The larger estates would have their own smith, saddler, miller, and builder. Wood from the forest would provide the material. Workers were paid mostly in kind, with only a very small money payment. Even in the towns the food and clothing were provided to a large extent within the home. Sombart speaks of butchers' shops being almost unknown because people killed and salted their own meat. Itinerant women boiled soap, made candles, and brewed for town households. The furniture, the leather for shoes, the feather bedding, and the hair for the cushions and sofa were nearly all prepared at home. Two-thirds of the population were predominantly engaged in agriculture and one-third in industry and trade—a proportion maintained till 1850. Only about one-fourth of the people lived in towns, and even the towns had an agrarian aspect. In Prussian towns in 1802–3 there were no less than 63,486 barns. The country was sparsely populated. The big towns were few. Berlin had 153,128 inhabitants and of the 1016 towns of Germany 998 had less than 10,000 inhabitants. Industry was scattered and there were no districts that could be called industrial, although Silesia had its linen industry and Saxony had its spinning and weaving of wool. In every sense Germany up to 1850 was a poor country, and it was a poverty that extended to all classes. Among the mass of the people, whether urban or rural, there was misery and want which often became famine. Nowhere was there anything approaching luxury or display. Trade was chiefly carried on at the great fairs, in particular at those of which Frankfurt-am-Main, Frankfurt-am-Oder, Leipzig, and Nuremberg were the great centres. Living was exceedingly cheap in Germany. In 1837–9 about one-fourth of the German exports were food and raw materials. About one-fourth of the wheat harvest was exported and 6 per cent of the rye. Next to corn, timber was the principal export, and the surplus of the wool produced for home consumption was also exported. The manufactures exported consisted of handwoven cotton, wool and linen wares, and wooden goods, but these were beginning to feel the effects of English machinery. The imports were yarn, pig iron, and colonial products, especially sugar. About one-fourth of the imports were cotton yarn, and German economic history is full of the attempts of the cotton spinners and iron manufacturers to free themselves from foreign imports. After speaking of the appalling filth of the streets of Berlin, Sombart refers to the very little movement that would go on in a German town: "The workers did not need to go miles to their workshops; their workplaces and homes were the same. The thousand requisites of everyday life were not brought together by an everlasting running round; shopping had not yet become the sweet occupation of women of all classes, who then found sufficient work in house and garden and care of the children and never dreamed of a walk within the town. In the evening people seated themselves in the shade in front of their houses or on Sundays went outside the town gates. . . . In the streets there were no shop windows."[1]

[1] *Die deutsche Volkswirtschaft im neunzehnten Jahrhundert*, p. 19.

Not only was Germany in a backward economic condition, but all circumstances were calculated to prevent any attempt to progress. Amongst the chief obstacles to economic advance were the internal divisions. There were, in 1803, 300 princes and overlords in Germany. They were reduced in 1815 to 38, but each territory had its own system of customs and tolls. Analogous to this was the confusion of systems of coinage and weights and measures. The so-called banks were as a consequence profitably occupied in moneychanging and when uniformity of coinage and weights and measures was established in 1833 for as many States as had joined the Zollverein, and in 1868 for practically all parts of Germany, they all announced their impending ruin. There was, further, no such thing as a common law. Each petty State had its own laws, and they were of the type that suited a feudal organization and were based largely on a natural economy.

The impression of Germany which is envisaged at this period is one of inextricable confusion in economic life. The Thirty Years War and the Napoleonic Wars arrested its progress, and Germany, that had been one of the foremost states of the Middle Ages, declined so that at the beginning of the nineteenth century it was sunk in mediaevalism. England had practically fifty years start of France. It had two hundred years start of Germany. The wonderful thing about Germany is that it should have accomplished its regeneration so quickly. The interest of the nineteenth century lies not merely in the tremendous advances made by England and France, but in the resuscitation of Germany and its appearance as a world power. This was the work of Prussia

The Leadership of Prussia

The kingdom of Prussia started from two centres, the Mark Brandenburg and the conquests of the Teutonic knights along the Baltic. The Mark Brandenburg, founded by Albert the Bear between 1134 and 1170, was transferred to the Hohenzollerns in 1411–17. John Sigismund (1608–19) obtained possession of the Duchy of Cleves and laid claim to Jülich and Berg, that is to say, Duchies in the West. In 1618 he was invested with the Duchy of Prussia and so united Prussia and Brandenburg. The Teutonic Knights—a Crusading Order like the Knights Templars—set out to conquer territory from the heathen Prussians for Christendom in the early part of the thirteenth century. They founded Königsberg in 1255 and took possession of Danzig in 1311. The religious side of the Order declined and its rule in effect came to an end when Albert of Brandenburg, its Grand Master, secularized the dominions of the Order in East Prussia in 1525. Frederick William, the Great Elector (1640–88), obtained at the Peace of Westphalia (1648) part of Pomerania, which brought him to the sea with, however, no port of any importance, and also the Bishoprics of Halberstadt and Minden and the Archbishopric of Magdeburg. His reform of the administration and his creation of a standing army enabled him to consolidate the power of Prussia. "The awful scourge of the Thirty Years' War had left the naturally sterile soil of the Mark Brandenburg desolate, with a population sunk to 210,000 souls. . . . Berlin was little better than the centre of a desert through whose sands a traveller might plod by the hour without meeting either man or beast." To fill the void Frederick William, the Great Elector, began the system of home colonization which was continued by his three successors. "The Dutch . . . taught the impoverished and disheartened inhabitants of the Mark how to drain their lands, to manage dairy farms, and to cultivate potato fields . . . and stimulated the Brandenburg Government to dig canals." [1] The Huguenot element, encouraged by the offer of houses and land tax-free and even money bribes, introduced skilled industries like the woollen, silk, metal, and glass manufacture, and encouraged horticulture. To this French element was due the quick rise of Berlin and a great increase in the strength and efficiency of the army. How well and truly the Great Elector laid the foundations of the Prussian State was seen when, in 1701, his son became its first King as Frederick I. Without some such great personality Prussia might very well have shared the fate of Poland.

Under Frederick the Great (1740–86) Silesia was added and the acquisition of part of the territory of Poland in 1772 united Prussia proper and Brandenburg. Frederick William III secured the Rhineland in 1815. The aim constantly kept in view by the heads of the Prussian State,

[1] A. W. Ward, "The Great Elector and the First Prussian King," chap. xxi, in *ambridge Modern History*, vol. v, p. 645.

whether Electors or Kings, was to weld their territory into one industrial and commercial system. The difficulties were enormous. Nowhere were there any natural borders, nor was the kingdom anywhere near a good outlet to the sea. An army was an absolute necessity to defend the kingdom against the attack of hostile neighbours, and this was an enormous burden to so poor a country. Sweden held a strong position in Pomerania, and controlled the Baltic; England was enormously powerful in Hamburg. Owing to the absence of anything like a frontier German industry was crushed by the competition of French, English, and Dutch goods. The Great Elector and the Kings of Prussia aimed from 1640 onwards at three things, namely, to accomplish the economic unity of their scattered territories; to make Prussia and Brandenburg the intermediate country between East and West; and to protect and develop their own industry and agriculture.

Economic unity was best secured by good communications. To do this trade routes had to be deflected and altered; for instance Stettin, acquired from Sweden in 1720, had to be diverted from Swedish trade interests. Magdeburg, connected as it was by the Elbe with Hamburg and Saxony, was the centre of a great salt and corn trade and a woollen trade with Saxony. In order to make Prussia the centre of this trade her rulers set to work to alter the roads, tolls, and shipping, so as to make communication within the country easier than with outside, and to build canals and improve the waterways. Movement between the different territories under Prussian rule was permitted, but the tariff barriers between them were continued for the reason that it was impossible to collect a revenue without them.

To make Prussia the intermediary kingdom was also a matter of improving the communications. But to this end other and more drastic steps were taken. By imposing tolls at Magdeburg, Frederick the Great diverted to Prussia the trade between Hamburg and Silesia which used to go *via* Saxony and when he had acquired Silesia the whole of the trade between Saxony and Poland was made to go *via* Brandenburg and the customs were rearranged so as to make Poland dependent on Prussia for exports and imports. There was a conscious effort on the part of the rulers of Prussia to unify their territory and to make it the great intermediary between East and West.

The devastation wrought by the Thirty Years War has already been mentioned. There followed the efforts of the Kings to attract immigrants. Industries, introduced by the immigrants, were fostered by a strictly protective system. There was a prohibition on the import of cloth and a prohibition more or less enforced on the export of wool; and there was a system of bounties under Frederick the Great. Every encouragement was given to agriculture; the marshes were drained; new methods of cultivation prescribed. Fruit trees were planted in waste places; and hops, vines, and flax were cultivated. It was estimated that in 1786 not less than one-third of all the inhabitants of the monarchy were either immigrants or descendants of immigrants, mainly Dutch or French.

As far as industry was concerned Frederick superintended everything from the greatest to the smallest. He founded iron, steel, and cloth factories. The home market must be secured for home merchants and foreign goods were practically shut out, while merchants and consumers were forced to purchase. Industry was carried on by home workers in gilds. The import of corn was prohibited and corn was stored up in great corn magazines to ensure low prices.

During 1763–73 Frederick the Great founded 264 establishments for the velvet, silk, satin, woollen, leather, iron, and sugar industries. He spent £300,000 on the two first.[1] "Let it be known," said the King, "that if an economic enterprise is beyond the powers of my subjects, it is my affair to defray the costs and they have nothing further to do than to gather in the profits."[2] Eight hundred new villages were created. The acquisition of Silesia and Polish Prussia doubled the population and resources of the kingdom. In 1744 the port of Emden was secured and the Bank of Prussia was created in 1765. But it never seems to have occurred to Frederick to unite his kingdom by abolishing tariffs. There were said to be 67 different tariffs in this kingdom alone. In the different parts of the kingdom the prohibitions and permissions varied, the Eastern provinces, Prussia, Brandenburg, and Silesia having by far the strictest system. At the end of the reign of Frederick the Great, Prussia was

[1] Emil Daniels, "Frederick the Great and His Successor," chap. xx, in *Cambridge Modern History*, vol. vi, p. 719.

[2] Ibid., p. 720.

still primarily an agricultural state, 80 per cent of her inhabitants being engaged in agriculture.

During the American War the ports of Northern Germany carried on a large trade with England in wood and corn. After it was over they opened up direct communication with the United States, fetching tobacco and rice and sending their linen there in return. The ports of Germany were flourishing.

In so far as it could make headway in spite of wars, Austria, too, was building up its trade, and a great development took place there in the eighteenth century, especially under Maria Theresa and her son Joseph II. Up to 1792 there was great commercial development until the Napoleonic Wars checked all progress. At the end of the eighteenth century there was a great revival of trade and commerce in Austria under the Hapsburgs as in Germany under Prussia.

During the eighteenth century then, Prussia was developed by a mercantile policy into a kingdom and there was considerable economic progress in the country up to 1806. In spite of the divisions between the different parts of their dominions, Prussia had a race of rulers who for 150 years devoted themselves to the economic development of their kingdom. They subdued their feudal underlings and turned them into officials or officers dependent on and loyal to the Crown. They had not merely united and nationalized their territories, but they had deflected them from their foreign connections. Prussia stood for something German and national in Germany; for something united and progressive when the rest of Germany was still in a backward condition.

Then came the Napoleonic Wars and a second period of devastation for Germany. In 1807, after the battle of Jena, Prussia was shorn of half its territory by the Treaty of Tilsit and Napoleon created out of it the Kingdom of Westphalia. Its population was reduced to 4½ million people and French troops were to remain in Prussia till it had paid the indemnity France demanded. That indemnity was fixed at such a figure that the Prussians could never pay it off although they seem actually to have paid 601,227,000 francs,[1] an almost incredible amount for

[1] J. Holland Rose, "The Napoleonic Empire at its Height, 1807–9," chap. xi, in *Cambridge Modern History*, vol. ix, p. 325.

so small a territory devastated by war. So utter were the prostration and discouragement that the Prussians had surrendered garrisons without any resistance. It was obvious that it was necessary to re-form the whole *morale* of the people if there was to be effective opposition to the French. Moreover, where Napoleon erected his new kingdoms on the Rhine, there he established the French ideas of liberty, law, and central and communal government. He was modernizing those territories. It is true they did not feel particularly grateful to the French because of the corresponding burdens of French taxation and military levies. But it was clear that if any effective opposition were to be offered, the Prussian people must not merely be improved in *morale* but the whole system must be changed. A mediaeval state must be made modern. So what France had done from below by a revolution, 10 years' chaos, and a Dictator, the two able Prussian Ministers, Stein and Hardenberg, set out to do from above. It is characteristic of the way in which Prussia stood for something national that it was able to attract to itself Stein, the type of the practical man, a Rhinelander educated at Hanover, and Hardenberg, the theorist, an Hanoverian, as was also Scharnhorst, the reorganizer of the army, while many others of the great men of the time were Saxon, and Blücher was a Mecklenburger.

In the work of modernization Prussia carried out six reforms. It reformed education, founding new universities where culture and civic duty should be taught. It united Prussian territories with a low tariff outside and free trade within. It freed the serfs. It abolished gild restrictions and permitted free choice of trades. It reformed municipal administration. And it executed great legal reforms. Of the six the gilds and the municipalities are the most important here.

The establishment of industrial freedom by the changes effected in the gild system was one of the most important of Prussia's reforms, and between 1810 and 1845 the gilds were shorn of most of their powers. The gilds were originally associations of small masters who carried out the police regulations and the industrial law of their time. They therefore had to have compulsory powers and if anyone desired to follow an industry he had to belong to one of these groups. In countries like France and England, with a strong central power, the worst abuses of the gilds were kept in check. In Germany, where no such thing as uniformity prevailed, the gilds became close corporations, limiting members, limiting trades, confining the right to enter a trade to a small privileged class and keeping the whole government of the town in their hands. On the other hand, the gilds undoubtedly performed certain useful functions. They were institutions for training apprentices, for helping members during sickness, for deciding disputes, for controlling unemployment. They had many social uses, and the policy in Germany was, for the most part, not to abolish the gilds as in France but to maintain them, especially on the side of apprenticeship, but checking the abuse of their powers. But as long as the gilds existed it was not possible for industry on a large scale to grow up. Entrance to a trade was only obtained after serving an apprenticeship of so many years, then surviving a difficult examination, and finally obtaining the right, which was often delayed or denied, of setting up in the industry.

If the factory owner had to wait till a man had got through all these stages the whole scope of his enterprise would be limited. Accordingly, public opinion in Prussia, and to a lesser degree in the rest of Germany, alternated in the course of the nineteenth century between faith in industrial freedom and faith in gild regulation. Until the middle of the century faith in industrial freedom was predominant, as the employers felt the restrictions of the old-fashioned system. After the middle of the century faith in gild regulation was revived, as the gilds were reformed as instruments of state policy, particularly as regards social insurance.

Gilds, in their old-fashioned and restrictive form, remained in many parts of Germany until 1860 and even in certain parts of Prussia until 1845. The reason was that the years after the peace were so unfavourable for economic development that industrial freedom seemed to be of no effect and therefore no one agitated for the abolition of the gilds. There was no question of setting up factories and therefore no occasion for demanding the abolition of the old system and for the construction of a new one. The small masters had not increased in number and there was scarcely any factory development.

In the formation of the Zollverein and the greater expansion of the area in which industry on a large scale could work is seen the movement for greater freedom on the one hand and, on the other, an outcry is heard from the small masters for the strengthening of the gild system as a protection against capitalism. For the very fact that the gilds were a restriction on capitalist enterprise meant that they afforded the small master a certain amount of defence. Absolutely unrestricted competition, as in France among the knitters and in England among the hand-loom weavers, was apt to thrust the greater part of the handworkers lower and lower.

In the period 1850–60 began industrial development along factory lines and the growth of railways, and the general characteristics of an industrial revolution made their appearance. A crisis set in among the handworkers, due not so much to the competition of the factories as to the changes in transport which began in 1840–50. In earlier times all industrial activity was localized. Production was confined to the worker's own house, to the village, to the town, or to the district. With increased transport facilities the whole mass of things needed became more accessible. The provision in the way of linen, clothes, and food, that had to be laid in, was bought ready-made. When it became easy to buy everything in a shop, the small handworker was ousted. He no longer worked for a number of families more or less known to him. He kept a workshop and speculated in a stock of things to sell. But capital and business training were needed and so the small man was ousted by the large scale production which improved transport brought to the very door.

When the small handworker first began to feel the squeeze there was a general outcry that it was due to the fact that too many people could set up in industry, and after the revolution of 1848 there was a restriction of industrial freedom. Membership of a gild became compulsory and persons could only set up as masters after an examination test. Apprentices could only learn their trade with a master, and the setting up for themselves of men who were not masters was forbidden. Councils of Industry were set up to supervise the gilds. All existing gilds were confirmed but members might leave the gilds at will. No one could be refused admission provided he paid the entrance fee and submitted to the tests of efficiency. They were put under the supervision of the communal authorities

In 1869 there was again a Liberal reaction, and when the

North German Union was founded it became important to make the laws uniform throughout the territory and a very much more liberal Industrial Code applying to the whole of North Germany was the result. The gilds again became voluntary associations of a private character. It was not until 1881 that the gilds were again reconstituted as public corporations with various objects, one of the chief being that of training apprentices.

The reform of the administration was the other great reform in Prussia and it was again the prelude to reform elsewhere. The control of the towns was in the hands of the gilds in which the greater number of the inhabitants had no part or lot, as in England before 1835. The municipal government was absolutely incompetent. In 1808 Stein's edict reformed the municipalities along the lines of self-government. The system as it existed left no room for local or individual initiative, and the system of local taxation was most oppressive. An attempt was made to set up in the towns a government enjoying a greater degree of freedom and to abolish the caste system as it had been abolished on the land and to a certain extent in industry.

In these reforms Prussia pointed the way to the rest of Germany, though the rest of Germany was slow to follow. And yet, despite the reforms, Prussia made slow progress economically, until the middle of the century, at any rate. But if progress were slow in progressive Prussia, it was still slower in the other German States.

During the period Germany was largely organized on the lines of natural economy, and there was little opportunity for capitalism to build up large undertakings or machine production. There was no internal market, no trained workpeople, and practically no capital for the foundation of undertakings. There were no banks in the modern sense, only places for money-changing. Factories were few, and machinery uncommon, despite the efforts of the Prussian Government to acclimatize machinery by means of the *Gewerbe-institut*. Most industries were organized in small workshops, and masters were as numerous as men in many industries. The period of 1815–50 in Germany was a weary time. The prices of nearly all articles sank. Industry was threatened by English and French competition and Germany had no protection against English machine-made goods.

Between 1850 and 1870 the industrial situation improved

somewhat. The Zollverein, but particularly the railways, played their part in cheapening costs and widening the market for industrial goods. During this period the Industrial Revolution really took root in Germany, even though the roots were but shallow. Coal, iron, steel and textiles began to change over to machinery and mass production methods, but it was not till after 1870 that industrial development really went ahead. During the first 70 years of the century industry in Germany was almost stagnant, but in those years Prussia laid the foundations of a united Germany and of the great industrial advance that was to follow. The record of that great industrial advance between 1871 and 1914 must now be traced.

Industrial Development after 1871

In 1871 Germany became at last a united nation. Pride in the achievement, pride in the victorious wars that had led up to the unification, pride in their nationality constrained the Germans to find other outlets for their energy and enthusiasm now that the period of the wars was over. If they had been victorious on the battlefield, why should they not prove victorious now in the factory and the laboratory ? Accompanying these events there had been a change in the German character. The Germans of the eighteenth and early nineteenth centuries were poets, philosophers, and musicians. It was the age of Schiller and Goethe. The new Germany was radically different from the old Germany. The struggle was not now for " intellectual or political ideals, or ideals of any kind, but a struggle for sheer mastery in the realm of matter and for political ascendancy amongst the nations ".[1] A cult of force had grown up, and the State was elevated to a position of importance which it had never held before. A young and vigorous nation had turned from idealism to believe in force, and now under the pressure of a rapidly expanding population directed its energies into the channels of industrial and commercial development. And behind loomed the all-powerful State, not indifferent to industrial progress as the government in *laissez-faire* England, but eager to aid the progress of industry by all means, by tariffs, by bounties,

[1] W. H. Dawson, *Evolution of Modern Germany*, p. 11.

by preferential rates. Such was industrial Germany under the Empire.

In this period of industrial development coal takes pride of place. Coal began to be developed on a large scale about 1860 with the building of railways, which not only required coal themselves but also increased the demand for coal by transporting it where it was wanted at cheap rates. Germany had supplies of both bituminous coal and lignite, a brown woody coal with only one-third the heating capacity of bituminous coal, but more easily mined. However, with the turn of the century lignite became more important, since it was used in the generation of electricity. Accordingly, while the output of bituminous coal between 1871 and 1913 increased from 29·4 to 191·5 million tons, that of lignite increased from 8·5 to 87·5 million tons.[1]

The late development of coal mining in Germany enabled it to learn the lesson of England's experiences. As a result German mines were well-equipped and efficient and generally large scale, the average personnel being 800 per mine.

Germany became a considerable exporter of coal, principally to Denmark, Russia, Belgium, and Holland. In 1913 Germany exported 34·5 million tons, but it imported 11·3 million tons, mostly from England, for iron-smelting in the Ruhr, since English coal is the best coking coal in the world.

The German iron and steel industry was built up largely as a result of the invention of the Gilchrist Thomas process in 1878, which permitted the use of the very impure ores of Germany. In addition, the process yielded a valuable bye-product in basic slag, which was an excellent chemical manure. Here again the German industry had the advantage of starting late and learning from England, so that the industrial units are generally large scale and well equipped. Further, as part of government policy, the railways gave cheap rates and permitted the coal and iron to be brought together very economically. Shipbuilding also made tremendous strides. The engineering industry followed in the wake of the developing industries of coal and iron. Germany thus was able to produce most of the engines and machinery that it wanted for its own industrial development, with

[1] J. H. Clapham, *Economic Development of France and Germany, 1815–1914*, p. 281.

the exception of cotton machinery, which it imported largely from Lancashire, and of agricultural machinery, which it imported from the United States. Engineering has made rapid progress with the development of electricity. England again pioneered the way, but did not have the same openings for electricity, so Germany took it up and expanded it tremendously.

Chemistry was yet another industry developed by England and taken up by Germany. In heavy chemicals England continued to lead the world with Germany a good second, but in light chemicals Germany took first place. In chemicals Germany had a great advantage in the supplies of potash found within its boundaries. Its exports of potash grew from 375,000 tons in 1871 to 9,600,000 tons in 1911.[1] The development of dyes was due to the excellent technical education in Germany.

Textiles passed through four stages during this period of German industrial development. First, spinning was done by machinery. Then weaving was done by machinery. Next the industry entered the small factory. Finally, the industry entered the large factory and combine. The different textile industries had, during the period, curiously different fortunes. Linen, the oldest of the German textile industries, shrank considerably with the transition from the workshop to the factory. The woollen industry, after depending on home-grown wool, took to importing wool, and an important cloth industry was built up on a factory basis, which exported abroad. Cotton was really founded in the 'fifties and 'sixties, but went ahead rapidly after 1871 with the incorporation of Alsace with its developed cotton industry within the Empire. In silk, Germany came second only to France and exported as much as £10,000,000 of silk goods per annum.

A striking feature of industrial organization in Germany before the War was the growth of "Kartells", joint bodies representing a number of different businesses which arrange price, sale, and output policies. Like all recently emancipated countries, Germany has a great capacity for co-operation amongst equals. The United States, on the other hand, with its rooted individualism, formed trusts, or virtually one-man businesses. The Kartells were

[1] J. H. Clapham, *Economic Development of France and Germany, 1815–1914*, p. 305.

formed to eliminate waste and competition in the home market and to achieve a unified policy as regards the foreign market, where dumping can only be successful by united action. Moreover, they had the blessing of the government, since they were supposed to stabilize prices and employment. Kartells were commonest in such exporting industries as coal and iron and steel. If they were confined to one industry they were known as "pure" (horizontal), while if they covered a number of successive industries, they were called "mixed" (vertical).

Banking in Germany also assisted in the building up of Kartells. Banking was late in developing in Germany, the Darmstädter Bank being founded in 1853, the Discount Bank in 1856, the Deutsche Bank in 1870, the Dresdner Bank in 1872, and the Reichsbank in 1875. But it has made up for its lateness by developing a vigorous industrial policy. The peculiarity of German banking in contrast with English banking is the policy of financing industry. German banks and German industries are indissolubly linked together, and German banks direct industrial policy to a considerable degree. Thus German banks encouraged the formation of Kartells when they saw it was to the interest of both finance and industry.

Social Insurance formed a prominent part of state legislation affecting industry in the 'eighties and 'nineties, and comprises Germany's greatest contribution on the side of state aid. On the other hand, Germany was very backward in the matter of industrial legislation affecting hours and wages and working conditions. There Bismarck drew the line and refused to carry further interference in the relations between employers and employed. The chief landmarks in the programme of Social Insurance were the Law of 1883 insuring workers against sickness, the Law of 1884 providing for compensation to workmen for industrial accidents, and the Law of 1888 insuring against incapacity and old age. These insurance schemes were on a contributory basis, and England drew on German experience when it set up its own insurance schemes some quarter of a century later.

With the industrial development of Germany the German workers have built up a strong labour movement, organized in trade unions on the one hand and in the Social Democratic Party on the other. Germans, like Frenchmen and unlike Englishmen, are capable of enthusiasm for an abstract idea. That idea Karl Marx supplied. Unlike both Frenchmen and Englishmen, Germans are capable of discipline to a high degree and will accept centralized authority readily. Trade unions in Germany have grown outwards from the centre and are strongly centralized, whereas in England they tend to be federations which only delegate so much power to the centre and in France they tend to be organized on the basis of almost complete local autonomy. Thus the German labour movement was far more capable of a concerted national policy than either the English or the French. The English trade union and labour movements grew up in an atmosphere of comparative freedom and prosperity, and they bore the marks of it in their comparative peacefulness and reformist programmes. The German and French trade union and labour movements, on the other hand, grew up in an atmosphere of repression, and they showed the marks of it in their revolutionary and sometimes violent spirit. It was not till 1892 that trade unions were properly legalized in Germany, and by that time the Marxian doctrines of class war and revolution had obtained firm hold. In the years that followed, however, as in France, opinion split into hostile schools, the reformist or revisionist and the revolutionary, and as concessions were granted and conditions were improved, the revisionists became stronger and stronger. In addition to the Social Democratic trade unions there were also Christian trade unions which were friendly to the existing system and did not desire to overthrow it either by peaceful or violent revolution and Liberal trade unions which concentrated on an immediate economic programme. The employers, however, were still more strongly organized—they insured each other against strikes and lock-outs—and this explains why trade unions achieved so little.

The reasons for the great success of Germany in its industrial development in the period of the Empire, apart from its natural resources and strong government, were manifold. The protectionist tariff gave confidence to industrialists to expand their production. Technical education and the attention paid to research were bound to yield fruit. The railways and canals were used as State instruments for the helping of industry by means of exceptional tariffs. The German workers were cheap, well-disciplined, and highly efficient. The German women also played their part, as they are the best housekeepers in the world. The banks assisted, by their policy of industrial loans and of entering wholeheartedly into co-operation with industry. The German Jews played an important rôle in finance and commerce and also in industry, with the exception of coal and iron. Finally, the Kartells enabled German industries to make the most of the tariff-protected home market and also to develop marketing abroad to the utmost. All these factors help to explain why a country that was mediaeval at the opening of the nineteenth century, and was only emerging from mediaevalism in the middle of the century should, by the beginning of the twentieth century, have become one of the leading industrial countries of the world.

CHAPTER 3

RUSSIA AND THE INDUSTRIAL REVOLUTION

The economic reconstruction of Russia in the nineteenth century.

The year 1856 (end of the Crimean War) is the dividing line between mediaeval and modern times in Russia.

The three great factors are :—

(1) The emancipation of the serfs. 1861–6.
(2) The coming of the railways.
(3) The transition from natural to money economy.

Significance of geographical conditions in Russia in relation to its economic history.

Climate.
The forest zone.
The Black Earth Zone.
The steppes.
The proximity to Asia.
The rivers.

Industrial organization before the Emancipation.

(*a*) State factories to provide manufactures necessary for national safety—armaments—army clothing.
(*b*) Seigniorial factories on nobles' estates. Influence of serfdom on the modern factory system in Russia. Industry and agriculture connected. Fundamental difference in Russian and W. European factory organization.
(*c*) Co-operation (the *artel*) as a feature of Russian social organization.
(*d*) The co-operative workshop (*svietelka*) and the home work trades (*kustari*).

The Industrial Development of Russia.

Growth of the cotton industry—Knoop.
Opposition of Moscow and Polish cotton regions.
Development of iron industry in the South in Donetz basin by Hughes.
Development of naphtha industry.
Foreign capital in Russian industry.
Vigorous ministry of Witte (1893–1903).
Social legislation.
Trade Unions repressed until 1906.

OF the European Great Powers France began to modernize itself as a result of the French Revolution : Germany followed in the first half of the nineteenth century ; but Russia, immune from the effects of the French Revolution, did not begin to become modernized till after the middle of the century. The three great transforming processes were the emancipation of the serfs, by which the bulk of the

Russian population became free, the coming of the railways, and the transition from a natural to a money economy. Of these three processes the emancipation of the serfs has already been dealt with.[1]

The second transforming process, the advent of the railways. materially modified the situation consequent on geographical conditions in Russia. There is no country in the world to which railways have meant and will mean so much as to Russia. The country is very flat and experiences great extremes of climate. The rainfall is small and there are no mountain ranges to shelter Russia from the winds from the North Pole. Thus the cold and the drought between them make the country unsuitable on the whole for canals. The greatest river, the Volga, flows into the Caspian and does not lead to the open sea. The Sea of Azof, into which the Don flows, freezes over in winter. The White Sea is closed a large part of the year by ice. Even the Baltic ports are frozen up in the winter months. Hence there is not only no coasting trade, but access to Russia is very difficult during the winter season except over the land frontier. The North American colonies at the end of the eighteenth century communicated with each other by way of the coast. Russia was only connected in winter by sleighing over the snow. In Russia the railways compensate for the lack of coast ; they counteract the ice and the drought ; they unite the country and they make the transport of bulky goods possible.

While Russia as a country has always had to grapple with transport difficulties, its very variety of regions and products has demanded that these difficulties be overcome.

In the north of Russia there is a great belt of forest in which very little corn is grown. Below that comes a stretch of some of the richest agricultural country in the world—the Black Earth Zone, which was supposed until recently to be so rich as to need no manure and to be inexhaustible. It is a treeless region and in the past has been largely dependent on the forest zone for fuel and for building materials. Then below the Black Earth Zone comes the zone of treeless steppe. It is capable of being tilled, but the great difficulty is the absence of rain. Rain falls in the spring and autumn but there are sometimes intervals of a year with no rain at all. This region, too, suffers

[1] See *Russian Agriculture*, part ii, chap. iv.

from lack of wood and building materials. Further south and east, again, comes a region of treeless, salt, stony steppe only suitable for grazing and inhabited by nomads. The North therefore needs the grain of the South and the South needs the wood of the North. To these regions the railway came as the great necessary link for transport and colonizing purposes. It made fuel available and enabled the iron, coal, and petroleum deposits to be exploited. Also it made it possible to extend the cultivation of cotton. The railway has accordingly been the great economic power in Russia, developing industry on the one hand and on the other enabling the cultivation of the Black Earth Zone and the steppe to be extended. It has also been the great factor in extending Russian trade in the East. The sea approaches are practically in the hands of the English, but the land route is a monopoly for Russia. Hence, largely, the Siberian railway, the penetration into Persia, and Russia's interest in Manchuria. The railway made possible the expansion of Russia's cotton industry by permitting Russian manufactures to reach the wider markets of Asia, when the home market was too poor to absorb more.

The third transforming process in Russian development in the middle of the nineteenth century was the transition from a natural to a money economy. One of the most characteristic features of Russia before 1850 was the absence of money. Peter the Great and his successors had been possessed by the dominating idea of getting money into the country. Their purpose was to export more than they imported, so that money should flow into Russia. Prohibitive tariffs were imposed to prevent the buying of foreign manufactures and to stimulate the export trade so that there should be a balance payable in bullion. The policy achieved little success, since the country as a whole, and even the economic units within the country, were largely self-sufficing. Before 1850 the basis of practically all transactions was still services and payments in kind. There was no market inside Russia, since the people had no wants. It was really in the same position as Western Europe before the time of the Crusades.

The foundations of a money economy were laid when Russia began to export wheat to England through Odessa. The railway greatly facilitated the development of wheat and other bulky exports, and Russia received the bullion in return and was able to raise the loans which were necessary for introducing money payments. Finally, the emancipation of the serfs necessitated a money economy. The freed peasants had to pay in money the taxes with which their land was burdened. In so far as the lord hired them, he had to pay them wages. All this meant that the land had to produce a surplus which had to be marketed and converted into cash, and of this the railways were the instruments. Nevertheless, so unused was Russia to a money economy, and so short was the supply of money, that it was one of the constant pre-occupations of the Russian Government during the remainder of the century to bring about a favourable balance of trade and to keep within the country the bullion which was the necessary basis of the new society.

The development of a money economy meant the reconstruction of society in Russia. Relationships based on status and custom gave way to new relationships based on contract and law. Self-sufficiency yielded to production on a scale providing a surplus for a market. Competition began to operate. Middlemen grew up to bridge the gulf between country and town. Partial mobility was permitted to the peasants who could now move to the towns and enter industry if they received the permission of their fellows. Modern industrialism began to grow up, and the divorce commenced between agriculture and industry.

The father of industrialism in Russia was Peter the Great (1689–1725). As a result of his travels in Europe he was very anxious to develop Russia along the lines of the mercantile system. But there was no money in the country to pay an army or a fleet, nor was it possible without capital to start the necessary manufactures of clothing, gunpowder, and cannon for the army, let alone to pay the ordinary expenses of the administration. In Europe, in the ordinary way, the towns and the rich merchants stood by the King and provided the necessary money in the way of advances or by paying taxes. But in Russia there was no middle class since the trade was in the hands of foreigners, at first of the Hanse League, and later of the English and the Dutch. To provide the things required, factories had to be started by the State. Peasants from the State and Crown lands formed the first source of labour supply for industry. An additional labour supply was found in prisoners of war, beggars, criminals, orphans, and the wives of soldiers on service. In this way was started a cloth manufactory to clothe the army. The State taxes were taken in wool, which was taken to the royal factories. In the same way was established the manufacture of saltpetre, gunfounding, sailcloth, arms, and other necessary things. The peasants were frequently attached to a factory for ever and were sold with it. Later on they were handed over to private manufacturers. While the State thus made its serfs into permanent factory hands in what were termed "proprietary" factories, it regulated their hours of labour, gave them legal rights against their masters, and forbade their being sold apart from the factory. The work in these factories, not being voluntary labour, was not of a high order, and little progress seems to have been made until after the middle of the nineteenth century, when it became possible to work a factory with free labour.

So great was the lack of enterprise that, in order to encourage them, special privileges were granted to factory owners. They were free from military service and their produce was sold to the State. At the close of Peter the Great's reign there were 233 State and private factories and foundries.[1]

Another class of industrial establishments consisted of the "estate" factories which grew up in the eighteenth century. The nobles set up certain manufactures on their estates and a certain number of serfs were made to work in the workshops, instead of giving labour in the fields. The nobles who had no such factories would sell or hire out their manufacturing serfs for service elsewhere. In Russia, therefore, manufactures were primarily a State or aristocratic affair. There was no special class of manufacturers.

A third type of industrial unit sprang from the estate factories. In these factories the peasants learned the arts of manufacture and in their turn taught those arts to the members of the family who remained at home. Home industries sprang up at which the peasants worked in winter, and the noble often found it more profitable to give out work to be done in the peasants' homes rather than to force people into the factory. Thus the factory and the domestic workshop developed side by side.

On the emancipation of the serfs the freed workers gave up working in the nobles' factories and the nobles lacked the

[1] J. Mavor, *Economic History of Russia*, vol. i, p. 124.

training or the capacity to carry on the factories on capitalistic lines. Sometimes they were sold, but more often they died out. The State or proprietary factories, on the other hand, had to take on wage-earning artisans, and they developed along modern capitalistic lines. They were in many cases glad to be rid of the obligation to employ the workpeople attached to the factory. Thus the emancipation of the serfs prepared the way for a wage-earning class. There were, however, features which made Russian industrial life quite different from that of Western Europe. These features were the close connection between industry and agriculture, the Russian workers' faculty for co-operation, and the importance of home work.

In the first place, the object at the emancipation was to make every Russian peasant a landowner. There was to be no proletariat class divorced from the land. The result was the slow growth of a definite factory class, since the attraction of the land remained and work in factories was deemed only temporary. Housing attached to the factories or located in the big towns was generally bad, but then residence there was only temporary. The extraordinarily low rate of wages was explained by the fact that the workers carried on agricultural work in summer and were not entirely dependent on the employer for their maintenance. Again, the very long hours of work would have been impossible had it not been for the yearly change to agricultural employment. At the same time, despite the low wages and long hours, the Russian worker was so inefficient and required so much supervision that the Polish worker who received higher wages was far cheaper.

Secondly, the Russians showed an extraordinary capacity for combining under a leader to do definite work. This form of organization was called the *artel.* It was known in the tenth century, and in the nineteenth century was to be found on every side of life, in industry, agriculture, lending societies, and insurance societies. The principle was that each member had to perform his share of the work and shared equally in the profits, and there was no capitalistic element. They selected a headman who did the bargaining—the *starosta.* They were to be found in mining, agriculture, and transport, and all the work connected with loading and unloading was contracted out to artels. There were also travelling artels of carpenters and masons, consisting of from 20 to 200 people who could not obtain work in the village all the year round. "They consist of peasants who are unable to obtain means of subsistence in the villages during the whole year and are obliged to seek work in the towns for several months. Each artel includes from 20 to 200 persons who live in the same village or in neighbouring villages. Preparations for the migration to the towns are made several months before it takes place. Towards the middle of January, the president of the artel (*starosta*) proceeds to the town to negotiate with a contractor (*riadtchik*) and arrange the terms of agreement. If he succeeds in obtaining work the members of the artel set out together from their homes on a certain day, generally some time after Easter, and travel to the town. Cheap special trains are run for their benefit. The contracts expire on October 8 for carpenters, and for masons on November 22, and the artels then return to the village for the winter. The *starosta* receives the whole amount of wages due to the artel and divides it among the members, according to their age and ability. . . . Difficulties rarely arise between the members of the artel and their employer, or amongst the members. All differences between the members are arranged by the *starosta* or by the general meeting. . . . By belonging to an artel the peasants secure certainty of work and a fixed wage as long as the association continues; and as the members are drawn from the same locality, they are never in the isolated position of single workmen, even when they are at a distance from their own homes. From a social point of view the artels appear to be very beneficial. As has been shown, the members as a whole are responsible for the work and general conduct of each individual member; consequently they keep strict watch over one another to see that none are idle or disorderly while the others work. The carpenters and masons and other temporary artels are instrumental in preserving the rural character of the working population of which they are composed. As all the members return every year to spend several months in their own province, the artels help to diminish the number of workmen who are periodically thrown out of employment and are entirely cut off from their native locality."[1] The employer is under no obligation to pension these people and they find it easier to deal with

[1] *Royal Commission on Labour: Foreign Reports*, vol. x. Russia [C–7063–xiv], 1894, p. 60.

one man. It will thus be seen that Russian workers were nomadic to a degree little realized in Western Europe.

The third peculiarity of Russian industrial life was the *kustar* or home-work trades carried on very often in co-operative workshops (*svietelka*). During the long winters the peasants had plenty of time on their hands and the more enterprising among them formed co-operative associations for the production of every kind of manufactured article. They formed themselves into an artel and started a workshop. Every kind of spinning, weaving and metal work, and the production of almost every article that could be made out of wood, bone or leather, was made in those *svietelka*. The number of people thus employed at the beginning of the century was stated as between 7 and 8 million at a time when 3 to 4 million were employed in factories.[1] In Russia accordingly home industries remained more important than factory industries. It was thought possible, therefore, on account of the three features described, that Russia might evolve along lines different from Western Europe, and that some alternative system to capitalism might be established. Sir D. M. Wallace, however, was of opinion that the artel was becoming capitalistic—the headman being a contractor.[2] Others believed that even home work was developing on capitalistic lines. Finally came the land reforms in the first decade of the new century, and the link between agriculture and industry was at last in the fair way of being snapped.

Up to 1850, then, Russia was a peasant Empire living by agriculture of a primitive type and supplying its wants by home industries or from the estate factories of the nobles, or from proprietary factories. Only one industry was being organized on capitalistic lines, that is to say, cotton. In the latter half of the nineteenth century the emancipation put on the market a supply of cheap labour; the construction of railways in all directions increased a hundredfold the means of communication; new banks and credit institutions were opening up; there was a great influx of foreign capital; coal and oil, iron and cotton went ahead and the South developed a great iron industry. The industrial revolution in Russia had begun.

In the great protectionist period after 1824 the cotton

[1] G. Drage, *Russian Affairs*, p. 185.
[2] Sir D. M. Wallace, *Russia*, p. 92.

industry settled round Moscow. The Oka and the Volga connect the district with the South and East while the forest zone on the North furnished both fuel and labour, and Nijni Novgorod with its great annual fair supplied a great market. By the Volga supplies of raw cotton could be got from the Levant and Persia, and when wood began to get scarce naphtha oil could be procured for fuel by the same route. Moreover, cotton goods suit the Russian peasant because they are cheap and bright.[1]

The Russian cotton industry owes much to a German, Ludwig Knoop, who was sent out to Russia in 1839 by an English firm to sell yarn. Instead of that he devoted his life to establishing and building up the industry of cotton spinning by machinery, until it was said that spinning factories were as numerous in Russia as churches.[2] But there was another district which also took up cotton spinning, and that was Poland. Poland possessed certain advantages over Russia, inasmuch as it could get American raw cotton and also it had a supply of more intelligent labour. The result was that the Moscow manufacturer began to agitate for an import duty on raw cotton, they themselves being supplied by Asia. For the same reason they agitated for duties on coal. They were supplied by the Volga with naphtha.

After the freeing of the serfs a system of utilizing foreign capital and home savings for industrial development was instituted. Neither the landowner nor the serfs had the energy, enterprise, or intelligence to carry out great undertakings—that had to be done by the foreigner. The railways from the 'sixties onward were partly instrumental in attracting foreign capital and awakening a capitalistic instinct in the country, and the foundation of banks was another cause. But till the 'eighties neither the freeing of the peasants, nor the railways, nor the banks, did much for industry. The peasantry stuck to agriculture and the railways chiefly stimulated the export of corn. As a matter

[1] G. Drago, *Russian Affairs*, pp. 158–9.

[2] "When the mills were started about forty-five years ago British carders, weavers, and spinners, as also managers and assistant managers, were brought over from the United Kingdom to set things going and organize the cotton industry on a stable basis. The managers and foremen in many mills are still Lancashire men, and the result has been that the machinery ordered has been and still is almost exclusively of British manufacture, the small balance coming from Alsace."—*Consular Report, Moscow*, for 1910, p. 9.

of fact the emancipation led to industrial retrogression, since the peasantry after the emancipation left the old estate factories, and the Ural iron works languished for want of hands.

Up to the end of the 'seventies the railways were almost completely built out of foreign material. The existing works were given large orders by the Government at high prices, concessions for new undertakings were given on very favourable terms, but nothing seemed to make the iron industry flourish till an Englishman, John Hughes, who was given extraordinary privileges, built iron works in 1871, in the South at Ekaterinoslav, where iron and coal lie near together. In 1876 the railways had to take half their rails from the home factories. For 12 years the steel factories had bounties on steel production. Then it was found that factories were importing foreign iron and were working it up. This was stopped by a continuous rise in the iron duties. The desire to develop their own resources and attract foreign capital was the foundation idea of the protectionist movement.

One great effect of the high tariff was to tempt in foreign capital to develop industries inside the tariff wall, and a great industrial development which had begun in the 'eighties was continued in the 'nineties. Russia began to develop the great coalfields and the iron mines of South Russia as well as the naphtha industry. This southern district has been almost entirely developed by foreign capital. In 1879 Nobel's, the Norwegian firm, founded the Society of Petroleum Industry, and in 1883 a French company, the Society of the Caspian and the Black Sea, was established with the support of the French Rothschilds. A great deal of English capital was also invested in Russian petroleum companies, both at Baku and Grozny.[1] The district of Ekaterinoslav, where John Hughes built his works in 1871, was entirely desert. It became a settlement for some 10,000 workmen. In 1880 a French company with a capital of 5,000,000 francs set up an iron works in South Russia and a great deal of Belgian capital was put into this part of the country in 1889. In 1891 a French company set up an iron and steel works and this was followed up by an ambitious Russo-Belgian company. The coal industry was started in the same way by foreign capital.

[1] M. S. Miller, *Economic Development of Russia, 1905–14*, p. 266.

It will thus be seen how great a part was played by foreign capital in the industrial development of Russia. Not only did foreign capitalists create new industrial centres: they contributed to the diffusion of technical knowledge, they gave an example of initiative, and they developed a spirit of enterprise. The reason for the enormous industrial development was to be found in the great railway construction which was going on. Great quantities of rails were needed and the Government made it a condition of obtaining orders that the works should be set up in the country itself. On the other hand, the railways, when built, enabled commodities to be carried cheaply and thus further advanced industrial development.

The industrialization of Russia that was proceeding during the 'eighties and 'nineties reached its height during the vigorous ministry of Count Witte (1893–1903). The building of the Siberian Railway not only reacted on agriculture and settlement but caused a boom in the iron and coal industries by reason of the demand for railway material. The completion of the railway between 1900 and 1905 led to increased sales of Russian cottons in China, but on the other hand it meant a slump in iron and coal. Industrial depression set in about 1903 and lasted till 1908. It was accentuated by the Russo-Japanese War, and culminated in the labour strikes and demonstrations of 1905. Gradually the depression lifted, and from 1908 to 1914 there was a period of very rapid industrialization in Russia. Fresh capital was invested in the industries, labour was being trained to run machinery, native capitalists were arising, and the output of all the chief industries increased, with the exception of naphtha or petroleum. Cotton spindles rose from 7,350,683 in 1905 to 8,448,818 in 1911, and cotton looms from 178,506 in 1905 to 220,000 in 1911. Between 1904 and 1913 South Russia expanded its output of pig-iron from 110·6 million poods to 189·7 million poods and its output of manufactured iron from 72·8 million poods to 141 million poods. The coal mined in the Donetz coalfield increased from 785·3 million poods in 1905 to 1,506·9 million poods in 1913. Petroleum, however, fell from 631 million poods in 1900 to 455 in 1905, rose again to 588 in 1910, but fell again to 561 in 1913.[1] It seems that the progress made by Russian industry under

[1] M. S. Miller, *Economic Development of Russia, 1905–14*, pp. 285–92.

capitalism in the years before the War is quite comparable with the progress planned for Russia in recent times.

In Russian industry paternalism was strong, both on the part of the employer and the State. This paternalism dated from the beginnings of industry in the proprietary and estate factories. From the earliest days houses or barracks had to be built to house the workers, and in the case of the proprietary factories the State interfered to regulate hours and working conditions. It was only in the later days that workers were left to fend for themselves. More typical was the following description: "On the employer fell the heavy financial responsibility of housing his workmen in barracks, of providing hospitals, theatres, recreation grounds, evening lectures for them, day nurseries in which their children might be cared for while the parents worked in the factory, and schools where they could be educated." [1] During the 'eighties social legislation began to be passed, and gradually hours and conditions were regulated, inspectors were appointed to enforce the law, workmen's compensation was introduced, and even health insurance was established. So *pari passu* with the development of industrial technique went the development of industrial and social legislation. This legislation was quite in the Russian tradition, and was never a battleground between conflicting schools of opinion as in *laissez-faire* England and individualistic America.

The tradition of autocratic paternalism in Russia meant on the one hand that the State protected the vital interests of the workers, but on the other hand that the State would scarcely allow organizations of the workers to protect themselves. Factory industry developed late in Russia, but trade unions developed still later on account of the government's repressive policy. Thus it came about that trade unions in Russia were as much political bodies as economic organizations, and their ancestry was the blood-stained one of secret societies, such as the Narodniki, the Narodnaya Volya, and finally the Bolsheviki. The governmental fear of trade unions was political rather than economic, and recalls the period of trade union repression in England at the beginning of the nineteenth century. Trade unions in England, however, grew up largely out of friendly societies, but under a system of autocratic

[1] Miller, p. 230.

paternalism there was little need for friendly societies, and Russian trade unions from their birth were fighting organizations. Although repressed, trade unions continually sprang up in Russia but as speedily collapsed after a riotous stoppage, police raids, imprisonments, and transportations to Siberia. Then came the great upheaval of 1905, which was partly economic and partly political. One upshot was a law of 1906 permitting the existence of trade unions as economic organizations but forbidding strikes.[1] Despite this prohibition strikes broke out, and then they became sedition and attempted revolution. Nevertheless, with the growing prosperity of 1908–14 strikes became less common, though the strike in the Lena goldfields caused a considerable stir in 1912 and 1913, and it seemed possible that the Russian labour movement might ultimately develop along peaceful, evolutionary lines. Then came the War and the Revolution, when the Bolsheviki were able to seize power through their secret society organization and through the organization of the industrial workers.

The industrial development of Russia after the middle of the nineteenth century is a record that is dramatic in the extreme. It is comparable with the industrial development of the United States, Russia being 50 to 100 years behind. Both countries required capital, but while both borrowed the capital the United States had skill, initiative, and enterprise of its own as well as a better climate and better communications, and thus its development was the more rapid of the two. During the first half of that century Russia was a mediaeval country with its economic life based on serfdom and a self-sufficing economy. Then came the rapid transformation of Russia into a modern State. The serfs were freed, railways were built, money was introduced, production of crops for the market became important, large industries grew up in cotton, iron, coal, and oil, banks were opened, capital was borrowed from abroad, and a large class of town workers developed. Industrial development had begun in the 'eighties and after a short interruption in 1903–8 was proceeding more rapidly than ever up to 1914. Into this rapid transformation burst the War, bringing the work of modernization very definitely to an end for the time being.

[1] Miller, p. 235.

CHAPTER 4

Industrial Development in the United States

I. 1783–1865, i.e. to end of the Civil War.
The creation of a nation out of thirteen colonies.

II. 1865–1914.
The Rise of the United States as a world power.

Period I is concerned with the question of uniting the States so as to form an economic whole, with the tariff policy to be pursued by the new State, with the expansion into hitherto undeveloped territory, with the growing divergence on economic questions between the North and the South, ending in war.

Period II is concerned with the reconstruction after the war. The Tariff policy becomes fixed as protective. Cotton growing is enormously extended in the South, cotton manufacturing is started in the South on a large scale. There is a rapid development of railways, iron and coal are brought cheaply together, steel develops. The problems to be solved are the control of the railways, the control of trusts, immigration.

Period I. 1783–1865

1783–1816.

Reconstruction after the War of Independence.

The Question of Union.

The essential divergencies between the States.

The necessity for economic union and a strong central government—

(i) To enforce the observance of treaty obligations.

(ii) To strengthen the economic position of the nation.

Federal Constitution agreed on, 1788. Abolition of tariffs between States. Reconstruction along national lines begun by Alexander Hamilton.

Foundation of National Bank.

Expansion of American trade to 1808.

Embargoes by France and later by England on American trade lead to War of 1812 and the foundation of an industrial system.

Effect of the War, 1812–14.

(*a*) Almost complete cessation of imports. Growth of home manufactures. Ruin of these after the peace. Result: Protective tariff of 1816.

(*b*) Increased migration West owing to depression.

1816–33.

Struggle over high or low tariff.

Antagonism between North and South emerges.

1833–65.

Crises of 1837 and 1857.

The expansion West and the Californian gold discoveries.

Development of Factory System.

Industrial development rapid after 1850, but still "Cotton is King".

Climax of antagonism between North and South.

Period II—after 1865

Unrestricted industrial development and unrestricted competitive methods until the 'nineties.

- Emergence of a great manufacturing nation.
- Growth of iron and steel industries spectacular.
  - New iron deposits discovered suitable for Bessemer steel.
- Growth of cotton and iron manufactures in the South.
- Formation of Trusts.
- The Labour Movement and its discouraging conditions.

After the 'nineties, controlled development.

- Trusts and Railways brought under control.

THERE have been two conspicuous turning points in the economic history of the United States. First there was the revolt from England and the subsequent task of forming the thirteen States into some sort of a Union. The second great landmark is the Civil War in the 'sixties with its final outcome of the Union, economic and political. In the United States, as in Germany, the nineteenth century is important as the era of State building.

After the peace of 1783, the pressure of economic events made it essential that there should be some authority capable of negotiating treaties and regulating trade, and, largely owing to the influence of Alexander Hamilton, this power was gradually entrusted, although amid great opposition, to the central government. Then the Government, having assumed responsibility for trade, the next question was what should be its policy, free trade or protection ? Should the American Government encourage manufactures or should the country be primarily a producer of raw materials ? Among the other problems were some resembling those which Russia had to face. Both countries have vast land areas which have only been welded into unity by the railway. Both have had great empty lands to settle.

After the Civil War the abolition of slavery led to a change in the whole character of the South. The great slave plantations were broken up and the methods of production altered. Northern capital was invested in the South and the development which took place made for homogeneity. In the place of two regions, differing radically from one another, the rise of a nation is seen. Another result of the war was to throw the United States back to a system of protection. After the war there was an extraordinary expansion in iron, cotton, and other manufactures; a great grain export grew up; and with these there emerged the vast and difficult questions connected with railroad combinations, business monopolies, and immigration.

Before the Civil War, American economic history falls into three main periods: (1) A period between 1783 and 1816, when the chief questions are those connected with the economic union of the States, the tariff (the policy on which swings round from free trade to protection), and the settlement of public lands. (2) The period 1816–33, during which the tariff is the dominating issue. It is here that the divergence of the North from the South is strongly brought out. The South is intensely jealous of the North, and, as an agricultural exporting country wishing to buy its manufactures cheaply, is free trade. If it pays duty on manufactures it is subsidizing the North. A protective tariff is regarded as a tribute paid by the South to the Northern manufacturers. The North is protectionist. From 1789–1815 there was a system of low tariffs; from 1816–33 a protective tariff. In 1833 the South forced a series of low tariffs on the North and the outcome of the Civil War was to send the whole country back to protection. And, quite distinct from the antagonism on the question of high or low tariffs, there is the strong opposition on the part of the South to any sort of encroachment by the central government on their State rights; and during this period there emerges the difficulty as to whether the new States should be "slave" or "free", ending with the Missouri Compromise of 1820.

The third period (1833–65) is the period of national expansion. The chief questions which arise during this period are those connected with the movement westwards, the struggle as to whether the new territories should be slave states or free, and the development of manufactures. It is also the era of low tariffs. The period closes with the secession of the South.

1783–1865

Throughout the whole period of the War of Independence the States were not a nation but merely a loose and jealous confederation of States. There was a Council of State representatives, which was a Congress not unlike the German Diet, but each State was independent of its neighbours. Each had the right of regulating its own customs and there was no machinery and no law by which a State could be forced to do anything it did not care to do. Congress was not a governing body; it was merely a Council of allied States. It is true that it had to raise an army, build a fleet, issue paper money, and raise loans; but these things were only done because of the exigencies of the war. In action it was feeble, irresolute, and ineffectual.

The aim of the States in taking up arms was independence, and they had no more idea of vesting in Congress part of the sovereignty thus acquired than they had of vesting it in King George. They had fought for freedom, and once the war was over each State was determined to go its own way as a sovereign and independent body.

At the end of the War in 1783 the tie which had bound the States together was loosened and a central government had to be created. There was a bitter and intense feeling of jealousy between the different States. The tariffs of each State varied as their economic condition differed. The East wanted a Navigation Act; the South wanted free imports; the Central States objected to both. The States with free trade or low duties smuggled goods over the land frontiers into the protected States. Congress was powerless, and until it had the right to deal with trade matters there could be no effective action.

Meanwhile American trade was suffering from the closing of the West Indies. Having broken away from the mother country they had to take the consequences, which were serious enough. The shipping between the West Indies and England was confined to British ships and the carrying trade of the North Americans was extinguished. The access to the fisheries which England had conceded was of no value, since the sale of salted fish in the West Indies had ceased. No united front as against England was possible owing to the intense mutual jealousy that existed among the States.

Nor was American industry or agriculture flourishing. Before the war America produced nothing but coarse domestic manufactures for home consumption and even they did not satisfy the home demand. In the South were the great estates producing tobacco, rice, and some cotton and indigo. In the Middle Colonies and New England there was a system of small farms and the produce raised was corn, butter, cheese, and cattle. The chief trade had been with the West Indies. There was a large fishing and shipbuilding trade, and ships could be built much cheaper in the United States than anywhere else. Tropical agriculture in the South and subsistence agriculture in the North were the characteristics of America. When the colonies broke off from England they were suddenly deprived of their sources of manufactured supplies and they were thus forced to attempt to supply themselves with the things that were found to be lacking. Subsidies and prizes were given for the manufacture of woollens and iron. Congress itself established several manufactures. Gradually a few manufactures began to develop, but very slowly, as capital and workmen were both lacking. But after the peace the shipbuilding trade was ruined; quantities of goods poured in from England; there was such a glut that English goods were sold cheaper in the colonies than in the country of their origin, and the whole of their industries collapsed. Agriculture suffered too, for the farmers could no longer sell at fancy prices to the British, French, and American armies; and the fishing trade had been ruined during the war. And even had they wished it there was no hope of being able to put on a tariff against England, as the States were hopelessly divided, and indeed were carrying on a tariff war amongst themselves.

But not merely was there this collapse in trade, manufactures and shipping. There was also a currency crisis. The British merchants declined to supply goods except for specie or other goods, since there was no means of enforcing the collection of debts. Specie flowed out, so that the country was reduced to barter in pork, tobacco, whisky, and salt. The coin was so clipped that it had to be weighed. Foreign loans were not to be had on any terms. The interest on loans already raised was not paid. Congress could get no money, and not merely were American applications refused in Europe: they were derided. In 1786 Congress issued paper money. The exchange value of the dollar was a penny. Laws were passed, as in France, to coerce the shopkeepers. The judges held that such laws were illegal and in Rhode Island they were dismissed. In Massachusetts there was civil war.

Once American commerce was deprived of the powerful protection afforded by the British fleet, it began to suffer from the depredations of the Barbary pirates who infested American harbours and sold captured Americans into slavery. Both Washington and Hamilton saw that a strong central government was needed to rescue the country from anarchy and to restore credit and regulate trade.

The forces of disunion were very powerful. The States were on the verge of war with each other; their economic interests were conflicting; and in addition there was the difficulty of communication. In 1787 Boston was as far removed from Philadelphia in time as New York is to-day from London. South Carolina was as remote as Cape Town. The remotest dependencies of Great Britain are now more accessible than the North and the South were to one another in those days. Bad roads, rivers without bridges or ferries, roving Indians and highwaymen, were some of the difficulties in the way of easy communication.

The Federal Constitution was agreed on at the Convention of Philadelphia of 1787 and confirmed by the States in 1788. To consolidate the Union the debts of the various States were assumed by the Central Government. To this there was determined opposition by the States that had low debts, who objected to have to pay part of the interest of the States that had heavy debts. The States with low debts were in the South, and the South was placated by the placing of the capital, Washington, there. But the purpose of Hamilton, who was responsible for this policy, was "to bind the moneyed classes firmly to the central government; to induce them to look to that quarter for the security of their capital and the punctuality of their dividends; to fix their interests in it rather than in the State governments." [1]

He further established a National Bank in 1791—another step towards allying property with, and creating credit under the guarantee of, the Constitution. This was bitterly opposed by the Democrats because they saw it was tending to centralization. They opposed it as an invasion of State rights and as something contrary to the Constitution. But with the power to regulate commerce vested in Congress and with its assumption of responsibility for financial obligations, confidence in the new nation began to grow, and when the Federal Government was fairly established there was a steady increase of prosperity. In 1791 a loan of 2½ million florins was successfully and speedily taken up in Holland and the subscriptions to the National Bank were covered without much difficulty.

The period following the establishment of the Union

[1] F. S. Oliver, *Alexander Hamilton*, p. 224.

was characterized by a remarkable expansion of American commerce. During the Napoleonic Wars, up to 1808, the United States as a neutral picked up the greater part of the carrying trade of the world. They had always possessed a shipbuilding trade and fisheries—two of the best training grounds for seamen. They did the trade between the French colonies and the mother country and a large part of the trade of Russia, Sweden, Germany, France, and even England. Their ships, being those of a neutral, were not liable to capture. Accordingly the shipments of West Indian sugar increased from 75,000 pounds in 1791 to 35,000,000 pounds in 1796. The tonnage of American vessels rose from 127,329 tons to 848,306. Also the United States had a great entrepôt trade in all colonial products. The capital possessed by the country was not very great, but what existed was nearly all absorbed in shipbuilding, and there was little for investment on any substantial scale in manufacturing concerns. Still, great changes were in progress which prepared the way for the introduction of capitalist industry. One of these was represented by the invention of the cotton gin by Whitney in 1793. Then Samuel Slater, who had worked in a cotton machinery manufactory in England, was able to reproduce from memory Arkwright's machine, and he set up the first cotton plant in 1790 in Pawtucket, Rhode Island. These innovations encouraged the supply of cotton in the South, so that the value of the cotton crop increased from $30,000 in 1792 to $15,000,000 in 1810, an advance which was bound materially to increase the capital of the country. Tobacco, as a crop, gave place to cotton, and this led, as will be seen, to the expansion westward of the American nation. But it was a change to a system which was well adapted to slave labour and it gave a firm economic foundation to the slave system. As during the period of the industrial revolution in England [1] so in America, the accumulation of capital and the opening up of markets were the main factors which brought in machinery. Capital reserves were gradually being built up out of the profits from shipping and cotton. A market was being created by the improvements in internal transport. Owing to the absence of roads, internal trade was more difficult than foreign commerce. It was easiest to bring goods by sea.

[1] See Knowles, *Industrial and Commercial Revolutions*, p. 28.

Roads were built partly with government grants and partly by turnpikes; canals were constructed, especially after 1812; and it became possible to supply an internal market. But the shipping industry, which absorbed so much of the available capital, suffered a grave check in 1806–7 with the Orders in Council and the Berlin and Milan Decrees. Neutral traders were shut off from the continent and American commerce suffered almost complete suspension.

America tried retaliation. England wanted corn and cotton; France wanted colonial produce and saltpetre; and the United States hoped, by cutting off all trade, to force the hands of France and England and to make their position impossible. Accordingly the Embargo Act was passed in 1807 forbidding any American or foreign vessel to leave the ports of the country. A certain amount of smuggling went on, but American commerce suffered heavily, and the Act failed to accomplish its purpose of coercing France and England into withdrawing their prohibitions. The Act was replaced in 1809 by the Non-Intercourse Act, which prohibited commercial intercourse between the United States and France and Great Britain. The great struggle ended in war. France was trying to force England on to her knees and England was bound in sheer self-preservation to attack French trade. She could not, therefore, tolerate that trade should be carried on in neutral ships. War broke out in 1812 and only ended with the Treaty of Ghent in 1814–15. The war produced the almost complete cessation of the trade of the United States.

The great diminution in imports into America brought about a rise in the price of manufactures. It was by trade that the American demand for manufactures was satisfied and all trade was cut off. Instead of protection it really meant prohibition, with the consequent high prices. Hence the American capital which had been invested in the carrying trade was withdrawn on account of the risk, and was attracted by the prohibition into developing manufactures at home. "Just in proportion as the embargo laws, and other kindred measures, were effective in destroying American shipping, did American manufactures strike deep root, and rankly grow." [1]

The industrial revolution, therefore, began in America in these years. Between 1806 and 1814 fifty companies

[1] A. S. Bolles, *Financial History of the United States*, vol. ii, p. 285.

were organized and incorporated in Massachusetts to carry on textile manufactures. Woollen goods increased in value from $4,000,000 in 1810 to $19,000,000 in 1815. The number of cotton spindles rose from 4,500 in 1805 to 87,000 in 1810, and to 130,000 in 1815. The iron, glass, and pottery industries shot ahead, though iron was still smelted mainly by charcoal till 1840, and Pittsburg became the centre of a rising iron industry.

The result of the peace in 1814–15 was a great increase of imports. Imports rose from $12,000,000 in 1814 to $113,000,000 in 1815 and $147,000,000 in 1816. Manufacturers felt themselves threatened with ruin by the fatal fall in prices. Many manufacturers failed and works were closed. Foreign demand for cotton raised the price beyond what American manufacturers could pay so as to manufacture at a profit. The upshot was the protective tariff of 1816. Despite the tariff English manufactures still flowed into the country, and there was a cry for further protection. The depression merged into the crisis of 1819, towards which speculation and bad banking also helped. Prices fell still further and unemployment became worse. All parts of the country felt the ill-effects except the West, into which those displaced in the East were rapidly flocking. Another tariff, affording greater protection to the metal and textile industries, was introduced in 1819 but was not passed till 1824.

After 1824 the woollen industry was very depressed and half the machinery in the New England factories was idle, due to the fact that English manufacturers could undersell American manufacturers. In fact, English competition was all along felt most severely in cotton, woollen, and iron manufactures. Nevertheless, the period was one of growth, even if vegetative growth. The cotton industry increased its number of spindles from 130,000 in 1815 to 1,246,000 in 1830. The output of pig-iron rose from 54,000 tons in 1810 to 165,000 tons in 1830. Even the woollen industry, the "poor relation" of American industry, revealed growth. Finally, trade revived about 1833 and remained prosperous till the crash of 1837.

The outstanding features of the period of 1833–61 were the crises of 1837 and 1857, with the very prosperous years between centring round the discovery of gold in California in 1848. On the whole the period was marked by rapid industrial development.

The crisis of 1837 was largely brought about by the consequences following President Jackson's decentralization of banking. Of the two parties, the Democrats stood for State rights and resisted centralization, and the Republicans supported a closer union and therefore greater centralization. Jackson, the Democratic leader, was for decentralization, and he attacked the United States Bank as being a centralized institution. The United States Bank had been established in 1791, but it was not certain that the Constitution gave powers for a centralized government bank and so it was dropped in 1811, but it had proved so useful that it was revived in 1816. The Treasury subscribed one-fifth of the capital and it was the depository of the Federal revenues. Its notes were legal tender for all payments and it was bound to redeem them in specie on demand. It was partly financed by the Government. The President nominated one-fifth of the directors; it did the Government business and the Government was responsible for the validity of the notes. The Democratic party were hostile to the bank. They held that it was unconstitutional and they charged it with exercising political influence on the side of the Republicans. President Jackson vetoed the Bill renewing the charter, and in 1833 he decentralized the bank. He withdrew the Government deposits and deposited them in various banks of the individual States of the Union. The result was that between 1833 and 1836 there was an extraordinary increase in the number of banks. The States exercised no control over them; they issued paper freely; the country was flooded with depreciated paper, as many of the banks had no capital to back their issues; and prices rose rapidly. Meanwhile the Treasury was disposing of its lands on a large scale. Speculation in land was brisk and excessive credit was given. Bad harvests in 1835 and 1837 caused distress amongst the farmers. Then the Treasury, as a measure of self-protection, demanded payments in cash and not in notes. This increased the difficulties of the times; and a fall in the price of cotton when anticipations were for a rise brought about a general crash.

After the crisis there was stagnation and recovery was slow. A reform was instituted in the banking system. State banks had to deposit with the Treasury securities to the amount of their note issue—a step which guaranteed to a certain extent sound money; and the Treasury kept the revenue in its own hands and no longer made use of any bank.

However, these measures did little to relieve the financial distress. Three crises followed in four years. In 1841, 55 banks became insolvent; and between January and April, 1842, 32 other banks.[1] A journal of the time [2] said that there was a degree of gloom in commercial circles seldom witnessed. Remittances from the country could not be obtained; goods could scarcely be sold for money at any price; and the accounts from abroad gave but little indication of a speedy revival of a demand for American produce. And the evil was universal. It affected all parts of the country, the industrial North, the agricultural West, the plantations of the South, farmers, manufacturers, traders, bankers, and labourers.

The great iron development of the United States had begun in the 'forties. Anthracite coal had been used in 1840 in smelting instead of charcoal and a revolution was taking place in the iron trade similar to that which had taken place in England in 1780. The tariff of 1842 put heavy taxes on English iron and the revival of trade increased the demand for American iron so that the industry became well established and the lower duties did not prevent a steady growth in the iron industry. The country was developing rapidly and needed iron. Especially there was a demand for rails. At the same time there was a considerable export. The cotton trade, too, was flourishing. Between 1845 and 1855 the quantity of cotton used in the mills of the United States doubled and there was a steady export to China, the East, and South America. The woollen industry was rather differently situated, since the United States was deficient in the raw material and it did not progress very strikingly. But the carpet trade received a great impetus from the invention of a power loom for weaving in 1848, and Brussels carpets were made by machinery. Machinery was also introduced into the hosiery trade. Shipping was also flourishing and American shipbuilding developed ships of a very high class. In 1861 the tonnage of the United States was a third of the tonnage of the world, that of the British Empire being a little over one-third. A large revenue was earned from the carrying trade of other nations.

[1] Stanwood, quoted by P. Ashley, *Modern Tariff History*, p. 167.
[2] *The Merchants' Magazine*, May, 1842.

Generally speaking, then, by 1850 the factory system was completely developed, and a great iron industry had begun. But the cottons and woollens were mostly low grade goods for general consumption. It was partly due to the strong industrial position of the Northern States that they were able to emerge victorious in the Civil War. At the same time, the high tariffs of the Civil War period and after still further strengthened that industrial position.

After the Civil War

The reconstruction of the South, the expansion in the Middle West, the railways, and the growth of an iron and steel industry fill the economic horizon after the Civil War. Disputes arose over the stabilization of the currency, one party believing in the greatest possible extension of the currency in order to finance the great expansion that was going on, the other supporting a stable currency. The dispute soon merged into a dispute over free silver. Then the tariff came in issue, a protectionist policy being looked upon as alone suitable for a great nation. Moreover, labour was on the same side for the reason that the workers wanted to be free from the competition of what they termed the pauper labour of Europe. The exceptions that were made were based on the idea of the free breakfast table.

With this dislike of the pauper labour of Europe went the restriction of Chinese and Japanese immigration. American national policy had never been tolerant of diversities of race, but it had the most profound belief in free competition. Although all were voters, no attempt was made to restrict the power of capital. For at least sixty years the tendency was all in the other direction, that is to say, the strengthening of the power of capital and respect for the rights of property. A western settler might kill half a dozen men and still enjoy the respect of his fellow citizens, but the theft of a horse was punished by the loss of all standing in this world and the next. There was scant respect for the rights of man, but much for the rights of property, and accordingly Factory Acts, Employers' Liability Acts, and Income Taxes were all unknown. Every possible privilege was granted to those who had capital for investment. If a man could only get capital there was land and opportunity and he became a member of a chosen race, and companies or corporations commanded specially favourable treatment. The mobility of labour was great, and, where all could get land and were potential capitalists, no labour movement could be very virile.

Although this tradition lingered until the end of the nineteenth century, a change had been developing. The South had been reduced to poverty; the railways began to combine; and it became obvious that free competition would not solve the great transport problem.

Then towards the end of the nineteenth century the trusts began to form, and they threatened the very existence of competitive industry. It was no longer so easy to rise in the world. The new immigrants did not understand the tradition of the older Americans and were far more willing to listen to anti-capitalistic arguments than the older generation. A humanitarian movement grew up as the factories developed, women and children, as in England, being the first to be given protection. In 1873 the farmers wanted State control because they alleged railway rates to be inequitable, but labour did not support them. By 1883 labour was demanding protection against Chinese immigration, but the farmers supported *laissez-faire*.

American labour movements had always been unpopular with the general public. They had begun badly by way of railway strikes and were regarded as a public danger and a menace to society. The Knights of Labour attacked land ownership—the sacred thing—and so the farmers became their enemies.

Meanwhile it had been impossible to carry out any degree of Government supervision. Posts were allotted on the spoils system. Salaries were quite inadequate, it being understood that officials paid themselves during the short time they were in office. No efficient administration was possible and the Government was not trusted. After 1900 all this changed. The Spanish-American war of 1898 created a feeling of unity and in war-time America got accustomed to the idea of Government direction. Accordingly, after 1900, laws that had been dead letters before were enforced against trusts and railways. A new code of labour legislation developed; trade unions acquired strength; new government departments for commerce and labour and for agriculture were inaugurated; and above all the railways and the trusts were brought under control. The Civil Service was rendered more responsible by putting a certain number of posts outside politics.

Accordingly, in the history of industrial development in the United States between 1861 and 1914 there seems to come a dividing line about the 'nineties. Till that time there is a period of unrestricted growth and unrestricted competition, which frequently led to trusts and combines. After that time there is a period of controlled development, as revealed by the government regulation of trusts and the policy of government conservation.

Between the Civil War and the 'nineties the United States became one of the great manufacturing powers of the world. Behind the tariff walls was built up a great iron and steel industry, and also great silk and cotton industries. On the other hand, the woollen and clothing industries did not prosper to the same degree, and shipping declined. The causes of this expansion of trade were various. There were the great natural resources of coal, iron, and cotton. There was the tariff, which stimulated rapid development. The enormous internal market secured to the American manufacturers made it worth while to introduce improved methods because of the very security of the home market. Then the scarcity and high price of skilled labour encouraged the introduction of machinery of every kind, and also standardization. Finally the unimportance of labour legislation, the few restrictions, and the absence of strong trade unions enabled the American manufacturer to develop his industry in his own way.

The most spectacular development of the period took place in the iron and steel industry. In 1870 the United States turned out 1·5 million tons of pig-iron as against England's 6 millions. In 1890 the United States produced over 9 million tons of pig-iron, surpassing England for the first time. The big factor in this development was the railway, which brought together the great deposits of coal round Pittsburg and iron ores on the western shores of Lake Superior. The two minerals are separated by a thousand miles of land and yet are brought together for the manufacture of iron on the largest scale known in the world's history. The history of the American iron trade is therefore the history of transportation. The cheap carriage of the ore and coke has been an indispensable factor for the smelting of the ore by the other. There were so many competing railways that they vied in offering facilities for conveying these goods and developed wonderful efficiency. The ore is loaded on cars at the mines by mechanical appliances. At the Mesabi mines the very steam shovel that digs the ore from the ground deposits it in the adjacent car. At every step direct manual labour is avoided and machines and machine-like devices enable huge quantities of ore to be moved at a cost which is astonishingly low. In the matter of competition the United States was hampered by distance. That has been removed. Steel enabled railway plant to be made larger and stronger; and larger engines and longer trains in their turn lowered the cost of transport.

Another great iron producing region has sprung up since the Civil War. On the borders of the States of Tennessee, Alabama, and Georgia there are great deposits of ore and near them great deposits of bituminous coal. Before the Civil War these natural advantages were not utilized. The regime of slavery and the lack of means of transportation prevented their being developed. When once the Civil War was over the mineral resources were developed on a rapidly enlarging scale. Alabama became a great iron producing State, the ore again making its journey to the coal. There was a large supply of negro labour paid at piece-work rates. It was freedom and the break-up of the old system and transportation that developed the Southern iron industry. It has been used for general foundry purposes, as it has rather too much sulphur for the Bessemer process.

Not only the iron and steel industries, but textile and other manufactures advanced rapidly after the Civil War with the growing market that was to be found within the United States itself. The cotton industry was greatly assisted by the fact that it drew its raw material from within the country. One feature of the period was the southward trend of this industry. Until the Civil War almost all the cotton mills were to be found in New England. After the Civil War cotton mills were opened in the South, where a plentiful supply of negro labour was available. Silk and woollen manufactures and the clothing industry also made considerable strides.

Towards the end of the period, and particularly in the 'eighties, the trusts made their appearance in American industry. Appearing as they did on the railways, in iron and steel, oil, sugar, whisky, these trusts were the result of the cut-throat competition of the period. Moreover, it was argued that the high protection aided and encouraged the formation of trusts; as was said: "The tariff is the mother of trusts." Certainly most of the trusts of national importance were to be found in the protected industries. The movement began with the formation of the Standard Oil Company in 1882. No doubt trusts have their bad points: they can exploit the consumers and the workers; they can use unfair business methods; and by their wealth they can corrupt politics and pervert the law. On the other hand, they have their virtues: they eliminate waste, reduce costs, have greater foresight, and have used some of their wealth to extend their foreign markets. Action against the trusts really belongs to the next period of controlled development.

During the period of controlled development from the 'nineties to 1914 industry continued its phenomenal growth. The value of manufactured products, which had been 1,886 million dollars in 1860 and 9,372 million dollars in 1890, rose to 24,246 million dollars in 1915. New industries opened up, old industries expanded, and all the while the home market continued to extend and the supply of raw materials seemed almost inexhaustible. Nevertheless, the distinctive character of the period is not that of growth, but of control.

The trusts had begun to develop in the 'eighties. In 1890 the first Federal attempt was made to control the situation by the Sherman Anti-Trust Act. Under this Act the Standard Oil Company and the Tobacco Trust were dissolved, but the trusts simply reconstituted themselves so as to be within the law, and in the years that followed the law played a losing game with the trusts. In 1914 another anti-trust measure was passed, the Clayton Act. A useful purpose was served by the publicity given to the doings of the trusts, even though legal action against them failed. Another example of more successful State control was the regulation of railway rates by means of the Inter-State Commission which was set up first of all in 1887.[1]

Trade unionism has never been a powerful force in the United States. The first attempt at a national organization of workers was the body called the Knights of Labour, which was founded in 1869. It was a secret society and was intended to include all classes of workers, but after 1886 it declined and gave way to the American Federation of

[1] See part iv, chap. iv, *post*.

Labour. This latter body consisted of skilled craft workers and was built up on sound, conservative lines. It accepted capitalism and such features of capitalism as scientific management, and attempted to get the best possible terms for its members. In disgust with the pusillanimous policy of these aristocrats of the labour world, another organization was formed in 1905, called the Industrial Workers of the World. It was a revolutionary body based on the syndicalist doctrines of Sorel and believing in direct action to subvert the existing social order. It also tried to unite unskilled and skilled workers, whether native or foreign, with a view to common action. By 1914 the movement was inconsiderable and its success small.[1]

The absence of a labour movement in the United States is not due to the lack of those problems that afflict other industrial countries. There have been the massing on the coal areas, the rapid growth of insanitary towns, the overcrowding and bad housing, the existence of slums, the overwork of children and the insecurity of existence which were only too familiar in the old world. The reasons for the absence of any real, effective labour movement are to be found in the peculiarities of the American industrial and political situation. The American workman has not been actually hostile to the capitalistic system, and therefore never really wished to combine against it. The artisan lived a middle class life with good wages and a high standard of comfort, and did not feel the grinding discontent of the less-favoured European. He hoped to rise in the world, to become an employer himself, and the chances were good. He was, therefore, not dissatisfied with the world as it existed. There was always the possibility of migrating West and taking up land if other things failed, and the opportunity to change one's industrial occupation was always offering itself. American work was not so specialized as European, hence the ease of effecting a change. The American worker, moreover, could not make himself felt politically, because the two great parties of the State—the Democratic and the Republican—were too well organized to permit a third " ticket " to have any chance of succeeding. The United States deals with the labour questions by States: such matters do not generally form a part of the

[1] J. G. Brooks, *American Syndicalism*, pp. 119–21. L. Levine, " Development of Syndicalism in America," in *Political Science Quarterly*, 1913, p. 478. Levine estimated the membership at 70,000.

work of the Federal Government. With the great diversity of labour laws and standards in the various States, anything like a powerful national union would be extremely difficult to organize. Such unions as exist are, therefore, local, very often confined not even to one State but to one town.

The American Republic is moreover composed of many groups of emigrants speaking various languages and hailing from different parts of Europe.[1] These races do not understand one another, and they look down upon one another. Any effectual combination between them seems highly improbable owing to the barrier of language. Many of the workers do not intend to remain in the United States and have no interest in helping their fellows by sympathetic strikes, or by any strike which would diminish their earning power even temporarily. American industry is arranged for mass production by means of a comparatively small class of very highly skilled and well paid workers at the top and a large class of unskilled Poles, Russians, Galicians and other Slavs, Syrians, and Southern Italians at the bottom to do the bulk of the standardized work on simplified machinery requiring no special skill. These unskilled labourers can change their occupations quite easily, since the processes in most industries are adapted for unskilled work. This low grade class of labour could not hold out any length of time against capital. No combination between the aristocratic artisan at the top and this unskilled labourer below was possible before 1914, even without the race barrier.

When the United States broke off from England it was an agricultural country consisting of a few States along the fringe of the Atlantic. Its marvellous expansion has been witnessed by which the great central region was settled up and the Pacific and the Atlantic brought together by a great railroad system the control of which became a problem. The evolution of an industrial side to American life and the growth of its great iron, steel, and cotton trades have been traced. How it was enabled to pour its wheat into Europe and thereby upset the centuries old agricultural markets in these older countries has been seen. The transformation

[1] Figures supplied by the Immigration Commissioners show that in American industry 25 per cent of the workers were American born and with native fathers, 17 per cent were American born and with foreign fathers, and 58 per cent were foreign born. Lauck, *Conditions of Labour in American Industries*, p. 1.

of the South from the plantation system into one of small holdings and the growth of a great cotton industry there have been revealed, and how the heritage of a negro problem has been left. The other great problems to be solved are the control of the great giant monopolies and the settlement of the forms of government for colonial areas. Both these questions seem likely to lead to a modification of that prohibition policy in the matter of tariffs which the United States has adopted hitherto.

PART IV

THE REVOLUTION WROUGHT BY MECHANICAL TRANSPORT

CHAPTER I

TRANSPORT IN FRANCE

Roads.

Corvées of the eighteenth century.
Napoleon as road builder.

Railways.

Influence of English engineers in first half of nineteenth century.
Development under Government control.

Shipping.

State assistance and its forms.

BRITAIN was first in the field in modern roadbuilding, but its methods were in great contrast to those of France. Britain was making metalled roads with great energy after 1750, and her canal era was beginning in 1760, but it was all piecemeal and patchwork. Enterprising landowners would improve a stretch of road and charge a toll; a bit further on the road would be unimproved and full of dangerous ruts and sloughs. In France, when improved road-making was undertaken, it was undertaken on a more or less comprehensive plan by the central government. A great movement took place in the latter half of the eighteenth century to join Paris to the principal towns of the kingdom by means of good roads with a made surface. A school of roads and bridges was set up in 1767. France was divided into two sets of provinces, the *Pays d'Élection* and the *Pays d'État*. The latter had far more local autonomy than the former and it was in the former that the King was able to carry out the most comprehensive schemes of road improvement. The *Pays d'État* (Artois, Flanders, Burgundy, Brittany, and Languedoc) made their own roads, and the roads of Languedoc called forth the praise of Arthur Young. The road system of France was, therefore, by no means uniform, though far more so than in England. The labour for the roads was provided by *corvées*—the inhabitants of the country districts had to give thirty days a year to road-making. This was a comparatively recent innovation dating in most provinces from about 1750, though it was started in 1720.[1] It was an innovation of the *intendants*, the royal officials responsible for governing the districts. They wanted better communications and simply used their powers to demand the labour, and got it. Nobles and ecclesiastics were exempt and the towns escaped. The *corvées* were an onerous tax on the peasant and the work was unsatisfactorily performed.

Turgot substituted a money payment in 1764, but many districts preferred the *corvées* and retained them. They were finally suppressed in 1787, after which the roads fell into a state of utter disrepair lasting until the days of Napoleon.

Generally speaking, however, France, thanks to the *corvées*, was better provided with roads than any country in Europe. There were said to be 12,000 leagues of made roads in France in 1788.[2] The maintenance of these roads in good repair was a great difficulty as they degenerated from *corvée* to *corvée*. In winter practically all roads were unusable. The rivers were not improved during the eighteenth century, and although large schemes of inland navigation were planned by the Crown by which all the rivers of France should be joined up by canals, little had been accomplished when the Revolution broke out. Such canals as were built had been built by private persons. These canals were all closed in summer owing to lack of water and they were useless part of the winter owing to frost. It was calculated that they were only usable four months of the year. The state of the rivers was so bad that there were constant shipwrecks. Between 1784 and 1787 no less than 37 boats were wrecked on the Loire.

Thus in the eighteenth century there existed in France a network of important roads and waterways, but the state of repair rendered these means of communication impracticable for a large part of the year. The various districts of France had been little isolated self-sufficing economic worlds before 1750. The isolation was being broken down, although very imperfectly, and the scheme of improved communications was being planned by the State on a more or less uniform basis.

[1] In England men were liable to give six days' labour on the roads and substantial farmers had to furnish a horse and cart in addition. This dated from 1551.

[2] On the whole subject, Letaconnoux, "Les voies de communication en France au XVIII siècle," in *Vierteljahrschrift für Sozial und Wirtschaftsgeschichte*, vii, pp. 94 ff.

Following the outbreak of the Revolution and during the ten years that followed, all roadbuilding and canal construction and river improvement was at a standstill. It was left to the genius of Napoleon to realize the political and economic importance of good transport. Probably, after the reform of the administration and the financial system which supported it, his most urgent work was that connected with the improvement of communications. Napoleon was ruthless in suppressing the brigandage that had developed during the disorders. He sent mobile columns into the suspected districts to keep order; he put gendarmes into the diligences; and he devoted the proceeds of the salt tax to the construction and maintenance of the roads. The revolutionary governments had taken a toll from the road users. Napoleon made the roads free. He constructed great engineered paved roads from Paris to Mont Cénis (Italy) and the Simplon (Switzerland), from Paris to Hamburg, from Paris to Amsterdam, and from Paris to Madrid. These great high roads were deliberately laid out as we would lay out a railway line, and were, and continued to be, the best made roads in Europe. His engineers were the greatest road makers since the Romans. Between 1807 and 1812 no less than 308 million francs were spent on the roads, and the bridges cost 25 millions more. The roads were divided into *routes impériales* and *routes départementales*. The cost of the maintenance of the former was borne by the State, of the latter by the Departments. The canals planned before the Revolution were now carried out. It was the ease of communication on the new routes that created the economic unity of France.

While Napoleon had been a great roadbuilder and had completed the road plans of the *ancien régime*, the Restoration Kings and Louis Philippe saw to it that the roads were kept in good repair. By the 'thirties France had one of the finest road systems in the world, just when railways were coming to the fore. Indeed, both roads and canals were so well managed by the State that they may be said to have retarded the development of mechanical land transport, since people did not feel, as England did in the 'thirties, the urgent need for greater facilities.

In the case of the railways, as with industry generally, the influence of English technique can be traced. In 1838 Edward Blount, an English banker, undertook to raise the money to construct a line between Paris and Rouen. It was built by Thomas Brassey, the contractor who did so much to build railways in France [1] as well as in other parts of the world, and fifty English drivers took charge of the locomotives.

If the technique of railway building was English, the method of construction was French. Canals and roads in France were all regulated from the centre, and this naturally reacted on railway development. From the very first the railways were planned on a general system by government engineers, and the methods of establishment and management were thought out beforehand. "While other countries were acting and experimenting, France was reasoning," [2] and these debates filled the years 1837–40. In 1842 it was settled that there should be nine main lines, and that the State was to contribute about £10,000 per mile and make and own the rail bed and build bridges and stations, while private enterprise was to be encouraged to lay down the track and provide the rolling stock. After 40 years the whole was to revert to the State. This control of transport was regarded as part of the duty of the State. Therefore it was to be expected that the companies would appeal to the State for assistance and equally certain that they would receive it. Though costly in money, the railways were absolutely indispensable both from a military and a commercial point of view. Hence the State guarantee of interest and hence also the reversion to the State.

Thirty-three different railway companies started. Excessive speculation broke out, and then came the crisis of 1847 and the Revolution of 1848. The companies stopped because they could raise no more money. They then appealed to the State for assistance. The State already had deep commitments in the railroads with the preliminary work they had undertaken with regard to the road bed, and in order to attract further capital it agreed to guarantee the interest on the capital. Further concessions had,

[1] Of these railways Brassey built the Paris and Rouen (1841), the Orleans and Bordeaux (1842), Rouen and Havre (1843), Amiens and Boulogne (1844), Rouen and Dieppe (1847). After the Revolution he built the line from Mantes and Caen, Le Mans, Lyons and Avignon in 1852, the Sambre and Meuse in 1853, Caen and Cherbourg (1855), and the Dieppe second line (1860). The English influence on French railways is to be seen in the fact that French railways pass on the lefthand side as in England, while ordinary French traffic passes on the right. Sir A. Helps, *Life of Brassey* (Bohn ed.), p. 84.

[2] A. T. Hadley, *Railroad Transportation*, p. 190.

however, to be made to stimulate the building of the railways. The arrangement under the original agreement, by which the lines were to revert to the Government and all the stations, lines, and equipment were to become Government property in forty years, was amended, and the period was in 1851–2 extended to ninety years. In return the companies undertook to make the branch line extensions themselves; in other words, the State was not to acquire and make the road for them, as in the earlier arrangements. The branch lines were to be built entirely at the expense of the companies.

The companies had spent about £80,000,000 on these lines when the crisis of 1857 occurred. They were unable to borrow any more money and a fresh arrangement was made with the Government by which the State guaranteed the interest on the new lines up to 4·65 per cent.

During the decade 1850–60 the railways of France had extended, until in the latter year they totalled 5,907 miles. The net result was that they had provided new arteries for traffic all over France and were beginning to revolutionize the transport of persons and goods.

The railways had become consolidated into six large companies by 1860. Five of the great lines radiated out from Paris, the sixth operated in the South. Each had a monopoly in its own district. The disadvantages of this monopoly were that they felt no necessity to lay themselves out to secure traffic either by cheap rates or good facilities. If there was a chance of goods going from Italy *via* Germany or France, they laid themselves out to secure the international traffic, but within France itself there was no competition. The big lines did not develop the local traffic and the State had actually to build and work some of the branch lines itself.

In spite of the difficulties attending the working and extension of the French railways, they were among the greatest achievements of the period. They created national rather than local prices, especially in agricultural products: the prices of these had varied so widely from place to place, that the tariff had to take cognizance of them.[1] They also

[1] Before the days of the railways there had been enormous local variations in prices. In 1817 wheat sold for 37 fr. the Hl. in the Côtes du Nord and for 80 fr. at Colmar and even in 1847 for 29 fr. in l'Aude and 49 fr. in le Bas Rhin. The spread of the railway net equalized prices. (Forille, *La France économique*, p. 94, quoted by Marshall, *Industry and Trade*, p. 109.)

hastened the evolution of the " great industry " as they did in every country where the railway network was fully linked up into a connected system. " Perhaps nowhere else in the world has the territory been so completely parcelled, nowhere else so complete a monopoly of railway transportation " been set up as in France.[1]

One result of this monopoly has been that there is little communication between the different industrial districts in France. The traffic has to go to Paris and be redistributed from there. Thus each district is largely self-sufficing as regards its subsidiary industries.

After 1871 there came another spell of feverish railway building in France. Many Frenchmen believed that the 1870–1 war had been lost on account of the slowness and inefficiency of their railways as compared with the German railways. Accordingly within twenty years of 1871 the length of track was doubled. In addition to building some of the lines, the State under the guarantee arrangements had to make up deficits of some of the companies, and so came to own several of the lines. For a time it was a question whether the State should not own all the lines, but the Government was frightened at the financial transaction involved. A new arrangement was made in 1883 under which the companies and the State were to share the profits, if any, and the railways were to lapse to the State between 1950 and 1980. Following the new arrangement, the deficits were more plentiful than the profits for many years, which meant continual State subsidies to the companies. Reasons given for the unprofitableness of the railways were the prevalence of short hauls, the rigidity of the railway rates, and general lack of adaptability. However, only one main system was taken over by the State, and that was the Western line, which was nationalized in 1908–9. Thus in 1914 the French railways remained predominantly in the management of private companies. Neither railways nor canals in France have played the part of State instruments for the furthering of trade and traffic that they have in Germany.

In the matter of shipping France, in common with other countries, began to resent English mercantile supremacy, especially after 1870 when the use of steel ships gave such an overwhelming advantage to England. To encourage the

[1] C. L. Raper, *Railway Transportation*, p. 74.

French mercantile marine, the State developed a bounty system for the building, running, and purchase of ships. In addition, foreign ships were penalized in French ports by means of the *surtaxe de pavillon* and the *surtaxe d'entrepôt*. State policy, however, did not achieve as much as was desired, and in 1913 France occupied merely the fifth place in the world's shipping list.

CHAPTER 2

Transport in Germany

The Unification of Germany by Railway.

The diversification of the German railway system—"63 railway provinces."

Objects of unifying railways.

(1) To promote the unity of the Empire.
(2) To promote the extension of German industry.
(3) To prevent local discrimination.

Imperialization of the railways rejected.

(1) Revenue would make the Empire independent of the States;
(2) Increase its patronage, and
(3) Set up monopoly.
(4) Excessive centralization.

Prussia purchased the railways in the kingdom of Prussia. To prevent Prussia buying up the railways the other States purchased the lines in their respective States. Prussia controls the lines of the North and the outlet to the North. Uniformity of system largely attained.

The principle of special rates.

(1) To assist agriculture and industry by granting cheap rates for raw material.
(2) To assist the home market.
(3) To assist the German ports and the transit trade.
(4) To assist German exporters.

The Development of Canals.

From 1880 the entire rebuilding of canals was undertaken for steamer traffic. The canalization of rivers undertaken. Result: cheap water transport. Especially important in a country with short coastline.
Railways are relieved of low grade heavy traffic.

Shipping Subsidies.

As far back as the eighteenth century, it had been the aim of the Prussian monarchs to increase the trade of their kingdom by improving the means of communication. Prussia, as well as Germany, has a good number of navigable rivers. These rivers, especially the Oder, were improved, and canals were built linking up the rivers, so that towards the close of the century Prussia had a network of waterways such as no other State of the time possessed. A few roads were built but mostly for military purposes. Nevertheless, the utility of rivers, canals, and roads throughout Germany was largely nullified by the vexatious system of customs and tolls everywhere. There were no less than sixteen customs barriers between Dresden and Magdeburg, and to go from Hamburg to Austria or from Berlin to Switzerland meant passing through ten States each with its own customs. Princes, nobles, ecclesiastics, corporations, and private individuals all had the right to fix tolls and customs. So numerous and prohibitive were the tolls on the Rhine, which should have been one of the greatest highways of the world, that goods used to go overland for the sake of cheapness till the French made the river free in 1804. And as the spirit of the Zollverein spread throughout the first half of the nineteenth century these obstacles to traffic and trade lessened and disappeared, and Germany, as a whole, prospered accordingly, especially with the introduction of the steamship. But the real advance in German prosperity dated from the advent of the railways in the 'forties and 'fifties.

Whereas the railway system of France was systematically planned, that of Germany, and even of the constituent States, grew up without any plan whatever. This led to as great a confusion of rates and rivalry as the system of customs and tolls before the Zollverein, and again the lead for unity came from Prussia. Most of the South German States built their own railways, but Prussia, at first, left railway building to private capital. As the railway system did not develop, the State guaranteed interest on the capital invested, with a proviso that it might after a time undertake the running of the road itself. There were many lines, however, which no company would undertake, and so the State was forced to construct some of the railways itself. The roads that the State built itself were first of all built on military grounds without much regard to business considerations, for example, the line from Berlin to the Russian frontier. Then after a time they had to take over the management of others. Between 1862 and 1866 Bismarck wanted money, and so he granted concessions to railway companies on especially favourable terms. He absolved them from the condition by which the State could take over their lines. Accordingly there was a real chaos of State-built lines, State-subsidized lines, State-managed lines, and private lines. By 1866 there were 5,896 miles of road, of which the State had constructed 1,890 miles and was managing 1,000, while the remaining 3,006 were in the hands of private companies. A good deal of railway building was undertaken between 1866 and 1874, partly on account of the expansion of trade and partly of the military exigencies of the Austrian and French wars. Then, as Prussia annexed Hanover and Hesse, it owned their State lines also.

When the Empire was established in 1871 the German railroad system was a "mixed" one. "There were, first, the Imperial railways. Then there were the State railways pure and simple. There were private lines in private hands, and private lines managed by the State. Some State lines were, on the other hand, managed by private enterprise, and there were finally lines leased by the Empire, as in Luxemburg.[1] There were so many different lines that the Empire did not form a railway unity, but consisted of sixty-three 'railway provinces'." "The traveller from Berlin to Karlsruhe," says one writer, "had to pass through the hands of half a dozen independent railway administrations, while upon the sender of a parcel from Königsberg to Metz it was incumbent to calculate the freight of this consignment according to the rates of nearly 1,500 tariffs."[2] "In regard to railway communication," said Bismarck, "we have arrived at a state of things which has not been peculiar to Germany since the Middle Ages. We have, I believe, in Germany sixty-three different railway provinces—that is, however, saying too little, for they are more independent than provinces; I might call them railway territories—of which perhaps forty fall to Prussia. Each of these territorial governments is fully equipped with the mediaeval rights of staple right, customs and toll, and arbitrary imposts on trade, for the benefit of its own private purse—yes, even with the right of arbitrary retaliation. Nowadays we see that railway administrations, without benefit to the railways and the shareholders, and as it were, as a kind of sport, wage with each other wars which cost much money, and which are wars of power, without financial competition, more than anything else."[3]

Unification was necessary if Germany was to hold her own as an industrial nation. But there was a second motive

[1] W. H. Dawson, *Bismarck and State Socialism*, p. 73.
[2] Quoted by W. H. Dawson, *Bismarck and State Socialism*, p. 74.
[3] W. H. Dawson, *Bismarck and State Socialism*, p. 79.

for unification. It would increase the unity of the Empire and would tend still further to keep Austria out. A different railway tariff system for Austria as well as a different customs system all tended to assure the hegemony of Prussia. Accordingly, the railway scheme was to complete the work of the Zollverein as far as unity was concerned, and it was an additional safeguard against Austria. Austria could be used as a market to promote the extension of German industry and to neutralize by low tariffs the geographical advantages of England in the proximity of her coal and iron.

There was much public dissatisfaction with the rate discriminations of the railways for different localities, and it was claimed that the railways gave preferences to foreigners. In the Imperial Constitution of 1871, very considerable rights were given to the Empire in matters of supervision. Uniform arrangements were to be made for the working of the railways. The result was that in 1873 an Imperial Railway Board was set up which drew up an Imperial railway code to control and unify the railway system of the country, but it failed to pass.

Bismarck then embarked upon heroic measures. He at once proposed the imperialization of all the railways. They had the nucleus of the system in the railways of Alsace-Lorraine which the Empire had acquired from France, and it seemed that since the Empire was to administer these it might administer all the rest as well. So he proposed that all the States should hand over their railways to the Empire, and he was willing to begin with Prussia. Legislation to this end was brought forward in 1876, but not only did the other States decline to hand over their railways, they also refused to accept the Prussian lines. They were afraid of strengthening Prussia, and moreover they were unwilling that the Empire should take out of their hands the making of thousands of appointments to the service and the placing of contracts. They were also afraid that Prince Bismarck might buy up the railways behind their backs and accordingly, to prevent any such action, several of the States began to buy up the private lines. The result was that the German States gradually went over to a State-owned system.

The objections they alleged to an Imperial system were, in the first place, the excessive centralization that would result. Then the revenue from the railways would perhaps enable the Empire to be financially independent of the constituent States. Again, the increase in the number of State officials would place at the disposal of the Imperial Government an enormous amount of patronage and so increase its political influence. And, perhaps most important of all, by abolishing competition the interests of the public would be sacrificed. The State is not susceptible to those motives of private interest which act as a spur to private enterprise.

These reasons carried the day, and Prince Bismarck began the acquisition of the whole of the railways of Prussia. He soon acquired possession for Prussia of practically all the main routes of railway communication in North Germany, whether they were in the Prussian boundaries or not. The companies were offered such extravagantly good terms that they were willing to sell. Between 1880 and 1884 this policy of the State acquisition of privately owned lines was so thoroughly pursued that, whereas in 1880 the Prussian system comprised 3,760 miles of railway, by 1900 the State-owned lines were 16,725 miles in length, and the Minister of Public Works exercised supervision over 2,127 miles more. In 1897, Hesse-Darmstadt combined her railway system with that of Prussia. Thus Prussia practically controlled the railway system of the whole of North Germany, and in time of war she had control of the whole system of Germany. Her influence was so preponderating that it was impossible for the Southern States to pursue an independent railway policy and although Saxony, Bavaria, Wurtemberg, and Baden were independent, their systems had of necessity to be reasonably uniform.

One reason which enabled Prussia to dominate the railway system of Germany and placed her in a position to compete successfully with the railway systems of Saxony, Bavaria, Wurtemberg, and Baden, was the fact that she owned her own coal mines. She was thus enabled to work her system at a considerably lower cost than the smaller States in South Germany.

One of the objects of nationalizing the railways was to assist the export trade. The Minister of Public Works drew up in 1884 a memorandum as to the principles on which preferential rates should be granted. They were to assist agriculture and industry by granting cheap rates for raw material; to assist German manufacturers in competition with foreign importers at home, and to assist

German trade abroad; and to assist the German ports. Preferential rates were only to be granted to foreign goods if no injury thereby resulted to any domestic industry.

Instances of special assistance to exports for the purpose of competition abroad are found in the case of coals to German ports and thence to Russia, Roumania, Austria, Belgium, the Netherlands, Italy, and France; manures for the relief of agriculture; ores to German industrial centres and for export; pig and other special kinds of similar iron to foreign countries, especially to enable competition with English iron; iron and steel products to aid exports generally; grain to assist places inland in exportation; spirits and alcohol to aid exports, especially to foreign ports and German colonies; increased exportation of yarns and tissues to Italy; glass to German ports for exportation by sea and especially to Italy; and for sugar to Switzerland to assist competition there with Austrian sugar.

There were also special seaport freights to aid the development of German ports. But besides these rates there were also other special deviations from ordinary railway freights for traffic with the Danube districts outside Germany; with the lower countries of the Danube, including Turkey, Roumania, Servia; with Russia (except Poland); with Italy and with South Africa.

By means of their control over railway rates the Ministers of State had an additional weapon to the tariff for the encouraging of exports and the discouraging of imports, and they have not scrupled to use it. Prussia has been the pioneer in this use of the railways, and the idea came from Bismarck.

Accompanying this nationalization of the railways was an enormous extension of the canal system. When canals were first built they were built as competitors to the roads and were therefore soon outdistanced by the railways. What was undertaken in Germany from 1880 onwards was the entire rebuilding of the canal system and its extension to accommodate steamer traffic. Now a canal vessel of 600 tons carries as much as sixty railway wagons and requires only one-thirtieth of the haulage power; it is one-third cheaper in carriage per ton, is worked at a lower rate of expenditure for men and materials, and can load or unload at any place *en route*. The disadvantages are the slowness, the unpunctuality, and the stoppage of traffic in winter. The State made the canals and improved the waterways.

The constitution provided that traffic on rivers should be free and that tolls should be taken only for the cost of improvements and maintenance. There was no element of profit in the canals.

It was rather strange that the State should create a competitor with itself in the canals. Indeed, the real reason canals became popular in Germany was the dissatisfaction prevailing with the railway rates as being too high, and many were glad to avail themselves of the low freights on the waterways. Germany always has an alternative method of transport. If the rates are too high on the railways canal rates are low and the haulage is in private hands.

The reason why the State encouraged canals was that the canals relieved the railways of the low grade bulky traffic. The State railways were unwilling to lay out large sums to increase the rolling stock, to enlarge stations and so forth, and they therefore preferred an extension of the canal system to take the low grade traffic.

Then in the second place the Government, realizing how important to mining, to agriculture, and to manufacturing was cheap transport, and knowing that water transport was by nature cheaper than by railway, decided that for the sake of the country the railways ought to be reinforced by canals.

There was another way in which the canals relieved the railway problem. One of the objects with which the State railways were founded was the prevention of local discrimination, it being impossible for the Government to give special rates to special areas. To reduce the rates on iron ore to the Ruhr district would be to have Silesia up in arms. The East Prussian landowners in 1888 petitioned the Government to reduce the rates on grain. It was done in 1891 between East Prussia and the Rhine Provinces, as there was a harvest shortage. Saxony immediately protested that this action destroyed the local market in the State. Bavaria, Wurtemberg and Baden lodged similar complaints. The millers of Mannheim said that they had spent a good deal of capital in building up a big grain import business for the Ruhr district from Argentina and the United States of America and that they would be ruined if East Prussia could come into the market, and finally these rates were discontinued. The difficulty constantly arises, but it can be got over by means of canal construction, and the onus of allowing discriminations rests on the people who do the haulage.

Accordingly, by reason of the great increase in technical knowledge, the canal system of Germany was brought into effective competition with the railways. Transport was not wholly in the hands of the State. It relieved the inelasticity of the State system and took the heavier class of traffic, the accommodation of which would have involved a very large outlay of an unremunerative kind.

To state in summary form the general transport position in Germany: The traders engaged in export business enjoyed very material advantages by the concession to them of exceptionally low rates, while the traders who did an exclusively home business were worse off under a state than they would have been under a company régime. The former, in accordance with the German national policy of commercial expansion abroad, got every possible help and encouragement in the consignment of their produce or their manufactures to foreign markets: the railway tariff has therefore been worked so as to stimulate as far as possible German transit trade and German exports. Moreover, they have been able to check the favouring of foreigners by the railways. The acquisition of railways by the State has meant additional protection for German industry.

As a paying concern the Prussian State railway system has been most successful and Bismarck soon realized that he had secured a revenue producing machine, which in 1912 yielded £56,550,000 surplus. The Government has been accused of fearing to bring the system up to date lest the surplus should be reduced and the national finances disorganized.

The result was that the German trader was driven more and more to use the waterways of which there was a great extension. Water carriage grew enormously and the railways became the feeders of water transport.

It remains to notice how Germany endeavoured to develop her oversea communications. In April, 1884, a measure was proposed for establishing and subsidizing a service of mail steamships between German ports, Australia, and Eastern Asia. The grounds urged for this proposal were the advantages which would accrue to German trade; the desirability of establishing direct and indirect postal communication with those parts of the world; and the national gain by reason of an increase in the material for forming an efficient Naval Reserve and the supply of first-class sea-going steamships which could be utilized by the Government as cruisers in a naval war.

This measure failed to pass the Reichstag, but in 1885 a similar measure was carried and subsidies were allocated for steamships to Eastern Asia, Australia, and to the Levant. The Chancellor was unable to include the West and East coasts of Africa as he desired.

The Government thus decided to give powerful support to the new colonial and commercial aspirations of Germany. It was made an essential condition that the steamers to be placed on the new lines should call in either at a Dutch or Belgian port, those ports being the natural outlets for the trade of the Rhine Provinces, Westphalia, Hesse, Baden, and Alsace.

No one had contended that the 1885 subsidy represented the value of the new postal service; it was looked upon as money paid for that service combined with the many and important interests of the German export industries; the requirements of the navy; a colonial policy; and the increase of German prestige in distant lands. In 1890 a further grant was agreed to for an East African line from Hamburg to Rotterdam, Lisbon, Naples, Zanzibar, and Delagoa Bay. The measure of 1885 had the most satisfactory result. The weight of the merchandize carried was trebled and the value nearly doubled in the first eight years of the subsidy.

The indirect advantages derived from the subsidy system were as great as the direct. From the institution of this system dates the success of German shipbuilding. Until then all large ships for German firms were ordered in England. Thereafter the ships for the transatlantic lines were built in German yards.

CHAPTER 3

Transport in Russia

Early transport difficulties.

1857–81—Railways chiefly built by private enterprise, with Government guarantees.

After 1881—Era of State railway construction.
The Siberian Railway.
Capital raised abroad.
Deficits.

Efforts to develop national shipping as adjunct to railways.
Corn export stimulated.

TRANSPORT in Russia is an aspect of economic history in which the influence of the French Revolution and of Napoleon is clearly visible. In agriculture and industry, Russia pursued the even tenor of its way, while the entire economic system of the German States was overhauled as a result of the French Revolution. Only in the matter of communications did France affect Russia at all seriously.

In 1809, Alexander I established the Institute of the Means of Communication and staffed it with French engineers and professors sent specially by Napoleon. Not only so, but the first head of the Department of Public Works was a Frenchman, de Béthancourt. In addition, the first railway of importance constructed in Russia and the first permanent bridge over the Neva at St. Petersburg were both built by engineers trained at the Institute on French lines.[1]

In 1809 communications scarcely existed in Russia, apart from the rivers which froze in the winter and ran shallow in the summer, and the earth roads which were generally quagmires in spring and autumn. Russia has a wonderful system of natural waterways, but is handicapped by its climate. Again, the country on the whole is flat and presents no problems of gradients, but it lacks stone and gravel for road-building. Under the influence of the Institute

[1] J. Bloch, *Les finances de la Russie au XIXe siècle*, pp. 169–70.

P

some progress was made in the first half of the nineteenth century. Some roads were built on the *corvée* system, and some canals were constructed, linking together different river systems, but it was not until railways began to be built that real progress was made in the means of transport.

The first railway line in Russia was built in 1836 from St. Petersburg to Tsarkoe-Selo, and was only 27 kilometres long. Then between 1843 and 1851 St. Petersburg and Moscow were linked together by a railway which cost 300,000 roubles per kilometre. Progress was very slow, and the terrible sufferings of the Russian Army during the Crimean War on account of defective transport clearly revealed the need for more railways. A special organization was set up after the war, called the General Company of Russian Railways, to develop railways in Russia, and the length of track increased from 1,165 kilometres in 1858 to 2,191 in 1861, to 3,484 in 1864, to 4,720 in 1867, and to 10,643 in 1870. Russia was rapidly gridironed with lines.[1]

The first line had been built by private enterprise. The line from St. Petersburg to Moscow was constructed by the Government. In the railway "push" after the Crimean War a policy of concessions was adopted, whereby the right to build railways was given out to private companies and the Government guaranteed the capital of the companies. The policy of concessions entailed great inefficiency and waste and was an intolerable burden on the Treasury. After the abuses of the concessions policy had been exposed, the State took a closer interest in the management of the railways, and when the leases fell in the State took the lines over. Accordingly the lines under State control rose from 23·5 per cent in 1889 to 60·5 per cent in 1900, and to 67·5 in 1913.[2] Count Witte was energetic in taking over railways and developing new lines, so as to build up an adequate Imperial system, since he realized the primary importance of railways to Russia.

State interference with railways in Russia took the shape not only of supervising the building and management of the lines but also of controlling the rates. Before 1889 there was free competition, and the result was, as in the United States, rate discrimination, which led to grave abuses and bitter complaints. At last in 1889 the State brought railway

[1] M. Kovalevsky, *La Russie à la fin du XIXe siècle*, pp. 853–5.
[2] M. S. Miller, *Economic Development of Russia, 1905–14*, pp. 183–4, 208.

rates under the control principally of a special Tariff Committee, which in the course of four to five years overhauled and unified the whole system.[1]

Strategic considerations entered into many of Russia's railway projects. Of course, strategic railways often proved to be of commercial and social importance. Railways enabled troops to be hurried to the outposts of empire in Europe and Asia, and traders and settlers frequently followed the soldiers. Railways were constructed throughout Asia. Of these the most important as well as the greatest achievment was the Siberian Railway. Sanctioned by an Imperial rescript in 1891, it was completed between 1900 and 1905, ran for 3,800 miles, and cost £100,000,000. It played the same rôle in Russia as did the Canadian Pacific Railway in Canada. Both railways linked together East and West, terminated at a warm-water port, and connected the Atlantic and Pacific Oceans by a band of steel. It opened up new regions to trade and settlement, and was a great empire-builder. On the other hand, the railways were typical of the two countries, for while the Canadian Pacific Railway was built by private enterprise, the Siberian Railway was a State undertaking.

One reason for feverish railway building in Russia was the Slavophil dream of a self-sufficing and economically independent Empire. Yet, by one of history's ironies, this very railway policy, designed as it was to sever the links with Western Europe, bound Russia more closely than ever to its western neighbours. Whether the State built the railways itself or gave out concessions to private companies, the bulk of the capital required was raised in Western Europe, particularly in France, since there was not the capital available in Russia itself.

Moreover, the railways were a heavy drain on a poor country, since in a sense they were built ahead of needs, at any rate of ability to pay their way. Between 1890 and 1913 Russia led the rest of Europe in railway construction, building 31,200 kilometres as against 20,800 kilometres by Germany, which came second. By 1908 the total railway debt was 4,107 million roubles, and till that time deficits were more or less constant, the deficit in 1908 amounting to 118.5 million roubles. After 1908 management and the financial situation both improved, and Dr. Miller reports

[1] Ibid., pp. 190–1.

that " on the outbreak of the War, Russian railways were just beginning to be a paying proposition ".[1]

One great development of the end of the nineteenth century was the subsidizing and encouragement of national shipping. This naturally followed when the development of the railways brought out corn for export. When Russian statesmen first woke up to the importance of shipping they realized that all the exports and imports of their country were carried on foreign ships and they determined to capture the trade. They reserved the coasting trade, they gave subsidies to various lines and paid their Suez Canal dues (1876). Iron vessels might be imported duty free.

In 1898 further encouragement was given to shipping by the creation of a Department of Commercial Navigation. The proportion of British shipping in Odessa fell from 50 to less than 25 per cent, while the proportion of Russian tonnage rose. Hitherto Russia had no ice-free port, but it undertook to develop the harbour of Ekaterina which is ice free all the year round, and a general attempt was made to improve the other ports, while a new bureau of Shipping, Shipbuilding and Harbours was created in 1902. The situation before the war was that in inland waters, such as the Caspian, Russian shipping naturally predominated, but that where the ports were open to the mercantile marine of other countries, Russian shipping lagged behind. Even then the bulk of the Russian shipping was foreign-built. This applied to steel ships, since the Russian iron and steel industry was badly placed for shipbuilding. In the case of wooden ships, Russia supplies practically all its own requirements.

[1] Op. cit., pp. 193–200.

CHAPTER 4

Transport in the United States

To 1812. Communications depended on a few turnpike roads.

To 1850. Steamboats and Canals
  Robert Fulton's first steamboat, 1807.
  Erie Canal, 1825, the economic link between East and West.

The railways and their part in the expansion of the 'forties and 'fifties.
  West linked to East.
  New lands opened up.

After the Civil War the great railway era sets in.
  First transcontinental line, 1869
  Expansion in the South—cotton ; and in the West—agriculture.

In the 'seventies the steel rail introduced.
  The refrigerator car.
  Elevators.
    Their significance.

Railway Rates. Evils of excessive rates.
  ,, discriminations.
  ,, pooling arrangements.
  Government control.
  Interstate Commerce Commission, 1887.

Shipping. Boom period of Napoleonic Wars.
  Embargo and Non-Intercourse Acts and consequent slump.
  Boom period of 1840–60.
    The " clippers ".
    Change from wooden to iron ships gives England permanently the advantage.

THE westward flow of settlement in America necessitated means of communication. Before migration could assume large dimensions there had to be a market for the purposes of the settlers, and the existence of a market depended on good communications.

During the period up to 1812, communication had depended on turnpike roads. These were, however, few and such as there were did not reduce the cost of transport much. From Philadelphia to Kentucky the carriage added one-third to the price, and articles like grain and flour could not be transferred any great distance. There were turnpikes which were erected by private persons, and turnpikes constructed by State aid. Congress constructed the National Road which ultimately, by 1840, extended from Pennsylvania to Vandalia, Illinois.

The second stage in communications came with the steamboat and the canal, and these were responsible for the bulk of the traffic to 1850. Magnificent waterways existed in the middle of the continent. But by the only boats available it was a forty days' journey from St. Louis to New Orleans. Return cargoes were not available, and the heat often spoiled the goods. Then, in 1807, came Robert Fulton, who placed the first successful steamboat on the Hudson. By 1816 steamboats were running freely on the Mississippi. This made it possible for a cotton belt to be fed and a market became available for the people of the North-West. The North-West fed the expanding South. The East sold manufactures to the North-West but did not buy from it, since the cost of transport across the mountains made it unprofitable to send grain eastwards. The South again exported three-fourths of its crop to England.

The most important diversion of traffic took place when the Erie Canal was built connecting Lake Erie and the Hudson River. Completed in 1825, the canal opened up the grain regions around the Great Lakes and reduced freight between Buffalo and New York from $100 to $15 a ton, and the time taken from twenty days to eight days. It became the economic link between East and West.

There then began a rivalry in canal building between the different States, and by 1835 there was canal communication from Philadelphia to Pittsburgh, the break at the Alleghanies being traversed by a portage railway. The funds for canal building were partly obtained by the States from the amounts the Federal Government gave them in respect of sales of the public lands. But this was not sufficient. The States began to pile up debts. Then when the financial crash of 1837 came, the States sold their public works and determined to undertake no more. Indeed, such enterprises were forbidden in future by amendments of their constitutions, so that the railways were built by private enterprise.

The great expansion of the 'forties and the 'fifties was to a great extent the result of the railroad. In a land of such vast distances the great problem was necessarily transport. The farmers who went West could not sell to the East because of the barriers of the mountains, except those who settled round the Great Lakes and could ship by the Erie Canal. The system of small farms and the absence of slavery were characteristics which connected them economically with the East, but corn and cattle are bulky things to transport and they were shut off from their natural market—the Eastern States. They could not have expanded at all before the advent of the railways, had it not been that the great expansion of the cotton belt was going on at the same time and they could and did supply the plantations by the Ohio with food.

The effect of the railroad was to link the West to the East and not to the South. Had it not been for the railroad the Middle States might have thrown in their lot with the South. As it was, traffic was diverted from North and South to East and West. Canals are not very suitable in a country like America, especially in the cold winters and hot summers. It was the railroads that enabled the great distances to be bridged and the settlers to be taken away from rivers. They made settlement beyond the Mississippi possible. The railways opened up fresh lands and the pioneers followed them. Between 1831 and 1853 the lines were chiefly built in the Eastern States. After that they appeared West of the mountains.[1] It became possible to organize a corn export.

As early as 1834 a transcontinental railway had been proposed but was deemed impracticable. The discovery of gold in California quickened the traffic between the Atlantic and Pacific coasts and strengthened the demand for a transcontinental line. The Civil War, instead of putting railways in the background, brought them into the foreground, since the Northern States found ready communication with outlying districts most important. Thus the first transcontinental railway was sanctioned in 1862 and completed in 1869. At the end of the Civil War the real era of railway-building began on a large scale.

A great development of cotton growing took place when the South had recovered after the Civil War. In the same way a tremendous agricultural development took place in the 'seventies in the middle West. This expansion was intimately bound up with the construction of the railways and still more with the invention of the steel rail and steel ship. The steel rail and the steel ship reduced the cost of transport and gave the American corn grower an opportunity in all the world's market. In manufactures the

[1] By 1840, 2,755 miles had been completed. By 1850 the mileage had reached 8,571. At the time of the Civil War 28,919 miles had been built.

idea was to retain the home market. But the home market was not sufficient for the American agricultural producer who had now become dependent upon export. Export was in turn dependent upon the development of cheap transport. There is no country that owes its development to railways to such a degree as the United States.

The flatness of the country facilitated the construction of railways. In this respect the United States is in the same category with Russia. The land was cheap; the road system was undeveloped and the canals inadequate. In winter many of the waterways froze. The need for railways was so great that they were built in America without any State interference. The States and the lesser public authorities supported the new undertakings with loans and guarantees of interest. They never troubled how the rails should be laid and there was no State regulation as to rates, building, or safety. Under these circumstances railway companies multiplied. The Federal Government began to make enormous gifts of public lands to the companies. Through these land grants the interest of the railway companies was bound up in the most intimate manner with the colonization of the district, since the hope of the companies lay in settling their districts and attracting population.[1] Some of the railways were run through an absolutely barren country. The companies gave cheap tickets to land-seekers, and cheap rates for seed for farmers. They sold the land under an easy repayment system and in order to facilitate traffic erected great grain elevators. They found their reward in the increased goods traffic. The general rate tariff was high as long as there was no competing line.

The American railways therefore do not, as in Europe, merely provide better trade arteries: they have also created new productive districts and commercial centres. In the latter part of the nineteenth century the prairie district west of the Mississippi, the pasture district of the mountains and Cordilleras, and the fruitful fields of the Pacific coast were opened up by the railways. Solidity and safety were not characteristic of these early railways, nor was their financial position of the best. If there was a prospect of good traffic two or three parallel

[1] Between 1850 and 1871 the Federal Government granted 159 million acres of land to the railways, while the State Governments granted 55 million acres.

lines competed for it and there would be bitter rate wars. The history of American railways alternates between periods of feverish over-speculation and heavy depression, since good trade stimulated railway building and then cut-throat competition followed. The railways, economically speaking, conquered the land, united it politically for ever, and in half a century made the Union one of the most powerful empires of the earth.

Early in the 'seventies a great advance was made in railway development by the substitution of the steel for the iron rail. The significance of this improvement is that it permits the indefinite increase of the train load so far as the track is concerned, whereas the iron rail would bear but a limited burden. The increase in the train load means a vast saving in the cost of transport, since it decreased the relative proportion of dead freight. The decline in freight rates was very marked. The lowering of transport rates to the seaboard indeed had several important results. In the first place, the Western farmer could now raise grain for the European market. In 1867 only about 8.3 per cent of the entire wheat crop was exported. In 1870, 20 per cent of the crop was exported and over 40 per cent in 1880; or, to put it in another way, the value of agricultural exports increased from $361,188,483, in 1870, to $685,961,091 in 1880. The closing of the South as a market led the farmers to look out for new openings for wheat and they found one in Europe.

With the completion of the Pacific railroad in 1869 began the system of big ranches in the Far West, and this cattle traffic was favoured with low freights. This was specially favourable when the truck could be made larger. The introduction of refrigerator cars in 1878 was the next great improvement in transport: this opened new markets in Europe for American meat and stimulated the cattle interests in the far West and in the corn growing and cattle and hog raising sections of the central West.

After cheaper carriage and cheaper production came the elevators built by the railways for the storage of corn. They have had the effect of saving the expense of putting up great barns and have facilitated the working of the land with a small amount of capital.

The development of the railways is essential in a country that has to move heavy goods in order to live. Freight and not passenger traffic has always been the more important consideration in American railway history. In 1900 the earnings from freight were almost three times as much as from passengers and there were forty times as many freight cars as passenger cars. The movement of heavy articles like minerals, cattle, wheat, and cotton was their main function.

The lines were at first short lines : very few exceeded 500 miles. A railway undertaking could be started more easily then in America than a company or factory in England to-day, and all sorts of expedients encouraged railway magnates to build. Subsidies were freely given ; they got land grants and exemptions from taxation ; the Government subscribed to their shares and guaranteed their bonds. There was much speculation and a good deal of chicanery. To get railways was the one thing that interested the public. How they got them and on what terms and what sort of a railroad it was, so long as there were two rails on which a locomotive could run, they cared not. As a result railroads spread out over the West at the rate of thousands of miles per annum.

The achievement was magnificent. The country was opened up at a rate hitherto inconceivable. But there were grave abuses. Vast fortunes were accumulated by methods which were more than questionable. The railway magnate who could make or break a town by providing or withholding a line of railway was a despot not always of a clean-handed type. Where a railway had a monopoly, or where a group of railways formed a monopoly, rates became exorbitant. Where railways competed, then the great evil was that of rate discriminations. Against both those evils of excessive rates and discriminating rates the customers of the lines, particularly the farmers, lifted up their voice.

Regulation of railway rates was in the hands of the separate States in 1869. This was soon found to be unsatisfactory, as so many of the railways crossed State frontiers and passed out of State control. Effective control of railway rates only began in 1887, when the Federal Government set up the Interstate Commerce Commission, and forbade discriminations and pooling agreements. The functions of the Commission were akin to those of the Railway and Canal Commissioners in England. They generally acted on complaints, but could initiate investigations on their own account.

Great opposition to the Commission was manifested by the railways and the powerful interests[1] who had received favourable rate discriminations. Obstacles were placed in the way of decisions, and the Commission became a byword for inefficiency and delay. The Federal Government made further efforts to meet those evils and to tighten up the administration of the law. By the Elkins Act of 1903, not only railway officials but the railway companies themselves and the shippers were liable to prosecution for illegal rates. By the Hepburn Act of 1906 the powers of the Commission were extended to cover facilities connected with railways, to demand reports where required, and to fix " just and reasonable maximum rates ". Further powers still were granted under the Mann-Elkins Act, of 1910.

An effective system of governmental regulation was gradually built up in what had once been regarded as the stronghold of free competition and private enterprise—the railways. At the same time, some of the success of this policy of State control must be credited to the mere fact of publicity in connection with the Commission's proceedings and also to the greater respectability which comes to trusts and monopolies in their old age.

The history of American shipping has been marked by great vicissitudes. The coasting trade has always been important and was particularly important in the early days when internal communications were so defective. American shipping enjoyed a great boom during the earlier part of the Napoleonic Wars, and the United States became the second carrier of the world. The Embargo and Non-Intercourse Acts and the War of 1812 put an effective stop to American shipping prosperity, and thereupon a slump ensued, lasting till about 1840. Between 1840 and 1860 American shipping again came upon a great boom. The trade of the United States and of the whole world was increasing rapidly ; the discovery of gold in California caused traffic with the Pacific to expand ; and the American shipbuilders brought to perfection during the period the construction of fast sailing ships, called " clippers ", for which they could draw on a plentiful

[1] The railways settled down into groups controlled by big capitalists :—

Vanderbilt .	21,353 miles	Gould . .	16,520 miles
Hill . .	20,242 „	Harriman .	14,725 „
Morgan .	18,879 „	Moore . .	13,028 „
Pennsylvania .	16,836 „	Rockefeller .	10,293 „

local supply of cheap timber. The period of the Civil War marked another turning point from boom to slump.

The effect of the Civil War was to throttle for a time the cotton manufacture of the United States and almost to destroy its export trade. The decline in American shipping which set in about the same time can only partially be ascribed to the war. A great revolution was then going on, in that the iron steamship was being substituted for the wooden sailing ship; and, moreover, while the United States was preoccupied with the war and the question of reconstruction, England had still further developed her carrying trade. The very change from wood to iron and later to steel as the building material handicapped the American shipbuilders. No longer could they draw upon their local supplies of cheap timber, wherein they had a distinct advantage over England: now they had to use iron and steel, materials in which England then had the very distinct advantage over them of cheapness.

The duties on shipbuilding materials and the absence of Navigation Acts are the reasons to which the decline of American shipping is ascribed by the American Commission on Marine Subsidies of 1904–5. Also it was the only industry to which the general protective measures then in favour were not applied. During the Civil War, American shipping lost ground and the new industry of iron shipbuilding was left without protection and never established itself against the competition of Great Britain. The decline in American shipping was startling. In 1861 American ships had carried 65 per cent of their own bulky goods, whereas in 1904–5 they carried only 10 per cent, and each year they paid abroad £30,000,000 in freights.

The Commission recommended very drastic measures, and an enormous mail subsidy out of all proportion to the services rendered was given, while the coasting trade between the United States and the Philippines was reserved for American vessels as was also that between Cuba and the United States. The results were on the whole negligible. American shipping continued to occupy a subordinate rôle in the external commerce of the United States. Even as late as 1912 American shipping carried less than 10 per cent of American exports and imports, and only 23 per cent of the shipping that entered and cleared the ports of the United States consisted of American shipping.

PART V

NATIONAL COMMERCIAL POLICIES

CHAPTER I

French Tariffs

Abolition of internal tariff barriers as a consequence of the Revolution.

Under Napoleon.

- Protection developed.
- "Continental System."

After Napoleon.

- The intensification of Protection. Industrial protection increased—agricultural protection added. Tariffs 1816, 1820, 1822, 1826, 1836, 1841.

The Free Trade Movement under Napoleon III.

- Freer Trade by Proclamation.
  - 1853–55. Various decrees reducing the duties on coal, iron, steel, and other raw materials. Confirmed by Chamber in 1856.
- Freer Trade by Treaty.
  - Treaty with England 1860. Duties reduced to 30 per cent *ad val.* maximum in France. England reduced wine and brandy duties, abolished protection of manufactures. Most favoured nation clause.
  - Other Treaties. Belgium 1862, Zollverein 1862, Italy 1863, Switzerland 1864, Sweden and Norway 1865, Hanse League 1865, Holland 1865, Spain 1865, Austria 1866, Portugal 1867.
  - Result—France focusses the Free Trade movement for Europe.
- Freer Trade by Law.
  - Lowering of the general tariff in France on raw materials, 1860–1861. Reduction of duties on corn 1861, cattle 1863, cotton and coal 1864. Reduction of duties on sugar, coffee, cocoa, and tea.
  - Reform of the colonial system: colonies to control own tariffs. Colonies allowed to trade freely with foreign countries in any ship.
  - Protection for shipping abandoned 1860 and 1866.

The Return to Protection.

- 1870–81. The reaction and the renewal of the treaties; agricultural support for protection.
- 1881–90. Agricultural and industrial interests joined by silk and wine industries in demanding protection.
- Méline Tariff 1892: definite return of protection.
- The tariff of 1910. Increased protection, especially on manufactures.
- Progress of French agriculture rapid. Increase in French trade, but at slow rate.

DURING the second half of the seventeenth and the first half of the eighteenth centuries the influence of Colbert was paramount in French economic policy. Colbert believed in State omnicompetence so far as industrial and commercial regulation was concerned, and called forth the famous protest of the merchants of his day, "*Laissez faire, laissez passer.*" But in the second half of the eighteenth century there began a definite reaction from the State regulation of trade and industry towards freer trade. The *philosophes*, particularly the physiocrats, inspired the movement; ministers of State, such as Turgot, took up the ideas; and the government of the *ancien régime* was sufficiently autocratic to be able to put those ideas into force against the will of industrialists and merchants. The chief token of the ministerial conversion was the famous Anglo-French Commercial Treaty of 1786, which reduced the century-old prohibitive duties on trade between France and England and by the great increase of trade helped to bring about the economic crisis in France which paved the way to the outbreak of 1789. The conversion of the ministers had not meant the conversion of the merchants, and when the Revolution put the middle classes into power this policy of economic liberalism was speedily reversed. In fact, one of the great reputed sins of the *ancien régime* was its freer trade policy. The comparatively low tariff of 1791 was followed by the almost prohibitive tariff of 1793, which in some features anticipated Napoleon's famous Continental System. The law of October 9, 1793, forbade entirely the importation of English commodities.

While the Revolution meant the re-erection of high tariffs in external trade, it led to the abolition of internal tariffs and barriers. There were in 1789 three distinct economic areas in France.[1] The area known as "the five Great Farms" comprised the twelve provinces mainly round Paris between the Somme and the Loire. Inside that area trade was free except for local tolls. Any goods passing out of that region or coming into it, whether from other parts of France or from foreign parts, paid duties according to the tariff of 1664. Another customs region consisted of a group of provinces "reputed foreign". They comprised Brittany, Auvergne, Franche-Comté, Artois, and Flanders.

[1] See map in *Historical Atlas of the Nineteenth Century*, Oxford University Press.

In the East was yet another group of provinces *de l'étranger effectif*, consisting of Alsace and Lorraine, Metz, Verdun, Avignon, Marseilles, Dunkirk, Bayonne, Labourd, and Gex, and these again were hedged off from the other two by a tariff. In some of these regions the tariff of 1664 applied; in others those of 1667 and 1671; but all were isolated economic regions in matters of customs just as if they had been separate kingdoms. Necker deplored these internal customs divisions and would have abolished them, but the local opposition was too strong. France did not offer a single internal free market to the producer, only a protected area. Inside these customs areas there existed a mass of tolls taken by *seigneurs* or municipal and ecclesiastical corporations. "The Baron de Coméré, who published in 1789 a treatise on finance, prepared a map showing the intricate divisions and subdivisions of France for the purpose of customs and excise duties, but declared it impossible to indicate the multiplicity and complexity of the barriers where transit dues were collected." These internal private tolls were numbered by thousands and required an army of collectors. They "seriously fettered the interior commerce of the country. . . . A boat from Languedoc to Paris laden with wine lost a fortnight in paying some forty tolls." [1] The money paid in tolls often exceeded the value of the articles.

The law abolishing all internal tolls and customs ran as follows:

"Inasmuch as a national constitution and public liberty are of more advantage to the provinces than the privileges which some of these enjoy and inasmuch as the surrender of such privileges is essential to the intimate union of all parts of the realm it is decreed that all the peculiar privileges of the provinces, principalities, districts, cantons, cities, and communes, either pecuniary or of any other description are once and for all abolished and are absorbed into the law common to all Frenchmen." [2] Thus the internal customs were abolished and internal free trade was set up.[3]

The return to protection on the part of the Revolutionary government was partly a matter of principle and partly a

[1] H. Higgs, "Finance," in *Cambridge Modern History*, viii, pp. 69–70.

[2] Buchez et Roux, *Histoire Parlementaire*, ii, pp. 259 ff.

[3] "The territory of France in all its extent is free, as also the persons who inhabit it." (Decree of 28th September, 1791. Levasseur, op. cit., i, p. 15.) In 1792 the *péages* or local tolls were suppressed, in 1793 the coinage was unified, and in 1795 the metric system adopted.

matter of war-time expediency. The long continuance of war compelled Napoleon to follow the policy which reached its culminating point in the Continental System of 1806–12.[1]

Owing to the English blockade Napoleon had to turn French trade inland and create new routes for it. He had no idea of making Europe a free internal market. His idea was that French goods should have preferential access to other lands, but that the French market should be shut to the foreigner.

In 1806 he planned a system of trade treaties, which should give French goods this preference. Only the treaties with the Italian territories materialized, and there the Emperor was able finally to obtain such good terms that, in the kingdom of Italy, he succeeded in excluding all foreign manufactures except the French. He secured not merely the exclusion of English goods, but German, Swiss, and Austrian,[2] while the way was paved for the entry of French goods by a low tariff, which enabled them to compete with Italian products. Italian raw materials, especially silk, were diverted to France by the fact that, if silk were exported to France, it paid no export duty; if exported anywhere else, it was subject to duty. Even the Italians could not obtain their own raw silk; it went to France, where, however, their manufacturers encountered a heavy tariff, while they had to put on a light one on French goods.[3]

In Spain there had been a heavy tariff on French goods, but in 1810, when Joseph Bonaparte became King, a much more favourable position for those goods was obtained.

With Germany no treaties were made, but the German princes, who owed so much to Napoleon, admitted French goods on very favourable terms. In Baden, for instance, the transit and import dues on French wines were lowered. There was also a preference in Poland. In order, however, to get an absolutely supreme position for French goods, it was necessary to shut English goods out.

The Continental System started in 1806 with the prohibition of the import of any goods from England, whether colonial goods or manufactures; the English were to be

[1] There is a complete study by E. F. Heckscher, *The Continental System*.

[2] P. Darmstädter, "Über die auswärtige Handelspolitik Napoleons I," in *Vierteljahrschrift für Social- und Wirtschafts Geschichte*, vol. iii, p. 128.

[3] P. Darmstädter, ibid., p. 133. French exports to Italy rose from 40,600,000 francs in 1807 to 51,600,000 in 1810 and 52,600,000 in 1811.

"blockaded in their island ". As a matter of fact, it was the English who blockaded Europe. All goods of English origin were to be confiscated, and any vessel, whatever its nationality, that touched at an English port, should not be received in any continental port, or if it did come, should be good and lawful prize. This decree applied not merely to France, but to the kingdoms allied to France and to the occupied countries ; in other words, English goods were to be excluded from Europe. When Lisbon opened its ports to English goods, Portugal was to be annexed. No less than 18 to 20 million francs' worth of English goods were seized in the Hanse towns.

The Continental System divides itself into two periods. During the period 1806–10 the System was tempered by smuggling and licences issued by both the French and the English governments. From 1810–12 it was strictly enforced and English goods really were excluded. The English, however, held certain strategic posts round Europe —Heligoland, the Channel Islands, Gibraltar—and from there and friendly places like Hamburg, Holland, the Balearic Islands and Sicily, they carried on a brisk smuggling trade.

" American ships laden with British goods were escorted to the continent by British cruisers and British merchantmen masqueraded under the flags of Spain, Denmark, Russia, Sweden, and even of France, and were provided with French consuls' certificates which were openly forged in London.

" Out of the 2,000 ships which entered the Baltic this year, says Napoleon, not one was a neutral." [1]

Moreover, the English were in a position to retaliate. They could and did cut off the French export trade to her colonies and they also hampered the supplies of raw cotton and colonial goods coming to France. Napoleon set out to provide new markets to compensate for those that had been closed and new sources of raw material. He obtained raw cotton from Italy and a little from Southern Spain, and he tried to grow it in Corsica and the Rhone valley. As a substitute for cane sugar the French scientists produced sugar made from beet, a process which had been discovered by a Berlin chemist, Achard, but which was improved by the French chemists in this period. French sugar factories were set up at Lille in 1810.

[1] A. Cunningham, *British Credit in the last Napoleonic War*, p. 61.

French industry seemed for a time to flourish enormously. In 1810 Napoleon made the System much more stringent. He wished to stop the smuggling and get more revenue which he badly needed. He therefore drew up a tariff, called the Trianon Tariff. This imposed very heavy duties on certain classes of imports, notably colonial goods. Up to now colonial goods and manufactures had only been prohibited if they came from England, and other countries had been free to send their goods, and the French allies might determine the rates of duties they would charge on colonial goods. They had carried on trade through neutrals, and were not over-particular as to the origin of the goods, which was often English. The new Trianon Tariff fixed the rates for all the conquered and allied countries, and Napoleon put his gendarmes into the foreign customs houses to see that it was really kept, and any breaches were harshly punished.[1] A vigorous campaign was undertaken against smugglers. Search was made for English goods, and when found they were confiscated and burnt. In October, 1810, bonfires were lighted with English products in Bayonne, Nantes, Antwerp, Zurich, Civita Vecchia, Ratisbon, Leipzig, Königsberg, and Memel. Russia declined to enforce the Trianon Tariff and refused to help to make Europe an economic dependency of France. She prohibited French cloth, silks, lace, and porcelain, and allowed colonial goods to come in freely if brought by neutrals, and was not a careful scrutinizer of ships' papers. Napoleon could not afford to leave such a loop-hole for the English, and the defection of Russia was serious as she had been an excellent market for French goods.

It was important also for Napoleon to be able to carry on the System a little longer, as England seemed at her last gasp. There was growing unemployment, Luddite riots, bread riots, and general disorder in 1811. Napoleon wrote as follows to Alexander of Russia in October, 1810: "The English are suffering much from the annexation of Holland and from my occupation of the ports of Mecklenburg and Prussia. Every week there are bankruptcies in London which cause confusion in the city. The manufacturers are without work; the warehouses are crammed." In December he writes: "Bankruptcies are multiplied, the exchange has fallen 25 per cent; the public funds

[1] R. Zeyss, *Die Entstehung der Handelskammern und die Industrie am Niederrhein*, p. 155.

have fallen, and the alarm of the manufacturers and merchants can no longer be hidden."[1] Nor was he exaggerating. The situation in England was deplorable. Unemployment was wide-spread, prices were high, there was scarcity of grain, reduction of wages, and high taxation. Fortunately for the United Kingdom, the year of its greatest difficulty, 1811, saw the weakening of Russia and a great financial collapse in France. The Continental System failed to bring about the downfall of England, but it ultimately wrought the downfall of France.

With the fall of Napoleon the progress of French industry was threatened by the competition of the English machine-made goods produced with cheap coal and iron. The French manufacturers accordingly demanded and obtained a high protective tariff. The real evil, of course, was not the protective policy itself but the exaggerated form it assumed in France owing to the prevalence of the ideas of the Continental System, which had aimed at exclusion. It would have been fatal to the Bourbon régime, on the other hand, to throw France open freely to the developed industrial production of England as it would have undone Napoleon's work for the reconstruction of French industry and might have caused that unemployment which would so easily start another Revolution.

Thus protectionist tariffs succeed one another in 1816, 1820, 1822, 1826, 1836, and 1841, despite the protests of the Government which, whether Bourbon or Orléans, was always more liberal in these matters than the bourgeois Chambers. And so matters continued until Napoleon III.

The nature of the tariffs during the *monarchie censitaire* from 1815 to 1848 was determined by the complexion of the legislature. The Chambers then were dominated by the landed class, who accordingly gave protection to such agricultural produce as corn, wool, and flax. At the same time the industrialists were sufficiently powerful to demand consideration, and coal and iron were subjected to heavy duties, and the cotton industry also received protection. Despite much discussion in the Chambers and outside and despite the evident desire of the rulers to reduce the tariff seriously, very little was done in that direction, and protection seemed as strongly entrenched as ever in France in 1848.

[1] Quoted from Napoleon's correspondence by A. Cunningham, *British Credit in the last Napoleonic War*, pp. 59–60.

During Napoleon III's rule came another surprising *bouleversement* of fiscal policy—again a movement towards freer trade on the part of an autocratic government against the wishes of a bourgeois majority.

The French economists had been in favour of lower duties, so were the ports, as they foresaw more export and import business. Both wine and silk were exporting trades; neither of them feared English competition; both knew that French concessions would be met by concessions from other nations and that the silk producers and wine growers could not fail to enlarge their markets. They were accordingly the pillars of the free trade party. Napoleon III was a firm believer in free trade. He wished to convince Europe of his pacific intentions in general and considered that he could not do it better than by a commercial treaty with his great industrial rival, England. He had, however, no chance of converting his people. With the exception of the interests just referred to, the French manufacturers were solid for protection. Between 1853 and 1855 Napoleon III had made some minor relaxations in the tariff, reducing duties on such raw materials as wool, cotton, fats and oils, dye-woods, coal and iron, and the Chamber confirmed them in 1856. The *Exposition* of 1855 had shown how great had been the progress made by Frenchmen and how little they need fear competition. Napoleon then proposed to make further reductions. There was an "indescribable emotion". Terrible pictures were drawn of the effect of the flood of English goods upon French industries; no one would be able to continue at work, the mines would be closed, and universal bankruptcy would ensue.

As it was hopeless to get a reduction of the tariff by parliamentary means, Napoleon determined to lower the tariff by treaty. As Emperor he had the treaty-making power in his own hands. The obvious treaty was a treaty with free trade England. She was the great bugbear of the French manufacturer; but once English goods were admitted and it could be found that ruin did not ensue, there would be nothing to be said for excluding the goods of other nations.

The treaty of 1860 was negotiated by Cobden on the English side and Chevalier on the French.[1] The English were to admit

[1] There is a complete study of the Treaty by A. L. Dunham, *Anglo-French Treaty of Commerce of 1860.*

all French manufactures free and were to reduce the duties on French wines and brandies.[1] The French undertook to reduce the duties on English goods to 30 per cent as a maximum till 1864, after which they were to fall to 24 per cent. Compared with the prohibitive heights of the previous tariffs this was free trade. The Treaty was to last for ten years. Both countries agreed not to prohibit the export of coal.

When this Treaty was concluded Cobden said nine out of every ten Frenchmen were against it. No one but a man in such a strong position as Napoleon could have so completely changed the economic system of France against the will of so large a proportion of the French people. Nor was it a popular treaty in England, and there was considerable difficulty in getting it through the House of Commons. The English regarded a commercial treaty as tampering with free trade, which was so obviously right in itself that it needed no bargain.

The Cobden Treaty was epoch making. Not merely did a highly protectionist nation abandon her position, but in this treaty there was introduced the "most favoured nation" clause which was to make for the spread of low duties in Europe.

The Cobden Treaty meant the abolition in France of the high tariff that had been maintained, with additions as new branches of industry developed, ever since the days of the Continental System. But it also meant that Europe must follow suit. Unless other countries were to see Great Britain, already the predominant manufacturing country, enjoying still further advantages in the other great market of the Continent, France, they too must make advances to France and try to secure concessions by making concessions. It was, moreover, impossible for the reductions in France to stop at those agreed on in the Cobden Treaty. The French manufacturer, now confronted with English competition with but a small amount of protection, must be able to get their raw material free of duties, and they must be able to hire ships freely. It meant the overhauling of the whole tariff, not merely that part of it which applied to England.

The reductions followed in two ways. The duties on

[1] The wine duties were reduced from 5*s*. 10*d*. a gallon to between 1*s*. and 2*s*. according to the alcoholic content. The brandy duties were reduced 30 per cent.

English goods had been fixed at 30 per cent maximum. The actual duty had to be negotiated in each case. To find out what competition French goods could " bear " a great inquiry was undertaken into French industry.[1] From this Commission we can get some idea of the progress of French technique. We find that iron was still smelted by wood though the use of coke was increasing rapidly,[2] and that there was a great amount of home work in the textiles. In some cases, in spite of more antiquated methods, the French were superior to the English. They could work up short haired wools better ; and the English were inferior where taste and finish counted. This inquiry considered that there were 123,357 establishments in France employing 1,782,932 workmen with a business amounting to 9,756 millions of francs and employing 502,355 horse-power. Even these statistics were held to be incomplete, and the official view was that there were actually 150,000 establishments and 2,000,000 workmen, and that the business turnover was 12,000 million francs. Although these figures are criticized[3] they do give some idea of the great industrial position of France at this date.

Only in a few cases, such as the metal products, was the maximum of 30 per cent reached. Other duties came far below. Yarn duties were fixed at 8 to 10 per cent, cotton and woollen stuffs at 15 per cent, tools were reduced to between 10 and 12 per cent. Generally speaking, the tariff when actually fixed for England was much below the agreed maximum and was a low one—a very low one for protectionist France.

This, the conventional or treaty tariff, only applied to the countries with whom an agreement was reached. The general tariff, i.e. the tariff in general use from which the conventional tariff was a deviation, was the next to be altered, and this was the second line of reduction.

As industry was deprived of its protection, the taxes on coal and raw material went between 1860–1. Agricultural protection followed suit between 1861–3 ; duties were lowered on colonial products such as coffee, cocoa, and sugar. The colonial and shipping laws followed as a matter of course. Between 1860–1 the colonies were allowed to trade where

[1] *L'Enquête sur l'industrie, Statistique de la France,* 2 ser., lxix.

[2] E. Levasseur, *Histoire du Commerce de la France,* ii, p. 538. Between 1861 and 1869 the amount of iron smelted by wood dropped from 163,000 tons to 36,000, but the production of the coke ovens had doubled. It shows, however, how far France was behind England in iron smelting.

[3] Levasseur, op. cit., ii, p. 576.

they liked; they were not obliged to trade as hitherto exclusively with France. In 1866 they were given control of their own tariffs, Algiers being the only exception. Low duties were imposed in 1861 on ships constructed abroad, so that the protection French shipbuilders had enjoyed was withdrawn. In 1860 all the preferences given to French ships over foreign ships were abolished.[1] Some of these changes were carried out by proclamation and afterwards confirmed by the Legislature, their consent only being sought after some years. In other cases the reforms were lumped together and the Chambers had to accept or reject them *en bloc*. They ended by accepting them, although the whole free trade movement was unpopular. Napoleon had, however, come into power on a popular vote. He was indispensable to the middle classes as the maintainer of order and he forced a free trade system on France. The opponents of low duties were not organized, nor were the free traders themselves what the English would have called genuine free traders. They were not convinced advocates of free exchange under all circumstances. They only thought that protection had gone too far in France. They wished for less exaggerated protection, not free competition.

For anything to succeed in France there must be a leader, a personality. The free traders found this leader in Napoleon. The protectionists had no popular leader. Let the popular leader once cease to count and with the majority of Frenchmen convinced of the desirability of protection it was only too probable that France would react in the opposite direction. The free trade movement in France had none of the elements of permanence and no popular support. France did not want "cheap bread", which was the cry in England; it was self-sufficing as regards foods like meat and wheat; and although the progress was more rapid between 1860 and 1870 than it had ever been before, if one can judge by export and import statistics, yet it was not possible to say that the progress would not have been greater with a protective tariff. No one could prove or disprove it. So unpopular were these low duties that, with Napoleon's waning popularity and the growing power of the Legislature, two commissions were appointed to inquire into the effects of the Treaty system just before the outbreak of war.

[1] Levasseur, op. cit., ii, pp. 601 ff.

In spite of the unpopularity of the change Napoleon, during the six years after the Cobden Treaty, used his power to conclude a series of European commercial agreements, thus helping to spread the system of low duties far beyond France.

Belgium, which was a great manufacturing country, could not see Great Britain enjoying such a favourable position in the French market without trying to secure similar concessions for itself. Since 1844 a free trade party had been growing up in Belgium that was willing to meet the French half-way. They had hitherto been unable to make themselves effective, but now the Anglo-French Treaty gave them their chance. They could urge the solid advantages to be gained by a reduction of the tariff, and in 1862 a Treaty between Belgium and France was concluded. In order to effect this treaty, however, France had to make still further reductions on certain articles in addition to the tariff given to the United Kingdom. The specialities of the latter were not necessarily the things that most vitally affected Belgium. France got reductions from Belgium for its wines and silks, which shows why the silk and wine industries supported free trade. It also got reductions on leather goods. Both parties guaranteed most favoured nation treatment. France then extended to England the special reductions given to Belgium. But England could not afford to see France with a specially favourable position in the Belgian market and so England, too, approached Belgium and negotiated a treaty in its turn. Then the Zollverein, seeing the advantages Belgium and England enjoyed in France, made its approach to France also, and another Treaty was negotiated. Reductions were made in respect of wines and textiles and some other commodities. In return the Zollverein got the Anglo-Belgian tariff with certain further modifications to suit itself. The Zollverein was thus bound to a low tariff for ten years, which meant ten years gained for Prussia to work for the further exclusion of Austria. In 1863 a treaty was concluded on the same lines with Italy; in 1864 with Switzerland; in 1865 with Norway, the Hanse towns, Spain, the Netherlands; in 1866 with Austria ; and in 1867 with Portugal.

In each case these nations also hastened to make treaties with each other and with England, and as all contained a most favoured nation clause, any concessions became general for all. In 1866, when Prussia had defeated Austria, the commercial arrangements made between Prussia and Austria were extended to the other Powers with whom they had most favoured nation treaties.

Other countries also followed the French example and abolished shipping restrictions and threw open their colonial trade. There was a general levelling of restrictive barriers all over Europe. France was the nodal point of the new free trade movement and yet France as a whole was protectionist.

During the period following the war, the pendulum in France again swung back towards protection. As a result of the war the economic life of France suffered the gravest set-back. Alsace-Lorraine was one of the great manufacturing districts, and its severance involved an annual revenue loss of many millions of francs. Then there was the indemnity to be paid, and the re-arming and reconstitution of the Army and the rebuilding of the fortresses to be carried out with a consequent huge increase in military expenditure.

For all these things money had to be found, and Thiers, who was at the head of the government, was a protectionist. He could not, however, raise the taxes on imported manufactures as these had been for the most part settled by treaty with the leading European countries, and Germany and France in the Treaty of Frankfurt of 1871 guaranteed each other most favoured nation treatment for ever. Accordingly, only the things not affected by the treaties could be touched. And yet an additional annual sum of something like 22 millions sterling had to be raised.

The duties on tea, coffee, and sugar, and the harbour dues were increased, but the revenue was still insufficient. The remainder was then got in the form of excise and stamp and registration duties. As a result the Frenchman became the heaviest taxed citizen in Europe and the costs of production rose. Hence there arose a further outcry: "Our taxes are so heavy we cannot compete." The effect of the war accordingly was indirectly to strengthen the cry for protection, although the Treaty system held it back.

The next question to be considered was what course should France pursue when the Treaties ran out. By 1877 the cry for protection had grown still stronger. France was beginning to feel the effects of the great depression; exports were dwindling, and the cotton, linen, iron, and coal industries began to agitate against the renewal of the Treaties. An inquiry was held in 1877 as to the reason for the decay of French trade. The Commission reported after a year's work that production in certain trades could never be so cheap as in England, and in the case of the iron industry coal cost double and transport treble, and they proposed a tariff on the basis of compensatory duties. They also proposed protection for agriculture. The Chambers of Commerce had been consulted and most of them were against the most favoured nation clause and in favour of specific instead of *ad valorem* duties. Moreover, by this time the agriculturists were beginning to be alarmed by the growth of the American wheat export, and were ready to ally themselves with the manufacturers. Thus by 1879–80 all the great industries with the exception of silk and wine, as well as the agriculturists and the merchants, were on the side of protection. In this frame of mind the new tariff was discussed.

The tariff of 1881 turned out to be a great disappointment. For one thing, Tirard, the Minister of Commerce, announced that the Treaties would have to be renewed, and most of them were renewed in 1881–4 for 10 years. Although there was an average difference of 24 per cent between maximum and minimum rates, that was chiefly for bargaining purposes. The tariff remained substantially free trade.

During the 'eighties the agricultural and industrial depression continued in France, and predisposed agriculturists, industrialists, and merchants still more strongly in favour of protection. In addition, the two free trade stalwarts, the wine and silk industries, had turned protectionist. The *phylloxera* had ravaged the French vines, and not only did foreign wines establish a foothold in France, but the French wine-producers incurred enormous expense to replant their vineyards. Accordingly, they claimed protection against foreign wines. In the case of the silk industry the turning-point was the opening of the Suez Canal, which reduced freight rates and enabled Indian and Japanese silks to enter France and undersell French silks. Thus the silk industry also demanded protection.

Hitherto the French Government had held protection at bay by playing off the agriculturists against the industrialists. Now the agriculturists and the industrialists made common cause, and the result was the Méline Tariff of 1892. This tariff marked the definite return of protection in France.

Comparatively high duties were placed on both agricultural and industrial commodities on both the maximum and the minimum scales. Further, under a Treaty France did not guarantee to maintain the minimum tariff at a fixed level, but retained the option of raising minima. Thus the only favour that a favoured nation received was the guarantee that it would be charged the minima, whatever they happened to be at any given time. Specific duties, moreover, in the place of *ad valorem* duties gave the opportunity of further discrimination.

In the years that followed 1892, France pursued the policy outlined in the tariff and intensified the duties at what were felt to be weak points. The tariff of 1910 did not introduce any new principle, but simply carried further the Méline policy. The result was that at the time the Great War broke out, France was one of the most strictly protected countries in Europe. Despite that fact, the heavy industries did not flourish in France. Germany was able to pour its cheap mass production manufactures into the country, and France was only predominant in those luxury goods which, being the product of French genius, scarcely needed a tariff. On the other hand, agricultural protection undoubtedly furthered the prosperity of agriculture—but the rest of the community paid for it.

CHAPTER 2

THE GERMAN ZOLLVEREIN

Period I. 1819–34. The formation of three large free trade areas and their eventual amalgamation.

The Vienna Conference, 1819, brings out the fundamental divergences between the States.

Attempt to form a Southern Union—lead taken by Baden. Congress of Darmstadt, 1820–3, abortive. Divergences between the States seem to make union hopeless—tariff war.

Hesse-Darmstadt and Baden make a treaty, 1824.

Wurtemberg-Bavarian Union, 1828. It becomes the model of the Zollverein.

Absorption by Prussia of the Enclaves, 1822–8.

The Union of Hesse and Prussia, 1828.

The Central German Union, 1828.

Treaty between the Northern and Southern Union, 1829.

Treaty between Electoral Hesse and Prussia, 1831.
Break-up of the Central Union.

Foundation of the Zollverein, 1834, for eight years.

Period II. 1834–53.

The adhesion of other States. Baden, 1835 ; Frankfort, 1836 ; Nassau, 1835.

The economic policy of the Zollverein. Influence of List.

Interests on the side of protection: Iron, cotton-spinners. Districts on the side of protection : Baden, Wurtemberg, Bavaria.

Interests on the side of free trade: Agriculture. The merchants. The North largely free trade.

The question as to the admission of Austria to the Zollverein. This would mean a strengthening of the protectionist party and a counterpoise to the leadership of Prussia.

Prussia's counter-move—The adhesion of Hanover and Oldenburg, 1851.

Period III. 1853–70. Formation of United Germany, and the beginning of the Industrial Revolution.

The crisis of 1853. Renewal of the Zollverein. Treaty to be made between the Zollverein and Austria to last twelve years. Admission of Austria postponed.

The French treaty, 1862. Second crisis of the Zollverein.
  Bound the Zollverein to lower duties.
  Virtually excluded Austria.
  Renewal of the Zollverein, 1865.

The Free Trade era. 1865–77. Tariff reduced, 1865–8, in consequence of the treaty with Austria—to last till 1877. Reduced again, 1870–3.

Creation of the Empire.
  Control of commerce given to the Central Government.
  The Treaty of Frankfort.
  Alsace-Lorraine added to Germany. Great increase in cotton production and iron manufacture within the Empire.

Period IV. 1870 onwards. The return to Protection.

Causes of the change.
  The commercial depression of 1873.
  The position of the iron industry.
  The Central Union of German Industrialists.
  The growing influx of American corn, which brought the agrarians into line with the manufacturers.
  The question of Matricular contributions or Customs.
  Bismarck's preference for indirect taxation.
  Political exigencies and Bismarck's leadership in the protectionist movement.

The tariff of 1879.

The increase of duties on agricultural products, 1885 and 1888.

The Caprivi Treaties, 1892.
  Policy of lower duties.
  Object to extend German markets.
  Agricultural protection diminished.

The tariff of 1902.
  Higher duties all round.
  The *Industriestaat* the predominant policy.

THE history of tariffs in Germany is not merely a record of revenue-collecting or industry-building; it is the story of nation-building. Here, again, Prussia took the lead.

As early as 1802 Frederick William III of Prussia had brought forward proposals for abolishing the prohibitive external tariffs and introducing uniformity within Prussia. The idea was in the air. In 1806 Napoleon overran Germany and introduced tariff uniformity in all the provinces he conquered. This proved the object lesson for those statesmen who had grown up with the ideas of Adam Smith and who wished to abolish the system of small States. In 1808 a note was dispatched to the various provinces by Hardenberg declaring almost in the words of Adam Smith that industry was best left alone and that it was not necessary either to favour trade or make it difficult. In 1810 an attempt was made to unify Prussia as to tariffs and to create an 8⅓ per cent tariff through the whole territory. It was epoch-making in that it abolished the old prohibitive system, and the direct encouragement of industry and trade ceased; bounties and subventions were given up. The Continental System which Napoleon enforced in 1810 prevented the tariff really coming into operation. In 1812 Hardenberg returned again to the idea of lower taxes and gave utterance to the opinion that owing to the geographical situation of Prussia prohibition was impossible, for smuggling was so easy and this smuggling tended to destroy the national spirit and to lower political morality. However, in 1813 a war tax had to be imposed and the old taxes retained for fiscal reasons.

It was not pure theory that was driving the Prussian Government at the time towards a system of low duties. After the war the two great exports of Prussia, linen and corn, suffered from the competition of English cotton and the English corn laws. It was very difficult for Prussia to send its linen to the English plantations or abroad, as the English were the carriers and charged such heavy freights. Meanwhile, tariffs were raised in France in 1813 and in Russia in 1810, and the only market to which Prussia could look for the sale of its linen and the other manufactures that had developed during the Continental System—wool in Silesia and Saxony, cotton and metal working—was in Germany itself. Prussia was therefore driven to advocate low tariffs or no tariffs within Germany in order to get a market. So the Prussian advance towards free trade was due partly to the desire to extend her sales. Austria, on the other hand, had a large home market, since a large part of her dominions had been unified under Maria Theresa and Joseph II and she had an outlet for her goods in the Mediterranean and therefore was not so much affected by the tariff policies of France, Russia, and England.

The second reason leading Prussia to a system of free trade or lower tariffs was the impossibility of maintaining a high tariff where individual States were so numerous that it was possible to evade any tariff by smuggling. A low tariff was the only workable one in the then existing condition of Germany.

The third reason which compelled Prussia to take the lead was that her statesmen saw that unless a larger State policy were substituted for that of innumerable small territories, there was no possible economic future for the country. The greater cheapness of production in England rendered a divided Germany helpless. That country was at the beginning of the nineteenth century hopelessly outclassed by England and France, and it had no power of retaliation, each State being too small for any effective action. France had put on a high tariff against England. This was impossible for Germany. Germany's task in the early nineteenth century was to establish a position against the competition of the more advanced countries. It was impossible to introduce machinery unless there was a large market; if Germany was to become an industrial State like England or France it had to be united so as to offer a large internal free market to its own producers. Moreover, it could not hope to compete in machine production unless raw material were cheap. Unification was necessary, not merely of Prussia, but of Germany. And the Prussian statesmen realized this.

Most writers and thinkers were convinced that something ought to be done, but it seemed in practice impossible for the separate States to agree. Also the different States represented different stages of economic development. Then so many bits of Germany were owned by foreign powers; Hanover by England, Luxemburg by Holland, Schleswig-Holstein by Denmark. And many little States were *enclaves* enclosed around by other States, while the smaller States were exceedingly jealous of Prussia and Austria. The difficulties seemed to make economic consolidation an impossible task. And yet there was one progressive State with its liberal statesmen and its trained officials ready to take the initiative. Von Bülow, Stein's successor, continued lowering the taxes. In 1817 he presented a very comprehensive scheme which did not become law but which was followed up in 1818 and made Prussia a fiscal unity. The effect of the scheme of von Bülow, the Finance Minister, may thus be summarized: Internal customs were abolished. Importation of raw materials was to be free. There was to be a 10 per cent average duty on manufactured goods. Colonial produce was to pay 20 per cent. There were to be moderate imposts on the transit of goods passing through Prussia. Excise duties were to be levied on a limited number of articles. It will be understood what this meant when it is realized that at the time there were sixty local tariffs in Prussia involving 2,800 classes of goods.

The Zollverein

The Prussian tariff of 1818 was the first step towards forming the Zollverein. Although the tariff was low compared with that of England, it was so efficiently administered that it seemed much severer than the tariff had been previously. Moreover, the thirteen little bits of States enclosed in Prussian territory, the *enclaves*, had generally been allowed to receive their goods subject to either very low transit dues or none at all. Hence they had become great smuggling depots for goods into Prussia. The smaller States suffered from the unwonted strictness of the Prussian administration and from the higher and burdensome transit taxes over which they had no control. They had in fact to pay the Prussian import duties before they came to their own territory.

The great result of the Prussian tariff was to give point to the discussions which were being held to simplify the traffic between the different parts of Germany. This had been the aim of Article 19 of the Constitution of the Germanic Confederation and a conference was held at Vienna in 1819 to see what could be done towards carrying out this article and facilitating inter-State commerce. At this conference the representative of Prussia declared that Prussia did not intend to accept any common plan which did not include the tariff of 1818; nor would Austria give up her prohibitions; and Bavaria, who had just introduced a tariff similar to that of Prussia, declined to lower her tariff walls. With the two great States in this humour little could be done in the direction of facilitating commerce.

The smaller States, Nassau, Oldenburg, Anhalt, and Baden, were in hopeless opposition. They differed on nearly every point among themselves but were united in opposition to the new Prussian system. Baden took the lead and suggested the formation of a South German Zollverein. Bavaria was not disinclined, and it was agreed by Bavaria, Wurtemberg, Baden, Hesse-Darmstadt, Saxony, the ducal Saxon States (Saxe-Coburg) Nassau and Reuss to meet at Darmstadt to discuss a treaty on certain definite lines, namely: abolition of all internal taxes; equal regulations as to road and water tolls; freedom for every individual State to fix its own excise but such excise not to be levied at a higher rate on goods of other States; common suspension of the customs barriers and customs-houses; and division of the proceeds according to the extent and population of the States.

Here were laid down the foundation principles of a complete Customs Union: principles which were new inasmuch as so much freedom was allowed to each State. The Congress of Darmstadt lasted from 1820 to 1823, and only served to reveal the almost irreconcilable views of the assembled States. Instead of agreement, tariff wars broke out on the termination of the Congress.

In 1824 Baden and Hesse-Darmstadt concluded a tariff treaty, but the attempt of Wurtemberg, Bavaria, Baden, Hesse, and Nassau to come to tariff agreement in 1825 failed utterly. In 1827 Wurtemberg and Bavaria tried again, and, rejecting the method of the reciprocity treaty, decided to aim at a Zollverein, which, with modifications of the tariff on either side, was in fact attained in 1828. This Zollverein served as a model for all the other Customs Unions. Under the scheme the two Kingdoms united in a common customs system with a common frontier. The customs-houses on the common frontier were abolished and the customs on the frontier were to be raised for a common fund. They agreed not to treat singly with other States. The proceeds of the duties were to be divided on a basis of population. Each State retained its own customs administration under its own control, but in each there was to be a representative of the other State with the functions of the watchdog. There was to be a general conference once a year to settle alterations, tariffs, and other questions. Two representatives from each State were to attend and were also to sit as a Court of Arbitration.

Meanwhile Prussia was proceeding in the direction of unification on its own account and in its own way. It was faced by the problem that its industry was crying for protection. If Prussia was to become anything more than an agricultural State, some effort must be made to keep out English goods. On the other hand, its frontiers marched with those of so many other States that to stop the smuggling seemed an impossible task. Accordingly Prussia was only too anxious to absorb enclaves and make them part of her system. By a mixture of bullying and cajolery Prussia between 1819 and 1828 persuaded the various enclaves to come inside the Prussian tariff system, and so removed the first obstacle in the way of the complete Zollverein.

The next step in the formation of the Zollverein was the union of Hesse and Prussia, and in 1828 a Treaty between them was signed. This Treaty resembled the South German Union. Hesse kept its own customs administration but was obliged to adopt the Prussian tariff and model its customs administration on the same scale of expenditure as that of Prussia. Alterations in the tariff were to be settled in common; there was to be a division of the profits according to population; and all internal bridge, water, road, and canal tolls were excepted.

Meanwhile the movement was spreading and Saxony, Hanover, and Brunswick and the Hanse Towns (Hamburg and Bremen) formed the idea of constituting a Central Union with free trade internally and low tariffs. This was really a defensive movement against Prussia. The leader of the Central Union was Saxony, which was afraid of being isolated. The members of the Central Union formed it along lines different from the others. They did not agree to complete union; they only promised not to join any other Union for three years nor to raise the transit taxes, and materially to facilitate traffic.

By the Convention of Frankfort in 1828 Electoral Hesse, Saxony, Brunswick, Nassau, Schwarzburg, Reuss, Frankfort, and Bremen formed the Central German Union. They retained their old customs and tariffs with their mediaeval character. They would have liked to find some middle system between the Prussian system and their own, but they could not agree on a common customs system and the only change was that they agreed to make certain roads and facilitate trade in food-stuffs.

Thus, so far, there have been four stages in the tariff policy of Germany, that is to say: (1) The Prussian tariff; (2) the South German Federation; (3) the Treaty between Prussia and Hesse; and (4) the Central German Union.

The fifth stage came when the Northern and Southern Unions approached one another and made overtures for unity. There were many difficulties in the way of a complete Union. The Prussian Rhine Provinces were developed manufacturing districts, whereas Bavarian industry was still struggling and would have been destroyed if exposed on equal terms to Prussian competition. But in May, 1829, a treaty was concluded by which the duties on certain manufactured goods—cotton, silk, woollen, leather, copper, tin, iron, tobacco, wine, and sugar—were reduced reciprocally, and they were to be gradually lowered until they disappeared. Other things were free. Transit taxes between the two were abolished and the two customs systems were gradually to approach a common form designed to make eventual union easier. There were to be yearly conferences. Thus the way was prepared for eventual free trade.

On the other hand, the Central Union was beginning to break up. Now that the two great Unions were giving such favourable terms to each other the smaller States manifested a desire to join in, especially those which, like Saxe-Weimar and Reuss, lay between the two. They entered into an agreement with Bavaria that, as soon as their engagements with the others terminated, they would join. Coburg and Meiningen did the same. Between 1830 and 1831 the Central Union broke up. Saxony was one of the first to realize the impossibility of effecting the union of Central Germany and approached Prussia with a view to union, proposing meanwhile to reduce its duties as much as possible. Prussia was not over anxious to include Saxony, and the negotiations came to nothing. In 1831, however, Prussia admitted Electoral Hesse on the same terms as Hesse, and the secession of Electoral Hesse from the Central Union, in which system it formed the strategical point, led to the break-up of the Union. The Thuringian States also wished to join, but they met with a refusal since their frontiers would have opened the door to wholesale smuggling.

Then the Northern and Southern Unions determined to lay aside the Treaty with its reciprocal duties and come to a direct union, if possible, which should include the Thuringian States and Saxony. There were, however, many difficulties in the way.

After prolonged negotiations and several crises, the Treaty was concluded and came into force on 1st January, 1834, for eight years. It comprehended Bavaria, Prussia, Saxony, Wurtemberg, the two Hessen-Thuringian States, the Enclaves, and the Hohenzollern territories. These areas included 7,719 square miles and 23,000,000 inhabitants. Outside were still Hanover, Brunswick, Oldenburg, Mecklenburg, Baden, Nassau, Frankfort, Lippe, the Hanse Towns, Luxemburg, and Holstein-Lauenburg.

The main terms of the Treaty were these: (1) Equal

customs system ; equal tariffs ; the abolition of all internal customs and all staple rights, only cards and salt being excepted. (2) Certain articles were subjected to an equalization tax. The excise was higher in some States than in others and any reduction meant a loss of revenue. Malt in Bavaria was the subject of an excise for the purpose of extinguishing the public debt, and it was felt impossible to give it up. It was, therefore, provided that certain things coming from other States, where they were subject to a lower excise, could be taxed so as to equalize the excise on the imported article. The principle was that the tax should be adjusted to the tax of the country of import. It was a very complicated, hampering, and expensive system, and led to nearly all the difficulties that emerged. (3) Coinage, weights, and measures were to be standardized by future negotiations. (4) The revenue was to be distributed according to population. This was not altogether popular in Prussia as they consumed more colonial goods per head than in the South and the principal duties were on such commodities. (5) Each State organized its own administration, but each had the power to appoint certain officials in the customs departments of the other States. (6) A special body was created to examine into any defects and difficulties in working ; to appoint the officials ; and to discuss the proposals of the members and the alteration of the tariff laws ; and it was to meet yearly in general conference. (7) Each State could negotiate treaties as long as they were not contrary to the Zollverein. (8) Any change required unanimous approval. This was a weak point because it gave a veto to any small State. But the general result was to abolish many internal duties, to suppress smuggling, and to give all the members equal rights at markets and fairs. It lightened the water dues and road taxes and made commerce infinitely easier.

The success of the Zollverein did not stop with 1834, for in 1835–6 Baden, Nassau, and Frankfort joined the Union, and only Hanover, Brunswick, Oldenburg, Mecklenburg, and several small States and the Hanse Towns then remained outside. In 1842 the Zollverein was renewed by the contracting States. The benefits had been immense. Smuggling had disappeared, trade prospered, manufactures sprang up in favourable localities, and even agriculture felt the benefit of the growth of general consuming power. The Zollverein was looked upon as a German institution which collected round it all the national feeling of Germany. It began to represent the Fatherland to the German.

Brunswick, Hanover, and Oldenburg had formed a Union of their own called the *Steuerverein*. This was expiring in 1841 and Brunswick applied to join the Zollverein, thus breaking up a Union which had cut right into Prussian territory and commanded the sea. Lippe-Detmold, Schaumburg, and Luxemburg joined in 1842.

Then in 1844 the Zollverein, after a brief tariff war, concluded a treaty with Belgium on terms that were far more favourable than before. Obviously the Zollverein was beginning to attain to an international position.

But once the Zollverein was reorganized the great question was, should it be protectionist or free trade ? And this was not merely a question of tariffs. It was really a question of life or death for the German Empire. Prussia represented the enlightened system of the day. She was the great dominating personality in Germany. The Austrian system was the old system of the Middle Ages with its serfdom, gilds, tariff restrictions and prohibition. It could only come into the Zollverein if the Zollverein were protectionist. And if she did come into the Zollverein it meant the nullifying of the Prussian influence and a deadlock. Prussia was reforming and leading Germany towards Empire along the lines of economic union first. To admit Austria with an Austrian party always checking the Prussian party was to render all the work hitherto done almost useless. Only if the Zollverein tariff was raised could Austria come in. It was impossible for her to pass quickly into a low tariff system. Accordingly, if Prussia could steer Germany along the lines of low duties, Austria would remain outside. And the almost dramatic interest of the time lies in the struggle for German unity with free trade as a weapon. But Prussia could not carry with her a protectionist Germany. What were the forces making for free trade or protection ?

Frederick List, in his "National System of Political Economy" (1841) preached protection and this cry was taken up by the manufacturers and such manufacturing States as Bavaria and Wurtemberg. On the other hand, the agriculturalists, the merchants, and the middle classes were generally free trade, as was agricultural and mercantile Prussia.

Prussia's immediate object then was to prevent Austria joining the Zollverein when it should be renewed in 1853. The question of Austria joining was actually brought up at the General Conference in 1850 by Bavaria. The attitude taken by Prussia was that, first of all, the Zollverein must be renewed and then they would have a basis for discussion. The South German States wanted Austria included and the whole thing settled as part of the Zollverein renewal.

There were three possible plans. There might be a Treaty between Austria and the Zollverein on the basis of preferential trade to prepare the way for Austria's entry; a Zollverein or complete union; or a Southern Zollverein of Austria and the Bavarian States.

Negotiations along all these lines went on — for the Southern Zollverein of course, secretly. Prussia's answer was to consolidate the North.

The two most important States in the North outside the Zollverein were Hanover and Oldenburg which formed the Steuerverein. A Treaty had been made between the Steuerverein and the Zollverein in 1845 to stop the smuggling that had gone on. Now Prussia felt that Hanover and Oldenburg must be incorporated at all costs, and in 1851, on the offer of very generous terms, Hanover and Oldenburg threw in their lot with Prussia.

Hanover gained, inasmuch as the great trunk lines of railway were now planned to go through the State instead of leaving her isolated by going round it. The other States, however, were greatly perturbed, and a conference among them was summoned to discuss how best to oppose Prussia should she insist on Hanover being included on these terms on the renewal of the Zollverein.

Negotiations and counter-negotiations continued on the question of protection, the question of Austria, and the question of Hanover; and it seemed as if a renewal of the Zollverein was impossible, so divergent had the various interests become. The outcome was that the Zollverein was to be renewed as before, but a Treaty was to be made between Prussia and Austria on terms of such a nature as to prepare the way for union. This Treaty was signed on February, 1853, to last for twelve years, when a joint commission was to be appointed to consider plans for Austria's complete admission.

The Treaty was intended to stimulate commerce between

the two parties. There were to be no prohibitions between the two countries and most favoured nation treatment was to be generally applied. Many raw materials and half-manufactured articles were free, others were made subject to a very low tariff and a reduction of 25 or 50 per cent of the ordinary tariff was made on such goods as cottons, chemicals, and metals. The Treaty was to extend to all the Zollverein and to the Italian Provinces of Austria.

The Zollverein was accordingly renewed in April, 1853, and Hanover was included. The free trade movement went on vigorously in Germany although the Austrian Treaty was looked on as a protectionist victory, since it was a check to Prussia. Meanwhile Prussia had kept Austria out for twelve years, and when the time for the admission of Austria came the French Treaty had altered the whole position of affairs.

The question of Austria joining the Zollverein would come up in the middle of the 'sixties for determination. Meanwhile France was negotiating free trade treaties, and Germany had the choice whether she should form a great Central Union with Austria or whether she should join with the Western system. Prussia was only too anxious to do anything which should preserve her preponderance and she eagerly seized hold of the French Treaty to bind herself to the Western system and circumvent the idea of a Central Europe Zollverein in which she and Austria would struggle for the first place.

But it was one thing for Prussia to negotiate a Treaty and another thing to get the other States to accept it. First of all they did not want to reduce duties, which they would have to do to get the French Conventional Tariff. Secondly, some of them wanted a Central European Union and disliked joining the Western Treaty system. Both the protectionists and the pro-Austrians were against her.

Without consulting the other States, Prussia simply went her own way and in 1862 concluded the Treaty, which provided for lower duties and "most favoured nation" treatment. The Treaty was concluded for twelve years, and if the Zollverein were not renewed Prussia would go on with the Treaty alone.

Prussia then communicated the Treaty to the other States, by which it was promptly rejected. Prussia declared that she took this to mean that the States did not wish to continue in the Zollverein and made the acceptance of the

Treaty a condition of renewal. Austria was not strong enough to resist, and as the States had all profited by the Customs Union they finally accepted the French Treaty with the consequent overhauling and lowering of the Zollverein tariff. Finally, when the Zollverein was renewed in 1865, relations with Austria were settled on a "most favoured nation" basis. The Zollverein suffered, as the Austrian tariff was now higher.

In the same year the Zollverein generalized all the reductions made to the States with whom, after the French Treaty, a series of Treaties was concluded. Instead of two tariffs, there was only one. In the result, duties which could show no financial results or had no protective value were abolished; all raw and semi-manufactured goods were to be free; the duties on cotton goods were substantially reduced as also on iron, silk, leather, and cloth. The result of the Treaties was that a wider market was opened for German exports in the West.

The next two great events of importance are the reform of the constitution of the Zollverein and the merger of the Zollverein in the Empire.

After 1867, when Prussia had secured its predominance after its victory over Austria, questions were decided by a majority and a *Zollparlament* was set up which controlled the customs revenue for the whole Kingdom—a great step towards unity, because it meant financial unity. The Southern States had no option, for Prussia controlled the outlet of their goods. In 1867 Schleswig-Holstein was compelled to come in. Then Mecklenburg and Lubeck joined, and only Hamburg and Bremen remained outside. The majority vote meant that tariff changes and policies could be much more easily effected, and so Germany proceeded rapidly on free trade lines. The first step was a Treaty between Austria and Prussia in 1868. Austria was overhauling her system after the war and wanted to borrow and so was driven to come into the Western European system. Hungary, as an agricultural State with free trade interests, counted for more than formerly. In 1868 there were reductions of tariffs on the side of both Germany and Austria, Germany in particular reducing her duty on iron, and both tariffs were fixed till 1877.

The Empire and after

Then came the war with France, and with it the Empire, and the official recognition of German unity which was already an accomplished fact. The foundation of the Empire gave the army, navy and diplomatic service over to the Emperor, as also of necessity the customs for their maintenance. Commerce and commercial policy were matters for the Imperial Assembly. To the Imperial Government were entrusted the organization of a common protection of commerce abroad and of German shipping and its flag on the high seas, the establishment of a joint consular representation of the Empire, the supervision of the railway systems, the construction of roads and waterways in the interests of national defence and of general traffic, and the control over the condition and navigation of the common waterways as also over all dues levied on the rivers and other waters. The endless negotiations between the different States about any proposed change were at an end.

The Treaty of Frankfort with France included a most favoured nation clause and this rendered it impossible for Germany and Austria to form a Customs Union, for the reason that Germany could not allow Austria free trade within the Empire without extending the same privilege to France.

The reason why Germany continued free trade, although Austria was shut out in 1867, was again political. The Liberals were the only compact party in the State and they were free traders. Bismarck was Chancellor and he wished to carry out the reorganization of the Empire. He could rely only on the Liberals, with the result that he adopted their economic policy. Up to 1865 the Government headed the free trade movement in opposition to Austria. They had, of course, a large free trade party behind them—chiefly the agrarians who insisted on the reduction of the iron duties. They temporarily outpaced the Government. But once the Empire was an accomplished fact the policy of Germany was to undergo a change.

The industrial revolution was, moreover, beginning in Germany. Alsace-Lorraine had come in with its well-developed cotton and iron manufactures. The iron and coal industries were developing. In 1870 it was still an agricultural country and therefore inclined to free trade. In 1873 Germany had abolished all agricultural protection and all its export duties and only maintained revenue duties and a small duty on textiles. Its arguments were borrowed from England and it carried its system through largely under the influence of the French Treaty. In the thirty years which followed, Germany with extraordinary rapidity became an industrial power as well as a commercial and colonial power of the first rank.

In 1879 there occurred an astonishingly quick veer round in German economic policy. The existing tariffs on industrial manufactures were raised; numerous protective taxes dropped subsequently to 1865 were reintroduced; the era of an energetic period of agricultural protection set in. It was an extraordinarily sharp reaction. Just when the free trade victory seemed assured, Germany changed its mind.

The depression following the crisis of 1873 seemed to be specially felt in the iron industry, which was to go over to free trade in 1877. The cessation of the special demand was complicated by the fact that the English iron manufacturers were underselling the Germans, and even though Germans were exporting they got no profit but were only working to prevent the furnaces from going out. They could not, they urged, compete with England with its mines so favourably situated, its cheap credit and its canal system, and they demanded to be secured in, at any rate, the home market. Moreover, the railway rates for iron had been raised 20 per cent, and so they agitated to prolong the iron duties in order that they should not disappear in 1877. They formed an alliance with the South German spinners who were always protectionists, and they were joined by the soda and sugar manufacturers who were afraid that their turn was coming. They were also joined by all the trades affected by the crisis, hat makers, leather, paper, linen and wool manufacturers, and by all the industries of Alsace. These formed in 1875–6 the Central Union of German Industrialists. With great skill they gave an unselfish aspect to the movement. They raised the cry of protection for national work, and they combined in their programme not merely the protection of certain trades but the question of working-class reform, patent reform, and railway reform as well as tariff reform.

The free traders were a powerful party as long as they included the agrarians, and it was not until a series of political manœuvres detached the agrarians and united them with the industrial party that the protectionist movement was safe. Hitherto the iron manufacturers and the agriculturists had regarded one another as deadly enemies, and the former had been the great party that had carried the abolition of the iron duties. But the circumstances of their industry were changing. The growth of railways in America and in Russia had deprived the Germans and the Austrians of one of their best markets, England. The German agriculturists were ceasing to be exporters. Moreover the grain that Austria could not now get rid of she was pouring at low prices into Germany, and Russia was doing the same with rye. Prices fell and with them land values. Rents dropped and the area under wheat decreased. They did not begin to clamour for protection of agriculture but for a reform of the taxes which should save them from the heavy pressure of the land tax. This was to be compensated for by indirect taxes and customs and they proposed a 5 per cent duty all round. Their demand was that they should be put on equal terms and not be specially taxed. In 1878 the agrarians and industrialists met to work out a tariff.

A leader was found for the movement in Prince Bismarck. He wished to have at his disposal the weapon of retaliation, and as Russia and Austria could only be reached by agricultural duties, agricultural duties seemed to be the means indicated.

But the immediate factor in the situation was the condition of the finances. The expenditure of the Empire was increasing and the reform of the Imperial taxation was urgently called for. The States contributed to the Imperial exchequer and the amounts demanded as contributions were rising. In the years 1874–8, there had been an increase of 19½ million marks. Bismarck's object was to substitute Customs duties for these contributions. He always disliked exacting these contributions from the States. In the first place, they worked out disproportionately. The inhabitants of agricultural Thuringia had to pay as much as the wealthy citizens of Hamburg and Bremen, numbers being the test, not wealth Moreover, the system made the Empire depend upon the good humour of those who composed the States, since the money would be voted by their Legislatures. He wanted to make the Empire as independent as possible by providing it with ample resources and to replace the matricular contributions by Imperial taxes. Moreover, Prince Bismarck did not believe in direct taxation. He believed that indirect taxes were a preferable means of raising revenue. And he held that direct taxation and discontent went hand in hand.

Along with these views was the fact that Bismarck wished to rely on the support of a party which he could trust to carry out his wider Imperialist policy. As long as he had to rely on the Liberals he had to be " free trade ". But with the turn of events it seemed as if he could unite groups of interests to form a great party which he could control. Accordingly he put himself at the head of the protectionist movement partly because he wanted a majority, partly because he believed in indirect taxation, and partly because of the protectionist tendencies round him. It has also to be remembered that Bismarck belonged to the Agrarian Party. He was himself a Prussian Junker.

In October, 1878, a majority of the Reichstag signed a declaration in favour of a change in the fiscal policy. Bismarck brought the question up before the Federal Council the following month and appointed a committee to revise the tariff and empowered them to call in experts if they wished. In December, 1878, he published a reasoned case for his new policy.

The new tariff was carried in 1879, although the exporters and the seaports were against the change. The Socialist movement was growing rapidly in Germany, but its leaders were interested in social reforms and not in tariff reforms. On the whole they were inclined to think that protection would increase the demand for labour although they disapproved of any possible rise in the price of food.

The duty on pig iron was merely restored to one mark the 100 kilos, though that on fine and manufactured iron was raised. As regards agriculture, the duty on wheat, rye, and oats was the same as on pig iron. On the whole, great moderation was shown in the compilation of the tariff.

The immediate effect was a decline in imports and an increase in exports. The protectionist reaction in Germany was important, as it gave a great impetus to the general reaction, and in the 'eighties Russia, France, and Austria each increased their duties. The great feature of the supplementary tariffs of the 'eighties was the increase in 1885 and 1888 of agricultural protection, due to American competition. Both in France and Germany the 'eighties can be regarded as a time when agricultural protection was being systematized.

In 1892 the Treaties negotiated in consequence of the

French Treaty expired, and it seemed as if a complete revolution of the tariff system was imminent. In France there was a strong current towards protection, as also in Russia, and the United States, by the McKinley Tariff, was intent on making itself more and more self-sufficing. What course should Germany pursue? Should it try to rehabilitate the system of reciprocity? But such a series of tariff treaties as would stem the great protectionist reaction could only be purchased at the price of certain sacrifices. "Concessions at the hands of agricultural nations, such as Austria-Hungary, Italy, and Russia, were to be obtained only by the reduction of certain duties on agricultural commodities; concessions at the hands of manufacturing nations, like Belgium and Switzerland, by the reduction of certain German duties on manufactured products."[1] In the first case, which was by far the more important, certain branches of agriculture had to pay the price; in the second case, certain branches of manufactures. In either case, to stem the protectionist movement, Germany had to make tariff reductions.

Nor was Germany unwilling to do so at this particular period. Bismarck had quitted office in 1890 and Caprivi had succeeded him as Chancellor. The Anti-Socialist Law of 1878 was dropped; the International Conference on Factory Laws was called; the colonial system was no longer pursued with the vigour that had characterized it under Bismarck, and East Africa was left to Great Britain in exchange for Heligoland. A new and more conciliatory spirit was apparent in German politics. Then German industry had been growing, and it became necessary to try and keep markets open for the growing exports. To assure the maintenance and prosperity of the working classes markets must be found. "Germany must either export wares or men," Caprivi said in his speech to the Reichstag. The necessity for keeping open foreign markets for export was there, but in order to do this a change had to be made in the German system. The Germans had hitherto held to the autonomous tariff which gave them the right to raise their duties when they liked. If Germany became the negotiator, it would have to do as France had done and create two tariffs, a conventional one and a higher one, and be willing to bind herself for a term of years. The change

[1] H. Dietzel, quoted by Ashley, *Modern Tariff History*, p. 88.

of policy therefore involved a change from an autonomous tariff to two tariffs.

Then appeared an additional reason for calling upon agriculture to bear some part of the common sacrifice, and that was that in 1891 there was a shortage in the food supply and it seemed necessary, in order to secure food, to lower the agricultural duties. After 1886 there had been a steady upward movement in prices which was increased when, on account of the famine, the Russian Government prohibited the export of wheat and rye. Outbreaks in Berlin emphasized the necessity of securing food at lower prices. Caprivi in his speech declared that while he had no intention of abandoning agriculture it was his view that agricultural protection had gone too far. The two decisive factors then were the international situation and the food supply; the industrial interests were to predominate, but agriculture was to receive a certain amount of protection.

The manufacturers supported the policy and so did the working classes. The agrarians were not unnaturally opposed. The first Treaty was that with Austro-Hungary, which was an exporting State, and was therefore anxious to get reductions. Others followed with Italy, Belgium, and Switzerland, all of which were to remain in force till 1903. Germany reduced its duties on corn, dead meat, cattle and wood, wine, hogs, butter, and eggs. In no case did these agricultural duties go back to the level of 1885. On some industrial articles small reductions were made and on certain iron goods, textiles, and on paper, leather, and others. In return there were general reductions of duties on German manufactured goods. Where reductions were not made the other State agreed that there should be no increase. In this way Germany prevented any further advance of Central Europe towards protection, at any rate, for twelve years. The opposition to extending similar treatment to Russia was strong, as Russia was a great grain exporting country and the chief rival. But after a costly tariff war Russia came in on the same terms as the others, and bound its tariff for the first time for a term of years. The landed interest east of the Elbe, that is to say, the great grain producers and forest owners, the vine growers of the west, and the cattle raisers, were sacrificed, but Germany had gained stability and certainty in her international relations with Central Europe for twelve years. Feeling that their vital interests had been injured, the agrarians drew together in 1893 to form the Association of Agriculturalists. By constant lobbying they secured a number of small concessions in the 'nineties, and in 1901 they obtained higher and assured protection for their produce by fixing the minimum or treaty rates in the Act itself and not leaving the rates to be fixed by negotiating ministers who might concede too much.

In the further tariff of 1902 the principles embodied were the maintenance of the exemption of raw materials not produced in Germany; taxation on semi-manufactured goods only to such an extent as not to interfere with export; and increased taxation on manufactured goods. Although the German iron industry had reached a high degree of technical perfection, it was necessary to counterbalance the economic advantage of foreign countries, and so the duties on iron were raised. The duties on machinery were also raised.

This new tariff marks a great departure. Germany had become an industrial country and cheap food was important. Also markets were more important than a highly protected agriculture. Accordingly Caprivi's policy was that of England in 1846. The *Industriestaat* was to be the predominant policy. The tariff of 1902 intended to hold the balance and declined to sacrifice agriculture for industry.

The difficulty, however, for Germany was that the countries with whom it had to negotiate wanted lower agricultural duties, and it seemed as if the Treaties could not possibly be concluded and that instead a series of tariff wars would take place or that all countries would apply their maximum tariffs. The net result, however, was that Germany retained the minimum fixed for corn but reduced its duties on horses, cattle, and meat, keeping them in every case, however, higher than they had ever been before. This was calculated to alienate a large part of the agrarian interest, who were disposed to feel that they had been sacrificed to the corn growers. Even then reductions had to be made on barley and wood from Russia in order to conclude the Treaty with that country. Reductions, too, had to be made on brewing barley from Austria and on cheese from Switzerland or no Treaties could have been concluded. The general result was that the Russian, Austrian, and Swiss tariffs, which were raised largely for negotiating purposes, remained very high. It was claimed that while valuable reductions had been obtained for German exports, the great thing accomplished was stability, in that the treaties were to last till 1917.

But Germany was not successful in stemming the protectionist reaction in Europe, for the reason that her own concessions were so small. At the outbreak of the Great War, therefore, Central Europe was bound to a highly protective system.

CHAPTER 3

Russian Fiscal Policy

The central idea was to attract and retain money in the country by means of (*a*) a protectionist tariff and the development of home production and (*b*) an excess of exports over imports.

Four Periods

1800–1824. A period of prohibitive tariffs.
1824–1850. Highly protective substituted for prohibitive tariffs.
1850–1877. A period of lower duties.
1877–1914. Return to prohibitive tariffs.

1800–1824. The system of prohibitive duties before and after the Napoleonic Wars.

The tariffs of 1810 and 1816.
Relaxations in the tariff of 1819.
1822 tariff returns to strict protection or prohibition.

1825–1850. Transition from prohibition to protection.

The Ministry of Cancrin.
Trade Relations with Poland and the East.

1851–1877. The Liberal movement subsequent to the Crimean War.

Money economy.
Growing need for imports.
Lower duties.
Trade treaties.
The Pan-Slavists.

1878–1914. Return to protection.

The 1891 tariff.
The currency policy of Wischnegradski (1887–1893).
Building up a gold reserve.
The policy of de Witte (1893–1903).
Change from paper to gold currency, 1897.
Depression at close of nineteenth century.
Tariff War between Russia and Germany, 1893–4.
Tariff of 1903.

PETER THE GREAT, having organized his army on the Western model, and industry along the lines of natural economy, and having got the window into Western Europe that he so ardently desired, the next question was the policy that should be pursued with regard to trade and exchange with the Western nations.

A leading idea of Russian policy right through was the

bullionist one, the desire to attract and to retain money in the country. It was the natural aim of any country that wanted to evolve a money economy. This could be done, first, by a protectionist tariff restricting imports so that it was not necessary to send money out of the country to pay for them and establishing home manufactures so that there was no need to purchase from abroad; and, secondly, by exporting in excess of imports, so that the balance should be paid in bullion. In these two ideas is found the keynote of Russian commercial policy.

The history of the Russian tariff divides itself into four periods[1]:—(1) There was the period 1800–24, when the importation of foreign goods was either absolutely forbidden or hindered by prohibitive duties which were only temporarily relaxed by the tariff of 1819. (2) From 1824–50 a highly protectionist tariff was substituted for a prohibitive one. (3) From 1850–77 there was a series of free trade tariffs, i.e. lower duties. (4) Then the inevitable reaction set in and the prohibitive tariffs of 1891 and 1903 were the result.

Peter the Great and his successors were imbued with the principle of bullionist mercantilism. His chief aim was to export more than he imported so that money should come in. The policy therefore varied. At one time every effort was made to attract foreigners so that the necessary trade should grow by which money could be attracted. At another time there were prohibitions designed to help home industry and by preventing people from buying foreign articles of luxury to prevent money going out. The whole idea of the system was to try and make money come in and prevent it going out, for money was all important in a country where it was so scarce.

Catherine II (1762–96) was imbued with the free trade notions that were so prevalent at that period and somewhat lowered the tariff. By the end of the century there was quite a free trade movement in the government. She also introduced three reforms which tended towards preparing the way for Russia to become an agricultural and manufacturing State. She reformed the provincial administration and created towns in order to have centres of government. Banks were created and money was concentrated so that a certain amount of capital could be obtained, but at

[1] Schulze-Gaevernitz, *Volkswirtschaftliche Studien aus Russland*, p. 244.

enormous interest. A large working class was growing up who were free; generally they were serfs who had bought themselves off from the estate factories.

After Catherine's death the Emperor Paul reverted to the old prohibitive system and even extended it to corn, the most important article of trade with England. After Paul's assassination, the Czar Alexander was again anxious to carry on trade along freer lines. He threw open the corn trade and tried to make Russia into a great transit State for the East, especially over Odessa. But the Napoleonic Wars destroyed all these schemes, and with Alexander's adhesion to the Continental System was introduced the old system of prohibition, and this was followed up by a strictly prohibitive tariff in 1810. This was occasioned not merely by the war with England but by the shocking state of the internal finances. After the war the prohibitive system was not removed. The invasion of Russia by the French roused every nationalist instinct, so that it seemed only natural to try to shut out foreign stuffs and to encourage home industry. The national feeling was not congenial to the internationalism of free trade.

The expected financial results did not follow. Still, industry developed as it did all over the continent. But the people had to pay dearly for it; prices were very high and native industry could not satisfy all needs, with the result that there was an enormous smuggling system which was carried on largely through Polish Jews.

In 1816, after the war, when a new tariff replaced that of 1810, it was still highly protective. Iron and textiles might not be brought in, though the prohibitions on certain articles were removed. In other words, the tariff of 1810, which was directed largely against England but was also in part the result of the financial exigencies of the time, was continued in 1816 with a slight modification. In 1819 a far more liberal tariff was instituted, Russia here following the example of Prussia. It was said to be the lowest tariff Russia had evolved. It was still protective but more prohibitions were removed and on raw materials there was only a low duty. There was, however, a tremendous outcry. Industries were said to be ruined, and scarcely had the tariff come in when it was decided to go back to the old system. It was pointed out that England, France, and Austria held to a prohibitive system and that Poland and Russia had become a sort of dumping ground, while

England shut out corn as well as manufactures. Agriculture had no market and industry no encouragement.

The tariff of 1822 went back then to the idea of taxing and prohibiting everything that could be produced in the country and only allowing in those raw materials that were necessary and foodstuffs that could not be produced at home. The export of twenty-one and the import of 301 articles were forbidden. Accordingly, although the Czar was inclined to freer trade and lower tariffs, the old prohibitive system was maintained partly because the national policy of Russia was against foreign goods, and partly for financial reasons, that is to say, to preserve the balance so that money should not flow out by reason of exports falling below imports. His idea was to protect the country against too many imports, and as low duties seemed to mean a low revenue the high tariff system was more convenient. The only possible market for Russian manufactures was the East, and after the war Russia began to try and extend her trade in that direction. Again, Odessa was made a free port, and all merchants in Transcaucasia were free from taxes for ten years. All wares from Persia were only to pay 5 per cent. The result of these measures was that the Armenian merchants in the Caucasus busily took up the transit trade and a lively exchange of commodities took place between Persia and Russia.

From 1824 to 1850 was a period of transition from prohibition to protection. The period nearly coincides with the period of the ministry of Count Cancrin, 1823–44. He had published a book in 1821 combating the views of Adam Smith. He was not a prohibitionist, but a protectionist. He gave up, for instance, the system of bounties, but assisted the sugar industry to start by his protectionist tariff. His opinion was that to prohibit such stuffs as the country could not produce or could only produce in bad qualities, injured trade, decreased the customs, helped smuggling, and prevented the export of home products. There were six tariff revisions during his ministry—1825, 1830, 1831, 1836, 1838, and 1841. The results were that high duties were substituted for import prohibitions; many taxes were lowered, and the whole rearranged to help home trade and at the same time increase the revenue. The effects of this policy were very favourable. The customs revenue rose 250 per cent; the cotton industry more than doubled; the number of people employed increased from

47,000 to 110,000; the cloth industry showed the same progress; exports exceeded imports. But all the time the export trade was still in the hands of foreigners.

When Count Cancrin left the ministry it began to be felt that, although great progress had been made, the results were not adequate to the efforts, and a certain opposition had been growing against the system of rigid protection. In 1844 the English Ambassador raised the question of the export duties on several Russian raw products which could find a ready sale in England, especially if free access were given to English goods. At the same time a committee handed a memorial to the Czar pointing out that on account of the dearness of their goods they were being ousted in the world's markets. The new Finance Minister, Wrontschenko, was afraid for financial reasons of lowering the duties, but the Czar was convinced and ordered a reduction, thus ushering in the period of freer trade.

Many export duties were abolished and the import duties on many necessary raw materials were lowered in 1846 in a preliminary way. The year 1850 may be taken as the dividing line between the policy of high protection and the policy of freer trade. In 1850 many prohibitive duties were removed, sixty-four in fact, but those on pig-iron, refined sugar, tea, and spirits were still preserved. On 622 articles they were lowered, prohibitions on export were removed, and export duties on 151 articles either removed or lowered. Difficulties arose because under the tariff the barrier between Poland and Russia was broken down and the Polish manufacturers began to compete in Moscow. But Russia wished to raise an industrial middle class in Poland as a set-off to the landowners and did not wish at that time to place any restrictions on that country. The tariff was so arranged that there were lower duties on the land frontier than by sea. Thus Poland could get its raw materials cheaper from the neighbouring countries overland. Following 1850, too, special pains were taken to promote the trade with Persia and China, and bounties on the export of Russian goods to China were paid. In 1858 they concluded the Treaty of Aigun with China and were successful in founding two new trading centres.[1]

The great Liberal movement, which set in after the Crimean war and led to the emancipation of the serfs and

[1] G. Drage, *Russian Affairs*, p. 467.

the building of the railways, further strengthened the movement in favour of free trade and low tariffs. The customs yield had averaged, before the 1850 tariff reduction, 34 per cent *ad valorem*. In 1857 and 1867 the tariff was further reduced. For the first time the nobility had a little ready money; they moved into the towns and began to become consumers of imported manufactures. Before that Russia had really lacked the capacity to purchase, partly because it had so little to give in exchange owing to defective transport, partly because the demand was low. Now that the nobility became exporters of corn and consumers of goods, they desired to get manufactures as cheaply as possible. There was as yet no manufacturing class, and therefore, as in Prussia, the nobility agitated for reduction in the iron duties so that they could get machinery and ploughs. By 1861 iron was admitted free, partly for the sake of the nobility, partly for the railways. In 1868 the reductions on 1850 rates were 50 per cent, and applied to foodstuffs, to raw materials which Russia could not produce such as chemicals, cotton yarn, pig-iron, and also to manufactures.

In addition to reducing its tariffs, Russia came out of its isolation in 1857 and negotiated Treaties with France, with Great Britain, and Belgium. Following those it concluded Treaties in 1858 with Austria, in 1860 and later with Denmark, Spain, the United States, France, Holland, Italy, and Switzerland. There was, however, no treaty with Germany. But although these treaties contained a most favoured nation clause, none of them bound Russia not to increase its duties.

The fourth period, one of high protection, was ushered in during the 'seventies, when a great reaction began to take place. In the first place, the cotton industry was growing and was assuming the proportions of a great industry. Then the Slavophils, with their opposition to all things Western, began to be a great political power. They looked upon Russia as having reached a higher and truer stage of civilization than Western Europe. "European society, in spite of its brilliant exterior, is built on shifting sand; its coherence depends simply on considerations of personal interest, on the money tie. The fabric of Russian social life, on the contrary, is firmly knit together by the prevailing principle of community which everywhere pervades it." [1]

[1] Schulze-Gaevernitz, cited by G. Drage, *Russian Affairs*, p. 45.

Their ideas were taken up by the Pan-Slavists, who looked upon the Russians as the great missionary power of the future, whose idea was to destroy the individualism of the West and spread the true form of civilization. Their attitude towards Europe was one of indifference, if not hostility, and under their influence the great colonizing movement eastwards was begun and a great protectionist movement reorganized to keep out things Western. England was the great foe. All India was believed to be groaning under British oppression and the Pan-Slavists constantly spoke of the liberation of India.

There was, then, this great conservative movement to preserve Russia from the influences and tendencies of the West. And yet the very protective movement they inaugurated attracted foreign capital; and the increase of taxation forced the peasant to grow corn for export or become a factory hand. Count Witte [1] gave this national ideal a practical form and attempted to make Russia self-sufficing. In 1892 he became Minister of Ways of Communication. In 1893 he succeeded Wischnegradski as Minister of Finance and he concentrated almost all the business of the Empire in his own hands. He tried to make Russia independent of the West by developing its great natural resources, its iron especially. He pushed forward colonization by means of railways and banks. By means of the Russo-Chinese and the Persian Banks he established financial control over a large part of those regions. He reorganized the finances and the currency so that Russia was able to obtain money for all this enormous work.

The change, however, began before Witte's time. After the Turkish war in 1877 an increase in the revenue was necessary and all duties were required to be paid in gold, a condition which increased the tariff by 30 to 34 per cent, and from that time onwards till 1903 the tariff was increasingly protectionist. The leaders of the protectionist reaction were the cotton industrialists round Moscow, cotton being then the only modernized industry in Russia.

Meanwhile a protectionist wave had been spreading over Europe. In 1879 Germany became protectionist, a fact which helped the Russian National Party. In Germany protection was carried through by the manufacturers and the landowners uniting. The extraordinary thing about

[1] His *Memoirs* were published in an English translation in 1921. His friend Dr. E. J. Dillon, gives some account of him in *Russia in Eclipse*.

Russia was that it was carried through in opposition to the landed interest, who were 85 per cent of the nation, and against the wishes of the West. It was carried through by a small minority, and Schulze-Gaevernitz implies that bribery was freely employed. In 1881 the tariff was raised 10 per cent partly to facilitate the abolition of the poll tax and the salt tax and to help the peasantry, and partly for protectionist purposes. It was raised in 1885 an additional 10 per cent, that is to say, altogether there had been a 50 per cent rise since 1868. In 1878 iron for machine factories was admitted free of duty as an exceptional case. In 1880 this was stopped, and the pig-iron duties were continuously raised till they became prohibitive in the epochal tariff of 1891.

To understand the tariff of 1891 it has to be realized that it was part of the currency problems of the time. Wischnegradski was in power between 1887 and 1893, and he was exceedingly anxious to replace the Russian paper rouble, with its constant fluctuations, by a gold currency. During the Crimean War the convertibility of paper money into coin had ceased. The currency was the silver rouble. Silver depreciated during the 'seventies particularly, and, as a currency, had become of no more importance than token money. Meanwhile the currency suffered from all the fluctuations that accompany an inconvertible paper and this was intensified by the action of speculators, especially on the Berlin Bourse. In February, 1888, the rouble was quoted in London at 19*d.*; in September, 1890, it was 31*d.*; by December, 1891, it had fallen to 21*d.* The stability of the rouble had to be assured and the silver coinage exchanged for gold. The preliminary steps were taken by Wischnegradski.

To have a steady paper currency it was necessary that it should be based on gold reserves, and so the important thing was to accumulate gold. This could be done either by loans or by a favourable balance of trade. Wischnegradski aimed at a favourable balance of trade, so as to get gold into the country. Hence he facilitated the export of corn,[1] and restricted by tariffs the import of manufactured articles in a way which finally found

[1] As to the growth of the corn export:—

	1881	1886	1894
Corn . . .	202,8 mill. poods	278,5 mill. poods	617,2 mill. poods
Price per pood	119,4	83,7	59,3

expression in the tariff of 1891. There was no compulsion to export corn, but Wischnegradski lowered the railway tariff and, the taxes being taken immediately after harvest, forced sale. In addition elevators were erected and inspectors were appointed to ensure the standard of the grain That was one side of Wischnegradski's policy.

The tariff of 1891, on the other hand, was intended to develop home industries and so diminish imports and the amount paid out for foreign goods. The tariff was accordingly very wide in its scope. It applied not merely to finished articles but to half-manufactured like yarn and raw materials like cotton, iron, and coal; and to agricultural machinery and manures.

As the result of his policy Wischnegradski was able to heap up a great gold reserve with which Count Witte was able to fix the rouble on a firm basis in 1893 and to go over to a gold currency in 1897. After 1894 the value of the paper rouble remained practically constant. The importance of the gold standard was very great. It simplified questions of foreign trade, since the variations in the rouble had always been a hindrance to commercial transactions with Russia. Secondly, the possession of a gold reserve within a country was an element of power. It was a guarantee of solvency and made it easier to arrange for loans abroad. But it was a change effected at the expense of the Russian peasant.

The tariff of 1891 had been most carefully worked out during the four previous years. It summarized all the previous changes and was considered a pattern of State forethought, and the year 1891 a year of new birth. The tariff of 1891 surpassed everything that up to that time had been done by protectionism in Europe. The idea behind it was to create a great self-contained Empire.

The central point of Wischnegradski's policy, then, was to heap up the gold reserve, and to do that he hastened Russia along the path of industrial development. During the 'nineties the same policy was rigorously pursued. The development of industry had become the central point of Russian policy in order to make Russia independent of foreign nations and to provide employment in the country itself. But under Count Witte difficulties developed. The price of corn sank, and the surplus diminished between 1891 and 1895 from 236·6 to 158·0 million roubles, and between 1896 and 1900 it further sank to 90·8 million roubles. With this the interest on loans could not be covered. New taxes had to be raised and money exported, about 260 million roubles yearly being necessary as a surplus for Russia's financial solvency. Even if Russia raised more money by taxes, it meant the export of the reserves on which the currency was based. Count Witte accordingly speeded up Russian development in order to have other things to export as well as corn; he carried through the conversion of Russian bonds; he made treaties; he reformed the banking system; he increased the taxes; he pushed on the construction of railways; he attempted to help agriculture by special credits and by subsidizing lines of railway. The colonies, Amur, Persia, and Finland, were brought into the tariff system. Drawbacks and bounties were given on textiles exported to the East and on sugar and petroleum. The policy of new markets in China and Persia was eagerly pursued, and the export of butter, eggs, and poultry was stimulated by the introduction of cold storage trains. In some cases he lowered the tariff for things necessary to develop the country. In 1898 the duties were lowered on agricultural machinery and on the machines for the gold industry of Siberia and the Urals, and the import taxes on iron steamers, ice-breakers, and swing docks were abolished.

The tribute to foreign countries was the corner stone of the system, and the aim was that it should be paid by the balance of trade and not by the export of gold. In Western Europe there was an idea that Russia raised its import taxes to increase its revenue. This was quite true, but the real object on Russia's part was to help industry, to decrease imports, and to pay the interest on its loans in goods and not in money.

In 1900 the tariff was again raised in order to compensate for the expenses of the war in China. Raw cotton was chiefly affected. This was one of the articles which drew most heavily on the balance; it was also an article which could and was grown in the country; and there was the danger of the cessation of American supplies. Since 1893 the production of cotton in Asia had steadily gone up. According to the English consular report in 1903, between 1890–1900 the total consumption of raw cotton doubled, and the consumption of Russian grown cotton trebled. The great difficulty, however, was to get enough capital to plant cotton on a very large scale and to provide irrigation.

Few changes were made in the tariff up to 1914. On the whole the tendency was downward before the War. Even then the average *ad valorem* value of the tariff was about 30 per cent in 1912. Foodstuffs had to bear the brunt, averaging 67 per cent *ad valorem*. Russia then had the highest duties in the world.[1]

Count Witte entered into commercial agreements with a number of countries, and particularly one with Germany, after a severe tariff war. In the tariff of 1891 a great distinction was drawn between goods brought by land and by the sea frontiers—those brought by sea being cheaper—the object being to favour the Baltic ports and the Russian railway instead of German railways. Germany's policy, on the other hand, had been agricultural protection, and this bore specially hardly on the Russian export of corn. Russia, accordingly, was anxious to bring about the reduction of the German duties, but having started metallurgical industries Russia meant to protect them. Thus Russia was precluded from granting German trade any facilities which might prove fatal to the industries which Russia had established and for which it was responsible.

In 1891–2 Germany concluded a series of Treaties by which it lowered its tariff rates on corn and agricultural manufactured goods in return for freer admission of German manufactured goods. By the end of 1892 Russia was the only nation excluded and yet it was vitally important to Russia to get an outlet for its corn. Russia felt itself penalized, and its next move was by means of a specially high tariff to get the benefit of the most favoured nation treatment. Russia, therefore, raised its duties in August, 1893, 50 per cent on all German goods in order to force Germany to admit Russian corn, and charged extra dues on all German shipments. Germany replied by raising its tariff on Russian goods higher than the maximum tariff. The tariff war lasted till March, 1894, that is to say, nine months. Finally Russia lowered its tariff on 120 articles in which Germany was specially interested, gave up the distinction between the land and sea frontiers, and lowered the duties on coal and coke. Germany, for its part, gave Russia the conventional most favoured nation treatment. Remissions of duty in the case of Russia amounted to nearly double those of Germany. Germany further promised that

[1] M. S. Miller, *Economic Development of Russia, 1905–1914*, p. 51.

the tariffs of the State railways should be so arranged that no discrimination should be made between the transport of Russian and German goods.

The importance of this tariff war was not merely that the countries forced each other to reciprocal reductions but also that the treaty was concluded for 10 years and that Russia thereby fixed her tariff for that period so that an element of certainty was introduced in commercial relations. When the agreement expired in 1904 Russia, in the throes of the war with Japan, was most anxious to renew it. Accordingly, after some preliminary skirmishes and some sacrifices on the part of Russia, the agreement was renewed.

Other States have in their day been in an economic position similar to that of Russia in the 'eighties and 'nineties, for instance, France at the time of Colbert and Germany in the first half of the nineteenth century. Both stood towards England's economic power as Russia stood before the Great War to the industrial countries of the West. Economic help was then given in each case by government protection but not with government money. The revival, the impetus itself, came in Germany from the people. Men like Frederick List roused the slumbering powers of the populace and the Government had to follow their lead, not *vice versa* as in Russia. List had worked in Germany for railways and protective tariffs in a way similar to Wischnegradski and Count Witte in Russia, but List worked with material means which were already existent in the country and required only to be put in motion. Russia worked with sums which burdened the people with a large " gold tribute " payable abroad. List found a people well prepared for industrial labour and the consumption of manufactures. In Russia both these conditions were lacking.

The tariff history of Russia is in contrast with that of the United States. In the United States the tendency of the tariff, apart from minor interregna, was ever upward. In Russia the tariff has bewilderingly ranged upwards and downwards. Apart from the fact that Russia is an economically backward country as compared with the United States, one reason for the difference was the different types of government. In the American democracy the economic interests of powerful classes always told on tariff policy, whereas under the Russian autocracy a fiscal policy could be pursued in the supposed interests of the country as a whole and cutting athwart the economic interests of powerful classes. Under an autocracy, also, sudden and spectacular changes of policy can be made. Finally, the tariff, which had been the whim of Slav schools and among the crochets of Ministers, had from the time of Count Witte become a matter of grim importance. Not only was the tariff framed to protect the gold reserve and the monetary basis of the country : it was shaped so as to guarantee the payment of loan interest. Foreign borrowing was one of the dominating influences shaping tariff policy from the 'nineties to the outbreak of the Great War.

CHAPTER 4

TARIFF HISTORY IN THE UNITED STATES

The Tariff as (I) Means of Revenue and (II) as Instrument of Protection

First Tariff Act, 1789.

Alexander Hamilton's Report on Manufactures.

Protection movement after 1814.
- The "American System".
- Tariffs of 1816 and 1824.
- Divergent interests of North and South.
- The Tariff of Abominations, 1828.
- Return to lower duties, 1832.
- The Compromise Tariff Act, 1833.
- The 20 per cent tariff, 1842.
- Tariffs of 1846, 1857, 1861.

Effect of Civil War.
- Tariff of 1864.
- Increase of the tariff for purposes of revenue. Protection coincides with national sentiment evoked by war. To preserve the home market by a high tariff becomes the foundation of national policy.
- Resentment by agricultural interests.
- Protectionist duties replace revenue duties.

McKinley Tariff, 1890.
- Free breakfast table.
- Agricultural protection.
- The Reciprocity clauses.

Struggle over Silver Question interferes with Democrats' plan of lower tariffs.

Dingley Tariff, 1897 : stiff protection.

Payne-Aldrich Tariff, 1909, and Underwood Tariff, 1913.

ONE important feature in the history of American economic development is that the tariff was the chief source of revenue, so that the tariff system had to adapt itself not merely to the protectionist or free trade notions of the moment but also to the requirements of the Treasury. Many articles of prime necessity were taxed for purposes of revenue ; financial and tariff history were intimately connected ; and commercial policy was materially influenced by the vicissitudes of the Federal finances, so that at one time there is a protectionist policy intensified for revenue reasons while at another time a surplus revenue leads to a reduction of the tariff.

Congress having taken into its own hands the power to

regulate tariffs, the determination of the policy to be pursued became one of the most important of the questions which had to be dealt with.

The first tariff was embodied in an Act of 1789. The duties were partly *ad valorem* and partly specific. They averaged 8½ per cent *ad valorem*. Goods imported in American ships were given a reduction of 10 per cent and American ships paid lower tonnage dues. There was accordingly a moderate tariff and a Navigation Act. Controversy has raged among American writers as to whether this tariff was intended to be a protectionist measure or was only for revenue. The Act, however, says "that it is necessary for the support of the Government and the *encouragement and protection of manufactures* that duties be laid . . ." It was in reality a revenue rather than a protectionist scheme. The Americans at that time had been so busy resisting the taxation imposed by England that direct taxation and excise duties were an impossibility and the revenue could only be raised from the customs. Some American writers accordingly date the beginning of what is called the American System from 1789 and others place it as late as 1816. As a matter of fact the industrial condition of the country did not at the time require protection and it would have been almost impossible to maintain it. Nine-tenths of the whole population were engaged in agriculture. The Northern States had a carrying trade and that, too, desired freedom above everything. Industry was too little developed to supply home requirements; the scarcity of skilled hands, high wages, and the want of machinery and the dearth of capital prevented manufacturing enterprise, and there was no impulse for the protection of nascent industries. The agriculturists wanted cheap imports, so did the merchants. Moreover, the wretched means of transportation and communication made internal distribution difficult; roads were poor, canals scarcely existed, and the business centres were isolated. It is impossible for manufacturers to flourish unless there is a market. All these conditions combined to keep the United States in the path of free trade.

The tariff was therefore a slight concession to the protectionist party, but the duties were too low to be anything like a protectionist tariff. Meanwhile the United States had gained economic unity. The customs barriers between the various States had been removed and the country was in a position to retaliate effectively if it was wanted. The reasons for departing from free trade in any degree were the necessity for revenue and the desire to retaliate, as against Great Britain.

In the next year, 1790, revenue was needed, and the tariff was increased. Hamilton in his capacity as Secretary of the Treasury was directed to draw up a report as to how they could best encourage such manufactures as would render them independent in respect of military and other essential supplies, and in 1791 he presented the famous Report on Manufactures with its elaborate argument for protection. From it List drew many of his ideas; and it has been the foundation of the American protective system.

However much Hamilton's Report influenced later legislation, at the time it was issued it does not seem to have had much effect. The United States was pre-eminently an agricultural country. It had to get its manufactured goods abroad and naturally wanted to get them at the cheapest rates; while a manufacturing class with power to bring pressure to bear on the government had not yet emerged. From 1789 to 1808 there were twelve tariff Acts in which the duties were increased till they were nearly tripled, but the main object was revenue, and the increasing expenses of the United States could be borne in no other way. The extraordinary demands were met by loans, but they, too, necessitated the payment of interest. There was then an inevitable increase, so that the tariff actually became protectionist while the country was not yet convinced of protection.

At the end of 1814 the treaty of peace was signed between England and the United States. During the Napoleonic Wars manufactures had developed in the United States as a consequence of the interruption of commercial relations with England.[1] The first result of peace was a great increase of imports. The same thing happened as had happened before—there was a sweeping invasion of English goods. Imports rose from $12,000,000 in 1814 to $113,000,000 in 1815 and to $147,000,000 in 1816. Manufacturers saw themselves threatened with ruin. Prices had to be lowered, many works were closed, and manufacturers became bankrupt. The foreign demand for raw cotton brought about a rise in its price and American

[1] See Part III, Chap. 4, *Industrial Development in the United States.*

manufacturers could no longer get cheap raw material. Hence arose a great clamour for protection. President Madison reported to Congress that circumstances had given a powerful impulse to American manufactures, which were now developed and constituted a body of interests such as to require immediate protection. Hamilton's arguments for the protection of infant industries could now be seen in their practical working. Hence, to prevent the ruin of industry, the "American System" was initiated and the protective tariff of 1816, which began the really protectionist movement, was adopted. The duties were moderate and by no means prohibitive, although the tariff was higher than it had ever been before, averaging 20 per cent. Cotton manufactures only got 25 per cent for three years and 20 per cent after that. This scarcely availed to check imports and the cry for a still further increase was heard. The era of protection had begun.

Between 1816 and 1833 there emerges very clearly the antagonism between the economic interests of the North and of the South. In the South, in the region cultivated by slaves, manufactures were impossible, for only intelligent free labour could work machines. Accordingly the South had no interest in a protectionist tariff. Moreover, they were afraid that England might retaliate on their raw cotton. The two leading facts of the period are the growth of the protectionist movement till 1828 and then its decline owing to the opposition of the South.

In 1819 there was a crisis owing to the fall in agricultural prices, and a Bill was introduced in 1820 to increase duties, but was not carried until 1824. The duties on iron, lead, wood, hemp, and the textiles were increased, the general average of duties being something over 30 per cent. After 1824 the woollen industry was very depressed. The lowering of the duty on raw material in England had enabled the English to outsell the American manufacturers. Half the machinery in the New England factories was idle and the only hope was to increase the duty on the manufactured article. The Bill increasing the duty on manufactured woollen goods was lost in 1827, and immediately protectionist associations were organized and higher duties demanded for almost every industry, and the protectionists began what was called an educational campaign.

The tariff question thereupon entered politics and a peculiar series of political manœuvres led in 1828 to the passing into law of the highest tariff of the half century, the Tariff of Abominations. The low-tariff Jackson party introduced a high and hampering tariff in the hope that the high-tariff Adams party would reject it and injure themselves in the country. The Adams party did not dare to reject it, and the tariff, beloved by none, became law. The South especially was furious. They regarded the tariff as a direct transfer of wealth from the South to the North. Moreover, the South had another grievance which was closely bound up with the tariff. Public money got from the customs was being applied to develop the roads and canals of the North. The South seems to have been in less pressing need of communications than the manufacturing districts and the South got the notion that they were to pay for the improvements in the North. At that time the South was doing the chief exporting business and it seemed intolerable in such circumstances that the South should be penalized.

However, the Act was not popular with any section, and moderate men in the North were anxious to make some concession to the South. Duties were successively reduced in 1830 and in 1832, so that practically the old tariff of 1824 was revived. Even the free traders did not wish for the complete abolition of duties. They realized that revenue must be got from somewhere and that the American people preferred that it should be raised on foreign imports.

The tariff of 1832 went back to the old tariff, and it was put in such a shape that the advocates of protection hoped it might be permanently retained. But it was still protective, and the South was not satisfied. Cottons, woollens, and iron were protected, while for articles not produced in the United States there were low duties or no duties. But the prospective permanence brought the South into line and in 1833 the Compromise Tariff Act was passed. It provided for the retention of a large amount of protection for nine years and thereafter a reduction to a uniform 20 per cent, which was about as near to free trade as was possible when it was a question of revenue. There were to be reductions by 1842 on all duties in excess of 20 per cent. The South had won.

The way in which the Compromise had been forced on the North clearly foreshadowed the Civil War of the 'sixties. The Southern States denied the power of Congress to pass Tariff Acts and declared them unconstitutional. And they further argued that even if Congress had power to pass these Acts the further provision that all duties should be uniform was violated, since it was the South that paid and the North that profited. Hence certain States refused to enforce the Acts. South Carolina in 1832 declared the tariffs of 1828 and 1832 null and void and threatened that if the Federal Government enforced those Acts South Carolina would withdraw from the Union. This was met in 1833 by the Force Bill, authorizing the President to use the military and naval forces to enforce the tariff where necessary. But matters did not proceed to such extremities and the Compromise Act of 1833 saved the situation for the time being.

The tariff policy of the period 1833–60 is marked by great vacillation. There were two bad financial crises in 1837 and 1857 which brought a period of depression and a clamour to return to higher duties. During this period American industry steadily developed and it could no longer be urged that cotton and woollen were infant industries. Still, with this very progress there had grown up a class of manufacturers with protectionist interests who about 1840 changed their ground, and the wages argument emerged which has had such enormous influence in America ever since. The argument was that American labour should be protected as against the competition of the less highly paid foreign labour. The protectionists asserted that high duties were necessary to keep out the competition of the ill-paid labourers of Europe and to maintain the high wages of the workers of the United States.

It is an essential principle in tariff policy that the tariff should not be constantly changing. It may be low or it may be high, but uncertainty as to what the next year will bring forth is disastrous. And uncertainty was the characteristic of the American tariff. There was a high tariff (1832), then a period of low duties. Then another high tariff (1842), then two low ones (1846 and 1857).

It was when the country seemed to be making for free trade that the whole revenue system was upset by the crisis of 1837. The crisis of 1837 was primarily due to the reckless banking which was encouraged by the Federal Government and followed President Jackson's policy of decentralizing banking. This led to a depreciated note issue. The resulting general rise in prices brought about over-production, land speculation, and ultimately the fatal fall in cotton prices.

American protectionist writers alleged that the crash came about as a result of the gradual diminution of the tariff, but there is no evidence to prove that the movement towards free trade was really injuring the manufacturers. Indeed, till the storm burst they were flourishing.[1]

This depression would necessarily produce a decline in the customs duties and therefore a decline in the Federal revenue. Meanwhile the Federal revenue was suffering from another cause. The Government had been selling land, and so great was the return that they extinguished the National Debt with the proceeds in 1836. The next consideration was what to do with the surplus, and they decided to distribute the money among the various States. This was done, but done in such a manner as to leave a deficit in the revenue. Something had to be done, and a temporary Tariff Act was passed in September, 1841, laying a duty of 20 per cent on all merchandize paying less except tea and coffee.

In 1842 they were faced by the fact that the customs duties were all to come down to 20 per cent, but the financial situation had become acute. Six States were bankrupt. The result was that a higher tariff was put on to secure revenue, but it was framed so that it was really protectionist. It increased the duty on cottons, iron, and woollens, and raised the average to 33 per cent, instead of the 20 per cent to which it was to fall. On manufactured goods the rate was higher.

After this there was a revival in trade, a fact which was ascribed by the protectionists to the higher tariff. Even Professor Taussig admits that the Tariff Act no doubt helped, in that it introduced certainty. It probably helped to expand profits in certain manufactures such as cotton and iron. Prosperity in these spread to the others and there was a general revival of confidence. It probably temporarily lightened the pressure. It probably emphasized the revival which must have come in a country which was developing so fast as the United States.

But this particular tariff was not to last long. It was superseded by a free trade era between 1846 and 1860. In 1844 the Democrats came into power. President Polk soon made his views plain. Duties there must be for revenue, but no duty should be put so high as to diminish

[1] E. Stanwood, quoted by P. Ashley, *Modern Tariff History*, p. 210.

imports, nor must they be raised up to that limit, as a margin must be allowed. Under this line there might be discriminations but not so as to affect the manufacturers of articles in general use. The protectionism of the President would apply to none of the great manufactures of the country.

The result was the Walker Tariff Act of 1846. All minima and specific duties were abolished and commodities were divided into a number of classes. Iron and wool manufactures paid 30 per cent, cotton paid 25 per cent *ad valorem*. Items in Schedule A, consisting of brandy and spirits, paid 100 per cent. It was a lower tariff than that of 1842. Then followed a period of exceedingly good years which was ascribed to the tariff just as the revival between 1842 and 1846 had been ascribed to protection, although other causes were operating as well, such as emigration and railways. Moreover, the great iron development of the United States had begun.

The country was becoming gradually accustomed to lower duties during the 'fifties, and the Treasury had a surplus, so great was the increase of trade. But the question of tariff revision was superseded by the more burning question of slavery. The manufacturers were prosperous and did not agitate for protection, and the result was that a further lowering of the tariff was comfortably carried in 1857. There was a reduction of about 25 per cent all round, duties on certain raw materials were reduced with advantage to the woollen manufacturers, and the free list was extended. It was the lowest tariff for half a century.

Then followed the crisis of 1857 for which the tariff was blamed. In fact there had been over-speculation, especially in railways, with the inevitable slump. There were small reserves in the bank to meet the paper currency—only about 9 per cent. Specie payments were suspended and imports dropped. The result was that the Treasury was crippled for money and the revenue declined by about one-third. Necessarily this brought with it the question of higher duties. The protectionists were rallied, and the result was the Morrill Tariff of 1861 which returned to the tariff of 1846. The main object of it was to restore the deficit in the revenue. But by this time the Southern States had seceded; the Civil War broke out; and the whole course of American tariff policy was altered.

The Morrill Act of 1861, passed just on the eve of the outbreak of the Civil War, merely aimed at restoring the tariff of 1846. But in fact this tariff was in a greater degree protectionist than that of 1846 for the reason that there was a change over from *ad valorem* to specific duties, and in the course of the change the specific duties imposed were in effect more than an equivalent for the *ad valorem* duties for which they were substituted. Between 1861 and 1865, while the war was raging, duties were imposed on many articles hitherto free. "No session, indeed, hardly a month of any session, passed in which some increase of duties on imports was not made . . . A huge national debt was accumulated . . . an inconvertible paper currency was resorted to . . . an enormous system of internal taxation was created; the duties on imports were vastly increased and extended."[1] The rule seemed to be: "Wherever you see a commodity, tax it." In 1862 specific taxes were imposed on the production of iron and steel, paper, leather and other goods, and a general *ad valorem* tax on other articles of manufacture. Furthermore, the country had to submit to an income-tax.

In 1862 compensation, so it was felt, had to be given to manufacturers for the disabilities under which they were producing: "If we bleed manufacturers, we must see to it that the proper tonic is administered at the same time."[2] So, partly as compensation, the tariff was raised. Now, as this compensation was very liberally calculated, it amounted to more than compensation and was in fact an increase of protection which was made possible by the realization of the need of revenue for the war and the general feeling in favour of vigorous measures. Most of the European countries turned to protection after 1878. That the United States preceded them by about 15 years was due to the causes stated.

In 1864 was adopted what Taussig calls "probably the greatest measure of taxation that the world has seen".[3] The need of revenue for the carrying on of the war, the desire to offset the internal taxes, the protectionist leanings of those who manipulated the tariff, and the general dishonesty and disorganization all combined to bring about a very high tariff. The average rate on dutiable commodities was 47·06 per cent and "it contained flagrant abuses in the shape of duties whose chief effect was to bring money into

[1] F. W. Taussig, *The Tariff History of the United States*, p. 160.
[2] Morrill, quoted by Taussig, p. 162, n.
[3] Taussig, pp. 163–4.

the pockets of private individuals ".[1] It was rushed through both Houses in five days. This was not intended to be permanent; it was an emergency measure, but it has never been gone back on. The war itself called forth a great feeling of national sentiment wholly alien to free trade. "Above all, the habits engendered during this period of comprehensive protection to everything led to a crystallization of the sentiment in favour of national exclusion and isolation." [2]

But not merely was the tariff not reduced after the war; it was expanded. The first great task was financial reorganization; specie payments had to be resumed, the banking system remodelled, and the internal taxes swept away. By 1872 the latter had disappeared. But no effort was made to reduce the protective duties which had been originally only a compensation for the internal taxes. It was intended to reduce the tariff later on, but the squabbles in Congress, the political struggles between the President and legislature, the readmission of the Southern States—all these things diverted attention temporarily from the tariff. The internal taxes had been reduced, revenue had to come from somewhere, and it was desired to accumulate revenue for the resumption of specie payments and to reduce the deficit piled up in war times. Meanwhile the war had given a great stimulus to certain manufactures such as clothing, and these manufacturers urged that since they had been called into existence by the war they were entitled to protection. Capital had been embarked in undertakings whose existence was bound up in the existence of the tariff and it became very difficult to change. It became accepted as the national policy for America.

In 1867, therefore, was enacted the Woollens Act, which increased the duty on manufactured woollen goods by amounts running up to 100 per cent. In 1869 the duty on copper was raised. Previously there had been a very low duty on the metal, and an extensive smelting industry had grown up in Boston and Baltimore, the ore being imported from Chili. About this time the copper mines of the Lake Superior region had come into production, and to help their development a duty was put on Chilian ore.

In 1870 duties again were raised on steel rails. As the

[1] Taussig, op. cit., ibid.
[2] Mayo-Smith and Seligman, quoted by Ashley, p. 233.

price of steel rails declined in England the duty, which was a specific one, became equivalent to 100 per cent by 1877 and consumers in America "were compelled to pay twice as much for steel rails as they paid in England".[1] The enormous profits which were made led to a great extension of production, and it is in this period that the great American steel development began. Gradually, with the increased production, prices eased.

In 1870 a few reductions were made on revenue articles, tea, coffee, cocoa, sugar, spices, also pig iron. The result was that the Federal Government came to depend more and more on the strictly protective duties for revenue.

Meanwhile discontent was growing among the farmers, especially in the west, who felt that they had to pay dearer for their manufactured goods as the result of protective measures, and as the surplus revenue was so large a 10 per cent reduction was made in 1872 on all protectionist duties, on cotton, wool, metals, paper, glass, and the duties on tea and coffee were abolished. This measure indicates the further tendency of America to give up revenue duties and to stick to protectionist duties. The policy so inaugurated was that known later as the free breakfast table.

In 1873 there was a crisis. It was felt all over the world and most severely of all in the raw material producing countries. An acute panic came about in the United States and the imports and the customs revenue fell off. In 1875 the 10 per cent reduction was repealed, so that the war duties as they were imposed in 1864 remained and the extreme protectionist character of the tariff was preserved and even intensified. Between 1875 and 1883 little alteration was made in the tariff.

The period after 1883 is remarkable for its great intensification of protection; a great industrial expansion equal almost in importance to the great agricultural expansion of the 'seventies and 'eighties, one of the chief features of which was the great growth of the steel trades, so that the United States became the chief producer of steel; the growth of trusts; colonial expansion; and the attempt to secure foreign markets for American manufactures.

In the history of tariff policy the landmarks are the McKinley Tariff of 1890, its reduction in 1894 by means of the Wilson Tariff, then the Dingley Tariff, a higher one

[1] Taussig, op. cit., pt. ii, chap. iii.

again, in 1897, which continued for the record period of twelve years and was largely reaffirmed by the Payne-Aldrich Tariff of 1909, and finally the Underwood Tariff of 1913, which revised the tariff rates downwards. The free breakfast table principle was largely adhered to, and the McKinley Tariff included not merely protection of manufactures but protection for agriculture, and a system of bounties was persevered in. Free Trade and Protection become definitely the rival policies of the two great parties, the Democrats and Republicans. At the same time the United States, while fencing off its market, vigorously seconded England in the attempt to maintain the open door in China while shutting out the Chinese, and undertook to strengthen her position in Pacific waters by building a canal across the Isthmus of Panama. The defence of the home market and the expansion of the foreign market by every means have since continued to be the commercial policy of the United States.

In the Presidential election of 1889 protection was made a cardinal issue by the Democrats under Cleveland, who went to the country on a policy of lower tariffs. The result of the election was a victory for President Harrison and a popular verdict for protection. But the Republicans had gone to the country not merely on the question of maintaining protection but of increasing it, and they were bound therefore to bring forward a tariff measure increasing duties. The result was the McKinley Tariff. It could not be urged that the manufacturers were suffering, for the value of their output had more than doubled between 1870 and 1890. The production of steel had increased from 34,000 tons in 1871 to 1,871,000 tons in 1890. The infant industries, argument, as Cleveland had pointed out, was quite out of date, and the great argument which carried the day was that of the home market and national self-sufficiency. It now became the main argument. To develop internal resources and make the most of them the protective system was represented as necessary. The argument which told at the polls was the argument of protecting the American labourer against the competition of ill-paid European labour.

The McKinley Tariff of 1890 lowered the duties on various foodstuffs such as sugar and on certain manufactures that no longer required protection such as iron and steel products and the coarser textiles, but on other manufactures and certain farm produce which were thought to require protection duties were raised. The finer textiles, pottery, glass, dress goods, tin plates, on the one hand, and wheat, barley, oats, potatoes, hay, eggs, apples, flax, hemp, and wool, on the other hand, were all protected further under the McKinley Tariff.

The most interesting part of the McKinley Tariff lies in the reciprocity clauses and the way in which the sugar duties were utilized to assist the United States. The enormous development of American manufacturing industry, as has already been indicated, was beginning to look for markets abroad and to try to obtain favourable terms by treaty, or, as an American writer has termed it, to seek expansion through reciprocity.

The first reciprocity Treaty which the United States made was with Great Britain on behalf of Canada in 1854, the Elgin Treaty. It established free trade in natural products between the two countries. In 1866 it was not renewed. This decision had important reactions not only on the relations between Canada and the United States but also between Canada and the Mother Country. The non-renewal of this Treaty was an indication of animosity between Canada and the United States which, if not created, was emphasized by the Civil War. During the disorganization and stress of the war, Canadian imports into the United States increased enormously. The men were fighting, and food was needed. Meanwhile the Canadians increased their duties on manufactures which were outside the Treaty, a proceeding which was regarded by the Americans as "wholly unwarranted and inequitable". But what so incensed the Northerners was that Canada actively sympathized with the South and gave hospitality to Southern refugees. Moreover, when the war was over revenue was needed, and Canada's free list was a possible source of revenue if taxed. The feeling of having been overreached and resentment at Canada's sympathies with the South were the considerations which primarily led in 1866 to the abandonment of the Treaty which has never been renewed. The non-renewal, in turn, had much to do with alienating Canada from the United States and keeping her within the British Empire.

With its tremendous industrial expansion, the United States about 1884 began to awaken to the fact that it might outgrow its home market and that it was in a position to supply Latin America with the same things as Europe, but that Europe had already got the trade. The result was that three Commissioners were appointed to ascertain the best modes of securing more intimate commercial relations between the United States and the countries of Central and South America. It marks the first step towards the deliberate extension of the export trade. The Commissioners recommended a conference at Washington and eighteen Central and South American countries met at Washington in 1889. They recommended better communications by steamboat, an intercontinental railroad, an international bank and monetary system, and treaties of reciprocity. The result was that in the McKinley Tariff of 1890 a clause was inserted in the Senate authorizing the President to take off the free list, in respect of sugar, molasses, coffee, tea, and hides, any country that levied duties on produce of the United States which in his opinion were inequitable and unreasonable. Any country whose fiscal arrangements were unfavourable to America would be penalized and the consumer would not be affected, since more would come in from other countries that treated the United States in a manner which was in its opinion fair. It was an ingenious plan. The United States gave nothing away, nor did it injure the consumer, since, for example, coffee, if not got from Brazil would come from Ceylon, and sugar from Cuba if not from the English West Indies. This weapon of retaliation proved very effective in securing privileges for American products. Brazil agreed to admit free of duty a list of important articles—wheat, flour, pork, fish, coal, agricultural and mining machinery, and railway material, and reduced by 25 per cent its duties on butter, cheese, canned meats, lumber, and cotton goods. Cuba granted free entry to thirty-nine classes of articles, a 50 per cent reduction on seventeen classes, and 25 per cent on fourteen classes.

It was by means of sugar that the United States was able to put pressure on Germany and Austria-Hungary. The threat to penalize beet sugar secured from Germany the removal of the prohibition on hogs, pork, and sausages imposed since 1883, "notwithstanding the strenuous and persistent efforts of our Legation for its modification and repeal." Moreover, the United States obtained the same rate of duties for its wheat which had been granted to Austria-Hungary in 1892. The latter country promised to apply most favoured nation treatment to the United

States, and from France was obtained in 1893 the minimum tariff in respect of wood and dried fruit. In all, treaties with ten States were concluded in the years 1891 and 1892, and in all cases either goods were removed to the free list or reductions of 25 or 50 per cent were secured. The only nations that were penalized were Colombia, Venezuela, and Haiti. The United States threatened to penalize Argentina, but did not, chiefly because it wanted the hides for the boot and shoe trade.

The elections which were held soon after the tariff of 1890 went in favour of the Democratic Party, who favoured lower duties. The question of the tariff was, however, inextricably mixed up with the silver question. The crisis of 1893 was ascribed to the excessive issue of silver currency. During the Civil War the currency was largely one of greenbacks, and gold in 1864 reached 185 per cent. Prices and rents naturally rose. This paper money continued to be the only money in use till 1879, when specie payments were resumed. Meanwhile the value of silver had gone down enormously and in 1873 silver had been demonetized. Then the Bland Act of 1878 required the Government to purchase and coin not less than $2,000,000 nor more than $4,000,000 worth of silver per month, a measure which partially remonetized silver. The idea was partly to keep silver up and partly to enlarge the coinage. The real strength of the agitation was that the community had not enough money. In 1890, by the Sherman Silver Act, the United States went still further on the road to bimetallism, requiring the Government to purchase 4,500,000 ounces of silver monthly and with this as a basis to issue as many notes as this silver was worth in gold. When these notes were brought up for redemption the Treasury officials changed them for gold; the result was that the gold was depleted and the silver remained. Then came the crisis of 1893, attributed to the excessive issues of silver, and the law was hastily repealed. The struggle over free silver or its restriction shattered the Democratic party, a great many of whom were in favour of free silver, and left them less able to carry through a modification of the McKinley Tariff. Nevertheless, a Bill was brought in in 1894 to lower duties considerably. It was so tinkered at in Committee and in the Senate that the Wilson Tariff, as it was called, was much less revolutionary than the President intended. It made no " deep reaching change ". " A slice was taken off here, a shaving there, but the essentially protective character remained."

In the Presidential election of 1896 the Republicans fought and won on the silver question, but once they were in office they began to alter the tariff once more. In 1897 the Dingley Tariff was adopted, and under it the duties reached the highest level they had ever attained in the United States. Duties on wool and woollen goods were re-imposed, and hides and flax were also taxed. Silks and linens received higher protection, and the McKinley duties on glass and pottery were restored. Metal goods remained as before, but tin plates received an increase of duty. The tax on sugar was doubled. Reciprocity was once more encouraged. The Act of 1897 "pushed protection in several directions further than ever before".[1] As a financial measure it is said not to have been very successful, but of course finance was complicated by the Spanish-American War. In 1897, too, the reciprocity system was again revived but on a new plan. Certain dutiable articles were selected and the President was authorized to reduce them for any country that granted the United States reciprocal and equivalent concessions. As a result, in the years that followed the United States Government was able to negotiate reciprocity agreements on favourable terms with France, Germany, Italy, and Portugal.

The interval between the tariff of 1897 and that of 1909 was the longest hitherto on record in the United States. The Spanish War and the growing expenditure of the Government were two matters that tended to divert attention from the tariff. Then came the crusade against the Trusts. It was thought that they were largely sustained by protective tariffs and that if duties were lowered and foreign competition stimulated the Trusts would have to lower prices. Revision, taken to mean reduction, was promised at the Presidential election of 1908. There was a general acceptance of the protectionist principle: the only question was whether the tariff was "unreasonably high". Such duties were to be imposed as would equal "the difference between the cost of production at home and abroad together with a reasonable profit for American industries". The result was the Payne-Aldrich Tariff of 1909. Amongst other things the duty on hides and the duties on coal were removed. Rates

[1] F. W. Taussig, *Tariff History of the United States*, p. 358.

on iron ore and lumber were slightly lowered as also were rates on iron and steel and on leather, shoes, harness and saddlery—all industries where there was no real competition.

To balance these there were advances on cotton goods, hosiery, razors, pocket-knives, and silk goods. No change was made in the wool and woollen duties. The duty on raw sugar was maintained to compensate the beet growers—300,000 tons were, however, to be admitted free from the Philippines. Summing up, it may be said that despite alterations in details and some slight revision downward, the general features and the degree of protection of the Dingley Tariff were maintained.

So bitter was the disappointment with the Payne-Aldrich Tariff on the part of people who favoured lower tariffs, that the history of the McKinley Tariff and its aftermath was repeated. Just as the McKinley Tariff led the way to the Wilson Tariff with its revision of duties downwards, so the Payne-Aldrich Tariff led to the downward-revising Underwood Tariff of 1913. The Democrats had been returned on the wave of indignation following the Payne-Aldrich Tariff, and they promptly took action. Believing that high tariffs served to bolster up monopolies that exploited the American consumers, President Wilson declared that "the object of the tariff duties henceforth laid must be effective competition, the whetting of American wits by contest with the wits of the rest of the world". The Underwood Tariff did not mean free trade, or even low tariffs necessarily: it simply meant lower tariffs on the ground that existing tariffs were unnecessarily high.

From a low-tariff country the United States has become the leading protectionist country of the world. As a matter of fact, for the United States, with its great resources and extensive home market, the problems of tariffs and of foreign trade are of less importance than for almost any other country in the world.

CHAPTER 5

National Expansion

French Colonial Policy.

British and French methods of colonization compared.

Policy of "assimilation" after French Revolution.

Liberal movement after 1848 Revolution; all slaves freed in French colonies.

Liberal era, 1861–6; French colonies allowed to work out own economic salvation.

Growth of French Colonial Empire after 1870.

Tariff assimilation.

German expansion.

Early policy of home settlement.

Germany joins in the scramble for Africa in the 'eighties.

Colonies regarded as means of acquiring control of tropical products

Russian expansion.

Growth of population necessitating an increase of the food supply. No physical barriers to spreading out. Result: expansion north-east into Siberia, where expansion was comparatively safe. Conditions of life difficult.

Expansion south-east. Danger from hostile tribes. The State had to follow up its people to ensure their safety.

The desire to get ports.

This led in Peter the Great's time (1689–1725) to the acquisition of a seaport on the Baltic from Sweden and to the acquisition of a sea outlet on the Black Sea from Turkey. Finland acquired.

The desire to get an ice-free port led partly to the expansion in Eastern Asia and towards the Persian Gulf by railway.

The desire to get markets in Asia, as the effective demand of the Russian peasant is so low.

Russian expansion has been peasant colonization by migration.

American expansion.

Inland expansion.

Public lands policy.
The Homestead Act, 1862.
The gold discoveries and their consequences.
Emigration from Europe.
American migration.
By 1890 inland expansion practically completed.

Expansion overseas.

The Spanish-American War.
New problems.

French Colonial Policy[1]

DURING the eighteenth century French colonies had been developed by monopolistic chartered companies. The economic policy was one of exclusion of foreigners and foreign goods. The trade of the colonies was therefore confined to the mother country as was the case with all the other colonial Empires—Holland, Spain, or England. The trade of France with its colonies was very important in the eighteenth century, being reckoned by M. Girault as two-thirds of its external commerce.[2]

Before 1763 France owned Eastern Canada, the whole of the Mississippi valley, and important islands in one of the two richest trading regions in the world—the West Indies. France had numerous and important settlements in the other great trading region—India. It had in addition settlements in West Africa, the great depot for the labour supply of the West Indian islands. It owned the islands of Bourbon and the Ile de France and had claims on Madagascar. By 1814 it was left with a mere remnant of its former Empire, Guadeloupe, Martinique, Réunion, and French Guiana being the principal French possessions. The interesting thing about the colonial expansion of France is the fact that France followed the same evolution as Great Britain and developed another great Empire in the place of the one it had lost. Whereas England eventually offset the loss of New England by a New South Wales and of Virginia by Canada, the French have offset Canada by Algiers and their losses in India by the development of possessions in Indo-China. In Algeria, acquired by penetration between 1830 and 1847, there is the expansion of the French race or *colonie de peuplement*, while in further India and West Africa there are examples of *colonies d'exploitation*. Therefore in both cases France and England have had a parallel development of an Empire of Race and an Empire of Rule.

The fundamental distinction between the two great colonial Powers lies in the fact that the expansion of the French race is so small. There were only 200,000 whites in the whole of the French Colonial Empire in 1907 when M. Girault published the third edition of his *Principes de*

[1] See, for full treatment of the subject, S. H. Roberts, *History of French Colonial Policy, 1870–1925*, 2 vols.

[2] A. Girault, *Colonial Tariff Policy of France*, p. 10

Colonisation.[1] This seems a small number beside the English 14 millions of 1911. France is essentially a ruler of coloured peoples and her colonial problems are mainly those of a tropical or semi-tropical Empire, i.e. of an Empire in Trust. The truth is that the Frenchman emigrates very unwillingly. He explores brilliantly; he is not unwilling to be an official and a soldier in the colonies; but the French settler is absent, and the French commercial houses in the colonies have great difficulty in keeping their French employees. The small size of French families, the general diffusion of comfort and property, the prospect of inheriting land under the law of the distribution of property—all combine to keep possible French colonists at home.[2]

In yet one other respect the two countries differ. France is primarily an Asiatic and African power. It is only an American power in virtue of Guiana apart from her West Indian islands, but she is essentially the great Mediterranean colonial power. Unlike England, France has shouldered an enormous financial burden in her Empire and, again unlike England, she has evolved a compromise between paternal rule of the colonies and self-government; she has devised the plan of "assimilation", i.e. a plan by which the colonies should be treated as if they were French provinces and their inhabitants as if they were Frenchmen. The idea is that, being French to all intents and purposes, they would not wish to break off and become independent units.

The English are not an assimilating race; their motives of expansion are almost wholly economic. The English colonies were founded in the seventeenth century by merchants grouped in chartered companies and they received no monetary support from the Crown. In the nineteenth century British expansion depended again on individual effort and chartered companies. There was very little of the missionary spirit, a great deal of commercial enterprise, and practically no desire for glory or prestige. The British

[1] He calculated that there were in addition 360,000 coloured persons in the West Indian Islands who were completely assimilated in sentiment as well as in law to Frenchmen, 17,000 criminals in the penal colonies, and 43 millions of *indigènes*—22 million in West Africa, 18 million in Indo-China, 2½ in Madagascar, and 500,000 in the other colonies. *Principes de Colonisation*, vol. i, p. 368. For comparison with Great Britain, see Knowles, *Industrial and Commercial Revolutions*, pp. 328–9; Knowles, *Economic Development of the British Overseas Empire*, vol. i, pp. 65–6, 152–3.

[2] J. E. C. Bodley, *France*, pp. 186–9.

have not attempted to transform native societies and have allowed a great deal of local autonomy, and therefore the British Empire is essentially an Empire of diversities as contrasted with the French, the ideal of which is to mould all the inhabitants to the pattern of a Frenchman.

The policy of assimilation was inaugurated at the time of the French Revolution. With its abrupt break with the past, the legislators swept away, on paper, many of the old limitations on French colonial trade. The colonies were to to " assimilated " to the mother country. Guadeloupe was to be as much a part of France as Brittany, therefore the policy to be aimed at was free trade between the mother country and the colonies and a tariff for the world outside. Just as the Revolution had swept away the internal barriers within France, so the barriers between France and its colonies were to be removed. All the monopolistic privileges of the chartered companies were abolished and the colonies were to share in " the fruits of the happy regeneration which has taken place ". The slaves were also freed, as slavery was incompatible with liberty, equality, and fraternity. They, too, were Frenchmen.

The British fleet, however, interfered with the free intercourse thus planned.[1] Napoleon, moreover, could not afford to have the production of the sugar islands destroyed by the abolition of slavery, and revoked the decree. With the attenuated Empire left in 1814 France reverted to the old policy of exclusion of foreign goods. Trade between the mother country and the colonies was regulated by Navigation Acts. The colonies, however, received a preference on their sugar in the home market and slavery continued. The colonies being so insignificant, Frenchmen ceased to feel interested in them and the same disgust with colonies, though for different reasons, was felt both in France and England up to 1870.

In 1830, in order to distract the political attention of Frenchmen, an expedition was undertaken to punish the Dey of Algiers who had insulted a French Consul. The conquest of the interior was carried out gradually within the next seventeen years.

In 1848, under the liberal impulse of the revolution of that year, the slaves were freed in all the colonies as they

[1] The consumption of sugar fell from 30 million kilos to 8 million kilos and was bought by the ounce at the chemists. Levasseur, *Histoire du Commerce*, ii, p. 127, n.

had been freed in the English colonies in 1833. This alteration of the basis of production in the tropical islands created great economic loss. Following on this came the competition of beetroot sugar, which again affected the colonies so adversely that it was felt better to let them work out their own economic salvation, if they could, unhampered by regulations imposed by the mother country.

The result was that the French colonies between 1861 and 1866 were allowed to trade with any country they liked in any ships they liked. They were also given control of their own tariffs. The colonial trade of the time was small. France was in a liberal mood as regards tariffs; the colonies were almost derelict; why trouble about their very small trade? Thus the policy of "tariff autonomy" instead of "tariff exclusion" or subjection was inaugurated. One precaution was, however, taken. In the islands of the Antilles and Réunion the colonies were not allowed to levy customs duties on imports which were the products of France. They were, however, allowed to levy wharfage dues on both French and foreign goods. The colonies then abolished all customs duties and levied enhanced wharfage dues which taxed French goods equally with foreign. This aroused much resentment in France. During this liberal period Napoleon III acquired Saigon and the neighbouring province in 1862, but, being distracted by European politics, little was done to follow this up.

Just as this movement to let the colonies work out their own economic destiny was the outcome of the Liberal era, so the Protectionist era involved a reaction towards closer relations and the favourite catch-word was again "assimilation", a return to the ideas of the French Revolution. The colonial policy of France since the Franco-Prussian war must not, however, be looked upon merely as part of the general tariff policy. The French have always had great missionary aspirations and have always held that a State no less than an individual should seek *la gloire*. The French revolutionary armies tried in 1793 to compel other peoples to be free. Napoleon, as we have seen, changed mediaeval into modern States by abolishing serfdom and gilds and by providing a modern system of law, finance, and administration to take the place of feudalism. He, too, went in for a policy of "assimilation" in Europe. Napoleon III stood for liberal ideas in commerce and for the defeat of Russia in the Crimea and Austria in

Italy. He posed as the patron of nationalities. The defeat of France by Germany and the loss of Alsace and Lorraine drove France to look elsewhere to realize both its missionary aspirations and its ambitions in respect of glorious achievement. Hence a great recrudescence of colonial expansion. Why should not France spread its great civilization in Africa and Asia and obtain there some compensation for the loss of the Eastern provinces ? To these two motives—glory for France and the spread of French civilization—came the desire to extend markets for French goods. In the 'eighties there is something romantic as well as something almost incredible about the rapid extension of the French rule in West Africa, the Sudan, Indo-China, and North Africa. Tunis became a Protectorate of France in 1881. Working down to the South from Algeria and up to the north from Senegal with a railway pushed out into the desert to back up the troops, the French founded a great African Empire in the Sudan, consisting of two million square kilometres, to which their claim was recognized by England in 1890. The way had been prepared by a whole generation of brilliant explorers who made known Dahomey, the table-lands of Nigeria, and who penetrated to Timbuctoo and Lake Chad just as the *coureurs des bois* had opened up the interior of Canada and made known the Mississippi valley to Europe in the seventeenth and eighteenth centuries. French Congo was another region obtained by France in 1885. The island of Madagascar had also accepted a French Protectorate in that year, which was transformed into direct rule in 1896. Annam and Tonkin also became definitely French Protectorates in 1885, and by agreement with England in 1896 the French protectorate over Cambodia was recognized.[1] The French sphere of influence in North Africa was rounded off by the protectorate assumed over Morocco in 1912. In this way France became the second great colonial power of the world.[2]

[1] It is worth noticing that the French seem to have an especial liking for the form of government known as a Protectorate, e.g. Tunis, Morocco, Magadascar, as well as Indo-China. As M. Girault puts it, " France prefers to hide the hand of iron under the velvet glove of a protectorate. A people," he says, " who would fiercely have resisted annexation submits to the educational influence of those who appear not as conquerors but as elder brothers." *Principes de Colonisation* (3rd ed.), vol. i, p. 370.

[2] The figures given by M. Girault (1907), of the extent of this Empire: 8 million sq. km. on the African Continent, 600,000 in the Indian Ocean, 700,000 in Indo-China, 100,000 in America, and 25,000 in Oceania. In Europe herself France does not possess more than 536,000 sq. km. Total given as 9·5 million sq. km. Op. cit., vol. i, p. 12.

The strength of the idealistic motive combined with the idea of bringing the blessings of French civilization to native races is well brought out by M. Leroy Beaulieu in his book, *De la colonisation chez les peuples modernes*. In the preface to the first edition, 1822, he says: " Colonization has been relegated to the second place in the national consciousness, it ought to be put first and foremost. Our continental politics ought henceforward to be essentially defensive; it is outside Europe that we must satisfy our legitimate instincts for expansion. We ought to work at founding a great African Empire and a lesser Asiatic one. It is the only great enterprise that destiny now permits us to indulge in. At the beginning of the twentieth century Russia will count 120 millions of prolific inhabitants occupying enormous territories, nearly sixty million Germans supported by thirty million Austrians will dominate Central Europe. One hundred and twenty million Anglo-Saxons will occupy the fairest countries of the globe and will impose their language on almost the whole civilized world. . . . By the side of these giants where will France be? Of the great rôle which she has played in the past, of the influence —often decisive—which she has exercised upon the progress of civilized peoples, what will remain to her? A memory, growing fainter day by day. Our country has a means of escaping from this inevitable decline, it is to colonize. . . . Colonization is for France a question of life or death, either France will become a great African power or she will be in a century or two only a second-rate European power, she will count as little more than Greece or Roumania in Europe."

In his book he set out the advantages of colonization and went on to say: " The prestige of a people which has imposed its direction, its language, its habits, and its tastes on extended territories has its reaction on life generally (*dans les affaires*). Under these conditions colonization at the moment of writing forms part of the mission of the great Western States." In the fourth edition of the book in 1891 M. Leroy Beaulieu states that his publishers told him when he first wrote the book in 1874 that no book on colonization would sell and he records the enormous change that had taken place in the French attitude towards colonies in seventeen years.

The same view was put by Gide in 1897. " Colonization is not a question of interest but a question of duty. It is necessary to colonize because there is a moral obligation for peoples as well as individuals to employ the forces and the advantages which they have received from Providence for the benefit of humanity. It is necessary to colonize because colonization is among the number of those duties which are incumbent on great nations and from which they cannot withdraw without failing in their mission in the world and engendering a veritable moral decadence."[1]

In no country has colonization been so systematically studied as in France. The whole philosophy of those who were urging France to take up her mission in the world rested on the idea that French civilization and French culture was something that was right in itself and therefore must be a benefit to all others, black or white. Hence, there is in French colonization an attempt at assimilation all round, not merely in the matter of tariffs. The Frenchman was good, therefore make the *indigène* good by the institutions which had produced a good civilized Frenchman. Attempts have, therefore, been made to give the natives a personal status, to break up the tribal or communal land-holding, since it was the first principle of a liberal policy to recognize the right of the individual to deal with his property as he liked. They were prepared to introduce French representative institutions into tropical colonies under the idea, inherited from Rousseau, that man was fundamentally good and only made bad by bad laws. The French considered that an institution once declared rational must as such be applicable at all times and in all places, and if the natives be liberated from superstition they must be raised to a higher plane of civilization by being induced or forced to adopt methods which make for personal liberty or justice. Therefore the great ideal was to apply French law and to treat the colonies as part of France and the *indigènes* as Frenchmen. That this might mean a complete revolution of their whole mode of life which might not necessarily be to their advantage does not seem to have occurred to the colonial enthusiasts. The policy of assimilation meant that the natives should adopt the language, the religious and political beliefs, the morals and the *esprit* of the French conquerors, and this philosophy applied to races as different as Negroes, Chinese-Annamites, Kanakas, and Arabs.

[1] Quoted Girault, *Principes de la Colonisation*, vol. i, p. 31.

"One party says, 'It is by religious beliefs that we will transform the *indigènes* to our own image.' Another, 'The conversion of Mussulmans is unrealizable, it is by institutions that we will assimilate them.' Others again, 'Assimilation by institutions is insufficient, it is in giving them our morals our *esprit français* that we will attract them to us.' They all agree that the gulf between the races can be bridged." [1]

M. Girault considers that the policy of assimilation "sacrifices neither the interest of the colonies nor that of the mother country . . . It is the only ideal possible where autonomy is impracticable or dangerous. . . . Tempered by a large decentralization, going as far, if need be, as federalism, it procures all the advantages of autonomy but has the incontestable moral superiority over federalism in that it unites instead of dividing. A single Parliament, composed of men speaking the same language in spite of their difference of origin, coming from all parts of the world where floats the same flag in order to discuss the general interests of their common country, is an eloquent and obvious manifestation of this unity. . . . The establishment of a federal parliament is to-day perhaps the only means which remains to England to keep Canada and Australia." [2]

This policy of assimilation did not work out as favourably as was hoped,[3] and another colonial school has arisen which maintains that a negro is not a Frenchman with a coloured skin but a person with a racial history and customs of his own who must be approached from the basis of ethnology and whose tribal customs and habits cannot lightly be interfered with. Others began to claim that the plan of submitting the colonies to the tariff system of France did not necessarily suit regions in such different stages of economic development and that their commercial development had been retarded by their subjection to the assimilating policy. A notable instance of want of success

[1] L. de Saussure, *Psychologie de la colonisation française dans ses rapports avec les sociétés indigènes*, p. 302.

[2] *Principes de Colonisation*, vol. i, p. 88.

[3] "In Indo-China, the French began by remodelling and destroying the native institutions and even attempting to introduce the entire legislation of continental France. . . . Wherever the French elective and representative institutions have been introduced into tropical colonies they have led to the most grotesque results. In the Indian possessions as well as in Senegal, the elections have become a pure formality. Thus, while thousands of votes are officially returned, hardly a native is seen to enter the polling-place on election day, the entire reports being prepared in advance by public officials." P. Reinsch, *Colonial Administration*, p. 19.

in the policy was seen in that pursued regarding the land system of Algiers, which had led to the expropriation of a large number of natives. In the Protectorate of Tunis it was impossible to gallicize native habits and customs since it was merely a Protectorate, and it was held by many that this enforced respect of native institutions had been beneficial to the colony. In West Africa where, owing to treaty agreements, it was not possible to apply the tariff system of France as was done under the policy of assimilation in Indo-China, it was urged that trade had developed much more rapidly, satisfactorily, and spontaneously. At the beginning of the twentieth century an attack was made on the whole idea of assimilation, and the idea was growing that "personality" was the thing to aim at in commerce, land system, habits, and customs; in other words, that each colony was a problem to itself and should be studied as such. Meanwhile, if France was to pursue its great civilizing, assimilating mission, it was obvious that it would have to spend money. French colonies have been very costly to the national exchequer and part of the crusade in favour of colonial personality has received its impetus from the fact that the English colonies which have been let alone and not developed according to a definite logical theory have as a rule paid their way and enjoy a larger trade with the mother country than the French colonies. "Colonization is a work of sacrifice and devotion. It demands a long series of persevering and painful efforts, and it will be long before the reward will be seen. Our generation will have disappeared when the results of what it prepared will have been accomplished."[1] The fact is that the French have never made their colonial revenue meet the expenditure and the deficit has been made up by France, but they have been inspired by these high ideals of the spread of French influence and have apparently thought the effort worth while. Meanwhile they tried to secure the economic compensation of markets reserved very largely for the mother country by a colonial tariff system giving free entry to French goods.

The argument was that so many sacrifices of men and money had been made in the acquisition of these new regions that they ought to make some return. Once public opinion was focussed on the colonies it did not seem as if they

[1] Girault, *Principes*, vol. i, pp. 370–1.

patronized French goods as they ought, and the idea grew that it was necessary to take definite steps to secure these markets to which France had a sort of moral right. It was noticed with dismay that the value of French goods imported by the older colonies was declining and foreign goods were increasing.

Imports 000 francs[1]

	French Merchandize.		*Foreign Merchandize.*	
	1865.	1880.	1865.	1880.
Martinique . . .	17,334	14,037	9,963	17,327
Guadeloupe . . .	18,890	11,631	3,819	13,624
Réunion . . .	14,431	9,198	12,010	28,707
Total . . .	50,655	34,866	25,792	59,658

It will be seen, therefore, that exports from France had declined while foreign imports had risen. Moreover, while France was the best customer for the products of her colonies, they bought in 1890 nearly twice as much from foreign countries as they did from France.

000 francs

In 1890,	210,790	total imports into French colonies.
	70,903	imports from France.
	3,293	,, ,, French colonies.
	136,594	,, ,, foreign countries.
	191,386	total exports.
	100,845	shipped to France.
	3,538	to French colonies.
	87,003	to foreign countries.

The result was the new tariff assimilation, the general feature of which was that French goods were to go into the colonies without payment of any duty, and that foreign goods were to pay the French tariff as applied in France. Colonial goods in the French market were to have a preference.

The policy of tariff assimilation was first applied to Algeria. In 1884 foreign products imported into Algeria were made subject to the same duties as if they were imported into France. French goods going into Algeria and Algerian products coming into France were free, and the trade between France and Algeria was in 1893 reserved for French vessels. Algeria was looked upon simply as

[1] Girault, *Colonial Tariff Policy of France*, p. 89.

three French departments. From the standpoint of navigation and tariffs Algeria was treated as national territory. The French tariff was applied to foreign goods going into Algeria. Each country, however, keeps for itself the revenue from the customs and the other duties collected on the frontier.

Then the other colonies were coerced by threats of the withdrawal of subsidies for public works and cajoled by preferences on colonial sugar, into re-establishing their customs duties, which of course did not apply to French goods, the wharfage dues remaining, however, for French and foreign goods. This was done by Guadeloupe in 1884 and Martinique and Réunion in 1885. They received in 1886 in return a 12 per cent abatement on their sugar while an additional tax of 7 francs per cent *ad valorem* was imposed on sugars imported from non-French sources.

In 1887 the French tariff was applied to Indo-China for foreign goods, French goods entering free, and the imports fell from sixty million in 1887 to forty-two million francs in the following year. The whole tendency towards tariff assimilation was summarized in the Law of 1892. The colonies were divided into two groups, the assimilated and the non-assimilated colonies. The assimilated colonies were Martinique, Guadeloupe, Guiana, St. Pierre and Miquelon, Réunion, Mayotte, Gabon, French Indo-China, and New Caledonia. The non-assimilated colonies, which were regarded as quite exceptional, were those regions where France was bound by treaties, as in West Africa, and later on in Morocco, where she was merely in possession as "Protector" as also in Tunis, or where the tariff of France would have been evaded by wholesale smuggling, owing to a long frontier with foreign neighbours on either side. Four English colonies, one Portuguese, and one German colony were enclosed in French West Africa, and to attract commerce to French instead of to the foreign ports it was not desirable to have a rigid tariff system. Therefore the non-assimilated colonies included West Africa, Tahiti, the French establishments in India, Tunis, and Morocco.

In 1897 Madagascar became an assimilated colony with the little islands of Nossi Bé, Diego Suarez, and Sainte Marie. Three-fourths of the colonial commerce was conducted under the new régime of assimilation. Not merely do imports from France enter the assimilated colonies freely, but also the products from one French colony to another.[1] Although foreign imports pay at the same rates as the French tariff, certain exceptions are permitted to fit the circumstances of each colony, though it is not intended that these exceptions shall be large and they apply mainly to food-stuffs. When the French tariff was revised in an upward direction in 1910 this new protection also applied to the colonial tariffs.

While France has no export duties, the colonies have them for fiscal reasons, and it is interesting to notice that Indo-China after 1898 decided to exempt from export duties those products sent to France and the French colonies or from one part of Indo-China to another. This is a parallel development to the preferences on export given by some of the British tropical possessions.[2]

If French goods were allowed into the colonies freely, colonial goods ought to have been allowed freely into France, but this was not done. Sugar, coffee, and cocoa formed an important branch of the French revenue and France could not afford to admit these free. In 1892 colonial commodities other than sugar paid half the ordinary duties. As the rates on the articles were very high, half the ordinary duty made a considerable difference, for instance, coffee paid 78 fr. per 100 kilo instead of 156 fr. Sugar was, however, excepted, foreign and colonial sugar being treated the same except for a surtax of 7 fr. upon sugar of European origin. The native beet-sugar growers had to bear an excise and it would have been impossible to allow in colonial sugars to swamp native beet-sugar growers. Sugar was, however, favoured by an export bounty in 1897 till it was abolished by the Sugar Convention in 1902.

While the non-assimilated colonies apply their own special tariffs to both French and foreign goods, they do not enjoy the reductions in France[3] which the goods of the assimilated colonies enjoy. They merely enjoy the minimum tariff as any other most favoured nation, but the products going from one French colony to another, whether assimilated or non-assimilated, are free. Decrees of the Council of State can also make exceptions for the imports

[1] This does not apply to French India after 1904. The products of French India are treated as those of most favoured nations.

[2] T. E. Gregory, *Tariffs*, pp. 284–90.

[3] In French West Africa there are surtaxes on foreign products. Girault, *Colonial Tariff Policy of France*, p. 111.

from the non-assimilated colonies; for instance, palm oil from French West Africa in 1892 was exempted from duty.

A reaction has, however, developed against the policy of assimilation. In the first place, foreign countries made it the ground of objection when France wished to secure Morocco. She not merely did not keep the "open door", but she shut it and locked it against foreigners while keeping it open for herself. Many of the persons interested in colonization in France considered that the colonies did not thrive under the assimilation system and that the French tariff, suitable perhaps for a highly developed Western country, was not suitable for undeveloped tropical areas. It seems to have been the opinion of foreign observers that French commerce did not expand as it should and that the colonies were unduly handicapped by the commercial system.

"France has succeeded in securing for herself the bulk of the commerce of her dependencies, but she has at the same time seriously handicapped their economic development. . . . French manufacturers, made sure of a market and of high prices, exert no energy to develop colonial commerce. They do not adapt their manufactures to the needs of local populations, nor do they realize the advantages that might be gained by making such towns as Saigon or Hanoi entrepôts for general Oriental trade. On account of the high customs duties all transit trade is discouraged, and commerce is confined to the local population, who are given few economic opportunities that would make them become better customers. Matters are not helped by the administrative system; the importing merchant is obliged to go through endless formalities to get entry for his goods and special caution moneys are exacted at every turn."[1]

Girault considers that the tariff policy has worked very unfavourably for the small colonies such as the islands in the Antilles, New Caledonia, French Guiana, and St. Pierre and Miquelon. Their external commerce has remained stationary or has declined. The natural place for the West Indies to trade with is the United States. The new tariff made American goods dearer, while French goods which could come in free of tariff were handicapped by the freights of the long voyage. Consumption fell off, customs revenue declined, and new taxes had to be imposed to get revenue.

[1] P. Reinsch, *Colonial Administration*, p. 238.

He says, " From all standpoints, tariff assimilation is, for the small colonies, deliberately devised misery. This policy, applied to small countries unable to defend themselves and whose attachment to the mother country is traditional, is unworthy of a great nation like France." [1]

Again, "The colonists are forced to bring goods from a great distance and pay very dear for them, when it would be easy to buy them at low prices in the neighbourhood. They are forced to undergo the inconvenience of serious delay in the securing of products for which they have urgent need. This creates among them a feeling of irritation against the mother country." [2]

The system, however, works better in Indo-China and Madagascar. In Indo-China the French manufacturer has gained, since French fabrics have completely supplanted other European fabrics. The whole trade of that region increased fourfold, from 127 million francs (export and import trade) in 1888 to 533 in 1912. Thus " assimilation is at most a handicap, it is not a cause of distress " in Indo-China. There are complaints that the high French tariff has hindered the transit trade from Siam and South China, that without the tariff Saigon would have developed as a great free port like Singapore or Hong Kong and that Indo-China cannot make reciprocity treaties with the Far Eastern countries. But one unexpected result has ensued, and that is that the tariff has hastened the development of a cotton industry in Indo-China itself. Protected against India and Japan by the high French tariff and against competition from the mother country by distance, and possessing coal and cheap labour, the colony has started its own textile manufactures, which is a source of much dissatisfaction to French manufacturers.

In Madagascar French merchandize has completely displaced foreign, and English fabrics have been ousted from the markets of an island which is as large as France.[3] Cotton fabrics constitute half the imports. The trade (export and import) rose from 67 million francs in 1909 to 109 in 1912. M. Girault, however, considers that " the discrepancy between the advantages gained by the

[1] *Colonial Tariff Policy*, pp. 199, 200.
[2] Girault, *Colonial Tariff Policy of France*, p. 283.
[3] Ibid., p. 221.

manufacturers and the sacrifices imposed upon the colonials is truly shocking ".[1]

West Africa is a non-assimilated region. When the various regions were united in 1895 it contained 3,913,280 sq. km. The import and export trade has risen rapidly and it is always quoted as the stock example of the success of a non-assimilated region.

Million francs

	Imports.	*Exports.*	*Total.*
1895	46·8	31·9	78·7
1910	153·1	125·2	278·3
1912	134·7	118·5	253·2

The imports of French merchandize

were in	1895	nearly	20	million francs.
	1908	„	40	„ „
	1910	„	70	„ „

Of these, textiles constituted half the value. " The external commerce of West Africa has developed with a rapidity much greater than that of the other colonies," is the verdict.[2] The prosperity of the natives has improved and their capacity for buying has increased. On the other hand Miss Mary Kingsley, in her *Travels in West Africa,* considered that the whole range of tariffs in French West Africa was too high and impeded trade.

The great success of the system of assimilation has been in Algeria, where trade has increased a hundredfold since 1834. Since 1871 it has risen from 300 millions to 1,217 in 1912. Four-fifths of the commerce of Algiers proceeds under conditions of freedom, since its exports go freely into France and the country receives its imports freely from France. It is really the commerce of one part of a nation with another part. The facts that many of the colonists are French, that the countries are only separated by a narrow strip of sea, and that there is no other neighbouring country from which its inhabitants could more advantageously obtain their goods—all make the system of assimilation very

[1] Ibid., p. 223.
[2] Girault, *Colonial Tariff Policy of France*, p. 234.

successful. By far the greater part of the whole French colonial commerce is done with Algeria. In general, the most important article exported from France to her colonies is cotton piece goods, and Algeria takes one-third of the cotton exports of France.

The alternative proposed by those who did not approve of the policy of assimilation was that for each colony there should be devised a tariff to suit its special needs by France, not necessarily the same tariff as France imposed for herself on the outside world. It did not mean colonial self-government or that the colonies should fix their own tariffs, but that France should fix them for each colony. A second line of attack on colonial policy involved the question that the colonies, while forced to admit French goods free of duty, were nevertheless obliged to pay half the French tariff rates when their goods entered France. In 1913, the half duty on colonial products was remitted, which meant the loss of 2½ million francs in revenue, sugar still being excepted. It was an attempt to buy off the opponents of assimilation, this great market now being completely free.

While the French colonies increased their imports and exports considerably, nevertheless when this increase is compared with the progress of the British Empire or the general growth of trade in the world, the result scarcely seemed commensurate with the effort. A skilled observer found that the external trade of all the French possessions, including Algeria and Tunis, was not one-third as large as the external trade of India.[1]

He also considers that the French colonies are overburdened with officials, that there is great difficulty in securing commercial agents since all want a post in the government, that French capital is shy of investment in the colonies, and that the few men who seek their fortunes there have not sufficient capital behind them, while the absence of banking and credit facilities largely accounts for the slow commercial development of some of the richest areas of the world. It is, however, not merely the colonies, but France also, that has paid the price. If it has carried out a policy of assimilation, if it has aimed at *la gloire* and the spread of French civilization, it has had to pay heavily for the privilege of carrying out what it conceives to be

[1] Reinsch, op. cit., p. 236.

its great mission in the expansion of French influence in the world.

German Expansion

During the seventeenth and eighteenth centuries Germany, and particularly Prussia, had pursued a policy of home settlement. The empty, or half-empty lands east of the Elbe had been filled up with Rhinelanders, with French, and with Dutch. During the nineteenth century, however, population in Germany increased at such a pace that there was not sufficient room for all and an outlet had to be found. Even in the seventeenth and eighteenth centuries German settlers had found their way overseas to North America. But in the nineteenth century they went there in their tens of thousands, helping to build up the eastern States, and later peopling Wisconsin and the Dakotas. Many Germans regretted this loss to the Fatherland, but a disunited Germany could take no remedial action.

Then in 1871 came the unification of Germany under the Empire and, on the part of some Germans, the hope of overseas expansion. But Bismarck was an adamantine opponent, saying, " I am no colonial man," and arguing that to maintain an overseas empire would require a powerful navy. However, in the 'eighties, the scramble for Africa began. France and Britain commenced to carve up Africa in their own interests, and at last public opinion in Germany grew so strong that Bismarck's hand was forced and, acting promptly, he took over the wide areas of East Africa, South-West Africa, Togoland, and the Cameroons.

While at the back of its mind Germany did not wish to be outdone by France, the impelling motives would seem to have been largely economic. Having no practical experience of tropical colonization, which was the only thing left for Germany to undertake since the temperate regions were occupied by England and others, it had an idea that it could develop a new German race in its African possessions which would prove as good a market eventually as the self-governing colonies and India were for England. Germany, too, like France, believed that colonies could be made to pay in trade and prestige. Germany also hoped that the German people would cease to emigrate to the United States and Russia and would go instead to the

Cameroons and South-West Africa and form a new German race which would retain its nationality and not lose it, as was the case with the German who crossed the Atlantic.

Both these hopes were destined to be disappointed. No German colony had up to 1913 paid its way. The deficits might be large or small, but a deficit there always was. Wars with natives had been costly of life and money; the Germans refused to emigrate to these regions, which were notoriously unhealthy, and as a market they were negligible. Then the Germans evolved a new theory. They had been made to realize the fact that there are two distinct regions of expansion—one where the white race can live and rear children and make a home in temperate climates, and the other the tropical belt which can be regarded, not as an area of settlement, but as an area which produces raw material for which there is a growing demand in the world—rubber, cotton, fibres, oils. They considered that tropical colonies were the economic regions with a future, and that to dominate them would be to "corner" some of the future supplies on which modern industry must increasingly depend. Hence, in spite of the failure of German colonies as areas of settlement, they might become important as areas for monopolizing tropical products for German benefit. This experiment had just begun when the Great War broke out, with its disastrous consequences to the nascent German colonial empire.

Russian Expansion

All through the eighteenth and nineteenth centuries Russia was a nation that never ceased to expand. "An insignificant tribe, or collection of tribes, which, a thousand years ago, was confined to a small district near the sources of the Dnieper and the Western Dvina, has grown into a great nation with a vast territory stretching from the Baltic to the Northern Pacific, and from the Polar Ocean to the frontiers of Turkey, Persia, Afghanistan, and China."[1]

The Russians were an agricultural people practising primitive methods. With an increasing population the

[1] Sir D. M. Wallace, *Russia*, p. 743. See G. Drage, *Russian Affairs*, map facing p. 1.

food supply became insufficient, and they had to spread out over an ever widening area. There was no barrier of mountains and they spread to the east and south. Religious persecution, the violent reforms of Peter the Great, the growing burden of serfdom and conscription, caused thousands to leave their homes and seek refuge in free territory. The State followed them and the colonists pushed further out still.

They could either push into the forest region or into the region of the steppes. The forest region was far the harder to cultivate, but the Finnish tribes who had settled there did not molest settlers, so that it was at any rate comparatively safe. In the steppe region lived the predatory nomadic hordes ever ready to plunder, attack, and carry off as slaves the peaceful agricultural population. As colonization pushed south, the government felt impelled to protect the population from the incursions of nomadic tribes, and to do this the Czars gradually annexed more and more territory, pushing further and further afield.

In the West, Russia was hemmed in by Poland and Sweden. There was little possibility of expansion in that direction. All the routes to the West passed through the territory of rival nations, and, accordingly, to open up a port communicating with the west became the great object of Russia's foreign policy. When Peter the Great became Czar in 1689 the Russian dominion already embraced about five and a half million square miles, but Archangel was the only sea port. Between Russia and the Baltic lay the Swedish Provinces. Between Russia and the Black Sea lay the Crimea. Between Russia and Central Europe were Poland and the Prussian Lithuanian Provinces. Peter the Great's foreign policy involved the weakening of Sweden and Turkey and the dismemberment of Poland. Sweden was defeated, and Peter got his footing on the Baltic and his point of communication with Western Europe. Catherine II pushed the boundaries west by sharing in the partition of Poland. In 1783 the Porte was forced to cede the Crimea to Russia. From this time onwards Russian merchants were able to export corn to the south. By the end of the eighteenth century Russia had three great outlets by sea. Its Baltic possessions were rounded off by the acquisition of the Grand Duchy of Finland which Russia obtained in 1809.

In 1725 the Russian Empire contained about 5,830,000

square miles. In 1897 it was 8,648,000 square miles, one-seventh of the land surface of the globe.[1] The population of fourteen millions in 1722 had grown to 171 millions in 1913. During the period the three great incentives to expansion were the necessity of increasing the food producing area, the defence of the population that this involved, and on the west the desire to get to the sea, so as to have access to the rest of the world free from ice and the interference of neighbouring powers.

The necessity for expansion for the purposes of food supply continued into recent history, and the necessity for defence led to increasing extension in Central Asia. In 1864, in a circular note, Russia explained "the dilemma in which civilized States in contact with wandering tribes are placed". They find it impossible to live in unity with such neighbours, and must establish a system of control or see their frontier a prey to chronic disorder. But when the frontier tribes are subdued, they in their turn are exposed to the aggression of more distant tribes, and hence the frontier line must be extended until it comes into contact with a regularly organized State, which can maintain order within its own borders.[2] A further reason for expansion into Asia was that Russia was foiled in its attempts to gain Constantinople in 1854 and 1877. Possession of Constantinople would have given Russia a free passage through the Dardanelles. But since it was not able to acquire that port, its territorial expansion in Asia went on with a view to getting to an ice-free port there. In Eastern Asia there is the Gulf of Pechili, and in the south-west lie the Persian Gulf and Indian Ocean. Hence is seen one great line of expansion pushed out in Trans-Caspian regions and another through Siberia. Russia obtained from China the right to push its great Siberian railway through Manchuria, having previously obtained the cession of the Amur region, and it thereupon began the Russification of the Province. In 1900 the Boxer troubles supplied Russia

[1]

Date.	*In Europe and Caucasia.*	*In Asia.*
	Square miles.	Square miles.
1725	1,738,000	4,092,000
1800	2,014,000	4,452,000
1855	2,261,250	5,194,000
1897	2,267,360	6,382,321

[2] G. Drage, *Russian Affairs*, pp. 488–9.

with an excuse for sending a large force into Manchuria, and Russia protected China against the demands of European Powers. It seemed as if the temporary occupation of Manchuria would become permanent when, in 1904, Japan made up its mind to check the advance of its gigantic neighbour by force. The result of the Russo-Japanese War of 1904–5 was to administer a check to Russian expansion eastwards. Russian expansion was for the time being thrown back on one of the other two lines of advance, to the Bosphorus or to the Persian Gulf.

The Russians are the only Europeans who have colonized in Asia in the sense that they have settled there. The characteristics of their expansion are, however, different, according as they have settled in the north or in Central Asia. In Europe and in Siberia Russian expansion has been a peasant expansion and the State has followed up the colonists. In the north of Asia the aboriginal tribes had no organized government with which to oppose the Russian advance. This made settlement easy. The immigrants, urged forward by stress of hunger, settled in the country destitute of education or capital. It was an informal and peaceful immigration, and it has been the great outlet for the surplus population of Russia.

The vast plains of Northern Asia were accordingly settled entirely by the Russian race without any such inter-mixture of foreign elements as characterized the colonization of the United States and Canada. Siberia has therefore homogeneity and cohesive strength: it is part of Russia as none of the British colonies is a part of Great Britain. The colonists began to go to Siberia at the end of the sixteenth century. For the most part it was voluntary emigration, being state-aided only to a small degree, though convicts and exiles formed no inconsiderable portion. A very much larger migration went on in the nineteenth century, especially after the emancipation of the serfs in 1861–5. Between 1807 and 1899 some 865,000 exiles were sent to Siberia, making up nearly a sixth part of the population, the remainder consisting of free settlers or descendants of exiles. Between 1893 and 1901 emigrants to Siberia numbered 1,318,000 persons. "In 300 years a vast country, presenting every difficulty which a severe climate, pathless forests, and the presence of unfriendly natives could offer, has been permeated from end to end by Russian psaneats, acting, until lately, almost entirely on their own initiative and without funds or support from Government."[1]

The Siberian Railway came as an enormous impulse to this colonization movement. It " united the east with the west, and opened up new markets for commerce and fresh fields for the expansion of western energy of every kind ".[2] The Russian occupation of Siberia must be regarded as a contribution to the material wealth, not only of Russia, but of the world.

Whereas the colonization of Siberia has been going on for over 300 years, Russian expansion in Central Asia has been mainly the work of the nineteenth century. The advance of Russia towards Central Asia was in progress in the eighteenth century, but it was in the years between 1864 and 1884 that Russia really made itself master of Central Asia. Central Asia was the seat of some of the oldest civilizations of the world. There was much fierce fighting with the peoples of Khiva, Bokhara, Kokand, and Merv before the Russians subjugated the older inhabitants. The whole of Central Asia, Lord Curzon reported, was like an " armed camp " when he visited it in 1889.[3] These dominions were already densely populated in places where it could be settled, the great want of the place being irrigation, and the field for emigration was restricted. " The hot dry climate is uncongenial to settlers from the north, and the frequent droughts, plagues of locusts, and entire failure of crops from one reason or another, make these regions unsuitable for peasant colonies."[4]

The importance of Central Asia lay, not in its openings for colonization, but in its capacity to absorb Russian wares on the one hand and to produce raw cotton on the other hand. It lessened the dependence of the greatest of Russian industries for raw material on foreign countries. Russia built the Trans-Caspian railway, primarily for strategical reasons but also for economic ends, and the cities of Bokhara, Khiva, and Samarkand, which some twenty years before were absolutely cut off from the world, had, in 1904, the price of cotton telegraphed to them every morning from Liverpool.[5]

[1] G. Drage, *Russian Affairs*, pp. 398, 410–11.
[2] *Ibid.*, p. 598.
[3] G. N. Curzon, *Russia in Central Asia*, p. 386.
[4] G. Drage, *Russian Affairs*, pp. 599–600.
[5] *Ibid.*, p. 601.

By the opening of the twentieth century the slave raids, which filled the prisons of Samarkand and Bokhara with captives who languished in torments for years, had been suppressed; the country was pacified and opened up and brought into contact with the outside world by the railway. There has been, therefore, great opportunity for internal development. The railway has given an impetus to trade in all directions.

The Russians have been such successful colonists in Asia for the reason that they are partly Asiatic themselves and can therefore get on with Asiatics. "Peace and submission to Russia are therefore assured conditions in Central Asia, but not merely because of the superiority in arms of the conqueror; the subtle instincts of race play their part in the work of Russification. The conquest of Turcomans by Russians is a conquest of Asiatics by Asiatics; the dishonesty, craft, and impassivity of the Oriental, which erect so powerful a barrier between ourselves and our Indian subjects, are qualities recognized by Russians as natural and normal; they excite no aversion, and form, in fact, a ground of mutual understanding." [1]

American Expansion

At the beginning of the nineteenth century, nine-tenths of the population of the United States lived along a narrow strip of sea coast hemmed in by the Alleghanies. In 1783 the population, white and black, was about 3,500,000. But there was that rage for migration that has always been characteristic of Americans. The stream of emigration pushed out in three directions. One stream pushed out into Central New York; another to Kentucky; and a third into Tennessee. In the south-west cotton growing had become exceedingly profitable. Another reason for the movement was that many of the soldiers of the army could not settle down again into ordinary life. Then as a rule men migrated west in times of slack trade and depression, and the commercial depression of the Embargo time, when there was no demand for American ships or sailors or for the produce of American farms, sent many to the west.

[1] G. Drage, *Russian Affairs*, p. 497.

"A wild rush for the west" began after 1816, when the great depression set in after the peace, and "the great western highways were choked with emigrants".[1] Between 1816 and 1821 six new States were admitted to the Union—Indiana, Mississippi, Illinois, Alabama, Maine, and Missouri. In 1803 Louisiana had been bought from France, and the navigation of the Mississippi secured to the United States. In all, the number of States had grown from thirteen to twenty-four by 1821.

This gigantic movement of population, which was continued and intensified throughout the nineteenth century, took place largely within the legal framework of the State public lands policy. At first there was trouble about the ownership of the new territories. The original seaboard States had claimed all the land to the west. They were, however, induced to cede the land west of the mountains to the Central Government on the footing that the proceeds of the land sold should be devoted to paying off the Public Debt.

A systematic survey of the land was undertaken. The country was mapped out into township sections and quarter sections. The land policy of the United States is attributable to that great organizer, Hamilton. He was asked to draw up a report on the administration and disposal of the public lands and did so in 1790. The first land ordinance was passed in 1796 embodying his suggestions. The land was to be surveyed, a land office was to be established, and the land was to be disposed of in large quantities.

As soon as a district was surveyed it was to be sold to the highest bidder. The reserve price was $2 an acre, and the land was to be sold in sections (640 acres), with one section as the minimum. It was therefore impossible for small settlers to buy at these land auctions. Hundreds of thousands of acres were sold at low prices to large capitalists and corporations, who either farmed the land themselves or sold it in small lots to settlers at high profit. The public lands were therefore really given over to speculators, and real estate speculation became a great business. An even more speculative element was introduced by the fact that the land was paid for in paper which varied in value. The crises of 1819–21 and 1837 were due in part to the excessive

[1] J. B. McMaster, "The Growth of the Nation (1815–28)," chap. xi, in *Cambridge Modern History*, vol. vii, p. 358.

speculation in land. Then, in 1800, a new system of sales in small lots of 160 acres on credit was inaugurated. The system of credit sales was not altogether happy in its results, and a Report commented: "The disastrous credit system spread over Ohio, Indiana, Illinois, Missouri, Alabama, Mississippi, Louisiana, and Michigan."[1] The settlers became encumbered with debts to the government, and by 1820 there were $22,000,000 of arrears. In 1820, however, there began a system of sales for cash and the price was lowered to $1·25 per acre, and the minimum area was reduced to 80 acres. Even then the price was too high for the majority of small settlers, and there was great dissatisfaction on the western frontier of settlement with the government policy. Nevertheless, 1820 is a real turning point in the history of land settlement in the United States. Until 1820 the policy was to sell the land at as high a price as possible in order to pay off the Public Debt. After 1820 the aim was to encourage settlement and development to the utmost, and the effect was to foster "small holdings at a low price, with deed in fee from the Government".[2]

In the north the land was heavily forested and not suited for large farms or plantations on account of the expense of clearing, and there accordingly the system was to sell the land to people who, owning the land, would clear it for themselves. In the south exactly the opposite was the case, the object being to keep out the small landowner and to retain extensive regions to be broken up with slave labour. But northern land was bought at a much higher rate from land speculators and a movement began to take shape that land should be sold at a low price in small parcels. This was the policy that won the approval of Jackson between 1829–37.

Many people had gone out and squatted on the land. These men, when land was bought, were either evicted or had to pay a big price to stay on. In 1830 the first Pre-emption Act provided that every squatter who had cultivated the land for a year should have the right to buy 160 acres at the minimum price before it was disposed of. However, this was only a small palliative. Land continued to be bought and then held up for higher prices and

[1] "The Public Domain. Its History," a Report by Thomas Donaldson, in *U.S. House of Representatives, Miscellaneous Documents*, 1882–3, vol. xix, p. 205.

[2] Ibid.

emigration west slowed down because of the capital needed for settlement.

In 1844 an Anti-Rent movement grew up with "free homes for free men" for its cry. From 1848 onwards measures were proposed to sell the land to settlers in small portions at nominal rates. The South was entirely opposed. It would upset all their traditional methods of agriculture. It was not till the War broke out that the Homestead Act of 1862 was passed, by which every person over twenty-one who was a citizen had a right to become the owner of 160 acres of land if he lived on and cultivated it himself for five years. Accordingly, the Civil War in its economic aspect was a struggle between the system of large farms and sparse population and the system of small holdings and vigorous colonization.

The Homestead Act constitutes one of the most important episodes in American history. Millions of acres were given away under this law to which, together with the railways, the United States owes its extraordinary progress. In particular it was found that nothing attracted the German emigrant so much as the idea that he could get free land. The Homestead Act meant the break up of the great capitalist landholding regime. As the prairie region was made accessible on the other side of the Mississippi by the railway, the land was reserved for small settlers. Public lands could still be bought in large areas, but there was not the same chance of re-sale when once people could get land for nothing.

In 1873 the Homestead Act was followed up by another measure giving a settler 160 acres if he would plant one-sixteenth of it with trees and protect them for eight years —the Timber Culture Act. The idea was to moderate the climatic extremes of the prairie by tree planting and to make available cheap material for building and fuel. Then in 1877 the Desert Land Act enabled grants of 640 acres of land unsuited for cultivation to be made for pastoral purposes. On this law the great cattle ranches of the west have been built up. Such is the framework of the State public lands policy.

The history of the United States during the nineteenth century was marked by rapid development territorially, as well as industrially and commercially. In the period 1800–20 the Ohio valley was settled during periods of depression. The period 1820–40 witnessed the expansion of the cotton States owing to the demand for their staple product. In the period 1840–60 the settlement of the Mississippi above the cotton belt took place. In 1810 the total population of the Ohio and Mississippi valleys was 1,078,316. By 1840 the population of the region occupied by the States of Ohio, Indiana, Illinois, Michigan, Wisconsin, Kentucky, Tennessee, Alabama, Mississippi, and Louisiana was six millions. By 1860 it had grown to 13,900,000.

Until the middle of the nineteenth century the two main factors in the expansion movement were depression and cotton. Discovery of gold in California hastened this extraordinary development. By 1848 there were some 6,000 men in the goldfields; by 1849 they had become 77,000. The result was the settlement of a new nation in the west which quickened commerce and industry by providing an ample supply of specie which, by raising prices, stimulated the development of industry enormously. It was the most powerful factor in bringing about the extension of the railroad and the linking up of the Pacific and the Atlantic. It made the United States a Pacific power; its boundary was no longer the Mississippi. The great economic event of the period then was the creation of a new America which was preparing the way, by reason of its enormous home market, for the transformation of America into a pre-eminently industrial State. But still more, it was preparing the way for that enormous agricultural development which was to pass like a storm over Europe and become a principal factor in all the tariff questions of the time.

At the same time the period was characterized by an enormous emigration from Europe without which this expansion would have been impossible. The European revolutions, especially those of 1848, the famines in the 'forties, and notably the Irish famines, tended to turn the stream of emigration to America. Between 1850–60 no less than 2,500,000 immigrants arrived and in 1860 there were 4,138,000 foreigners in the United States. Between 1860 and 1870 the number was rather less, being two and a quarter millions. Between 1871 and 1880 the numbers were 2,812,191; between 1880 and 1884, three millions. If a depression affected Europe and not the United States, people left Europe. If the depression was general, as in 1857, they stayed at home, as it was useless to go to a country where things were as bad. Among Europeans,

Germans, Irish, and English predominated. The Germans left because in the districts of Mecklenburg-Schwerin and Pomerania the large estates made it hopeless to acquire a holding. A great number of these Germans were agriculturalists. The Irish on the contrary kept to the towns. The majority of the English were skilled workmen, engineers and miners, and some went into cattle ranching. In so far as the western expansion is concerned it was the German element that was the chief colonizing element.

But the greatest development was carried through by the American himself. The bulk of the immigrants settled near their landing place, and it was the native population that moved out westwards. One of the most extraordinary features of American life is the migratory character of the population. The typical American would rather migrate than alter his way of living. With the increasing density of the population it became necessary to adopt intensive cultivation, and the frontiersman could not, or would not, adapt himself to it. There were among the farmer population many people who never found rest during their life, but broke up the homestead four or five times to go off hundreds of miles distant. It is almost impossible for us to conceive with our rootedness the comparative ease with which an American would give up or sell his farm and move west.

Between 1860 and 1870 the Civil War wrought great changes in the agriculture of the country. The organization of great armies increased the market demand for food products in the north, and agricultural production in the north was greatly extended. Meanwhile the repeal of the Corn Laws in England and the rapid development of manufactures there and in America gave American agriculture a great stimulus. At the end of the War many people moved west, especially soldiers of the Northern army. In 1873 came a great crisis and a period of depression. Works were closed down and merchants and artisans put their savings together and again moved west. Whole colonies went out from New York every week. A thousand families left Brooklyn in a year. The high wages had enabled most of the town workers to accumulate savings.

About a quarter of the population of Indiana, Illinois, Wisconsin, and Iowa were immigrants, that is to say, not born in the State, while of their own people, 22·5 per cent had pushed on west. They poured thence into

Minnesota, the Dakotas, and Nebraska. Even in the south they left Georgia for Texas. In no case, therefore, did the foreign element outnumber the native element. In no case was the native population less than seven-tenths of the whole. Therefore the foreign element was easily absorbed and in that way the national characteristics were preserved although the foreign element was so large. Of the Germans hardly more than 25 per cent became agricultural labourers, of the Irish 12 per cent, of the Scandinavians 40 per cent. The tendency of the foreign population was for a city life, mechanical and mining operations, hand-trades, and shopkeeping. The newcomer had generally to seek paid employment at once.

The Census of 1890 reported that the western frontier in the United States had disappeared. The empty lands had now been occupied, and fresh settlers would for the most part require to buy or lease farms. No longer were free lands to be a safety valve in times of depression and to serve for a retreat to the native Americans as the foreign immigrants came crowding in. The work of inland expansion was more or less complete.

The cessation of inland expansion coincided with the beginning of overseas expansion in the history of the United States. The overseas expansion of the United States, by the annexation of Hawaii in 1898, and by the cession in 1899 of Porto Rico and the Philippines, as well as by the establishment of a virtual Protectorate over Cuba as a result of the Spanish-American War, is epoch-making for many reasons. It has already been seen how all the century the United States had been expanding, but expanding into contiguous territory separated only by land distance. Louisiana was bought in 1803 from France, Florida was ceded in 1819. Texas and California were annexed in 1846. Oregon was also ceded in 1846, and the middle filled up by settlers. Then Alaska was bought in 1869. The expansion overseas, however, was something entirely different. The population is of a different race and type, and cannot easily be given free Republican Government at the outset but has to be governed on an aristocratic rather than a democratic basis. The virtual abrogation of the Monroe doctrine was implied in this new form of expansion. It meant the acquisition of colonies by a people who had always been strongly against such a system.

Thus the United States had to face entirely new problems

from those of settling the prairies. It had to deal with the question of tropical colonization as distinct from the expansion of the race. An Empire of Rule was added to the Empire of Settlement, and the new problems had to be faced by a federal country that was not itself a nation because of the vast alien groups only partly " Americanized " within its borders.

As far as the policy of the United States was concerned, the American based his whole scheme of colonization on education. Accordingly, in the case of the Philippine Islands, they devised an exceedingly expensive scheme of education but neglected roads, which are of primary importance. They proceeded on the assumption that what was good for the United States was good for the Philippine Islands. " The task which has been undertaken is, in fact, to make an American out of a Filipino ; and it is a task for which few people who have had any personal acquaintance with tropical races will be prepared to predict even a moderate degree of success." [1]

But to pay for this system of education a high tariff was maintained on goods. Chinese labour was excluded in the same way as the Chinese were excluded from the United States. The restriction on the Chinese tended to hold back the colonies. Moreover, the United States tried to prevent the advent of the Trust, with the result that the laws of the islands hindered the advent of capital. The Filipinos wanted good roads and economic prosperity, while the tendency of the Americans was to give them political instruction and legislation. The same attempt to reform along the lines of education and sanitation was made in Cuba, and the system was found to be very expensive.

The United States learned from its initial mistakes and adopted a policy of internal development within the colonies, and a policy of preferential tariffs so as to encourage trade between the colonies and the United States. Roads and railways were built, capital was invested in plantations and industries, and very liberal tariff reductions were given to colonial produce. The result was that in the period before the War the production of wealth in the colonies increased rapidly and the trade between the colonies and the United States expanded similarly. The colonies were bound to

[1] A. Ireland, *The Far Eastern Tropics*, p. 252.

the United States by economic as well as by political ties, and neither the economic ties nor the political ties were relaxed over the period. Apparently in 1914 the period of political schooling was not yet over for the Filipinos and other colonials, and the United States had still to play the rôle of the " big brother " to the members of its Empire of Outposts—its empire of islands and coastal strips guarding trade routes and serving as naval depots.

PART VI

GROWTH OF STATE ACTION

CHAPTER I

Aspects

Agriculture.
Industry and Commerce.
Transport.
Scientific Research.

ONE of the most striking events of the period beginning with the last twenty-five years of the nineteenth century is the growing influence of the State in the economic sphere. It is noticeable in almost every phase of economic life: in agriculture, in industry, in transport, in commerce, and in social welfare.

In agriculture the American corn exports had the effect of increasing government interest in all farming questions. On the continent it took the form of assisting farmers to grow beet by bounties, thus stimulating the introduction of rotation of crops and intensive agriculture. Co-operative societies for purchase and sale were encouraged to enable the small man to get over the disadvantage of being small. Co-operative credit societies were also assisted by the Governments by grants and in other ways, the idea being to relieve the peasant from the yoke of the middleman, the money-lender, and the burden of mortgage indebtedness. In Germany and Russia the Government had undertaken to rearrange the land so as to form compact holdings, and in Ireland it has financed the transfer of the land from one set of owners to another. The State has intervened on the continent to provide cheap transport facilities for agriculture, and has protected it by tariffs and readjustments of taxation. Even in the United States, a great grain exporting country, the farmer was protected in 1897 against imports from Canada, and the import of raw materials like wool that might possibly be produced at home. Among all the Great Powers the Governments have tried to encourage agriculture by assisting agricultural education and stimulating research.

In industry there are three aspects to be considered: there is first the conduct of the actual production, there is the control of combinations or monopolies, and there is thirdly the question of the training of the worker and his treatment when at work.

Up to the outbreak of the War of 1914 there was little State production. Where States owned railways they would erect locomotive works and repairing shops in connection with them. The State would necessarily undertake some manufacturing for purposes of post office equipment, army clothing, and ordnance production, and this tended to increase with the growth of European armaments after 1870.

Where the State did not itself engage in production it often subsidized it in various forms. In Russia the iron industry was started by concessions on favourable terms and by the promise of orders on a large scale. In Germany favoured industries, such as shipbuilding, were helped by cheap railway rates on the timber and iron required.

The control of joint stock companies and combinations has led to a greater extension of State activity. As these impersonal corporations developed, the Governments had to secure a standard of honesty in company promoting. There are, therefore, in the case of all the Great Powers, laws relating to the formation and sphere of action of companies. As these companies merged into kartells or trusts the question of the regulation of monopolies became more pressing.[1] The most drastic development in this direction has been the procedure of the United States, which not merely prohibited Trusts but, in 1912, set up a body, the Federal Trade Commission, the function of which was to dissolve monopolistic combinations after inquiry, with power to prosecute the members. Again, England, France, Germany, and the United States have all promoted technical education to a greater or less degree, thereby training workers for industry. This has become a pressing question with the decline of the domestic workshops, which were formerly the great training ground of boy labour through the apprentice system. With the growth of the factory system, certain branches of work have been taken over by boys, and as these occupations lead nowhere and are no training for after life, there has arisen the problem of "blind alley" labour. Technical training is an attempt to correct this.

[1] On the procedure adopted by the various countries, J. W. Jenks, "Report on Industrial Combinations," *Industrial Commission, U.S.A.*, vol. xviii.

The protection of the worker is provided for in the long series of factory, mining, compensation, and insurance laws adopted by the Governments of the Continental Powers and by the various State Governments in the American Federation. The efficient enforcement of these laws varies considerably in the different countries.

In transport the growth of State action has been marked. In two out of the five Great Powers the railways were started by private individuals, but both the United Kingdom and the United States have had to assume a progressive intensification of control of railway operations. The welfare of every country has come to depend so vitally on railways that it has become almost a question of national existence that the railways shall work smoothly, facilitate trade by rapid despatch, feed the towns, and assist the mobility of human beings as well as goods. In Russia, Germany, and France military considerations have also supervened, and in the first two countries the railways are owned and operated by the State; in the last the French Government owns and works part of the railway system and has so subsidized the rest that, though worked by private companies, they are dependent on the Government.

Under the head of social welfare come the sanitary regulations, education, and the assistance to the poor. In all these respects Russia was still backward in 1914, but in the case of the other Great Powers, increasing attention had been paid to these matters by either the central or local authorities.

The extension of the sphere of State activity to include scientific research in medicine and also for agricultural and industrial purposes has been marked in Germany, France, the United States, and the United Kingdom.

CHAPTER 2

Causes

Predisposition in certain countries to control from above.

Contrast of tradition of individual liberty in non-serf countries.

Facilities of communication, producing international rivalries and the scramble for markets and tropical products.

The Labour Movement.

Use of taxation to redress inequalities as between individuals.

The feeling of revolt against State interference with individual liberty as a factor in economic history.

WHAT are the causes of the great extension of State activity in recent times?

It is partly accounted for by a certain predisposition of certain States for control from above. In Germany, France, and Russia, the tradition of State action has always been strong. This is due in some measure to the fact that they were serf countries right down to the nineteenth century, and in serf countries there is little movement or training in initiative. The Germans, being poor, looked to their princes for help. France had always looked to its King, and, though the Revolution set up the idea of freedom and *laissez-faire*, Napoleon I revived the tradition and it has never completely died out. The autocrat of all the Russias necessarily did things from above when they were done at all, but he was hampered by the lack of a trained Civil Service on a salaried basis, a vast area to administer, a peasantry just out of serfdom, and indifferent communications. There having been no middle class in Russia till not long before the Great War, industry and commerce were carried on by foreigners and Jews. The problems the Czar had to face were quite peculiar. The will to act was there; the machinery was inadequate.

In the two non-serf countries, the United Kingdom and the United States, there was a strong dislike to State control, dating from the seventeenth century. The interesting thing is to see both groups of countries going in the same direction.

In the United States, the only State control tolerated

for a large part of the nineteenth century was a protective tariff. After the Civil War the Americans came to believe that a high tariff was necessary to develop their industry. In other respects America has inherited the old Puritan tradition of individual freedom. This has been intensified by the jealousy of the various States of the assumption of any power by the Federal Government. Her Civil Service has been untrained and inefficient, the appointments being largely the results of political loyalty rather than capacity for the job. Only in the twentieth century has she set up a Federal banking system and an efficient State control of monopolies, while the Inter-State Commerce Commission only got powers which would make its control of railways effective in 1906. All this, however, shows the growing tendency to *étatisme* even in the United States.

In Great Britain the tradition of individual liberty in economic matters coming down from the Civil War of 1642 was strong. England was organized in the nineteenth century for world trade, banking, exchange, and shipping, and she did not believe in putting barriers in the way of her world control. In spite of the growing importance of the colonial factor after 1870, which worked in the other direction for preferences, England remained free trade. In this respect she was not merely in striking contrast with the country that has followed so many of her traditions, the United States, but also with Germany, France, and Russia. The explanation lay in the fact that England was an international world power while these other countries were working out a national economy which England had outgrown.

Apart from these special peculiarities in each nation which might lead some of them to adopt State regulation more quickly than others, there were certain general causes at work, too strong even for the two Anglo-Saxon countries.

There was first the growing rivalry of the nations. No country could afford to be outdone; each felt that it must help its own citizens if the other country did so. Individuals cannot be pitted against the bottomless purses of foreign governments. No country wishes to fall behind and so the Government steps in to help, subsidize, control, or direct the action of its own people.

But this only raises the further question of what causes the foreign rivalry? This was due principally to the railways and steamships. The railways brought the continental countries—the countries with large land areas and small sea outlets—to the forefront. The industrial changes, too, led to a scramble for raw materials and markets and people began to look to their governments to help them to get their fair share. England was held, for instance, to dominate raw material through her shipping, which brought it to this country, and to gain a great advantage in foreign markets for her produce by the ease of access her shipping provided. Foreign governments considered that they ought to have their own shipping lines, not merely to secure raw material, but to carry on national trade in national ships. The result was shipping subsidies and other forms of encouragement in all the Great Powers.

The rivalry of the nations had led to the attempt to secure the unoccupied areas of the world to get markets and raw materials and enjoy a bigger prestige. Railways, as we have seen, made colonies more valuable by enabling them to be opened up and colonies again enlarged the scope of State activities. Tropical colonies had to be developed by railways and these had often to be financed by the State. Under the ægis of the State, science saw to the production of raw materials and made the tropics healthier places to live in. The great example of this type of State control was the sanitary regulation by the United States of the building of the Panama Canal. In certain regions, notably India and Egypt, irrigation is urgently necessary. The expenditure required is, however, so huge that only the State could undertake it and the State has afterwards to regulate the water supply it provides to see that everyone gets his fair share.

In all these directions the constructive imperialism of the thirty years before 1914 tended to train both the United Kingdom and the United States in State enterprises worked by their own officials. The paternalism necessary to govern tropical or semi-tropical areas, whether they be Algeria, Egypt, West Africa, or the Philippines, increased the tendency to abandon *laissez-faire*. If the State undertook great works of public utility for coloured peoples abroad why should it not also play the economic providence for its own people at home? The idea of the 'fifties and the 'sixties was that the government did everything extravagantly and inefficiently. The best government is the one which governs least, was the maxim, and yet, when it came to India, it was obvious that great development works were carried out by a bureaucracy with a success not usually attributed to governments. The increased interest in colonial matters after the scramble for Africa intensified the reaction towards constructive action by the State instead of *laissez-faire*. Railways themselves increased the whole sphere of State activity, as we have seen, either by raising the question of State control or State operation.

In yet another direction improved communications have operated to centralize and enhance the power of the Government. They have diminished distance and have broken down so much local life that it tends to throw more into the hands of the central government. In the period before railways it would take days to send or receive communications over quite short distances. Much had necessarily to be left to private initiative and local government, as in Russia before 1914. With telegraphs, telephones, and railways a nation is more easily administered than a county would have been in the days before 1850. Hence the tendency to concentration and uniformity on a central plan.

The Labour movement, too, has worked in the same direction. The whole Socialist movement has stimulated labour laws and the Government has had to see that they are carried out. Socialism favours the conduct of all economic activities by the State and has habituated men's minds to the idea of nationalization, and to an increase of State action as a compromise. The inspectorate, moreover, grew with the extension of the labour code and with it control and *étatisme*. In the United States, where labour laws are enacted and administered very differently by the various States, the Labour movement tends to increase the governmental activities of the States rather than of the central government.

In the United Kingdom, Germany, and France the administration became very efficient after 1870, and it was capable of carrying out State schemes as it would not have been at an earlier date. The United States is improving considerably in this respect. The Russian standard of central administration left much to be desired.[1]

[1] The Russian officials were said to be dilatory and inefficient and were accused of being open to bribery. On the other hand, I have been told of Russian officials who would not take money for important concessions, saying that they only desired the development of their country's resources.

A confusion of ideas often arises. In England in the seventeenth

It is quite obvious that the social services such as education, inspection, sanitary precautions, and insurance have to be paid for and this, combined with the growing expenditure of the State on armaments after 1870, led to increased taxation and with taxation, again, a growth of State control. Certain countries, France, Germany, and the United States, relied on an increase of the customs to meet the growing expenditure and thereby attempted to kill two birds with one stone. They considered that they were encouraging industry and agriculture by a high tariff as well as obtaining revenue. Free trade England, however, only levied duties on a few articles which could not be produced at home (tea, tobacco, coffee, sugar, wine, prunes, currants, etc.), and came to rely more and more on direct taxation and gradually elevated it into a powerful means of social control as well as a great financial engine.

The various Death Duties led to the appropriation by the State of a considerable portion of a man's capital on his decease. This tended to prevent the accumulation of large fortunes and accelerate the break-up of great landed estates.

Since 1894 the United Kingdom system of Income Tax has been a system of graduation by means of exemptions and abatements. Below a certain level a man does not pay Income Tax at all, only indirect taxation. In 1910 allowances for children, in abeyance since 1806, were revived and since 1907 the man with an earned income has paid at a lower rate than a man with an unearned income. In 1894 the tax was graduated, so as to press less hardly on the smaller incomes, and in 1910 a super-tax was imposed on incomes over £5,000, which limit was reduced to £3,000 in 1914, when the principle of graduation was made more elaborate.

century a State official was paid by the man who wanted the work done, and that was the way the official made his living, just as a barrister does now. He often bought his office and recouped himself from fees. As late as the beginning of the nineteenth century, if an Englishman wanted a thief caught he himself paid a Bow Street runner, as he also paid for passing over a piece of road mended by a Turnpike Trust. It is only recently that we have ourselves adopted the principle of a salary, devotion to the State interests only and services rendered freely when such services are deemed necessary for the general welfare of the community. Honesty in administration is very modern. Russia was still a mediaeval State in this respect before 1914. Knowing something of the seventeenth century administration in England, I should say that that of Russia was no better and no worse than that of England two hundred years ago. Prussia was the first country to reform its administrative methods in the eighteenth century.

In all this the English State through its officials has been taxing the rich for the sake of the poorer members of the community, a marked contrast both to eighteenth century taxation in France and Germany, where the poor were taxed and the rich escaped lightly, and the French revolutionary idea of equal taxation.

Even the United States, which had continuously opposed an income tax on the ground that it was inquisitorial and gave the State the power to pry into other people's affairs, had to come to a federal Income Tax in 1913 administered on much the same principles as the English, with a graduated tax according to the income. The Income Tax is also to be found in France. In pre-War Germany there was no Imperial Income Tax but such a Tax existed in the German States comprising the Empire. The German Empire, however, was dependent for its revenue on the customs and contributions from the States.

In all these countries, as appears from documents laid before the Royal Commission on the Income Tax in 1919, the Income Tax had an allowance for dependents, in France a very extensive allowance. The United States made no distinction between an earned and an unearned income, but this distinction was made in Prussia and in France, the earned income receiving preferential treatment.[1] The Income Tax, when worked in this way, is a remarkable example of action by the State to redress inequalities of fortune and assist the poorer man with a family to shoulder his burdens.

One of the most striking instances of State control was the assumption by Russia in 1894 of the manufacture and sale of alcohol. This brought in no less than £75,900,000 revenue in 1910, being 27 per cent of the gross revenue.[2]

While the widening sphere of the Government in economic matters has been largely due to the economic rivalries of States after 1870, aided by the pressure of the Labour movement and by the effect of railways in diminishing the barrier of distance, there were other factors making for *étatisme*.

The agricultural imports from America quickened the movement. In 1880 the continental Powers were agricultural, not industrial, and their agriculture had to

[1] Royal Commission on the Income Tax, 1919; Appendices 12–14.

[2] Report for the year 1910 on the Russian Budget [*Cd.* 4962—186], p. 11.

be saved if possible by the Government when the great drop in prices took place. Then, too, Germany, victorious in war, afforded the example after 1870 of a great industrial State that had attained a great position with the assistance of government railways, government canals and government organization generally, including a tariff. She was the very antithesis of *laissez-faire* and seemed to thrive on it. The Health Movement also tended to the growth of control both central and municipal, and this was intensified as the system of Sickness Insurance developed. The growth of the Trusts was leading the United States in particular continually to assume a greater control of industry, and the emigration movement tended in the same direction. The large numbers of Germans, Italians, Galicians, Russians, and Eastern Europeans who came to the United States all came from countries where State interference was a familiar aspect of their lives. They had no prejudice against government regulation as had the old settlers who had inherited the English tradition. It thus tended to become obscured and make the American people less hostile to government action in various forms.

All through the Middle Ages and right through the epoch of the monarchs as the directing power of economic life down to the rule of Parliaments in the nineteenth century, there has been a perpetual dispute as to the line to be drawn between the proper sphere of government action and that to be left to individuals.

The Reformation was a revolt against Church authority in economic as well as in religious matters. Puritanism was an extreme assertion of individual freedom arising out of the repudiation of ecclesiastical control and reflected itself in the demand for *laissez-faire* in industrial as well as in religious concerns.

The Civil War in England was partly a revolt against the system of "Thorough" in economic matters as carried out by Charles I, and England entered upon a period of freedom from government control after 1660. Only in matters of foreign trade and tariffs was that control effective till 1842–6. That tradition went from England to her colonies in America as did so much else in the economic sphere, and was reproduced in the intense individualism of the United States, where the belief that the State could do no good thing was strengthened by their resistance to the English Government, which was regarded as an oppressor.

Only very reluctantly did the separate States surrender even the control of the customs to the Federal Government, and they bitterly resisted a Federal Bank. Their individualistic leanings were strengthened by the fact that they had no trained civil service to exercise control and they felt that the less government interference they had the better. One might regard the American rebellion of 1776 partly as a revolt against government control in the shape of Navigation Acts and Stamp Duties, although it was really an assertion of a nationality that resented being dominated by another nation, and Navigation Acts and Stamp Duties were an expression of overlordship galling to a people with a tradition of independence.

The French Revolution was another revolt against autocratic regulation and in favour of complete freedom.

In the nineteenth century Russian anarchism and nihilism were also signs of reaction from control in favour of individualism, while French syndicalism also originated in a feeling of resentment against government. Nevertheless, the tendency towards an ever greater participation by the State in economic life has continued in a marked degree and was only intensified by the Great War and the subsequent reconstruction.

BIBLIOGRAPHY

INTRODUCTION

General

Birnie, A. *Economic History of Europe, 1760–1930.* 1930.
British and Foreign Trade and Industry : Memoranda, Statistical Tables and Charts. First Series : 1903, *Cd.* 1761. Second Series : 1904, *Cd.* 2337.
Cambridge Modern History, vols. 5 to 12.
Day, Clive. *History of Commerce.* 1922.
Fay, C. R. *Co-operation at Home and Abroad.* 1925.
Gregory, T. E. *Tariffs.* 1921.
Knight, M. M., Barnes, H. E., and Flugel, F. *Economic History of Europe.* vol. ii : Modern Times. 1930.
Ogg, F. A. *Economic Development of Modern Europe.* 1926.
Raper, C. L. *Railway Transportation* (based on A. T. Hadley, " Railroad Transportation "). 1912.
Renard, G., and Weulersse, G. *Life and Work in Modern Europe. Fifteenth to Eighteenth Centuries.* 1926.
Sombart, W. *Socialism and the Social Movement.* 1909.

France

Bodley, J. E. C. *France.* 1902.
Dickinson, G. Lowes. *Revolution and Reaction in Modern France.* 1927.
Elton, G. *Revolutionary Idea in France, 1789–1871.* 1923.
Fisher, H. A. L. *Bonapartism.* 1908.
Kovalevsky, M. *La France économique et sociale à la ve de la Révolution.*
Sée, H. *Economic and Social Conditions in France during the eighteenth century.* 1927.
—— *Esquisse d'une histoire économique et sociale de la France . . . jusqu'à la guerre mondiale.* 1929.
—— *La vie économique de la France sous la monarchie censitaire, 1815–48.* 1927.

Germany

Dawson, W. H. *Evolution of Modern Germany.* 1919.
—— *Germany and the Germans.* 2 vols. 1893–4.
Fisher, H. A. L. *Studies in Napoleonic Statesmanship : Germany.* 1903.
Marriott and Grant Robertson. *Evolution of Prussia.* 1915.

Russia

Beaulieu, Leroy. *L'Empire des Tsars et les Russes.* 3 vols. 1897.
Drage, G. *Russian Affairs.* 1904.
Kluchevsky. *History of Russia* (translated by C. J. Hogarth), vol. v. 1931.
Sering, M. *Russlands Kultur und Volkswirtschaft.* 1913.
Wallace, D. Mackenzie. *Russia.* 1912 (also many previous editions).
Vernadsky, G. V. *A History of Russia.* 1930.

The United States

Bogart, E. L. *Economic History of the United States.* 1922.
Jennings, W. W. *History of Economic Progress in the United States.* 1925.
Lippincott, I. *Economic Development of the United States.* 1927.
Oliver, F. S. *Alexander Hamilton.* 1915.

AGRICULTURE

France

Augé-Leribé, M. *L'Evolution de la France agricole.* 1912.
Clapham, J. H. *Economic Development of France and Germany, 1815–1914.* 1928.
Herbert, S. *Fall of Feudalism in France.* 1921.
Luchitsky, J. V. *L'état des classes agricoles en France à la veille de la Révolution.* 1911.
—— *La petite propriété en France avant la Révolution.*
—— *La propriété paysanne en France à la vielle de la Revolution.*
Sagnac, P. *La propriété foncière et les paysans, 1789–93.* 1901.

Germany

Cahill, J. R. Enquiry into Agricultural Credit and Agricultural Co-operation in Germany [*Cd.* 6626]. 1913.
Clapham, J. H. *Economic Development of France and Germany, 1815–1914.* 1928.
Goltz, T. A. G. L. von der. *Geschichte der Deutschen Landwirtschaft,* vol. ii. 1903.
Middleton, T. H. Recent Development of German Agriculture [*Cd.* 8305]. 1916.

Russia

Knudsen, Wieth. *Die Bauernfrage und Agrarreform in Russland.* 1913.
Pavlovsky, G. *Russian Agriculture on the eve of the Revolution.* 1930.

The United States

Brewer, W. N. History of Agriculture in the United States. *Tenth Census* (1880), vol. on Agriculture.
Carver, T. N. " Historical Sketch of American Agriculture," in Bailey's *Cyclopædia of American Agriculture,* vol. i. 1908.
Hammond, M. B. *The Cotton Industry,* 1897.
Hart, A. B. " Disposition of our Public Lands," in *Quarterly Journal of Economics,* vol. i, pp. 169–83.
Sato, S. *History of Land Question of the United States,* 1886.
Treat, P. J. *The National Land System, 1785–1820.* 1910.

INDUSTRY

France

Ballot, C. *L'Introduction du Machinisme dans l'Industrie française.* 1923.
Clapham, J. H. *Economic Development of France and Germany, 1815–1914.* 1928.
Forrester, R. B. *Cotton Industry in France.* 1921.
Harris, S. E. *The Assignats.* 1930.
Levasseur, E. *Histoire des Classes Ouvrières de 1789 à 1870,* 2 vols. 1903–4.

LEVASSEUR, E. *Questions Ouvrières et industrielles en France sous la Troisième République.* 1907.
LEVINE, L. *Labour Movement in France.* 1912. Second edition entitled *Syndicalism in France.* 1914.
MARRIOTT, J. A. R. *French Revolution of 1848 in its economic aspects,* 2 vols. 1913.
MONTGOMERY, B. G. DE. *British and Continental Labour Policy.* 1922
PIPKIN, C. W. *Idea of Social Justice.* 1927.
Royal Commission on Labour: Foreign Reports, vol. vi, France [*C.* 7063–ix]. 1893.

GERMANY

ASHLEY, A. *Social Policy of Bismarck.* 1912.
ASHLEY, W. J. *Progress of the German Working Classes.* 1904.
CLAPHAM, J. H. *Economic Development of France and Germany, 1815–1914.* 1928.
DAWSON, W. H. *Bismarck and State Socialism.* 1890.
—— *German Socialism and Ferdinand Lassalle.* 1888.
—— *Social Insurance in Germany, 1883–1911.* 1912.
—— *The German Workman.* 1906.
Royal Commission on Labour: Foreign Reports, vol. v, Germany [*C.* 7063–vii]. 1893.
SANDERS, W. S. *Trade Unionism in Germany.* 1916.
SCHMOLLER, G. *Geschichte der deutschen Kleingewerbe im neunzehnten Jahrhundert.*
SOMBART, W. *Deutsche Volkswirtschaft in neunzehnten Jahrhundert.* 1927.

RUSSIA

BLOCH, J. *Les Finances de la Russie au XIXe siècle.* 1900.
KOVALEVSKY, M. (ed.). *La Russie à la fin du 19e siècle.* 1900.
—— *La Régime Economique de la Russie.* 1898.
MAVOR, J. *Economic History of Russia,* 2 vols. 1925.
MILLER, M. S. *Russian Economic Development, 1905–14.* 1926.
SCHULZE-GAEVERNITZ, G. VON. *Volkswirtschaftliche Studien aus Russland.* 1899.
TUGAN-BARANOVSKY, M. I. *Geschichte der russischen Fabrik.*
Royal Commission on Labour: Foreign Reports, vol. x, Russia [*C.* 7063–xiv]. 1894.

THE UNITED STATES

BROOKS, J. G. *American Syndicalism.* 1913.
BRUCE, P. A. *The Rise of the New South.* 1905.
CLARK, V. S. *History of Manufactures in the United States,* 3 vols. 1916–29.
COMMONS, J. R. (ed.). *Trade Unionism and Labour Problems,* 2 pts. 1905–21.
ELY, R. T. *Labour Movement in America.* 1905.
JENKS, J. W. *The Trust Problem.* 1922.
KELSEY, C. "Evolution of Negro Labour," *Annals of the American Academy,* January, 1903, pp. 56–76. 1903.

TRANSPORT, TARIFFS, AND EXPANSION

FRANCE

ASHLEY, P. *Modern Tariff History.* 1920.
CLAPHAM, J. H. *Economic Development of France and Germany, 1815–1914.* 1928.

Continental Railway Investigation : Reports to the Board of Trade on Railways in Belgium, France, and Italy, 1910 [*Cd.* 5106].
DUNHAM, A. L. *Anglo-French Treaty of Commerce of 1860 and the Progress of the Industrial Revolution in France.* 1930.
GIRAULT, A. *Principes de Colonisation*, 3 vols. 1907.
—— *The Colonial Tariff Policy of France.* 1916.
HECKSCHER, E. F. *Continental System.* 1922.
LEVASSEUR, E. *Histoire du Commerce de la France*, 2 pts., 1911–12.
MEREDITH, H. O. *Protection in France.* 1904.
ROBERTS, S. H. *History of French Colonial Policy*, 2 vols. 1929.
Royal Commission on Canals and Waterways, vol. vi. Foreign Inquiry : Report on the Waterways of France, Belgium, Germany, and Holland, by W. H. Lindley, *Cd.* 4841, 1909.

GERMANY

ASHLEY, P. *Modern Tariff History.* 1920.
CLAPHAM, J. H. *Economic Development of France and Germany, 1815–1914.* 1928.
DAWSON, W. H. *Protection in Germany.* 1904.
HIRST, M. E. *Life of Frederick List.* 1909.
JAGTIANI, H. M. *The Rôle of the State in the Provision of Railways.* 1924.
LIST, F. *National System of Political Economy.* 1904.
LOTZ, W. *Die Ideen der deutschen Handelspolitik von 1860 bis 1891.* 1892.
—— *Die Verkehrsentwickelung in Deutschland, 1800–1900.* 1900.
Royal Commission on Canals and Waterways, vol. vi. Foreign Inquiry : Report on the Waterways of France, Belgium, Germany, and Holland, by W. H. Lindley [*Cd.* 4841]. 1909.
SCHNEE, A. H. H. *German Colonisation Past and Present.* 1926.
TOWNSEND, M. E. *Origins of Modern German Colonization.* 1921.
—— *Rise and Fall of Germany's Colonial Empire.* 1930.
WEHRSTEDT, K. *Die handelspolitische Bedeutung der deutschen Kolonien.* 1926.
ZEYSS, R. *Die Entstehung der Handelskammern.* 1907.

RUSSIA

KOVALEVSKY, M. (ed.). *La Russie à la fin du 19e siècle.* 1900.
KRAUSSE, A. *Russia in Asia, 1558–1899.* 1899.
MILLER, M. S. *Russian Economic Development, 1905–1914.* 1926.
WITTSCHEWSKY, V. *Russlands Handels-, Zoll- und Industriepolitik von Peter dem Grossen bis auf die Gegenwart.* 1905.
YARMOLINSKY, A. (ed. and trans.). *Memoirs of Count Witte.* 1921.

THE UNITED STATES

ASHLEY, P. *Modern Tariff History.* 1920.
DEWEY, D. R. *Financial History of the United States.* 1922.
IRELAND, A. *Far Eastern Tropics.* 1905.
JOHNSON, E. R. (ed.). "History of Domestic and Foreign Commerce of the United States": *Columbia-Carnegie Institution Publications*, No. 215A, 2 vols. 1915.
NEARING, S., and FREEMAN, J. *Dollar Diplomacy.* 1926.
RAPER, C. L. *Railway Transportation.* 1912.
STEPHENSON, G. M. *History of American Immigration, 1820–1924.* 1926.
TAUSSIG, F. W. *Tariff History of the United States.* 1914.
The Public Domain : Its History. A Report by Thomas Donaldson, in U.S. House of Representatives Miscellaneous Documents, 1882–3, vol. xix.
TURNER, F. J. "Rise of the New West": *American Nation Series*, vol. xiv. 1906.
—— *The Frontier in American History.* 1921.

INDEX

Administrative reform, **8**, **42**.
Africa, partition of, 22, 345.
Agriculture, reconstruction, 8–9, 15, 35, 43–6; revolution, 23–5; education, 339; tariffs, 339; improvements in France, 24, 44–5, 49–50, 55, 56–8; in Germany, 24, 44–5, 46, 66–8, 70–2, 73; in Russia, 45, 83; machinery, 96–7.
Alaska, 334.
Albert of Brandenburg, **161**.
Albert the Bear, 160.
Alexander I, 75.
Alexander II, 76.
Algeria, 306, 308, 315–16, 320–1.
Alsace-Lorraine, 147–8, 251.
American Federation of Labour, 203–4.
American system, 289, 291.
Armaments, 21.
Artel, 78, 180–2.
Assignats, 118, 119, 120, 121.
Austria, serfdom abolished, 8, 14, 20, 106; internal tariffs abolished, 19; shipping, 23; national policy, 158; growth of trade, 164; Maria Theresa, 164; Joseph II, 164; Zollverein, 263–6.

Baghdad railway, **13**.
Baku oil-fields, 184.
Bank of France, 127, 127 *n.*, 138; Raiffeisen banks, 70; Bank of Prussia, 163; German banking, 30, 156, 160, 168, 172; Russian land banks, 81–2; Russian banking, 182, 183, 281; United States Bank, 193, 197.
Bauwens, 129, 133.
Belgium, 18–19, 250, 263.
Berlin, 155, 159, 161.
Berlin Decree, 195.
Birkbeck, 56.
Bismarck, **4**; social reform, **26**; social insurance, 172; industrial legislation, 172; railway policy, 217, 218–21; fiscal policy, 267, 269–70; colonial policy, 322.
Blanc, Louis, 106, 141, 142–3.
Blount, Edward, 211–12.
Blücher, 165.
Boll-weevil, 11.
Bolsheviki, 186, 187.
Booms in trade, 185, **194**, 198, 201–2, 298.
Bounties, 19, 339.
Boxer rising, 325–6.
Brassey, Thomas, 212, **212** ***n.***
Bribery, Russian, 345 *n.*
Brigandage, French, 120.
British Empire, slavery abolished, 8.
Burghley, Lord, **4**.

California, 332.
Canada, 300.
Canals, French, 210; German, 221–3; American, 195, 230.
Cancrin, Count, 278.
Capital investment, 10.
Cattle, importance of, 37, 44.
Chaptal, J. A. C., 122 *n.*, 124-5.
Chevalier, 246–7.
Chicago, 97, 98.
China, 8, 325–6.
Civil Service, unreformed, **17**.
Civil War, 87–9, 91, 189, 333.
Coal-mining (*see under respective countries*).
Cobden, 246–7.
Codes, Napoleonic, 69–70, 109, 117, 126.
Colbert, **4**, **108**, **111**, 112, 240.
Colonial expansion, 21–2, 30–1; French, 7–8, 22, 31, 155, 306–22; German, 22, 31, 322–3; Russian, 325–8; American, 334–6.
Combinations, industrial, **7**.
Coméré, Baron de, 241.
Commercial Treaty, 1786, 113–14, 115, 240.
Commercial Treaty, 1860, 18, 107, 144–5, 246–7.
Commune, Paris, 109–10, 134, 147, 150.
Conseils de Prud'hommes, 134.
Consular service, 23.
Continental System, 109, 121, 124 *n.*, 130, 131–2, 240, 242–5.
Convention, French, 118, 120.

Co-operation, agricultural, 7, 57, 58, 339.
Co-operative movement, 146–7, 150.
Co-operative workshops, 142, 143, 182.
Cotton industry (*see under respective countries*).
Councils of Commerce, 126.
Councils of Industry, 167.
Crimea acquired, 324.
Crimean War, 20, 76, 226.
Crisis of 1837, 197–8, 293–4; of 1857, 295; of 1873, 298.
Cuba, 335.

Dantzig, 161.
Dawson, Sir W. H., 72, 154, 157, 169.
Declaration of the Rights of Man, 14, 117, 135.
Democracy, 13, 28, 172.
Depressions, agricultural, 24, 46, 73, 269.
Depressions, industrial, 113–14, 268; French, 251–2; Russian, 185; American, 191–2, 196, 290–1, 294.
de Saussure, quoted, 313.
Dingley Tariff, 298, 303.
Directory, French, 118, 120–2.
Disunity, French, 116–18; German, 154, 155, 160; American, 84, 86–7, 190.
Domestic workshops, French, 138, 149, 152; Russian, 179, 180, 182.
Douglas machines, 128.
Drage, quoted, 326–7.

East Prussia, 63, 64.
Economic nationalism, 6, 11–12, 13, 16–20, 28, 30 (*see also under* "Tariffs").
Ekaterina, 228.
Ekaterinoslav, 184.
Elbe, 60–4, 68–9, 73–4.
Electrical development, 148, 170, 171.
Elevators, grain, 95, 233.
Elizabeth, Queen, 4.
Emancipation Edict, 64, 65–6.
Embargo Act, 195.
Emigration, 322.
Engineering, 149, 170, 171.
England, home of inventions, 3, 4–5, 7, 27; personal freedom 4, 5, 12; Charles I, 4, 348; Industrial Revolution, 4–5; individualism, 6; industrialism, 6–7; free trade, 12, 16; population, 20; Imperial Preference, 23; American wheat imports, 24; Civil Service reforms, 29; health movement, 29; serfdom, disappearance of, 41; slavery abolished, 41; improved farming, 44; Gild Socialism, 107–8, 151.
English competition, 113–14, 196.
English crisis, 1811, 244–5.
Equality, meaning of, 135.
Erie Canal, 230.
Estate management, 38, 40, 48, 71, 73.
Expositions, 144.

Factory legislation, 109, 150, 172, 186.
Fairs, importance of, 159.
Fallowing, 68, 72.
Famine, emancipation from, 10–11.
Feudalism, 4, 6, 8, 20, 36–41, 48–51, 61–2, 63, 64, 65–6, 76–7, 175–6.
Finland, 324.
Fisher, H. A. L., 122.
Foreign capital in Russia, 182, 183, 184–5, 281, 284.
Foreign trade, 115, 116, 130 *n.*, 131 *n.*
Forests, German, 72.
Fourier, 106, 139–40, 141.

FRANCE:
Agricultural discontent, 50.
Agricultural improvement, 24, 44–5, 49–50, 55, 56–8.
Alsace-Lorraine, loss of, 147–8.
Banalités, 48.
Bank of France, 127, 127 *n.*, 138.
Birkbeck, 56.
Blanc, Louis, 106, 141, 142–3.
Blount, Edward, 211–12.
Brassey, Thomas, 212, 212 *n.*
Caisse des Comptes Courants, 127.
Caisse d'Escompte du Commerce, 127.
Canals, 210.
Cens, or *Champart*, 48.
Chemical industry, 130.
Coal-mining, 145, 146, 148.
Colbert, 4, 108, 111, 112, 240.
Colonies, 7–8, 22, 31, 155; chartered companies, 306; trade monopoly, 306; loss of early empire, 306, 308; Algeria acquired, 306, 308; *colonies de peuplement*, 306; *colonies d'exploitation*, 306; contrast to England, 306–8; small racial expansion, 306–7; Asiatic and African power, 307; assimilation policy, 307–8, 309–10, 313,

321–2 ; missionary spirit, 307–8, 309–10, 311–12 ; French Revolution, 308 ; Napoleon and slavery, 308 ; abolition of slavery, 308–9 ; tariff autonomy, 309 ; Saigon acquired, 309 ; Tunis acquired, 310 ; Sudan, 310 ; Madagascar acquired, 310 ; Indo-China, 310, 316 ; Morocco, 310 ; West Africa, 310, 316, 318, 320 ; Leroy Beaulieu quoted, 311 ; Gide quoted, 311–12 ; native policies, 312–14 ; de Saussure quoted, 313 ; Girault quoted, 313, 318, 319–20 ; tariff assimilation, 313–14, 315–20 ; tariff " personality ", 314, 321 ; colonial trade, 315–21 ; Algerian tariff policy, 315–16, 320–1 ; Guadeloupe, 316 ; Martinique, 316 ; Réunion, 316 ; assimilated colonies, 316 ; non-assimilated colonies, 316, 317–18, 320 ; Madagascar assimilated, 316 ; colonial export duties, 317 ; duties on colonial produce, 317 ; reaction against assimilation, 318; Reinsch quoted, 318 ; trade hindered, 318 ; burden on colonies, 319 ; success in Indo-China, 319 ; and Madagascar, 319–20 ; and West Africa, 320 ; Mary Kingsley, 320 ; success in Algeria, 320–1 ; slow progress, 321 ; officialism, 321 ; lack of enterprise, 321 ; *la gloire*, 321.
Combinations, forbidden, 117, 134, 140 ; tolerated, 147 ; legalized, 150.
Comèré, Baron de, 241.
Commercial Treaty, 1786, 113–4, 115, 240.
Commercial Treaty, 1860, 8, 107, 144–5, 246–7
Commune, 109–10, 134, 147, 150.
Compagnonnages, 112, 140.
Comptoir Commercial, 127.
Continental System. 121, 240, 242–5.
Co-operation, agricultural, 57, 58.
Co-operative movement, 146–7, 150.
Co-operative workshops, 142, 143.
Corvées, 49, 49 *n.*, 209.
Cotton industry, 110–11 ; English mechanism, 111, 128 ; revival under Napoleon, 128–9 ; Bauwens, 129, 133 ; Oberkampf, 129 ; collapse, 132, 133 ; revival after 1815, 136 ; progress under Napoleon III, 145, 146 ; loss of Alsace, 148 ; mechanization, 149.
Country industries, 112–13.
Crédit du Travail, 147.
Crédit Foncier, 144.
Crédit Mobilier, 144.
Depressions, industrial, 113–14, 251–2.
Domestic workshops, 138, 149, 152.
Dupont de Nemours, 52.
Electrical development, 148.
Engineering, 149.
English competition, 114.
English imports, 113–14.
Estate management, 40, 48.
Factory legislation, 109, 150.
Famines, yearly, 50.
Feudalism, 6 ; tolls, 48 ; hunting rights, 48 ; abolition, 50–1, 50 *n.* 1.
Foreign trade, 115, 116, 130 *n.*, 131 *n.*
Fourier, 106, 139–40, 141.
Free trade treaties, 107, 145.
Freer trade, 16, 18, 107, 240.
Généralités, 108, 116.
Gild system, 111–2.
" Great industry," 112.
Guesde, 150.
Hayes and Law, 111.
Henry IV, 4, 108.
Holker, 111.
Imperial Preference, 23.
Industrialization, 29, 56, 57, 136, 138–9, 139 *n.*, 148, 149.
Influence until 1870, 14–15, 16, 18–19, 20–1, 106–7, 108, 135–6.
Intendants, 108, 114, 116, 125.
Intensive farming, 49–50, 52.
Interventionisme, 110.
Iron industry, 110, 129, 136, 145, 146 ; Creusot, 111 ; Wilkinson, 111 ; armaments, 121.
Labour movement, lack of continuity, 140–1 ; fertility in theory, 140–1 ; spasmodic growth, 141 ; revival after 1880, 150 ; Syndicalism, 150–2.
Lack of capitalists, 111.
Land, hunger, 45 ; freedom of use, 51 ; sales, 53, 54–5 ; inheritance, 53–4 ; transfer, 54–5.
Leblanc, 130.
Liberty before the Revolution, 108–9.
Linen industry, 110, 138.
Lods et ventes, 48.
Louis XIV, 4.
Louis XVI, 108.
Manufactures royales, 112.
Marseilles, harbour frozen, 115.
Mechanization, 136–7 ; English machines, 137, 137 *n.*, 138,

138 *n.*; English managers, 137; Douglas, 137; Maberley, 138; under Napoleon III, 145.
Métayer system, 51.
Millerand, 150.
Milne, 111.
National workshops, 142–3.
Nationalization, 150.
Necker, 241.
Pays d'election, 116.
Pays d'état, 116.
Peasants and taxation, 35, 38, 48–9, 51; numbers, 47; improving status, 48; burdens, 48–9; payment in kind, 49; bound to the soil, 49; feudal burdens lifted, 50–1; taxation lightened, 51; support the Revolution, 52; apostles of equality, 52; increase in numbers, 53–4, 54 *n.*; *morcellement*, 58–9; peasant rescue, 59; bye-employment, 115; benefit from the Revolution, 118.
Poll tax, 49.
Population, 20, 126.
Potato production, 57, 58.
Proudhon, 106.
Railways, 138, 144, 180; English technique, 211–12; centralized planning, 212; state subsidies, 212; reversion to the state, 212–13, 214; economic crises, 212, 213; six groups in 1860, 213; absence of competition, 213; economic reactions, 213–14; renewed building after 1871, 214; prevalence of deficits, 214; Western line nationalized, 214; private management elsewhere, 214.
Revolution of 1848, 106–7, 142–3.
Roads, state-built, 209; school of roads and bridges, 209; *corvées*, 209–10; Napoleon, 211; Louis Philippe, 211.
Rousseau, 50.
Serfdom, 8, 35–6, 39, 47–8, 117.
Shipping, 23, 214–5; state bounties, 215; *surtaxe de pavillon*, 215; *surtaxe d'entrepôt*, 215.
Silk industry, 110, 129, 136.
Silk worm failure, 114.
Situation, favourable, 154–5.
Slavery abolished, 20, 41.
Social legislation, lack of, 149–50.
Socialism, Utopian, 135, 139–40; Marxian, 140, 147.
Société Centrale de l'Agriculture, 56.
Société Générale du Commerce de Rouen, 127.
St. Simon, 106, 139, 141.
Stability, industrial, 149.
Sully, 4.
Syndicalism, 107, 150–2.
Syndicate Law, 1884, 150.
Taille, 49.
Tariffs, 109; for agriculture, 58; of 1791, 119, 240; of 1793, 121, 240; of 1810, 132, 244; of 1815, 136, 245; internal tolls abolished, 240–1; Continental System, 242–5; protection till 1848, 245; Napoleon III and freer trade, 246; Parliamentary opposition, 246, 249; tariff reduction by treaty, 246; commercial treaty with England, 246–7; spread of commercial treaties, 247–9, 250–1; industrial inquiry, 248; colonial system, 248–9; shipping laws, 248–9; unpopularity of low duties, 249; Belgian Treaty, 250; Zollverein Treaty, 250; return to Protection, 251, 253; loss of Alsace-Lorraine, 251; military expenses, 251; influence of Thiers, 251; depression of 'seventies, 251–2; industrial inquiry report, 252; American wheat, 252; tariff of 1881, 252; depression of 'eighties 252; Méline Tariff, 1892, 252–3; increased protection, 253; tariff of 1910, 253; unsuccessful in heavy industries, 253; successful in agriculture, 253.
Tithe, 49, 51.
Tolozan, 111.
Trade unionism, slow growth, 150; tendency to violence, 150; bias against politics, 150; Syndicalism, 150–2; membership, 151.
Tradition of control, 108; of liberty, 108; of revolution, 135, 140, 141–2.
Turbilly, Marquis de, 52.
Turgot, 108, 210, 240.
Waste, extent of, 52; reduction of, 56, 57.
Wheat production, 57, 58.
Wine production, 57, 58; phylloxera, 148, 252.
Wool shortage, 114.
Woollen industry, 110, 120, 136, 149; in Lille, 110; in Picardy, 110; in Normandy, 110; in Champagne, 110; round Carcassonne, 110; expansion, 113·

Commercial Treaty 1786, 114; revival under Napoleon, 129.
Young, Arthur, 52, 113, 209.

Frankfort, Treaty of, 267.
Frederick I, 161.
Frederick II, 161, 163.
Frederick William, the Great Elector, 156, 161, 162.
Frederick William III, 161, 255.
Free competition, 199, 200, 201.
Free Trade, 7, 13, 15–20, 27, 95, 107, 145, 246–9.
Fulton, Robert, 230.

General Strike, 107.

GERMANY:
Agrarian politics, 71–2.
Agriculture, importance of, 158.
Agricultural contrast, east and west, 60–1.
Agricultural improvement, 24.
Backwardness, 160, 164.
Baden, 62, 65 *n*., 66 *n*.
Banking, 30, 156, 160, 168, 172; finance of industry, 172.
Bavaria, 62, 66 *n*.
Berg, Grand Duchy of, 62.
Bismarck, 4, 26, 172, 217, 218–21, 267, 269–70, 322.
Brandenburg, 63, 64.
Brunswick, 66 *n*., 68.
Canals, rebuilding and enlargement, 221; advantages and disadvantages, 221; state ownership, 222; canal and rail competition, 222–3; division of labour, 222; prevention of discrimination, 222–3.
Cereal production, 72.
Chemical industries, 156, 171.
Climate, 72, 155.
Coal-mining, 26, 155, 170, 172.
Coastline, poor, 155.
Code Napoleon, 69, 70.
Colonial expansion, 22, 31, 322–3.
Confederation of the Rhine, 62, 69.
Cotton industry, 26, 171.
Dawson, Sir W. H., 72, 154, 157, 169.
Depression, agricultural, 73, 269; industrial, 268.
Disunity, 154, 155, 160.
East of Elbe, 60, 61, 63, 68–9, 73–4.
East Prussia, 63, 64.
Economic ambitions, 28, 224.
Electricity, 170, 171.
Emigration, 322.
Engineering, 170, 171.
Estate management, 40, 60, 71, 73.
Fairs, importance of, 159.
Fallow, 68, 72.
Feudalism, 6, 160.
Foreign trade, 159, 164.
Forests, 72.
Frankfurt, Grand Duchy of, 62.
French influence on serfdom, 62.
Gilds, 158, 165–7.
Hanover, 66 *n*., 68.
Hesse-Darmstadt, 65 *n*., 66 *n*.
Hesse, Electoral, 62, 66 *n*.
Hohenzollern-Sigmaringen, 62.
Holstein, 63, 65.
Immigration, 64.
Improved farming, 44–5, 46, 66–8, 70–2, 73.
Industrial legislation, 172.
Industrial organization, 171–2, 174.
Industrialization, 9, 20, 25–6, 27, 30, 74, 154, 157, 169–72, 174.
Influence of wars, 30, 169.
Internal tolls, 217.
Iron and steel industry, 26, 155, 170, 172.
Jews, 174.
Junkers, 60, 63.
Kartels, 171–2, 174.
Labour movement, 172; influence of Marx, 173; repression, 173.
Large estates, 63–5.
Linen industry, 171.
Lippe, 66 *n*.
Manorial cultivation, 50.
Mecklenburg, 63, 65.
Mecklenburg-Schwerin, 65 *n*.
Mecklenburg-Strelitz, 65 *n*.
Migrants, agricultural, 74.
Milk scarcity, 68 *n*.
Münster, 62.
Napoleon, 62.
Nassau, 65 *n*., 68.
"Nation in arms," 156–7.
Natural economy, 158, 168.
Oldenburg, 66 *n*.
Open fields, 67–8.
Peasants, instruction, 69–71; credit, 70; state aid, 70; co-operation, 70–1; prevalence, 73; no agrarian revolution, 73; "land flight," 73–4; wage labour, 74.
Pomerania, 63, 64, 65.
Population, 20–1, 154, 155, 156, 159.
Potato production, 72.
Poverty, 156–9.
Predominance after 1870, 21, 23.
Raiffeisen, F. W., 70.
Railways, 155, 156, 170, 217–23

Redistribution of land, 68–9.
Rhineland, 61.
Rivers, improvement, 216.
Rotation of crops, 68, 69.
Saxe-Coburg-Gotha, 65 *n.*, 66 *n.*
Saxony, 66, 68–9.
Self-sufficiency, domestic, 158, 159.
Serfdom, 8, 61–6, 158.
Settlement, freedom of, 69.
Shipbuilding, 170, 224.
Shipping, 156 ; subsidies, 223–4.
Silk industry, 171.
Social Democratic Party, 26, 172.
Social Insurance, 172.
Soil, poverty of, 72, 155, 156.
Sombart, Werner, 156, 157, 158, 159.
State action, 157, 169–70.
State in 1815, 9, 160.
Sugar beet, 68, 70, 72 ; Convention, 68.
Tariffs, 20 ; nation-building, 255 ; Hardenberg's note, 255 ; Congress of Darmstadt, 259 ; tariff treaty of 1824, 259 ; Southern Zollverein, 259 ; Central Union, 260 ; Union of Prussian and southern Zollvereins, 260–1 ; dissolution of Central Union, 261 ; Zollverein of 1834, 261–2 ; renewed, 262 ; national institution, 262–3 ; *Steuerverein*, 263 ; further additions, 263 ; Belgian treaty, 263 ; fiscal policy, 263 ; Prussian opposition to Austria, 263, 264 ; List preaches Protection, 263 ; free trade Prussia, 263 ; Zollverein renewed, 264, 265 ; Austro-Prussian treaty, 264–5 ; French treaty, 265–6 ; further treaties, 266 ; reform of Zollverein, 266 ; merged in Empire, 267 ; Treaty of Frankfort, 267 ; free trade policy, 267 ; motives, 267 ; free trade progress, 267–8 ; change to Protection, 268 ; industrial depression, 268 ; English competition, 268 ; Central Union of German Industrialists, 268 ; Industrialists' propaganda, 268 ; Agrarians turn protectionist, 268–9 ; agricultural depression, 289 ; Bismarck's motives, 269 ; tariff of 1879, 270 ; German influence abroad, 270 ; lower agricultural protection, 272 ; commercial treaties, 272–3 ; Russian tariff war, 272, 285–6 ; tariff of 1902, 273–4.
Thirty Years' War, 63, 157.
Trade unionism, 172–3.
Waldeck, 65 *n.*, 66 n.
West of Elbe, 60–1, 62–3, 64, 69, 74.
West Prussia, 64.
Westphalia, 61, 62.
William I, 4.
Woollen industry, 171.
Workers, low wages of, 173.
Wurtemberg, 62, 66 *n.*
Zollverein, 160, 258–66.

Gide quoted, 311–2.
Gilchrist Thomas process, 26, 170.
Gild socialism, 28, 107–8.
Gilds, 4, 8, 40, 42, 108, 111–2, 117, 158, 165–7.
Girault quoted, 313, 318, 319–20.
Grozny oil-fields, 184.
Guadeloupe, 316.
Guesde, 150.

Hadley quoted, 212.
Hamilton, Alexander, 189, 190, 193, 290, 329.
Hardenberg, 165, 255, 256.
Hawaii, 334.
Hayes and Law, 111.
Henry IV, 4, 108.
Hohenzollerns, 160–2, 164.
Holker, 111.
Hughes, John, 184.
Huguenot settlers, 161.

Imperial preference, 23.
Imperialism, 13, 27, 344–5.
Indebtedness, rural, 89–90.
Indemnities, 126–7, 164–5.
Independence, War of, 190, 191.
India, 345.
Individualism, American, 6, 154.
Indo-China, 316, 319.
Industrial Revolution, 4–5, 9, 20, 25–6, 29, 56, 57, 123–5, 136, 138–9, 144–6, 148, 149, 154, 169–72, 174, 178, 182–7, 189, 195–6, 198–9.
Industrial Workers of the World, 107, 151, 204.
Institute of the Means of Communication, 225.
Intendants, 108, 114, 116, 125.
" International," 147.
Interstate Commerce Commission, 203, 234–5.
" Interventionisme," 110.
Ireland, 20 *n.*, 24, 41, 332.

Iron industry (*see under respective countries*).
Isnard, 124.

Jackson, Andrew, 197, 330–1.
Jacquard loom, 128.
Jena, demoralization after, 164–5; reconstruction after, 28, 165.
Jews, 174.
Junkers, 60, 63.

Kartells, 171–2, 174.
Kingsley, Mary, 320.
Knights of Labour, 200, 203.
Knoop, Ludwig, 183.

Labour movement, 9–10; French, 140–1, 150–2; German, 172–3; Russian, 186–7; American, 200, 203–5.
Laissez-faire, 6, 12, 13, 21, 24; origin, 108; abandonment, 344–5.
Land Banks, Russian, 81–2.
Laws of settlement, 40, 42.
Leadership of Prussia, 154, 155, 164, 168, 217.
Lena goldfields strike, 187.
Leroy Beaulieu, quoted, 311.
Levant, 183.
Liberty, before the Revolution, 108–9; and the Revolution, 4–5, 36, 106, 117; tradition of, 108; meaning of, 135.
Linen industry, French, 110, 138.
List, F., 16, 27, 263.
Lord Curzon, quoted, 327.
Louis XIV, 4.
Louis XVI, 108.
Louis Philippe, 211.
Louisiana purchase, 329, 334.

Maberley, 138.
Madagascar, 310, 316, 319–20.
Madison, 291.
Manchuria, 325, 326.
Mandats, 121.
Manorial cultivation, 38, 39, 40.
Marseilles, 115.
Marx, Karl, 26.
Marxian Socialism, 107, 173.
McKinley Tariff, 298, 299–300, 301.
Meat, transport of, 15; exports, 92, 97–8; statistics, 98, 103.
Méline Tariff, 252–3.
Mercantilism, 11, 13, 15, 17–18, 27, 164, 177, 276.
Mesabi mines, 202.
Métayer system, 51.
Milan Decree, 195.
Miller, M. S., quoted, 186.
Millerand, 150.
Milling, improved, 98–9.
Milne, 111.
Mississippi region, 332.
Missouri Compromise, 190.
Morocco, 310.

Napoleon I, Codes, 9, 109, 117, 126; industrialization of France, 29, 123–5; interest in agriculture, 55 *n.*, 55–6; roads and canals, 56, 109, 211; influence on Germany, 61, 106, 125; on Italy, 125; tradition of control, 108, 109; restoration of order, 109, 118, 122, 123, 125; tariffs, 109; Continental System, 109, 121, 124 *n.*, 130, 131–2, 242–5; characteristics, 121–2; Fisher, H. A. L., 122; Chaptal, J. A. C., 122 *n.*, 124–5; subventions to manufactures, 123; economic policy, 123; *Correspondence* quoted, 123; economic staff, 124; Isnard, 124; collapse of 1811, 125, 132–3; policy of centralization, 125–6; bureaucracy created, 125–6; Councils of Commerce, 126; Chambers of Manufactures, 126; indemnities, 126–7; interest in banking, 127–8, 132; Bank of France founded, 127, 127 *n.*; Society for the Encouragement of National Industry, 128; Jacquard loom, 128; Douglas machines, 128; inventors rewarded, 128; industrial revival, 128–32; interest in industry, 129; English blockade counteracted, 131; Non-Intercourse Act, 131; English-foreign trade, 131 *n.*; tariff of 1810, 132, 133, 244; fall due to economic failure, 133; lack of social policy, 134; combinations forbidden, 134; *Conseils de Prud'hommes*, 134; enduring influence, 134; beet sugar, 243; English crisis of 1811, 244–5.
Napoleon III, favours free trade, 16, 246–9; influence on Europe, 21, 107, 250–1; President, 143; becomes Emperor, 144; restoration of order, 144; industrial progress, 144, 145, 146; railways, 144, 145; *expositions*, 144; Commercial Treaty, 1860, 144–5, 246–7; low tariff treaties,

145, 246–51 ; trade progress, 145, 146 ; universal suffrage, 146; combinations suppressed, 146 ; and permitted, 147 ; co-operative movement, 146–7 ; "International," 147 ; increase in wages, 147.
Narodnaya Volya, 186.
Narodniki, 186.
National expansion (*see under respective countries*).
National workshops, 142–3.
Nationalization, 150, 214, 220, 222.
Navigation Acts, 11, 12.
Necker, 241.
Negro cultivators, 90–1.
Nicholas I, 75–6.
Nijni-Novgorod, 183.
Non-Intercourse Act, 131, 195.
North versus South, 84, 86–7, 190, 291, 292–3.

Oberkampf, 129.
Old Colonial system, 17–18, 19.
Open field system, 36–7, 44–5, 53, 67–9.
Orders-in-Council, 195.

Panama Canal, 344.
Peasants (*see under respective countries*).
Persia, 183.
Personal freedom, 4, 5, 8, 14, 28–9, 41, 42, 88.
Peter the Great, 65, 177–9, 275–6, 324.
Philippines, 334, 335.
Phylloxera, 148, 252.
Pittsburg, 196, 201.
Poland, 183.
Population, French, 20–1, 126 ; German, 154, 155, 156, 159 ; American, 21, 328, 332.
Porto Rico, 334.
Potato production, 57, 58.
Proudhon, 106.

PRUSSIA :
Albert of Brandenburg, 161.
Albert the Bear, 160.
Army, importance of, 161, 162.
Berlin, 155, 159, 161.
Blücher, 165.
Canals, 221–3.
Cleves, Duchy of, 160.
Councils of Industry, 167.
Dantzig, 161.
Development from above, 165.
Early industrial development, 163; immigration policy, 163; bounties and protection, 163.
Economic unity, 162.
Emancipation Edict, 64, 65–6.
Frederick I, 161.
Frederick II, and Silesia, 161 ; economic policy, 161 ; immigration policy, 163 ; agricultural improvement, 163 ; industrial development, 163 ; industrial decree, 163 ; port of Emden, 163 ; Bank of Prussia, 163 ; internal tariffs maintained, 163.
Frederick William, the Great Elector, 156, 161, 162.
Frederick William III, 161, 255.
French influence, 165.
Gilds, reform of, 165–6 ; revival of, 166, 167 ; weakening, 168 ; strengthening, 168.
Hardenberg, 165, 255, 256.
Hohenzollerns, 160–2, 164.
Home colonization, 161, 163, 322.
Indemnity, 164–5.
Industrial code, 168.
Industrial freedom, 165–6, 167.
Industrialization, 167, 169.
Jena, demoralization after, 164–5 ; modernization after, 165.
John Sigismund, 160.
Königsberg, 161.
Leadership in Germany, 154, 155, 164, 168, 217.
Loss of territory after Jena, 164.
Magdeburg, 162.
Manorial cultivation, 40.
Mark Brandenburg, 160.
Mercantilism, 164.
National policy, 158, 164.
Origins, 160–1.
Pomerania, 161.
Railways, 167, 169 ; private construction, 217 ; State guarantee, 217 ; State construction, 217 ; chaos, 217–18 ; Bismarck quoted, 218 ; need for unification, 218–19 ; "heroic measures," 219 ; Imperialization opposed, 219–20 ; nationalization movement, 220 ; State coal mines, 220 ; aid to export trade, 220–21 ; aid to ports, 221 ; protection to home trade, 223 ; canal and rail competition, 222–3 ; State railway profits, 223.
Redistribution of land, 68.
Scharnhorst, 165.
Stein, 165, 168.
Sterility of soil, 155.

Tariff of 1810, 255–6; Hardenberg and low duties, 256; war tax of 1813, 256; motives behind low duties, 256; need for German unity, 256–7; political chaos, 257; tariff of 1818, 257; towards the Zollverein, 258; abolition of internal tolls, 258; growth of Zollverein, 260–6; merged in Empire, 267.
Teutonic Knights, 160–1.
Thirty Years' War, 161, 163.
Transport improvement, 162, 167, 216.
von Bülow, 257.
Ward, A. W., quoted, 161.
Zollverein, 15–16, 154, 160, 166–7, 169; tariff of 1818, 257; Conference of Vienna, 258; absorption of enclaves, 259–60; treaty with Hesse, 260; union with southern Zollverein, 260–1; Saxony rebuffed, 261; Electoral Hesse admitted, 261; Thuringia rebuffed, 261; Zollverein of 1834, 261–2; Baden, Nassau, Frankfort join, 262; Zollverein renewed, 262; further additions, 263; problem of fiscal policy, 263; rivalry with Austria, 263, 264; free trade Prussia, 263; Hanover and Oldenburg join, 264; Zollverein again renewed, 264–5; Austro-Prussian treaty, 264–5, 266; French treaty, 265–6; further treaties, 266; reform of Zollverein, 266; merged in Empire, 267.

Raiffeisen, F. W., 70.
Railways, 5, 10, 11, 18, 22, 23; French, 138, 144, 150, 211–14; German, 155, 156, 170, 217–23; Prussian, 167, 169, 217–23; Russian, 30, 31, 176–7, 182–5, 226–7; American, 91, 92–4, 98, 190, 201–3, 230–5.
Revolution, French, 3, 4–5, 14–5, 106, 109; emancipating effect, 4–5, 36, 106, 117; Declaration of the Rights of Man, 14, 117, 135; gilds abolished, 108, 117; tradition of liberty, 108; causes, 115; disunity before, 116; uniting effect, 116–8; combinations forbidden, 117; privileged companies abolished, 117; serfdom abolished, 117; legal equality, 117; financial collapse, 118, 120, 121; *assignats*, 118, 119, 120, 121; maximum prices, 118, 119; reform of taxation, 118–9; inflation, 120; trade collapse, 120; brigandage, 120; indemnities, 120; *mandats*, 121; Convention, 118, 120; Directory, 118, 120–2; bourgeoisie benefited, 135; meaning of liberty, 135; meaning of equality, 135; return to protection, 241–2.
Revolutions, of 1848, 106–7, 142–3; of 1905, 187; of 1917, 187.
Roads, French, 209–11; Russian, 225–6; American, 229.
Rousseau, 50.

RUSSIA:
Agricultural reforms, 29, 45, 83.
Alexander I, 75.
Alexander II, 76.
Artel, 78, 180–2.
Baku oil-fields, 184.
Banking, 182, 183, 281.
Bolsheviki, 186, 187.
Boom of 1908–14, 185.
Bribery, 345 *n*.
Cancrin, Count, 278.
Climate, 176.
Coal-mining, 25, 182, 183, 185.
Cotton industry, 25, 182–3, 185, 281; Polish rivalry, 183; statistics, 185.
Crimean War, 20, 76, 226.
Depression of 1903–8, 185.
Differentiation, 83.
Domestic workshops, 179, 180.
Ekaterinoslav iron works, 184.
Estate factories, 179–80.
Expansion, 7, 31; continuous, 323; pressure of population, 323–4; lack of barriers, 324; religious persecution, 324; Peter the Great's reforms, 324; State burdens, 324; State follows, 324; Peter's acquisitions, 324; Catherine's conquests, 324; Crimea acquired, 324; Finland acquired, 324; expansion statistics, 324–5, 325 *n*.; access to the sea, 325; Central Asia, 325, 327; lines of expansion, 325; Siberian Railway, 325, 327; Amur province, 325; Boxer rising, 325–6; Manchuria, 325, 326; Russo-Japanese War, 326; racial expansion, 326; Siberian settlement, 326–7; Drage quoted 326–7; Lord Curzon quoted,

327; Trans-Caspian Railway, 327; economic development, 327, 328; Samarkand, 327; slave raids, 328; pacification, 328; success in colonization, 328; Russian Orientalism, 328.
Foreign capital, 182, 183, 184–5, 281, 284.
Grozny oil-fields, 184.
Hughes, John, 184.
Industrialization, 9, 25, 178, 182–7; Peter the Great, 178–9; foreign influences, 183–5; comparison with U.S.A., 187; late but rapid development, 187.
Iron and steel industry, 25, 182, 184, 185; bounties, 184; Belgian and French capital, 184; output statistics, 185.
Knoop, Ludwig, 183.
Kulak, 89.
Kustar, 182.
Land Banks, 81–2; land hunger, 45–6.
Landlords' compensation, 77–8.
Lena goldfields strike, 187.
Levant, 183.
Lithuanian nobles, 76.
Manorial cultivation, 40.
Miller, M. S., quoted, 186.
Mir, 77, 78, 79, 81–2.
Money economy, 176, 177–8.
Nadiel, 77, 79.
Narodnaya Volya, 186.
Narodniki, 186.
Natural economy, 176, 177–8.
Nicholas I, 75–6.
Nijni-Novgorod, 183.
Oil, 25, 182, 184; Nobel's 184; Rothschild's, 184; output statistics, 185.
Oka, 183.
Paternalism, autocratic, 186; employers' liabilities, 186; social legislation, 186; repression of workers, 186–7; secret societies, 186–7; revolutionary strikes, 187.
Peasants, emancipation of, 76, 180; immobility of, 77; redemption payments, 78, 80; backward methods, 78; improvement required, 79, 81; industrial retrogression, 184.
Persia, 183.
Peter the Great, 65; bullionist policy, 177, 276; industrial policy, 178–9; fiscal policy, 275; impulse to expansion, 324; foreign policy, 324.
Railways, 30, 31, 176; overcome frost, 176; compensate lack of coastline, 176; unite north and south, 177; link with Asia, 177; aid to industrialization, 182, 183, 184, 185; Tsarskoe-Selo line, 226; St. Petersburg-Moscow line, 226; Crimean War, 226; General Company of Russian Railways, 226; State control, 226; Count Witte, 226; rates control 226–7; Siberian Railway, 227; foreign capital, 227; heavy drain, 227; statistics, 227.
Revolution of 1905, 187.
Revolution of 1917, 187.
Riadtchik, 181.
Roads, 225–6.
Russo-Japanese War, 81, 185.
Schulze-Gaevernitz, 276, 280, 282.
Serfdom, 8, 20, 38, 43, 65, 76–7, 175–6.
Shipbuilding, 228.
Shipping, 23, 228.
Slavophilism, 75, 76, 82, 227, 280–1.
Starosta, 180, 181.
Steppe, 177.
Svietelka, 182.
Tariffs, periods, 276; Peter and bullionism, 276; Catherine and free trade, 276–7; Paul and prohibitive system, 277; Alexander I and freer trade, 277; Continental system, 277; tariff of 1810, 277; tariff of 1816, 277; liberal tariff of 1819, 277–8; tariff of 1822, 278; trade with East, 278, 279; prohibitive system abandoned, 278–9; Count Cancrin, 278, 279; Wrontschenko, 279; freer trade, 279–80; tariff of 1850, 279; tariffs of 1857 and 1867, 280; commercial treaties, 280; return to protection, 280; Count Witte, 281, 283, 284; Turkish War, 281; bribery, 282; tariffs of 1881 and 1885, 282; tariff of 1891, 282–3; Wischnegradski, 282–3; paper currency, 282; change to gold standard, 283; fall in corn prices, 283; need for new taxes, 284; financial reconstruction, 284; interest on foreign loans, 284, 286, 287; tariff of 1900, 284; high protection, 285; German tariff war, 285–6; German commercial treaty,

285–6 ; Russian economic backwardness, 286 ; contrast to the U.S.A., 286–7.
Trade unionism, repressed, 186 ; permitted, 187.
Transport, importance of, 176–7 ; lack of, 225 ; natural waterways, 225.
Ural iron works, 184.
Volga, 183.
Wage-earners, slow growth, 180 ; bad housing, 180 ; low wages, 180 ; long hours, 180 ; inefficiency, 180 ; artels, 180–2 ; nomadic nature, 182.
Wheat, exports, 24–5, 80 ; prices, fall in, 24–5, 80.
Wieth-Knudsen, 82.
Wischnegradski, 281, 282–3, 286.
Witte, Count, 4, 25, 27, 185, 226, 281, 281 *n.*, 283, 284, 286, 287.
Wrontschenko, 279.
Zemstvos, 81, 83.

Scharnhorst, 165.
Schulze-Gaevernitz, 276, 280, 282.
Scotland, 41.
Serfdom (*see under respective countries*).
Shipbuilding, French, 215 ; German, 170, 224 ; Russian, 228 ; American, 194, 198, 236.
Shipping, 5, 11, 12, 19, 23 ; French, 214–15 ; German, 156, 223–4 ; Russian, 228 ; American, 94–5, 194, 198, 201, 235–6.
Silk industry, French, 110, 129, 136.
Slavery, American, 8, 15, 20, 41, 46, 85, 88, 189, 194.
Slavophilism, 75, 76, 82, 227, 280–1.
Slater, Samuel, 194.
Smith, Adam, 16, 27.
Social democracy, 26, 172.
Social insurance, 172.
Sombart, Werner, 156, 157, 158, 159.
St. Simon, 106, 139, 141.
Standard Oil Company, 203.
State action, 6, 11–12, 21, 25, 27, 28, 157, 169–70, 178–9, 200–1, 204–5, 339–49.
Stein, 165, 168.
Sully, 4.
Syndicalism, 28, 107, 150–2.
Syndicate Law, 150.

Tariff (*see under respective countries*).
Taussig, Prof., 294, 296–7.
Taxation and peasantry, 38 ; reconstruction, 42.
Teutonic Knights, 160–1.
Tolozan, 111.
Trade unionism, French, 150–2 ; German, 172–3 ; Russian, 186–7 ; American, 107, 151, 200, 203–4.
Trading companies, 11–12.
Tradition, of control, 108 ; of liberty, 108 ; of revolution, 135, 140, 141–2.
Treaty of Ghent, 195.
Tropics, development of, 344.
Trusts, 200–3.
Tsetse fly, 11.
Turgot, 108, 210, 240.
Turnips, 44.

UNITED STATES OF AMERICA :
Agricultural machinery, 96–7.
Agricultural reconstruction, 46, 189.
Alabama, iron industry, 202.
American Federation of Labour, 203–4.
Berlin and Milan Decrees, 195.
Boom, in 'forties, 198 ; after 1865, 201–2.
California, 332, 334.
Canals, 195, 230.
Capital, power of, 199, 200.
Carpet industry, 198.
Cattle ranching, 98.
Central Pacific Railroad, 91.
Chicago, 97, 98.
Cincinnati, 97.
Civil War, 87–9, 91, 189.
Clayton Anti-Trust Act, 203.
Coal-mining, 198, 201.
Colonies, Hawaii annexed, 334 ; Porto Rico, 334 ; Philippines, 334 ; Cuba, 334 ; Spanish War, 334 ; changed outlook, 334 ; tropical colonization, 335 ; faith in education, 335 ; high tariff, 335 ; Chinese exclusion, 335 ; policy in Philippines, 335 ; in Cuba, 335 ; economic development, 335 ; preferential tariffs, 335 ; rapid progress, 335 ; " big brother " rôle, 336.
Condition in 1815, 9.
Controlled development, 201.
Cotton, 85, 89, 90–1, 91 *n.*, 103, 194, 198, 202.
Council of State representatives, 190 ; weakness, 191 ; disunity of the States, 191–3 ; Federal Constitution, 193.

Crisis, of 1837, 197-8 ; of 1857, 295 ; of 1873, 298.
Currency dispute, 199, 302.
Depression after 1783, 191–2 ; after 1815, 196, 290–1, 329 ; after 1837, 198, 294.
Desert Land Act, 96, 331.
Elevators, 95, 233.
Embargo Act, 195.
Expansion, 7, 91, 92–3, 100, 101, 190, 194 ; streams of migration, 328 ; motives, 328 ; rush to the West, 329 ; Louisiana purchase, 329, 334 ; growth of new States, 329 ; public lands policy, 329 ; land survey, 329 ; Hamilton's Report on Public Lands, 329 ; Land Ordinance, 329–30 ; credit sales system, 330 ; arrears of indebtedness, 330 ; cash sales system, 330 ; plantations and small holdings, 330 ; Jackson's policy, 330–1 ; Pre-emption Act, 330 ; Anti-Rent movement, 331 ; Southern opposition, 331 ; Homestead Act, 331 ; settlement of prairies, 331 ; Timber Culture Act, 331 ; Desert Land Act, 331 ; cattle ranches, 331 ; Ohio Valley, 331 ; cotton belt, 331–2 ; Mississippi region, 332 ; growth of population, 332 ; gold in California, 332 ; emigration from Europe, 332–3 ; European revolutions, 332 ; Irish famines, 332 ; German agriculturalists, 333 ; American migration, 333–4; "frontier spirit," 333 ; Civil War, 333 ; repeal of Corn Laws, 333 ; depression after 1873, 333 ; foreign element absorbed, 334 ; disappearance of the frontier, 334 ; Florida, 334 ; Texas, 334 ; California, 334 ; Oregon, 334 ; Alaska, 334.
Farms, statistics, 100 ; tenancy increasing, 101.
Free competition, 199, 200, 201.
" Free soil " party, 87.
Free Trade, by England, 95.
Freight rates, 94–5.
Fulton, Robert, 230.
Hamilton, Alexander, 189, 190 ; federal policy, 193 ; United States Bank, 193 ; federal loan, 193 ; Report on Manufactures, 290; Report on Public Lands, 329.
Homestead Act, 1862, 96, 331.
Immigration, 99 *n.* ; English, 99–100 ; Irish, 100 ; German 100 ; Scandinavian, 100 ; restriction, 199.
Imperial preference, 23.
Indebtedness, rural 89–90.
Individualism, 6, 154.
Industrial Revolution, 9, 20, 25, 189, 195–6, 198–9.
Industrial Workers of the World, 107, 151, 204.
Inefficiency, State, 200 ; " Spoils " system, 200 ; underpayment, 200.
Intensive cultivation, 101 ; State aid, 101–2.
Iron and steel, subsidies, 192 ; smelting by charcoal, 196 ; high protection, 198 ; anthracite smelting, 198 ; growth, 201 ; factors, 201–2 ; railways, 201–2 ; development in Alabama, 202.
Jackson, Andrew, 197, 330–1.
Knights of Labour, 200, 203.
Labour movement, 200, 203–5 ; Knights of Labour, 200, 203 ; American Federation of Labour, 203–4 ; Industrial Workers of the World, 204 ; reasons for weakness, 204–5 ; workers' prosperity, 204 ; traditional politics, 204–5 ; mixture of races, 205 ; mobility of labour, 205.
Land policy, 95–6, 189, 329–31.
Massachusetts, civil war in, 192.
Meat exports, 92, 97–8, 103.
Mesabi mines, 202.
Migration, American, 100, 333–4.
Milling, improved, 98–9.
Napoleonic War boom, 194.
Negro cultivators, 90–1.
Non-Intercourse Act, 195.
Northern States, 85–6, 190.
Ohio valley, 331.
Orders-in-Council, 195.
Oregon, 334.
Pawtucket, 194.
Personal freedom, 4.
Pittsburg, 196, 201.
Population, 21, 328, 332.
Railways, 23, 91, 92–4, 98, 190, 201–3 ; open up the West, 230–1, 232–3 ; influence of Civil War, 231 ; first transcontinental, 231 ; railway booms, 231, 232, 234 ; importance of cheap transport, 231–2 ; private construction, 232, 234 ; State aid, 232, 234 ; rate wars, 233 ; steel rails, 233 ; rates reduction, 233 ; ranching traffic, 233 ; refrigerator cars, 233 ; grain elevators, 233 ; importance of freight traffic, 233–4 ;

railway despotism, 234; rate discrimination, 234; rate regulation, 234–5; Interstate Commerce Commission, 203, 234–5; Elkins Act, 235; Hepburn Act, 235; Mann-Elkins Act, 235.
Refrigerator, 97–8.
Rhode Island, 192.
Roads, 229.
Sherman Anti-Trust Act, 203.
Shipbuilding, boom, 194, 198; slump, 236.
Shipping, 23, 94–5, 235–6; boom, 194; expansion, 198 235; decline, 195, 201, 236; "clippers", 235–6; Commission on Marine Subsidies, 236.
Slater, Samuel, 194.
Slavery, 8, 15, 20, 41, 46, 85, 88, 189, 194.
Southern States, 84–9, 190.
Standard Oil Company, 203.
State Control, 200–1.
Steamboat influence, 230.
Sugar, 85.
Tariffs, before 1861, 19, 190; Civil War, 21, 189, 190; problem in 1783, 189; growth of protection, 190; lower tariffs, 190; return to protection, 190, 199; "free breakfast" table, 199, 298, 299; chief source of revenue, 288, 290; moderate tariff of 1789, 289; American system, 289, 291; tariff of 1790, 290; Hamilton's Report on Manufactures, 290; rising tariffs, 290; Napoleonic wars, 290; industrial depression, 290–1; President Madison, 291; "infant industries" argument, 291, 299; tariff of 1816, 291; North versus South, 291, 292–3; tariff of 1824, 291; growth of protection, 291; "Tariff of Abominations," 291–2; Southern resentment, 292–3; "Compromise Tariff," 292; high wages argument, 293, 299; fluctuating tariffs, 293; crisis of 1837, 293–4; decline of revenue, 294; tariff of 1841, 294; protectionist tariff of 1842, 294; President Polk, 294–5; tariff of 1846, 295; lower duties, 295; crisis of 1857, 295; tariff of 1861, 295–6; Civil War influence, 296–7; increased duties, 296–7; tariff of 1862, 296; tariff of 1864, 296–7; high protectionism, 297, 304; Wollens Act, 297; copper duty, 297; steel duties, 297–8; farmers' discontent, 298; crisis of 1873, 298; industrial expansion, 298; McKinley Tariff, 298, 299–300, 301; Wilson Tariff, 298, 302–3; Dingley Tariff, 298, 303; Payne-Aldrich Tariff, 299, 303–4; Underwood Tariff, 299, 304; self-sufficiency argument, 299; Reciprocity with Canada, 300; Latin America, 300–1; Washington Conference, 301; Brazilian agreement, 301; sugar weapon, 301; commercial treaties, 301–2; Spanish War, 303; reciprocity agreements, 303.
Taussig, Prof., 294, 296–7.
Tobacco, 84–5, 194; Tobacco Trust, 203.
Transport improvement, 93–5, 194–5, 229.
Treaty of Ghent, 195.
Trusts, growth of, 200, 202–3; State control, 200, 201, 203; tariffs, 202–3; advantages and disadvantages, 203; legislation, 203.
Union Pacific Railroad, 91.
War of Independence, 190, 191.
War of 1812, 195.
Washington, George, 192–3.
Wheat, exports, 23–4, 35, 46, 91, 92–3, 103, 189; factors, 93–5, 96–7; spring and winter wheat, 99.
Whitney cotton gin, 194.
Woollen industry, 196.

Vienna, Conference of, 258.
Vienna, Congress of, 27.
von Bülow, 257.

Ward, A. W., quoted, 161.
Wars, influence of, 28–32; freedom, 28–9; machinery, 29–30; colonial expansion, 30–1; tariffs, 31; Civil War, 87–9, 91, 189, 333; Franco-Prussian, 169; Thirty Years, 63, 157–8; Crimean, 20, 76, 226; Russo-Japansee, 185; of Independence, 190, 191; Spanish-American, 334.
Washington, George, 192–3.
West Indies, slavery in, 41.
Wheat freights, 23; production, 57, 58; exports, 23–5, 35, 46, 91, 92–3, 103, 189.

Whitney cotton gin, 194.
Wieth-Knudsen, 82.
William I, 4.
Wine production, 57, 58, 148, 252.
Wischnegradski, 281, 282–3, 286.
Witte, Count, 4, 25, 27, 185, 226, 281, 281 *n.*, 283, 284, 286, 287.
Woollen industry, French, 110, 113, 114, 120, 129, 136, 149; American, 196.
Wrontschenko, 279.

Young, Arthur, 52, 113, 209.

Zollverein (*see under* " Germany " *and* " Prussia ").